Sociological Perspectives on Media Piracy in the Philippines and Vietnam

Vivencio O. Ballano

Sociological Perspectives on Media Piracy in the Philippines and Vietnam

Springer

Vivencio O. Ballano
St. Paul University
Quezon City, Philippines

Polytechnic University of the Philippines (PUP)
Santa Mesa, Kalakhang Maynila, Philippines

ISBN 978-981-13-5728-2 ISBN 978-981-287-922-6 (eBook)
DOI 10.1007/978-981-287-922-6

Springer Singapore Heidelberg New York Dordrecht London

Softcover re-print of the Hardcover 1st edition 2016

Printed on acid-free paper

Springer Science+Business Media Singapore Pte Ltd. is part of Springer Science+Business Media (www.springer.com)

Acknowledgments

This book on media piracy in the Philippines and Vietnam is a product of a long and painstaking fieldwork, sociological research, and writing. This would not have been possible without the generous help from several people and organizations.

The research data in the Philippines which focused on optical media piracy in Quiapo Barter Trade Center Complex in the city of Manila and its affiliate networks in Metro Manila and nearby provinces would not be a reality without the generous assistance and expertise of several people who assisted the author in his entire fieldwork. The author is thankful for the research grant of the Japan and Toyota Foundations which financed his postdoctoral fellowship under the Southeast Asian Studies Regional Exchange Program (SEASREP) in 2012. This grant enabled him to extend the scope of his dissertation research on media piracy to Vietnam. The author is particularly grateful to the SEASREP Executive Director, Dr. Maria Serena Diokno, and Program Officer, Ms. Imelda Adante, for facilitating the approval of his postdoctoral research grant application.

With regard to his fieldwork in the Philippines, the author is greatly indebted to a community organizer (name withheld for security reason) of a local nongovernmental organization (NGO) in Quiapo when he started his data collection in 2010. He assisted the author in his interviews with some key media piracy traders and Muslim leaders in the Quiapo Barter Trade Center Complex on the optical disc piracy trade operations. Without some of his inside knowledge of the trade—owing to his close association with some piracy producers and distributors in the Quiapo Muslim enclave—and guidance during the entire fieldwork in the area, the author's sociological analysis on the persistence of media piracy in the country would not have gone beyond mass media reports.

The author is also indebted to two former Optical Media Board (OMB) Chairmen and OMB key officers who graciously accommodated his interviews and shared their experience and personal knowledge on the optical disc piracy operations in the Philippines. The author expressed his heartfelt thanks to his key informants, Muslim leaders, and law enforcers for enriching his sociological analysis on the media piracy problem in the country.

His fieldwork in Vietnam was made possible by the generous help of his Filipino and Vietnamese friends. In particular, the author is greatly thankful to Sr. Azucena Nate, SPC, for introducing him to a Vietnamese contact (whom he cannot identify for security reason) who, in turn, introduced him through electronic media to his key informants in Ho Chi Minh City. The author is highly indebted to his interpreter and tour guide (name withheld for security reason) during his fieldwork in Ho Chi Minh City. He thanked his friends and key informants in Vietnam who shared their personal knowledge on media piracy and protection racket in the city.

Finally, the author is grateful to Dr. Ricardo Abad, his professor and dissertation adviser, and to all his professors and friends in the Sociology and Anthropology Department of Ateneo de Manila University for providing him the necessary sociological training and academic preparation to undertake this study. He is also grateful to Springer Science+Business Media Singapore and all the reviewers, editors, and editorial staff, especially Vishal Daryanomel, for making this book a reality. Lastly, he would like to thank his wife Emily and his children Joanne Faye and Johann Karl for their loving support and inspiration.

Sociological Perspectives on Media Piracy in the Philippines and Vietnam

Vivencio O. Ballano

Contents

Abbreviations

AmCham	American Chamber of Commerce Vietnam
ANT	Actor–network theory
APEC	Asia-Pacific Economic Cooperation
ASEAN	Association of Southeast Asian Nations
BEBA	Bureau of Economics and Business Affairs
CD	Compact Disc
DVD	Digital Versatile Disc
EDCA	Enhanced Defense Cooperation Agreement
EU	European Union
FTA	Free Trade Agreement
GATT	General Agreement on Tariffs and Trade
GSP	Generalized Special Preferences
HCMC	Ho Chi Minh City
IFC	International Financial Corporation
IIPA	International Intellectual Property Alliance
ILO	International Labor Organization
IMF	International Monetary Board
IP	Intellectual property
IPR	Intellectual property rights
MICT	Ministry of Information, Culture and Tourism
MoLISA	Ministry of Labor, Invalids and Social Affairs
OMB	Optical Media Board
PHDR	Philippine Human Development Report
PWL	Priority Watch List
QBTCC	Quiapo Barter Trade Center Complex
SEA	Southeast Asia
TRIPS	Trade-Related Aspects of Intellectual Property Rights
UN	United Nations
UNDP	United Nations Development Programme
UNESCO	United Nations Educational, Scientific and Cultural Organization
USDC	United States Department of Commerce

USTR	United States Trade Representative
VCD	Video Compact Disc
VHS	Video Home System
WB	World Bank
WB-IFC	World Bank-International Financial Corporation
WIPO	World Intellectual Property Organization
WL	Watch List
WTO	World Trade Organization

The original version of this book was revised. An erratum to this book can be found at https://doi.org/10.1007/978-981-287-922-6_8

Chapter 1
Introduction

1.1 Background of the Media Piracy Problem

Media piracy or the counterfeiting of copyrighted film, music, video games, computer and music videos, and other digital media products and services has become an urgent and serious concern of today's globalizing world, affecting not just the trading systems of developed countries but also of developing and emerging economies all over the world. For the United States whose economy is increasingly driven by innovation and intellectual property (IP) through the sales of IP products and services at home and abroad, curbing media piracy—as portrayed by some powerful copyright lobby groups—is a matter of life and death for the U.S. economy. Copyright piracy is said to have deprived the American economy of billions of dollars in sales and revenues, resulting in a loss of thousands of domestic jobs.[1] To combat piracy and protect the American IP exports from counterfeiting, the U.S. Congress amended the Trade Act of 1974 and included IPR protection in its Section 301 trade process, giving the U.S. President, through the United States Trade Representative (USTR) office, the authority to monitor the intellectual

[1] As a consequence of the global and U.S.-based sound recording piracy, for instance, it is alleged that the U.S. economy has lost $12.5 billion in total output annually and 71,060 jobs. Please see http://www.ipi.org/ipi_issues/detail/the-true-cost-of-sound-recording-piracy-to-the-us-economy. Supporters of stronger IPR protection in the United States estimated that online piracy alone can cost the U.S. economy between $200 and $250 billion a year and is responsible for the loss of 750,000 jobs. But some groups questioned the source and methodology of these estimates of piracy losses. Some claimed that estimates of piracy losses are replete with methodological errors, including double and triple counting that swell estimates (http://www.freakonomics.com/2012/01/12/how-much-do-music-and-movie-piracy-really-hurt-the-u-s-economy/). Sanchez (2012), for instance, argued that industry-sponsored estimates are dubious and lack sound empirical basis. See "How Copyright Industries Con Congress" at http://www.cato.org/blog/how-copyright-industries-con-congress. Some economists also argued that losses due to piracy do not really represent lost sales as people who buy fakes belong to a market segment which cannot afford to buy the original products and are not therefore the target market of the genuine goods in the first place (Chaudhry and Zimmerman 2013, p. 10).

V.O. Ballano, *Sociological Perspectives on Media Piracy in the Philippines and Vietnam*, DOI 10.1007/978-981-287-922-6_1

Fig. 1.1 World map background with U.S. flag (Image courtesy of Ohmega 1982 at FreeDigitalPhotos.net)

property rights (IPR) performance of all U.S. trading partners around the world, to create piracy watch lists, and to impose trade sanctions against violators (Fig. 1.1).

This strong stance of the United States against piracy is, however, resisted by some high-income and IP-consuming emerging economies in the Asia Pacific region, led by China and some Southeast Asian (SEA) countries known for piracy such as Malaysia, Thailand, Indonesia, Vietnam, and the Philippines. For these countries, curbing piracy, including copyright and media piracy, through the hegemonic pressure of the USTR and its powerful network of copyright lobby groups led by the International Intellectual Property Alliance (IIPA), is a form of neo-colonization and domination which deprives emerging economies the opportunity to free ride on the latest innovation in the global creative economy.[2] The USTR started listing these countries in its piracy watch lists in 1989. At present, some of these countries still remain in the watch lists except the Philippines. Vietnam and the Philippines which are both piracy hotspots in the SEA had, however, an opposing development in the USTR's watch lists in 2014. After long years in the Watch List (WL), Vietnam was elevated, for the first time, to the Priority Watch List (PWL), after being included in the Watch List for a long time, while the Philippines was

[2] The U.S. Trade Representative (USTR) is the lead government agency under the Office of the U.S. President, authorized by the U.S. Trade Act, to monitor the IPR performance of the U.S. trading partners, issue an annual Special 301 Report, and include violators in the Priority Watch List (PWL) and Watch List (WL). This annual report is usually based on the yearly findings and recommendations of the International Intellectual Property Alliance (IIPA), a powerful private sector coalition, formed in 1984, of trade associations representing U.S. copyright-based industries. Its members include Association of American Publishers, Entertainment Software Association, Independent Film & Television Alliance, Motion Picture Association of America, and Recording Industry Association of America. See IIPA home page at http://www.iipa.com/aboutiipa.html.

removed altogether from the watch list system of the USTR in 2014, after being a regular feature in the PWL and WL for almost two decades.[3] Despite the Philippines' removal from the watch list system and the government's modest efforts to reform the local IPR system, media piracy continues to persist in the country with impunity.

1.2 Media Piracy in the Philippines and Vietnam

As understood in the current copyright piracy literature, media piracy in the Philippines and Vietnam has a fairly long history in the USTR's watch list system, and its development follows some social and technological patterns experienced by other piracy-laden countries around the world. Media piracy in these two countries started with analog piracy through unauthorized viewing, copying, and sharing of copyrighted films and songs in the late 1970s and throughout the 1980s with the introduction of the analog technologies of the Betamax, Video Home System (VHS), cassette tapes, video players, and recorders. It flourished in the 1990s with the popularity of the illegal optical disc piracy using the compact disc (CD), video compact disc (VCD), digital video disc (DVD), and other formats of the digital technology and migrated to the online digital platform since the early 2000s with the growing sophistication of digital computing and popularity of the Internet—using the popular peer-to-peer (P2P) sharing method, cyberlocker, media boxes, deeplinks, and other cloud-assisted technologies (2014 IIPA Special 301 Report). With the massive Internet penetration in the world and the introduction of nanotechnology which miniaturizes computer hard drives, increases digital speed, and widens data storage a billion times, media piracy on the Internet has become easier and more difficult to regulate.

[3] The USTR has not provided a convincing empirical evidence to prove that piracy has indeed declined in the Philippines to justify the complete removal of the Philippines from the watch lists in 2014. In fact, the Washington-based International Intellectual Property Alliance (IIPA) and IP International Anti-Counterfeiting Coalition (IACC) recommended in 2013 that the Philippines should be retained in the USTR's Watch List for 2014 because of the continuing optical disc piracy and the rising online piracy in the country. Although the Philippines has requested the removal and has improved its IPR protection system, media piracy remains notorious in the country. The basis of the USTR was more on improvement of IPR legislation and judicial reforms made by the Philippine government rather than actual reduction of piracy goods and services in the country (please see 2014 USTR Special 301 Annual Report). Moreover, the removal coincided with President Obama's visit to the Philippines and the signing of the Enhanced Defense Cooperation Agreement (EDCA) in April 28, 2014, an executive agreement which allows increased rotational presence of American troops and military operations in the country and thus can rebalance the U.S. forces in the SEA and counter China's adventurism in the West Philippine Sea (for a more detailed explanation on EDCA, please see Thayer (2014) "Analyzing the US-Philippines Enhanced Defense Cooperation Agreement" at http://thediplomat.com/2014/05/analyzing-the-us-philippines-enhanced-defense-cooperation-agreement/). This agreement has created a suspicion that the removal from the watch list has something to do with the United States getting military favors from the Philippines rather than the substantial decline of media piracy in the country.

But Internet penetration in the world is uneven, and thus not all can connect with the web to illegally download one's favorite movies or songs. Moreover, the high poverty level in the Philippines and Vietnam has prevented people to buy the latest digital gadgets and to connect with the Internet to download or consume digital media. With increased supply and declining prices of discs, CD and DVD players, and recorders imported from China, those who are less computer literate and poor prefer to buy pirated discs as a means of consuming counterfeit media goods. Thus, despite the growing digitalization and Internet penetration of these two countries, hard goods piracy or optical disc piracy remains an important mode of illegal commercial and noncommercial consumption of optical media goods in developing countries of the SEA countries such as the Philippines and Vietnam.

1.2.1 Optical Disc and Digital Piracy

The optical media piracy in the Philippines and Vietnam started in the 1990s with the rise of digital technology using the CD, VCD, and DVD which replaced the analog technology of the Betamax and VHS cassette tapes.[4] Pirated discs containing copyrighted songs, films, or software with a price often ten times cheaper than the original copies became widely accessible and affordable to millions of people in the Southeast Asian region. In the early 2000s, the disc piracy has already created open piracy retail markets in Indonesia, Thailand, Malaysia, the Philippines, and Vietnam. In the Philippines, the Quiapo Barter Trade Center Complex in Manila was listed in the USTR's most notorious piracy markets in the world. Medium-sized malls in the country are also constantly being monitored by IIPA representatives because of rampant optical disc retail piracy. Vietnam's major cities such as Hanoi, Ho Chi Minh City (HCMC), and Danang are also being watched by stakeholders and antipiracy lobby groups for open optical disc piracy trade (Fig. 1.2).

In 2001, the physical and optical disc piracy in the Philippines and Vietnam had reached a critical level, prompting the powerful IIPA to recommend to the USTR to place Vietnam in the Special 301 Watch List (WL) and the Philippines in the Priority Watch List (PWL) for failure of their governments to address the growing problem of media piracy.[5] It alleged that Vietnam and the Philippines failed considerably

---

[4] Sony introduced the Betamax in 1975. But it was the VHS, popularized by Japan Victor Corporation (JVC), which became popular in the 1980s for video home viewing. Please see Chap. 7 of this book for a more detailed explanation on this.

[5] Being listed in USTR's watch list system implies that the foreign country has not satisfactorily complied with its obligation to TRIPS and international standards on IPR protection, a violation of its commitment to GATT or free trade agreement (FTA) with the United States. This entails continuous monitoring and pressure from the USTR of the country's yearly IPR performance and a possible suspension or termination of trading privileges with the United States under the Generalized System of Preference (GSP) which entails a possible loss of millions of dollars in trade value. The Philippines participates in the U.S. Generalized System of Preference (GSP) Program, which allows duty-free imports of certain products into the United States from developing

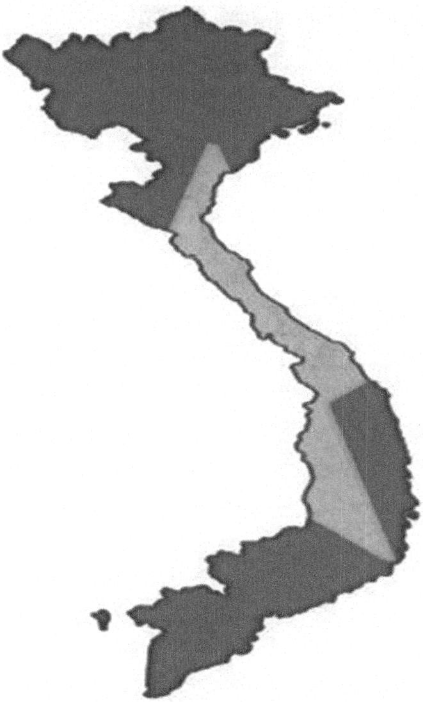

Fig. 1.2 Vietnam map on flag drawing, grunge, and retro flag series (Image courtesy of taesmileland at FreeDigitalPhotos.net)

to curb piracy and to comply with the international copyright standards. The local digital media markets of these countries remained counterfeit. The local courts were not deterrent against piracy, and the law enforcement system was often nonexistent and nontransparent. It also alleged that Vietnam's market, in particular, is almost entirely pirate and its antipiracy enforcement has been slow, uneven, and almost totally lacking in transparency. With regard to optical media piracy, the IIPA noted that it is rare to find a legitimate copy of a U.S. copyrighted work in both digital and non-digital formats in the communist state. Instead, pirated music, film, computer program, and other copyrighted materials are readily available on the Internet and in retail stores throughout the country. The optical media production lines in the country also exceeded Vietnam's low consumption levels and were believed to be used for piracy (2001 IIPA Special 301 Report) (Fig. 1.3).

The Philippines, like Vietnam, also received a strong negative assessment and a warning from the powerful IIPA in 2001 due to rampant optical media piracy. The IIPA report alleged that "[t]he Philippines is rapidly becoming a central battlefield in the increasingly intense campaign against optical media piracy in Southeast Asia; but the country remains ill-prepared to fight this battle" (p. 175). It also alleged

countries (IIPA 2001 Special 301 Report). In the first 11 months of 2000, for instance, over $687 million of imports from the Philippines entered the U.S. duty-free under this program (IIPA 2001 Special 301 Report). Vietnam has not yet participated in the program but has a pending application.

Fig. 1.3 Philippine map on flag drawing, grunge, and retro flag series (Image courtesy of taesmileland at FreeDigitalPhotos.net)

that the country's pirate production capacity continued to increase and its domestic market remained heavily infiltrated by pirate product in all segments, from software to audiovisual, music to books. Moreover, it observed that the Philippines lacked regulatory controls, updated legal framework, and strong enforcement mechanism against optical media business. The production, distribution, and sale of unauthorized music CDs, video CDs, and CD-ROMs containing illegal copies of business software applications and/or entertainment software as well as literary materials are damaging the legitimate market of the copyright industries in the country. In its overall assessment, the USTR concluded that the Philippines remained ill-prepared to fight optical media piracy as it lagged behind in meeting its international obligations under the Trade-Related Aspects of Intellectual Property Rights (TRIPS) of the General Agreement on Tariffs and Trade (GATT) (2001 IIPA Special 301 Report, p. 175).

1.2.2 *Government Response*

In response to the IIPA and USTR's assessment and international pressure to comply with the IPR aspect of their bilateral trade obligations to the United States, the Philippine and Vietnamese governments took some significant legislative and administrative steps to curb copyright piracy, particularly media piracy, in their own respective jurisdictions since 2001. With regard to copyright protection, the Philippines and Vietnam simplified and updated their respective IPR codes to comply with the international copyright standards demanded by the IIPA and USTR as well as strengthened their administrative machinery to address optical disc piracy.

The Philippines, in particular, amended its existing copyright law to increase the scope of, and the penalty against, unauthorized production and distribution of optical media. In February 2004, Philippine legislature approved the Optical Media Act of 2003 in order to criminalize media piracy and increased its penalty thereof.[6] To fight film piracy and illegal recording of feature films inside cinemas which often target American blockbuster movies to be distributed as camcords or masters for worldwide duplication, the Philippines also enacted the Anti-Camcording Act (Republic Act 10088) in 2010.[7] Finally, after a protracted negotiation and pressure from the United States to curb online media piracy, the Philippines passed into law the controversial Anti-Cybercrime Act of 2012 (Republic Act 10175).[8] In the administrative aspect, the Philippine government strengthened the enforcement powers of its lead agency against media piracy, the Video Regulatory Board (VRB) which was renamed as the Optical Media Board (OMB) in 2004. Moreover, to improve its fight against software and copyright piracy, the Philippine government created the Philippine Anti-Piracy Team (PAPT), a coalition of government agencies consisting of the National Bureau of Investigation (NBI), Optical Media Board (OMB), and the Philippine National Police (PNP) under the supervision of the new government's lead IPR agency—the Intellectual Property Office (IPO). This coalition led by the OMB is responsible for the continuous raids against optical disc piracy establishments throughout the country. It also played an important role in the closure of the Quiapo Barter Trade Center piracy market in the city of Manila in 2012, the top piracy production and distribution center of counterfeit media in the Philippines, long listed in the most notorious piracy markets in the world by the IIPA and USTR.

Vietnam, like the Philippines, also updated its copyright laws to combat media piracy and complied with many of the IIPA and USTR's antipiracy and law enforcement recommendations. With the determination to transform its centrally planned economy into a market economy, Vietnam introduced a series of reforms to update its IP laws and strengthen its IPR protection system in order to comply with the international standards. One significant IPR reform was the compilation and upgrading of its IP laws. With the intention of becoming a member of the World Trade Organization (WTO) through the help of the United States, Vietnam enacted its new IP Law in 2005 which consolidated and streamlined all its IP laws, scattered over 40 legal documents, into one version. It also updated its other laws and regulations which provide provisions related to IP such as the Criminal Code (1999), Science and Technology Law (2000), Customs Law (2001), Trade Law (2005), Investment

[6] http://www.papt.org.ph/uploads/file/RA9239%20Optical%20Media%20Act.pdf

[7] http://www.ipophil.gov.ph/images/IPEnforcement/Manual/Manual.pdf

[8] http://www.gov.ph/2012/09/12/republic-act-no-10175/

Law (2005), Technology Transfer Law (2005), etc.[9] It also issued implementing rules and regulations to enforce the new IP Law of 2005 and other related laws. On December 31, 2008, for instance, it issued Instruction No. 36/2008/CT-TTg which provided guidelines on strengthening copyright management and implementation of copyright and related rights protection.[10] In recent years, Vietnam removed from government offices pirated software and investigated, and in some cases raided and fined, businesses suspected of using pirated software.[11] To address the rising online media piracy, Vietnam, like the Philippines, also passed a similar Internet law signed by the Vietnamese Prime Minister Tan Dung on July 15, 2013, which primarily prohibits personal web page owners to take news from news media agencies and use it as if their own—Decree 72.[12]

Despite government efforts to improve IPR protection, fight media piracy, and regulate the Internet, Vietnam's online media piracy remains a growing problem. It is estimated that up to 90 % of all digital content provided to users on the Internet in the country such as songs, movies, e-books, and software and mobile phone applications is pirated. In 2012, Zing.vn, a portal run by a Vietnamese company, became the highly publicized infringing website in Vietnam with more than 30 million Internet users and was attracting investments from major international investment firms.[13] And in 2011, the U.S. embassy, owing to the absence of legal websites with huge following in the country, was forced to join this portal and maintain a "Zingme" account to network and to reach out to young people in Vietnam and to build closer ties with its former enemy.[14]

The growth of online digital piracy occasioned by the increasing Internet penetration in the country and the popularity of the broadband technology in mobile phones did not, however, decrease the popularity of the optical disc piracy in Vietnam. Optical media illegally copied on CDs and DVDs and sold to the public continue to grow in major cities by mobile vendors and by registered CD–DVD shops in Vietnam. The elevation of Vietnam from WL to PWL in the USTR's 2014 Special 301 Annual Report for the first time after being listed in WL for 16 consecutive years is an indication that media piracy has not declined despite copyright reforms in the communist state (2014 USTR Special 301 Report). This observation can also be applied for the Philippines. After more than 15 years of IPR reforms since the IIPA labeled the country as a central battleground of video piracy in Southeast Asia, one can still observe the same intensity of copyright infringement in the country—albeit shifting more, this time, in the cyberspace. Although the Philippines was removed from the Watch List of the USTR's 2014 Special 301

[9] http://www.wipo.int/export/sites/www/about-ip/en/studies/pdf/wipo_unu_07_vietnam.pdf/

[10] http://www.wipo.int/wipolex/en/profile.jsp?code=VN

[11] http://www.state.gov/e/eb/rls/othr/ics/2013/204760.htm

[12] http://thediplomat.com/2013/08/decree-72-vietnams-confusing-internet-law/

[13] http://36mfjx1a0yt01ki78v3bb46n15gp.wpengine.netdna-cdn.com/wp-content/uploads/2013/04/130208-USTR_Special_301_Submission_VIETNAM.pdf

[14] http://news.yahoo.com/vietnam-us-relies-pirate-network-082635699DOUBLEHYPHENfinance.html

Report, massive physical and online media piracy has not substantially declined even with the "closure" of the notorious Quiapo piracy market in 2011.[15] Thus, despite the Philippine and Vietnamese governments' continuous efforts to improve their respective IPR protection system, media piracy or the unauthorized copying, downloading, sharing, and trading of copyrighted media materials in digital and disc forms continue with impunity. By inspection, one can still observe the clandestine piracy distribution network of Quiapo and see the familiar site of illegal vending of pirated discs on the sidewalks, kiosks, wet markets, rented stores, and stalls in medium-sized malls in the Philippines.

The persistence of the media piracy, particularly optical disc piracy, in the Philippines and Vietnam makes one wonders: Why is media piracy enduring in these two countries despite the USTR pressure and government IPR reforms and renewed drive against copyright piracy? What are the major social forces which support and sustain this persistence in these two Southeast Asian countries? What sociological insights can we cast on this phenomenon?

1.3 Understanding Media Piracy

To understand media piracy in emerging economies of Southeast Asia such as the Philippines and Vietnam, theories abound to account its persistence. One popular theory points to the price: optical and digital media such as music, film, software, or video game downloaded from infringing sites in the Internet are free, while illegal discs sold on the sidewalks and in CD–DVD shops are ten times cheaper than the genuine copies. Thus, media piracy persists because people continue to patronize it. It is cheaper and more affordable to people, especially the poor, to just buy pirated CDs or DVDs on the sidewalk or download illegally copyrighted media online than to purchase original discs or genuine online files.

Related to this explanation is the view which sees poverty as the major factor why counterfeit disc business persists in developing countries. People sell counterfeit optical discs as a source of livelihood to overcome poverty (Baes 2002). Moreover, other explanations which are largely espoused by stakeholders, U.S. multinational copyright companies, and antipiracy organizations allude to the weak legal market, copyright law, and law enforcement system. The IIPA, the umbrella organization of the U.S. copyright industries, and the USTR in their annual Special 301 piracy assessment reports, for example, blame the persistence of media piracy primarily to the failure of law enforcement, noncompliance of local copyright laws

[15] A report revealed that less than a year after the Philippines was downgraded by the USTR from PWL to WL, in 2013, Quiapo piracy returned to its usual business albeit in a clandestine way (De Vera 2013). Interviews and observations by the author with some retailers also revealed that Quiapo Barter Trade Center piracy market remained the main source of pirated discs in Metro Manila and nearby provinces despite the closure ordered by Mayor Lim.

with TRIPS and the World Intellectual Property Office (WIPO) copyright treaties, and the slow government implementation of USTR's recommendations.

Finally, one popular explanation attributes the persistence of media piracy to the influence of organized crime and terrorism. For instance, the Optical Media Board (OMB), the Philippine government's main watchdog against illegal optical media, blames the Chinese syndicate or the Hong Kong triad for continuously supplying counterfeit discs to Filipino sellers nationwide. Chinese syndicates in mainland China were also blamed for the continued exports of pirated goods and replicating technologies to Vietnam. Some scholars claimed that piracy persists because it is a highly profitable crime and the proceeds are allegedly used to finance terrorism and criminality (e.g., Treverton et al. 2009).

Although these explanations can account for, to some extent, the persistence of media piracy in developing countries, their approach to the problem, however, tends to be narrow and one-dimensional. In particular, it tends to disregard in its analyses other relevant nonlegal and sociocultural forces such as the social resistance of developing countries against stricter IPR protection, role of the informal sector and informal trading which includes the media piracy trade in the economic development piracy-laden countries, bureaucratic red tape and regulatory burdens in legalizing optical media business, and monetary or bureaucratic corruption—to name a few—which sustain the relational nature of media piracy business. Current investigations and studies on the persistence of piracy, more specifically on digital media piracy, tend to focus more on the illegal and immoral aspect of counterfeiting and on the loopholes of law enforcement against piracy (Karaganis 2012), employing more often the prescriptive lens of jurisprudence rather than the holistic and empirical lens of sociology and of the social sciences. Finally, policymakers tend to adopt a normative and non-network approach in explaining the endurance of piracy, focusing only on weak legal market structure, inadequate IP legislation, and loopholes in the judicial system as the main factors facilitating copyright infringement. Rarely do they view the problem from a sociological perspective which can include the sociocultural and technological forces that facilitate media piracy in today's global society.

1.4 Analyzing Media Piracy in Contemporary Global Society

To understand media piracy sociologically and to come up with a more humane approach to the infringement problem, it is necessary to consider the bigger and dominant global forces that sustain its persistence. This requires analyzing critically the social construction of the current antipiracy campaigns, the U.S. hegemony in the global IP trade and the social resistance of emerging economies toward it through piracy, the growing urbanization and media urbanism in piracy-laden countries, and applying the development communication approach that democratizes the distribution of creative goods and allows access of the poor to copyright goods and services necessary for the poverty alleviation and social development.

1.4.1 The Current Antipiracy Campaign

How much of the current antipiracy campaigns is empirical and how much is a social construct? The issue of media piracy has often been simplified by stakeholders, antipiracy lobbying groups, and government regulators as a simple case of theft and criminal appropriation of privately owned copyright goods and services which must be addressed with urgency and iron-fisted law enforcement drive. The antipiracy discourse propagated by corporate- and government-sponsored public relations and media campaigns is being framed in an increasingly aggressive language, using strong phrases such as "war against piracy," "battleground for piracy," and "fighting piracy" or calling infringers as "pirates" to discourage people to participate in any form of copyright infringement (Mirghani 2011, p. 113). To combat piracy on the demand side, "campaigns are made to educate the buying public that acquiring pirated products is illegal, unethical, and socially unacceptable..." (Miyazaki et al. 2009, p. 71). These campaigns are so aggressively framed by corporate lobby organizations that the public seems to believe that infringement is theft, immoral, and illegal and that research on its underlying cause has been largely attributed to inadequate IP law, to defective law enforcement system, and even to people's weak moral formation (e.g., Hill 2007). Thus, Karaganis (2012) lamented that debates on media piracy are centered on law enforcement issues rather than on understanding its behavioral nature and the limited market structure of licit media trade. "When it comes to piracy, the boundaries of domestic and international policy conversation are exceedingly narrow… [T]he policy conversations on piracy are exceedingly narrow and focused on enforcement—on strengthening police powers, streamlining judicial procedures, increasing criminal penalties, and extending surveillance and punitive measures to the Internet" (Karaganis 2012, p. iii).

The weak independent research tradition on piracy to counter this tendency of industry-sponsored antipiracy campaigns has facilitated this enforcement approach to copyright piracy. Through their lawyer-dominated antipiracy teams, the powerful U.S. copyright lobby groups are able to shape the current debates and discourses on media piracy around its immoral and criminal aspect rather than understand its complex nature in today's technological age and find a more appropriate empirical response to the problem. Copyright infringement may be highly repulsive to people and authorities in American and Western cultures with their strong individualist, capitalist, and legalist cultural orientation as illegal and theft of privately owned creative work. But this may not be the case for people in Asian and Oriental cultures which prioritize the community over the individual and encourage communal sharing of artistic or creative work (Warshofky 1994). Thus, reducing the current campaigns against copyright and media infringement to their moral, legal, or law enforcement dimensions is like "tasting the icing but not the cake," i.e., understanding only one dimension of the problem and missing a whole range of other important sociocultural, technological, and network dimensions that sustain counterfeiting and media piracy. Media piracy is a complex and highly networked cultural phenomenon which is supported by various networks of the growing complexity of the global age that encourages fluidity and liquidity of things and information rather than stability and solidity of regulation (Ritzer 2010). Thus, the persistence of copyright infringement and media piracy could not be merely attributed to the moral defect and criminal culpability of individual and corporate "pirates" and to the country's weak IPR law and law enforcement system.

The persistence of media piracy needs to be seen in a more holistic way, i.e., as "part of the integrated aspects of modern society, equally situated in the urban, social space of the modern city and the global, geopolitical landscape of colonialism in the past and the present" (Fredriksson 2012, p. 1). Copyright infringement such as media piracy has to be understood within the larger context of power, hegemony, social resistance, urbanization, migration, media urbanism, and development communication in order to come up with a more empirical, holistic, and humane global antipiracy drive.

1.4.2 "Piracy" as a Social and Ideological Construction

Power analysis in understanding the persistence of media piracy is apparently absent in the current piracy research and investigation dominated by industry-sponsored studies. Yet critical scholars and sociologists see the centrality of power in the social construction of reality. They do not see social phenomena such as media piracy as "natural" and historically neutral but as social and ideological constructions by powerful interest groups which aim to control society's resources. Seen from this perspective, the current antipiracy campaign is, therefore, not a natural confluence of things but a social construction of reality that favors unduly the copyright industry. In sociology of knowledge, sociologists are more concerned with understanding the processes on how human "knowledge" is developed, transmitted, and maintained in social situations and everyday life (Berger and Luckman 1966). The current aggressive campaign of U.S. copyright stakeholders, corporate lobby groups, and government agencies led by the USTR that paints a serious and grim picture of copyright piracy as creating devastating losses in revenues and jobs is, therefore, a social construction that protects the vested interest of large conglomerates of U.S. copyright multinationals, rather than providing an empirical view of the "true state of things" in the global copyright production and consumption.

Portraying copyright infringement as a serious crime of theft that needs an urgent "military" response is a product of ideological discourses shaped by top U.S. copyright industries, corporate lobby organizations such as the IIPA, as well as the USTR. In the first place, the use of discursive language such as the term "piracy" which relates it to the crime of "piracy in the high seas" and its current antipiracy drive which employs military metaphors is largely a social construction by corporate lobby groups. After the September 11 terrorist attacks, corporate lobbyists were said to be successful in relating copyright piracy with terrorism, insinuating that the proceeds of the highly profitable piracy business are used to finance organized crime and terrorism (Mirghani 2011). But copyright legal texts seldom use the term piracy for infringement. And many of these so-called alleged "pirates" are not actually gun-toting organized criminals but poor and displaced people due to war such as the Muslim optical disc piracy retailers in the Philippines (Ballano 2011), migrants, students, and even professionals or scholars who have no adequate licit access to cultural materials necessary for their total human development.

Furthermore, the word "piracy" is a general label which does not immediately distinguish the various forms of copyright infringement and degree of human culpability from a mere copying of an image from the Internet or a short quote or idea from an author's work without attribution to a clearly illegal massive replication and commercial distribution of optical media. Film piracy, for instance, includes a broad range of copying and sharing activities which could not all be considered illegal: "hard goods" commercial piracy, consumer theft of pay TV signals, consumer copying and sharing of prerecorded videos and of pay TV programs, and—mostly in prospect—Internet file sharing. "All of these activities are illegal, with the exception of pay TV copying, which is permissible or within a gray area of law" (Waterman et al. 2007, p. 3). With regard to music, one study showed that most of the music file sharing is primarily done by young people for private use with their friends and family and not for commercial use (Karaganis 2012). But the current antipiracy campaign and industry research tend to disregard the various forms of unauthorized use of copyright materials and consider all those who use or share copyrighted work without permission as stealing and piracy and all people who use copyrighted content without authorization, regardless of intent and extent of use, as "pirates."

Industry-sponsored piracy studies are also full of ideological constructions to make it appear that piracy has devastating effects to legitimate sales and American jobs, thus intensifying the piracy scare of the public and the urgency to stop copyright infringement "at all cost." More often, the methodology used by corporate research is considered by some groups as replete with methodological errors and shrouded with secrecy. The use of "rippling effect" in computing losses by the Motion Picture Association of America (MPAA), for instance, has been questioned by one group for using one-directional ripple effect, i.e., counting only those that hurt the studios in terms of sales but not the other positive ripple effect of piracy such as cheaper movies for everyone, allowing them to spend more money elsewhere and therefore helping the economy. Tim Lee argued that the use of ripple effects of industry research is one-sided. It only considers the negative ripples but not the positive ones, thus merely double-, triple-, or quadruple-counting the actual losses.[16] Others argued that estimates are said to be inflated and based on a wrong assumption that every person who pirates a work would have otherwise purchased the work at full price. They said that some infringers may purchase the genuine work if they'd been unable to get a pirated copy, but a lot of others would have

---

[16] See "MPAA Actually Admits That Some Of Its Piracy Stats Are Bogus" at http://www.techdirt.com/articles/20080122/18164639.shtml.

simply done without it.[17] As already mentioned, some economists also argued that the sales of pirated goods bought by people who cannot afford to buy the original products must not be counted as losses as they are not part of the target market (Chaudhry and Zimmerman 2013).

Karaganis (2012) explained that the main problem with industry-sponsored piracy studies is transparency. The main industry associations publish general descriptions of their methods but little about the assumptions, practices, or data underlying their work. Without transparency, he argued, it is difficult to evaluate the research findings or claims without knowing what questions the surveys asked and how they calculated key variables, such as the substitution effects between pirate and licit sales and the like (Karaganis 2012, p. 61). The issue on the appropriateness and reliability of the methodology used in estimating losses would further complicate as piracy advances more to the cyberspace with new digital platforms owing to the evolving nature of technology.

In sum, the current use of military metaphors and exaggerations of losses due to piracy in antipiracy campaigns spearheaded by the U.S. copyright industry, therefore, aims to reconstruct the piracy problem in favor of corporate business interests rather than portray the empirical reality of copyright infringement. It aims to influence the public to see the world and its cultural resources as being endangered by callous pirates, thus needing increased legal restrictions and swift justice (Mirghani 2011, p. 114). With the use of this kind of metaphors and approaches, antipiracy conversations continue to focus on revenue losses and law enforcement issues and on how to stop or regulate the destructive force of piracy, rather than on tackling the broader macro issues about the structural determinants of media piracy and finding empirical solutions that address the underlying global forces which sustain it.

1.4.3 Global Forces Sustaining Media Piracy

1.4.3.1 U.S. Global IP Hegemony

One important global force that explains the persistence of media piracy in emerging economies is the U.S. hegemony in the global IP trade. Borrowing Antonio Gramsci's concept, Raymond Williams (1973) defines hegemony as "the central, effective and dominant system of meanings and values, which are not merely abstract but which are organized and lived…." and "which are experienced as practices which appear as reciprocally affirming" (Williams 1973, p. 9). In international arena, hegemony can refer to the cultural and economic leadership of one powerful economy in world trade which other economies view as mutually affirming.[18] The current global piracy trade is not a simple case of theft and criminality as antipiracy campaign and

[17] See "Texas-Size Sophistry" at http://techliberation.com/2006/10/01/texas-size-sophistry/.

[18] For a more detailed explanation on the U.S. hegemony in the global IP trade, please see Chap. 2 of this book.

industry-sponsored research would want people to believe. Rather, it is a manifestation of active and covert resistance against stricter IPR protection regime engineered by the United States to control the rising global IP piracy trade. The quest for a stronger global IPR protection against piracy emanates from the domination of the IP industry in the U.S. economy that is projected in a worldwide scale, making the United States the leader or hegemon of the global IP trade. If the currency of the old capitalist social order is gold, colonies, and raw materials, the currency of today's informational capitalism is said to be intellectual property or creativity in the form of ideas, innovations, and inventions (Warshofky 1994). And the United States is said to be the first country to realize that its economy is increasingly dependent on IP to maintain its economic superiority in the world. Thus, in the 1980s, the United States through corporate lobbying of top IP multinational corporations which are most affected by piracy and counterfeiting abroad with the weak global IPR protection system made a series of policies to require developing countries to adopt the U.S.-patterned IP protection. To hide its hegemonic designs and to make it appear that protecting IP is for the interest of all nations, the United States used the cultural mechanism of law, utilizing multilateral agreements, especially the General Agreement on Tariffs and Trade (GATT) and its Trade-Related Aspects of Intellectual Property (TRIPS); free trade agreements (FTAs), especially bilateral trade agreements with individual countries (BTAs); and multilateral and regional institutions such as the World Bank (WB) and the International Monetary Fund (IMF), to pressure developing and IP-consuming countries to adopt a stricter IPR protection system that favors U.S. IP companies and multinationals. And the most potent U.S. legal tools to counter the "scourge" of piracy at home and abroad against American IP are Section 337 of the Tariff Act of 1930 that allows punitive action against pirated imported products and Section 301 of the Omnibus Trade and Competitiveness Act of 1988 that allows the U.S. President through the USTR to create piracy watch lists and unilaterally impose trade sanctions against countries engaging in piracy against U.S. IP goods and services (Pugatch 2004).

1.4.3.2 Piracy as Resistance to U.S. IP Hegemony

The social resistance of emerging and IP-consuming economies of the Global South also constitutes a major global force that fuels the persistence of media piracy. The U.S. hegemony in the global IP trade did not unfold in the international stage without the opposition of emerging countries led by China and ASEAN countries in the USTR's watch lists, pressured by the United States to adopt a stringent IPR protection regime in the Asia Pacific region. Law is not only a maker of hegemony but also of social resistance. Thus, to counteract the U.S. hegemony in the global IP trade, resisting countries use the same IPR laws and their loopholes to engage in both active and passive resistance. To avoid losing trade benefits with the United States, emerging economies employ piracy as a form of passive or covert resistance or what James Scott calls as the "Weapons of the Weak" (Scott 1987). This covert resistance from below can occur in the legal and law enforcement loopholes. Passive resistance can include delaying tactics, tolerant attitude of government toward counterfeiting, publicity stunts in piracy raids by local law enforcers, underfunding law enforcement programs, nonenforcement of IP law such as the optical media law due to government's weak drive against corruption, etc. Since the multilateral agreement on the international standards of IPR protection called TRIPS and U.S.-patterned IPR system which are imposed on developing countries are new transplants in the legal culture of emerging economies, cracks in law enforcement and formalization process of digital media trade can result in covert resistance (Wei 2010). These cracks can manifest in the bureaucratic burdens and complex, time-consuming, and expensive requirements in formalizing the optical media business, nonenforcement of the optical media law, government's tolerance of corruption in antipiracy campaigns, and in the technological spaces created by the Information Communication Technologies (ICTs) that allow infringement strategies as a form of social resistance in the cyberspace.

1.4.3.3 The Rise of the Middle Class and Media Urbanism

The persistence of global media piracy must also to be seen within the context of the growing middle class in emerging economies and what Sundaram (2009) calls as media urbanism. The urbanization that took place over a period of several decades in Europe and North America is said to have happened in just a few years in East Asia and Asia Pacific, as shown by the emergence of megacities and hundreds of small and medium urban settlements (Yeung 2014, p. 3). The Asia Pacific region is not only the locus of the fastest-growing urbanism and migration in today's global age but also the primary focus of the U.S. IP hegemony and destination of American IP and digital media goods and services. This results in a new form of urbanism where the claims of/on the city are interpolated with the world of film, music, cable, software, advertising, and television. Urban life and consumption in Asia Pacific megacities are, therefore, increasingly mediated by U.S. digital media goods and services. The U.S. search engine giant Google and its multimedia social media platform YouTube as well as American social media such as Facebook, Twitter, and LinkedIn, for instance, are highly influential in the cultural life of the middle class in Asia Pacific.

It is highly recognized by economists and marketers that a rising demand for copyright and digital materials presupposes a growing urban society with a large middle class. Most consumers of digital goods and services belong to the middle class who have a high level of computer literacy, strong Internet connection, and financial capacity to buy the latest digital gadgets and computer applications to access the latest digital consumer products and services. And countries with a fast-rising middle class with strong appetite for copyright and digital materials are, coincidentally, concentrated in the Asia Pacific region, being the fastest and largest regional economy in the world, even surpassing the U.S. and European economies. China alone with its huge growing middle class and fast-growing economy which can even overtake the United States as the number one economy in the world is enough to attract the global U.S. and foreign copyright multinationals to Asia

Pacific. Moreover, the ASEAN countries join China to constitute the largest and fastest-growing middle class concentration in the world with a rising exponential consumption of U.S. media goods and services. Unfortunately, China and ASEAN are also the leading countries in the Asia Pacific region and in the world with the highest concentration of the world's poor and incidence of pirate consumption and illegal media trade, largely done and participated by the poor and migrants.

The rise of media urbanism has resulted in two major cultures of consumption in this region: the licit consumption of the affluent and middle class and the pirate consumption of the poor and migrants. Consumption is not just physical but also social: "You are what you buy" (Todd 2011). The way people consume goods and services such as digital media and choose their brands reflects their social class and stature in society. Piracy can, therefore, be seen as an illegal and counterfeit consumption of the poor who tries to improve their life and imitate the licit media consumption of the affluent and middle class. Struggling to survive in alienating cities and unable to buy genuine media goods and participate in licit media trade, many poor and migrants engage in illegal activities such as pirate media consumption and retail business in order to survive and meet social expectations. Hernando de Soto (1989) argued that the poor live, trade, manufacture, transport, or even use goods in the city illegally, at times, to overcome poverty. But such illegality is not antisocial in intent but is intended to achieve such essentially legal objectives such as building a house, raising a family, providing a service, or developing a business. Economically speaking, the poor and migrants who engaged in these activities are better off when they violate the laws than when they respect them (de Soto 1989, pp. 11–12). With the complex, rigid, and high cost of doing licit optical media trade as demanded by the USTR and government's antipiracy agencies and the high prices of genuine media products and services, the poor are forced to go illegal in their optical disc vending trade and consumption patterns.

1.4.4 The Development Communication Approach to Media Piracy

If many of those who engage in piracy trade and pirate consumption in emerging and developing countries of the Asia Pacific, including the Philippines and Vietnam, are migrants, poor, marginalized, or those who have no adequate access to licit copyright goods, services, and trade, then it is imperative that they must be part of the current global media market and development initiatives. The media are important contributors to social and cultural life and key components of democratic structures. They are a significant driver of growth in many economies. The business of producing content generates substantial income flows and jobs that contribute directly to the economy. Increased access to knowledge spurs higher levels of literacy, which strengthens human capital for higher productivity (Locksley 2008, p. 2). Development communication as one of the classical theories of communication research aims to place communication and media technology in the service of development. Its main focus is not just economic programs but the development of people. It assumes that in any strategy or program of development, it sees people as the prime target. The needs of the people predicate the delivery of development under this theory (Lagerway 1990). This approach seems appropriate in the current search for IP development paradigms. Minimizing media piracy, particularly optical disc retail piracy in emerging markets of Southeast Asia such as the Philippines and Vietnam which is dominated by the poor, requires the holistic approach of development communication that allows the participation of the less privileged and migrants in the licit market.

The capitalist colonization and privatization of the creative commons have blocked the licit access of the poor to genuine copyright materials and processes necessary for their human development, thus encouraging them to engage in illicit access through piracy. The demand for stricter IPR protection by the USTR and the hegemonic control of the United States and its rich trading partners of the global IP trade creates a global market that favors the affluent and middle class consumers and rich formal traders but discriminates the poor, the marginalized, and those who lack legal access to current technologies and business opportunities necessary for their human development. This has created overt and covert social resistance which resulted in various piracy strategies. Despite the mass production and lowering of prices of some ICT devices, the high-quality digital goods and services on the Internet continue to be unaffordable to the poor. Even Internet access remains elusive for the poor. In the Philippines, for instance, Internet connection which is controlled by private corporations is highly expensive and inaccessible to the poor. This partly explains why the use of pirated CDs and DVDs or optical disc piracy remains popular to the less privileged in the Philippines and other developing countries despite the rising online piracy in developed countries. The licit market for copyright goods and services is limited in developing countries and biased against the poor.

Capitalism endorses the primacy of the market for people's development and economic welfare. It is assumed that the more people are connected with the market, the more are their chances to be part of the global consuming public. Although the market is an important structure for development in capitalist societies, it is, however, structured in ways that make it both inclusive and exclusive as in the case of the current media market. It is inclusive in the sense that it caters to every community that can afford to buy or sell something. But it is also exclusive in the sense that it discriminates against people who live below the poverty threshold or those millions of people who cannot buy or sell in the market (UNESCO, p. 14). The current media market discriminates the poor and encourages them to engage in pirate consumption and illegal retail trade. The licit market for genuine IP and media products is clearly discriminatory against the poor especially to those piracy-laden developing countries of Southeast Asia. The price of an original DVD containing a feature film, for instance, is usually ten times higher than the pirated copy. The poor who cannot afford the original DVD copy usually buys the pirated version in illegal market. In Vietnam, for instance, those who buy pirated CDs which contain educational books or textbooks are usually poor students and parents who cannot afford

Fig. 1.4 Pirated educational CDs sold in a Vietnamese bookstore and usually bought by poor students and parents (Image courtesy of the author)

to buy the original copies. Thus, Karaganis (2012) argued that the high prices for genuine media goods and the low incomes of those who consume pirated products are some of the main ingredients of global media piracy. In Vietnam and the Philippines, the price of an original DVD can be equivalent to a week's food for a poor family. Thus, lowering the price of media goods in low-income developing countries can be crucial to minimize media piracy. The price structure of media goods and services must be responsive to the income levels and the living standards of countries to enable the poor to access the necessary copyrighted content for poverty alleviation and development (Fig. 1.4).

Restructuring the market also implies creating new business models that prioritize human development over maximization of profit. Limited piracy in new markets is actually a form of informal marketing that popularizes the product. Thus, what industry studies consider as losses due to piracy may not actually be lost sales but expansion of the product's market. Allowing piracy in poor and developing countries can create demands for copyright goods and services overseas, while legal and judicial infrastructures for the entry of genuine products into emerging markets are still on their way. Moreover, reforming the market also requires simplifying the registration and bureaucratic requirements for optical media trade to attain full formalization of the optical media trade, thus allowing the poor in developing countries to avail of the business opportunities of the licit media market especially for small optical media retail business. This requires dialogue and coordination between copyright and Internet service providers, soft and hard technology manufacturers, government and multilateral IP regulators, and the USTR in order to come up with a unified and more humane and pro-poor IP business model and development system.

Lastly, addressing media piracy problem using the holistic approach of development communication requires a more relational and sociological perspective, keeping in mind the growing complexity of the current network and global society. Media piracy is a complex phenomenon that intertwines with various human and nonhuman networks in different dimensions.

1.5 The Book's Sociological Approach

Sociological approaches do not only examine the legal and law enforcement systems of social phenomena but also the human and nonhuman networks, specifically the social and technological interactions between people and material environment. The socio-ecological model, for instance, considers the complex interplay between individual, relationship, community, and societal factors in understanding social phenomena. When dealing with economic actions such as the illegal optical media piracy, the economic-sociological perspective can examine networks, long been considered by scholars as an important component to business success and a significant information resource which can be critical in identifying and exploiting business opportunities (Hendry et al. 1991). Social networks, especially co-ethnic and kinship networks, are also relevant in overcoming informal barriers in international trade, i.e., weak legal international institutions or inadequate information about trading opportunities (Rauch and Trindade 2002, p. 116). The illegal optical media trade is largely controlled by networks of Chinese traders. These Chinese traders with global and local networks are known to be in the forefront of the piracy trade as suppliers and producers of pirated digital media in Southeast Asia, particularly in the Philippines and Vietnam. Thus, in an environment of network society, global business, and digital technology, the actor–network theory (ANT), a constructivist and relational network perspective in the sociology of technology, can be an appropriate theoretical framework to apply in investigating the human and technological networks that sustain the optical media piracy trade in the Philippines and Vietnam.

The sociological perspective which examines social phenomena in a holistic and empirical way can be a suitable lens to understand the complex and multidimensional problem of media piracy. Unfortunately, there is very little sociological and empirical work that examines media piracy, particularly in the SEA countries such as the Philippines and Vietnam, that uses the relational and network approach. Karaganis (2012) observed that there has been a good number of industry research on global media piracy funded by U.S. software, film, and music industry associations over the past two decades, but there is little and infrequent independent empirical research on media piracy (p. 15). The early major empirical work on media piracy, focusing on China and Taiwan, with a sociological orientation was published more than ten years ago by Shujen Wang (2003). This was followed recently by a comprehensive edited volume entitled "Media Piracy in Emerging Economies" which showed a lot of sociological underpinnings on copyright piracy in developing economies. It covered a lot of topics on IPR and copyright piracy of several countries, but did not include the Philippines and Vietnam in its analysis (Karaganis

2012). The most recent major empirical work on media piracy with sociological underpinnings is the book by Ramon Lobato entitled *Shadow Economies of Cinema: Mapping Informal Film Distribution* (2013). This study offers a more holistic bottom-up understanding of the dynamics of informal and illegal film distribution in the informal or shadow economies—from the informal distribution sites of Los Angeles, Lagos, and Melbourne up to Mexico City. Its main focus, however, is on film piracy and not on media piracy in Southeast Asia. The research does not also include the Philippines and Vietnam in its investigation and analysis.

This book which is based on the dissertation and postdoctoral research study of the author aims to address this need for more sociological and empirical studies on media piracy and attempts to account the persistence of optical media piracy trade in the Philippines and Vietnam using sociological perspectives, particularly those of the critical and network perspectives of sociology of law, resistance, and technology. Although this book applies an eclectic theoretical approach, the overriding sociological framework used in this book is the relational and network approach of the actor–network theory (ANT) of sociology of technology to interpret the interconnections of various human and nonhuman networks that sustain media piracy in the Philippines and Vietnam.

1.6 Objectives of the Book

The main objective of the book is to understand the persistence of media piracy in the Philippines and Vietnam from a more holistic approach of sociology. Beyond the arguments of defective law enforcement and copyright legal systems, this book examines the socioeconomic networks behind the persistence of media piracy in two developing countries consistently listed in the annual Special 301 Report of the USTR as piracy hotspots in Southeast Asia, namely, the Philippines and Vietnam. Using documentary and ethnographic data and the relational approach of the actor–network theory (ANT) in the sociology of technology as the overall theoretical framework, the book investigates how the following network forces contribute to the persistence of media piracy and impede the full formalization of the optical media trade in the Philippines and Vietnam: the government's positive attitude toward the informal sector, strong social resistance of developing countries to stronger IPR protection demanded by the USTR, unstable and sometimes conflicting trade policies on intellectual property and technology, burdensome business registration process, weak enforcement of business regulations, bureaucratic corruption and loopholes in law enforcement system, as well as trade ties of piracy-laden countries with China.

The book also attempts to provide a social background of the people behind the illegal business of counterfeit CDs and DVDs and why they persist in this type of trade. It also provides an overview of the media piracy through the years in both physical and digital formats as well as its future trends vis-à-vis technological advancement and innovation. Ultimately, this book invites policymakers, law enforcers, advocates of antipiracy groups, and the general public to use a more holistic lens in understanding the persistence of copyright piracy in developing countries and thus shifting the blame from the moral defect of the traders to the current problematic copyright policy and enforcement structure as well as the difficulty of crafting effective antipiracy measures in a constantly evolving technological advancement of the global era. Instead of focusing only "on enforcement—on strengthening police powers, streamlining judicial procedures, increasing criminal penalties, and extending surveillance and punitive measures to the Internet" in fighting media piracy, this book suggests that policy discussions and formulations to minimize media piracy must also include the technological and sociocultural factors which support it (Karaganis 2011, p. 5).

Although this book contains some inside information and social patterns on how media piracy is done and sustained by traders and their networks in the Philippines and Vietnam, it does not intend to be a handbook or intelligence guide for law enforcement, especially with regard to the social profile of traders (Chap. 5) and to the strategies used by traders and unscrupulous law enforcers to circumvent the optical media law (Chap. 6). The main intention of this book is largely academic: to theorize sociologically and to provide empirical illustrations thereof on how the media piracy trade persists in the Philippines and Vietnam as well as to expand the scope of the current debate and theorize on copyright piracy, one that includes the nonmarket and nonlegal sociocultural networks that sustain copyright infringement and media piracy trade.

1.7 Definition of Terms

This book uses three major terms which need conceptual definition and delineation of their scope to fully understand their usage throughout the text.

The first most important term which is often mentioned in this book is intellectual property (IP). The World Intellectual Property Organization (WIPO) defines intellectual property as "creations of the mind, such as inventions; literary and artistic works; designs; and symbols, names and images used in commerce." It has four general types: copyright, patents, industrial designs, and geographical indications. Since this book also mentions copyright and patent, a WIPO definition is further needed to clarify their scope as forms of IP. A "copyright" is a legal right given to authors for their creative works such as books, music, paintings, sculpture, and films, to computer programs, databases, advertisements, maps, and technical drawings. A patent is an exclusive right granted for an invention (Fig. 1.5).[19]

The second important term of this book is "piracy." This term has no direct, universal, or stable legal definition in official reports or current literature on copyright infringement. Most descriptions and definitions about it are shaped by American copyright industries and antipiracy organizations and often viewed from the legal

[19] http://www.wipo.int/about-ip/en/index.html#ip

Fig. 1.5 Patent, copyright license, and trademark show intellectual property (Image courtesy of Stuart Miles at FreeDigitalPhotos.net)

perspective. This is partly due to the nuances of the meaning of the various types of unauthorized use of copyrighted materials. Moreover, technology which carries copyright content is constantly evolving due to innovation. For instance, the term "VCD format" included in the optical disc piracy definition is no longer useful as this format has already become extinct with the invention of new formats. The constant change of type and format of optical media prevents the fixing of the definition of media piracy by authorities. The law which has the power of fixing social arrangement has always been behind innovations. Oftentimes, when a legal definition has been established, subsequent societal conditions would sometimes alter it significantly and necessitate an amendment of the existing definition. A conceptual or operational definition is also largely determined by the underlying theory or perspective which shapes it.

Most current definitions of piracy or media piracy are largely influenced by the prescriptive views of jurisprudence and ethics that dominate today's copyright piracy literature. Piracy, under these perspectives, is often seen as a theft of intellectual creation, an illegal act or crime, rather than a complex process that requires empirical assessment. Thus, it is better to view the current definitions of piracy as a social construction, a product of enforcement debates, rather than a description of a specific behavior (Karaganis 2012, p. 2). The term piracy as illegal copying of copyright products has various shades of meaning from a mere unauthorized downloading to a large-scale commercial activity. In this book, the term "piracy" as used in the Philippines and Vietnam primarily refers to the illegal large-scale and commercial copying and distribution of optical media as stored in digital disc formats such as DVD, DVD-R, CD, CD-R, and VCD. It can also mean as the unauthorized use, access, loading, downloading, selling, and sharing of copyrighted media on the Internet by individuals or groups.

Finally, the most important term used in this book is media piracy. Media piracy is an additional term and social construct in copyright piracy literature. With some popular works in the social sciences (e.g., Wang 2003; Karaganis 2012; Lobato 2012) and the frequent use of the term by corporate lobbying groups such as the IIPA, media piracy has gradually become a standard term in intellectual property infringement literature. But like "piracy," this term has no stable definition and often carries with it the moral undertone as a form of theft and crime. In legal terms, media piracy can be defined as the illegal or unauthorized mastering, manufacturing, copying, distribution, and sale of soft or hard copies of optical media containing copyrighted film, music, book, video game, business and computer software, and other materials on the Internet or in illegal retail stores using the various disc formats such as DVD-R, DVD, CD, CD-R, Blu-ray, and other storing devices in violation of the optical media law. Due to lack of existing sociological definition of piracy, this book adopts this working definition for media piracy, although its sociological analysis would go beyond and view it as an unauthorized process rather than a mere illegal act. Furthermore, this book would focus on the trade aspect of media piracy in disc format or on optical disc piracy trade. Although online piracy is popular in developed countries but has just started gaining ground in emerging economies of Southeast Asia, optical disc media still remain very popular in developing countries such the Philippines and Vietnam. The persistence of media piracy can be examined from various aspects and dimensions. This book focuses on the persistence of the illegal production of digital media and not on illegal consumption. Thus, it incorporates as much as possible the points of view of the law enforcers and of the optical media traders themselves, not consumers. It assumes that consumption of counterfeit media would not prosper without the persistence of the illegal media production and distribution (Fig. 1.6).

Media piracy can be classified broadly into two different types depending on the source where the copyrighted media were used and stored: optical disc media piracy if the digital media such as music, software, video game, or film are stored and

Fig. 1.6 Picture concept pirate discs (Image courtesy of jiggoja at FreeDigitalPhotos.net)

viewed in discs and online media piracy or Internet piracy if the content is viewed, downloaded, or copied directly from the Internet. If piracy is understood in the general sense as copying outside the copyright law, then optical media piracy is the unauthorized copying of optical media as defined by the optical media law. This type of media piracy is popularly understood as the illegal copying, distribution, and trading of optical media discs such CDs, CD-ROMs, or DVDs which contain copyrighted film, music, textbook, software, and other digital media content by illegal vendors in the sidewalks, kiosks, or retail shops of developing countries. The Philippine Optical Media Law of 2003 provides a technical definition of optical media as:

> a storage medium or device in which information, including sounds and/or images, or software code, has been stored, either by mastering and/or replication, which may be accessed and read using a lens scanning mechanism employing a high intensity light source such as a laser or any such other means as may be developed in the future. (Section 3 [i])

Online media or digital media piracy can be defined as the unauthorized use, copying, mastering, replication, and sale of copyrighted music, film, software, video game, and other copyright content uploaded, downloaded, or shared on the Internet. Although this book also mentions media piracy on the Internet or online piracy, its main focus is on the illegal manufacturing, sale, distribution, or trading of copies of optical media stored in DVD, DVD-R, CD, CD-R, Blu-ray, and VCD formats, or what is popularly known as the optical disc piracy. The term optical disc piracy, highly influenced by the definition of the Motion Picture Association of America (MPAA), is often popularly understood as counterfeiting of motion pictures or films. And since the greater bulk of pirated digital media are films, the term optical disc piracy is often synonymous with film piracy or counterfeiting of motion pictures. While it is true that film is one of the most popular media counterfeited in developing countries, this term, however, also includes unauthorized replication and distribution of other media content such as music, business and computer software, video games, textbooks, or e-books stored in a disc. In its broadest sense, the term "media piracy" as understood in this book is referring to the unauthorized or illegal use, uploading, downloading, copying, sharing, mastering, distributing, and retailing of copyrighted digital media such as film, music, books, video games, business and computer software, and other digital applications in disc or file format which are intended for online and/or offline social interactions or exchanges.

1.8 Theoretical Framework

This book uses a relational and network approach to the persistence of media piracy. It examines the connections of some major forces which sustain the illegal trade of optical media in the Philippines and Vietnam. It assumes that media piracy persists in these countries because there are key intertwining social and technological networks which support it. Human actors or groups do not only form networks with other actors or groups, they also create networks with a series of material and nonhuman networks to pursue a social practice (Law 1992). But unlike the approach of popular network theories which focus only on human social networks, this book also explores the nonhuman and technological networks. Media piracy as a social practice is highly mediated by digital technology. Media piracy could not be accomplished by humans without the indispensable cooperation of the latest digital and replicating technology and the information and communications technologies (ICTs) such as the Internet, smartphones, tablets, personal computers, and other high-tech gadgets. Thus, a pirate producer cannot master or replicate an optical media without replicating machines nor get the orders of distributors on the number of pirated discs from the provinces in the Philippines without the mobile phone technology.

In analyzing illegal or criminal act such as media piracy, many sociologists and criminologists tend to neglect the technological or material networks that accompany the performance of an illegal act in favor of the social. Yet in an informational society, the only things that appear to have real existence are machines: "transportation systems, cable and wireless networks, microwave channels, satellites and the Internet which are the 'scapes' that 'constitute' various interconnected nodes along which flows can be relayed" (Urry 2000, p. 35). In a digital world, machines become more and more linked in a symmetrical manner with human actors in heterogeneous networks, thus blurring the distinction between the human and technical agency. In this case, understanding novel crimes such as piracy and counterfeiting can no longer be analyzed adequately using the classical and popular approaches of criminology and the sociology of crime that apply the strict human and material dichotomy between the criminal and criminal tools and neglect the network components of organized criminality. Nigel Coles (2001), for instance, laments the failure by criminologists to adopt social network analysis techniques and concepts in the investigation of criminal networks. For him, such techniques offer significant potential advantages to criminologists seeking to analyze relational data.

Overcoming this dichotomy between the subject and object in crime as well as the apparent lack of social network analysis techniques in criminology, this study attempts to apply the ANT, a new theoretical movement in the sociology of science and technology, to show how the human and the material interplay and merge in the crime of copyright piracy. ANT's peculiar feature of resolving this dichotomy can greatly account for the accomplishment and persistence of the optical media piracy trade in today's cyber society. The primary tenet of actor–network theory (Callon and Law 1989; Latour 1993; Law 1992) is the concept of heterogeneous network that social life and technology are products of the interplay of material and human networks. A network is said to contain many dissimilar human (social) and nonhuman (technical) elements or "actants" which are considered inseparable from one another. ANT concentrates on yielding a unified theoretical perspective. It claims to deliver a nondualistic standpoint on how things are "stitched together" across divisions and distinctions. It seamlessly combines the social and the material world in a symmetrical way (Murdoch 1997). It attempts to understand how interactions are commonly framed through mixtures of the social and the material. For ANT, "material resources and technologies are as much more than simply the outcrops of human intention and actions, for they actively participate in processes of interaction. These resources frame, define and configure interaction. And without such resources humans could never hope to act upon others distant in time and space" (Murdoch, 1997, p. 329). Applying this approach, this book sees the persistence of media piracy as fueled by a smooth running of an intertwining network of some major social and technological networks which sustain the counterfeit trade in the Philippines and Vietnam, both legal and nonlegal as well as the macro and micro dimensions.

1.9 Methodology

This main bulk of the data of this book is based on the two subsequent research studies by the author whose fieldwork has spanned to more than 6 years. Most of the ethnographic data, particularly those in Chaps. 3, 4, 5, and 6, are based on the dissertation research completed in 2011 which dealt on the persistence of optical disc piracy in Quiapo Barter Trade Center Complex in the city of Manila and on the subsequent postdoctoral research project on the obstacles of formalizing the optical media trade in the Philippines and Vietnam, sponsored by the Southeast Asian Studies Regional Exchange Program (SEASREP) in 2012–2013. The Quiapo Barter Trade Piracy network being investigated in the dissertation is the central piracy network of production and distribution of pirated media discs in the Philippines, while the media piracy networks studied in the subsequent research are retail piracy networks in the Philippines and Vietnam. In the Philippines, one group of retail piracy networks included in the study was located in one municipality in the province of Rizal and the other group was situated in one major city of Metro Manila, two of the many satellite retail networks of the Quiapo piracy network in the country. In Vietnam, retail networks being studied were retail piracy outlets in Ho Chi Minh City which included some mobile piracy stalls and CD–DVD shops of various sizes that sell pirated media discs. These retail networks in the Philippines and Vietnam are among the notorious open piracy sites frequently mentioned by the IIPA and USTR in their annual Special 301 Reports. The book, therefore, aims to show the interconnection of the various types of networks in the piracy trade as well as to illustrate how a big production and distribution piracy network like the Quiapo piracy network interconnects with its small retail networks to persist in the illegal network of optical media trade.

Both research studies relied on secondary and primary data. The secondary data included official reports and records of private and public documents, books, newspaper reports, research articles in journals, and other online materials. The primary data came from the structured and unstructured in-depth interviews with the key informants, survey, and personal knowledge and observation of the author such as the giving of bribe money by DVD vendors to local policemen. The key informants in the dissertation included 1 community organizer in the Quiapo Barter Trade Center area, 2 producers, 2 former Optical Media Board (OMB) chairmen, 2 OMB agents, 5 policemen, 10 distributors and 35 retailers, and 4 local Muslim leaders. Triangulation was applied to test the veracity of information. Three criteria according to their importance were used in the selection of key informants: reliability, availability, experience, and referral from the lead key and trusted informant who have personal knowledge of the trade. Being a regular visitor and observer of the Quiapo Barter Trade Center piracy complex and an occasional buyer and former student of a nearby university law school for a couple of years, with a few Muslim classmates whose relatives were piracy operators in the barter trade area, the author gained some personal knowledge about the illegal trade and a witness on how the Quiapo Muslim trade area transformed from a commercial barter trade center of legal clothing and home and personal products into a "notorious" open piracy hub of pirated discs and counterfeit goods in the Philippines.

The description and analysis of the piracy network in Vietnam, culled from the author's postdoctoral research project report, were based on secondary and documentary sources and on the author's personal observations and in-depth interviews with some employees, mobile traders, and owners of CD–DVD shops in Ho Chi Minh City in October 2012 with the aid of two highly educated Vietnamese interpreters and guides who were familiar with the media piracy trade. These interpreters–informants toured the researcher and introduced him to the various retail networks in the Vietnamese city. The key informants on the *Giang ho* (gangster) protection racket have personal knowledge as their establishments have experienced dealing with the underworld. Relevant news reports and research studies on the informal Vietnamese trade, especially those connected with media piracy, were also examined and used to supplement or countercheck what informants have shared during the fieldwork. Of course, like any other research studies that deal with illegality, corruption, or the underworld, a gap can always be expected in the data. Nevertheless, some social patterns can still be identified by triangulating some trustworthy information which can suggest or provide a glimpse on what the entire empirical reality would probably look like. The names of key informants are withheld in this book to protect their privacy and security.

Lastly, this book would often cite the Special 301 annual assessments and reports of the IIPA and USTR to supplement its research findings, owing to the limited literature and data on media piracy in the Philippines and Vietnam—taking into consideration their limitations and the methodological issues raised by some scholars and researchers against industry-sponsored piracy statistics and studies.

1.9.1 The Roadmap of the Book

This book consists of seven chapters. The first two chapters provide an overview of the book and of the global context on the ongoing politics of intellectual property trade and piracy in the world between the United States, China, and the IP-consuming countries. The next four chapters would explain the major social and technological forces and networks which sustain the media piracy trade in the Philippines and Vietnam. The last chapter provides an overview on the evolution of media piracy through the years as well as some important future trends and trajectories of IPR protection and media piracy in the world.

In particular, Chap. 1 explains the background, objectives, theoretical framework, method of data collection, and roadmap of the book. Chapter 2 provides an introduction and overview of the ongoing politics of control and hegemony of the intellectual property (IP) trade in the world by IP-exporting countries led by the United States and the politics of piracy and social resistance by IP-consuming developing countries such as the Philippines and Vietnam. It highlights the centrality of power analysis in any sociological investigation of socioeconomic phenomena such as the persistence of media piracy in the world. Understanding the persistence of the optical disc piracy would not be fully understood without examining the dynamics of power and politics between exporting and importing countries of IP goods and services. Thus, this chapter broadly describes the global context of the ongoing politics of control and hegemony of the IP trade in the world by IP-exporting countries led by the United States and social resistance of IP-consuming and emerging economies led by China and some ASEAN countries such as the Philippines and Vietnam. It assumes that the prevalence of media piracy in the Philippines and Vietnam is primarily a form of passive resistance, the "Weapon of the Weak" of the IP-importing countries against the pressure and insistence of the United States and top IP-exporting countries on stronger IPR protection.

Chapter 3 argues that the tolerant attitude of the Philippine and Vietnamese governments toward informal work and trade, as reflected in their legislation and programs on the informal sector, supports informality and thus encourages informal business such as the optical disc piracy trade. Developing countries see the crucial role of the informal sector in employment generation and economic growth. Thus, they see no urgency to expedite the formalization of businesses including the illegal optical disc trade and comply with the demand of intellectual property (IP)-exporting countries led by the United States for greater IPR protection.

Chapter 4 explains the legal and bureaucratic obstacles as an important force which sustains the piracy trade. It argues that optical disc traders prefer to go informal in their business operations as it is easier, more convenient, and cheaper to maintain than going legal in the Philippines and Vietnam. It describes the overall cultural and business regulatory environment of these two countries and points out some of the major legal and bureaucratic burdens and difficulties of opening and maintaining legality in retail business and regulating the technologies of the piracy trade as contributory factors in the persistence of informality and illegality of the optical media business in the Philippines and Vietnam.

Chapter 5 opens up with the general profile of traders of optical disc piracy trade. Then it argues that these Filipino and Vietnamese traders participate in the piracy business because of some major social, economic, and technological factors other than weak legal, judicial, and law enforcement systems that encourage them to engage in counterfeit media business. This includes the "push" factors such as the adverse socioeconomic situations in the Philippines, for example, the ongoing war in Autonomous Region in Muslim Mindanao, massive poverty, and social discrimination against Muslim Filipinos, which drive the displaced Maranao and Maguindanao Muslims to migrate to urban centers and engage in optical disc piracy as an alternative livelihood, and the "pull" factors such as the opening of more trading opportunities facilitated by the *Doi Moi* (renovation) economic policy of the Vietnamese government, the lure of higher profits in optical disc piracy trade, and the ease of registering and maintaining a CD–DVD shops that sell counterfeit discs. The chapter ends with other important factors such as material networks that support the persistence of piracy: (1) technological network (the use of allied digital technologies that facilitate the piracy business operations for traders, particularly the Internet, the mobile phone, and other hardware and software digital technologies), (2) kinship network (the employment of social and kinship ties to manage the illegal trade and protect its secrecy), (3) ethnic network (the recruitment of informal workers and traders who belong to similar ethnolinguistic group to protect the secrecy of the trade and the use of local language as deterrence against raids and other law enforcement actions), and (4) religious affiliation (common religious ties among traders protect trade secrets and serve as deterrence against law enforcement).

Chapter 6 argues that the persistence of the optical disc piracy trade in the Philippines and Vietnam is not primarily sustained by lack of law enforcement action but by monetary and bureaucratic corruption and by the illegal alliance between law enforcers, illegal traders, and other illegal groups, resulting in inaction of law enforcers and nonenforcement of the optical media law. To support this argument, this chapter examines and analyzes sociologically some social patterns and cases of corruption, particularly bribery, in production and retail piracy, airport and mall operations, government antipiracy agencies, judicial proceedings, and conduct of raids. Ultimately, it argues that what the official law says "it is" may not be what "corrupt" law enforcers and other illegal groups say "it is" in actual social practice.

Finally, Chap. 7 provides some overview of the evolution of media piracy through the years and some future trends and trajectories of the optical media piracy. Media piracy is an evolving cybercrime which can easily adapt to the current technological and social environment. Optical disc piracy seems to be a transitory phenomenon in developing countries with underdeveloped IP culture and low Internet penetration. But as developing countries such as the Philippines and Vietnam increase in Internet penetration and computer literacy, media piracy shifts to online piracy. This chapter also traces the technological development in media piracy from analog to nanotechnology and the role of China in the evolution of copyright infringement and counterfeit trade in the world. Finally, it suggests some major directions and trends in media piracy as technology becomes more powerful and sophisticated. The advent of quantum computing and growing role of hacking in counterfeiting and media piracy is also being projected as one of the most serious challenges to copyright industries and law enforcement agencies in today's global and technological age.

References

Baes, J. (2002). *Toward a political economy of the 'real': Music piracy and the Philippine cultural imaginary*. Paper read at the conference on "media practice and performance across cultures", University of Wisconsin-Madison, Wisconsin, 14–17 Mar 2002.

Ballano, V. (2011). *Law, technology, and networks: A study on the persistence of the informal optical media piracy business in a Philippine Barter Trade Center*. Unpublished dissertation, Department of Sociology-Anthropology, Ateneo de Manila University.

Berger, P. L., & Luckmann, T. (1966). *The social construction of reality: A treatise in the sociology of knowledge*, Garden City: Anchor Books.

Callon, M., & Law, J. (1989). On the construction of sociotechnical networks: Content and context revisited. *Knowledge and Society*, *9*, 57–83.

Chaudhry, P., & Zimmerman, A. (2013). *Protecting your intellectual property rights: Understanding the role of management, governments, consumers and pirates*. New York: Springer Science+Business Media.

Coles, N. (2001). It's not what you know-It's who you know that counts. Analysing serious crime groups as social networks. *British Journal of Criminology*, *41*(4), 580–594.

De Soto, H. (1989). *The other path: The economic path to terrorism*. New York: Perseus Books.

De Vera, B. A. (2013, November 4). Less than a year after its 'upgrade', Quiapo back in anti-piracy radar. *Interaksyon*. http://www.interaksyon.com/business/74122/less-than-a-year-after-its-upgrade-quiapo-back-in-anti-piracy-radar. Accessed 15 Sept 2014.

Fredriksson, M. (2012). Piracy, globalisation and the colonisation of the commons. *Global Media Journal – Australian Edition*, *6*(1), 1–10.

Hendry, C. et al. (1991). *Human resource development in small to medium-sized enterprises* (Research Paper No. 88). London: Employment Department.

Hill, C. (2007). Digital piracy: Causes, consequences, and strategic responses. *Asia Pacific Journal of Management*, *24*, 9–25. Doi: 10.1007/s10490-006-9025-0.

IIPA. (2001). 2001 special 301 report. http://www.iipa.com/special301_TOCs/2001_SPEC301_TOC.html. Accessed 3 Aug 2014.

IIPA. (2014). Letter to Ms. Susan F. Wilson, Director for Intellectual Property and Innovation, Office of the United States Trade Representative. http://www.iipa.com/pdf/2014SPEC301COVERLETTER.pdf. Accessed 16 Jan 2015.

Karaganis, J. (Ed.). (2011). *Media piracy in emerging economies: Price, market structure and consumer behavior*. New York: Social Science Research Council.

Karaganis, J. (2012). Where do music collections come from? http://www.piracy.americanassembly.org/where-do-music-collections-come-from.

Lagerway, Fr. Cornelio. (1990). *Introduction to development communication: Its philosophy and approach*. Monographs on development communication. Manila: Communication Foundation for Asia. http://www.cfamedia.org/main/?p=2427. Accessed 5 June 2015.

Latour, B. (1993). *Re-assembling the social, an introduction to actor-network theory*. Oxford: Oxford University Press. http://www.ufrgs.br/ppgas/portal/arquivos/orientacoes/Latour,Bruno._2012.pdf. Accessed 15 Jan 2015.

John Law (1992) 'Notes on the Theory of the Actor-Network: Ordering, Strategy and Heterogeneity', SystemsPractice, 5 (1992), 379-93

Lobato, R. (2012). *Shadow economies of cinema: Mapping informal film distribution*. London: Palgrave Macmillan.

Lobato, R. (2013). *Shadow economies of cinema: Mapping informal film distribution (cultural histories of cinema)*. London: Palgrave McMillan.

Locksley, G. (2008). *The media and development: What's the story?* World Bank Working Paper 158. http://siteresources.worldbank.org/5EA1BC14-1762-41C0-A156-478520C1DCC3/FinalDownload/DownloadId-8EEA041D40C29CBB4464985E8A677505/5EA1BC14-1762-41C0-A156-478520C1DCC3/INFORMATIONANDCOMMUNICATIONANDTECHNOLOGIES/Resources/The_Media_and_Development.pdf

Mirghani, S. (2011) War on piracy: Analyzing the discursive battles of corporate and government-sponsored anti-media campaigns. *Critical Studies Media Communication, 25*(2), 113–134. Doi: 10.1080/15295036.2010.514933.

Miyazaki, A. D. et al. (2009). Price, scarcity, and consumer willingness to purchase pirated media products. *Journal of Public Policy & Marketing, 28*(1), 71–84.

Murdoch, J. (1997). Towards a geography of heterogeneous associations. *Progress in Human Geography, 21*(3), 321–337.

Pugatch, M. P. (2004). *The international political economy of intellectual property rights*. Cheltenham: Edward Elgar.

Rauch, J. E., & Trindade, V. (2002). Ethnic Chinese networks in international trade. *The Review of Economics and Statistics, 84*(1), 116–130.

Ritzer, G. (2010). *Globalization: The essentials*. West Sussex: Wiley-Blackwell.

Sanchez, J. (2012). How copyright industries con congress. http://www.cato.org/blog/how-copyright-industries-con-congress. Accessed 16 Jan 2015.

Scott, J. C. (1987). *Weapons of the weak: Everyday forms of peasant resistance*. New Haven: Yale University Press.

Sundaram, R. (2009). The new urbanism? Urban life in India and the problem of the copy. http://www.bilkent.edu.tr/bilkent/academic/crts/workshop/ravi_abs.doc

Todd, D. (2011). You are what you buy: Postmodern consumerism and the construction of self. *HOHONU 2012, 10*. http://www.hilo.hawaii.edu/academics/hohonu/documents/vol10x12youarewhatyoubuy-postmodernconsumerismandtheconstructionofself.pdf

Treverton, G. F. et al. (2009). *Film piracy, organized crime, and terrorism*. Santa Monica: RAND Corporation. http://www.rand.org/content/dam/rand/pubs/monographs/2009 RAND_MG742.pdf. Accessed 21 Dec 2013.

UNESCO. Communication technology and development. http://www.unesdoc.unesco.org/images/0008/000811/081109eo.pdf

Urry, J. (2000). Mobile sociology. *British Journal of Sociology, 51*(1), 185–203, http://services.carstensorensen.com/media/Urry2000.pdf. Accessed 16 Jan 2015.

USTR (2014). 2014 special 301 report. https://ustr.gov/sites/default/files/USTR%202014%20Special%20301%20Report%20to%20Congress%20 FINAL.pdf. Accessed 4 Jan 2015.

Wang, S. (2003). *Framing piracy: Globalization and film distribution in Greater China*. New York: Rowman & Littlefield Publishers.

Waterman, D., Ji, S. W., Rochet, L. (2007). Enforcement and control of piracy, and sharing in the movie industry. http://www.indiana.edu/D0AC37F9-8483-49C6-9FD4-B1F5FAE5018F/FinalDownload/DownloadId-84E30BB9E4A03E956B17E7AEF96633AE/D0AC37F9-8483-49C6-9FD4-B1F5FAE5018F/~telecom/people/faculty/waterman/Movie_Piracy_TPRC_8_07.pdf. Accessed 20 June 2015.

Wei, S. (2010). Globalization and indigenization: Legal transplant of a universal TRIPS regime in a multicultural world. *American Business Law Journal, 47*(3), 455–507.

Warshofsky, F. (1994) *Patent wars: The battle to own world's technology*. New York: Wiley.

World Intellectual Property Office. (n.d). WIPO Lex. http://www.wipo.int/wipolex/en/. Accessed 10 Dec 2014.

Williams, R. (1973). Base and superstructure in Marxist cultural theory. *New Left Review, 82*, 3–16.

Yeung, Y. M. (2014). Asia Pacific urbanism under globalization. http://www.researchgate.net/profile/Yue_Yeung/publication/253068580_ASIAPACIFIC_URBANISM_UNDER_GLOBALIZATION/links/543fcb160cf2fd72f99dac22.pdf. Accessed 2 July 2015.

Chapter 2
U.S. Global Hegemony in Intellectual Property and the Politics of Piracy and Resistance

2.1 Understanding Power and Hegemony

Recognizing the centrality of power in any socioeconomic phenomenon has always been at the heart of the sociological analysis. For Anthony Giddens (1985), all social systems are "power systems" and thus power is a fundamental concept in the social sciences. Power for him is domination in terms of acquisition and use of resources or capabilities and expressed in struggles and subordination: Power is generated in and through the reproduction of structures of domination (Giddens 1984). In the modern world, the most generalized and integrated structure of domination, both spatially and temporally, is said to be that of capitalism. Capitalism is not a thing, a system, or a model but, first and foremost, a process and a cluster of structures of systematic domination. And these structures of domination are not attributes of actors but "matrices of social power" that arise from a dominant mode of interaction (Stewart 2001). As a matrix of social domination, capitalism undergoes a historical structuring and modernization that implies subordination of social forms to the pursuit of a single goal of appropriating profit or the accumulation of capital (Stewart 2001, p. 67).

Scholars who use materialist theoretical framework models argue that power is central in the formation of capitalism and in the ability of its elites to transform economic institutions for their own advantage (Chirot 1985; Collins 1986; Hall 1985). In its late development, some authors argued that capitalist accumulation is linked to the extraction of surplus value from the Global South and the use of military Keynesianism to support capital accumulation in the core (Frank 1967; O'Conner 1973). But with its current global brand which Castells (2009) calls as "informational capitalism," accumulation has shifted in form and focus: from the physical plant to the knowledge embodied or used in that plant (Warshofsky 1994). In other words, accumulation in today's capitalism is not so much on acquiring physical goods and services but of the knowledge, copyright, patent, trade secret, or the intellectual property behind the creation of these goods and services.

V.O. Ballano, *Sociological Perspectives on Media Piracy in the Philippines and Vietnam*, DOI 10.1007/978-981-287-922-6_2

To account how states accumulate power and capital in today's global capitalist economy, a remarkable amount of writings has been published in recent years to apply the concept of "hegemony" in order to understand domination in international relations and trade. Domination in the current informational capitalism is said to employ a "diffused" rather than an overt type of power and coercion which suits to what critical scholars understand as hegemony. The concept of hegemony has its roots in the work of the Italian Marxist Antonio Gramsci who argued that dominant groups in society maintain power and protect common class interests, not through coercion but through the use of alliances with members of the elite and cultural institutions such as schools, law, the media, and the church to create a compatible version of reality which favors elite interests. Heavily influenced by this Gramscian view, Stuart Hall (Hall and Jefferson 1976) who further developed the concept of hegemony in cultural studies sees it as referring to "a situation in which a provisional alliance of certain social groups can exert 'total social authority' over other subordinate groups by 'winning and shaping consent so that the power of the dominant classes appears both legitimate and natural'" (Hall 1977). Simply put, "hegemony means moral and philosophical leadership, leadership attained through the active consent of the major groups in society" (Bocock 1986, pp. 27–94). As already mentioned in the previous chapter, Raymond Williams (1973) defines it as "the central, effective and dominant system of meanings and values, which are not merely abstract but which are organized and lived…" and "which are experienced as practices which appear as reciprocally affirming" (Williams 1973, p. 9). Hegemony, therefore, is a "diffused type of power that 'naturalizes' a social order, an institution, or even an everyday practice so that 'how things are' seems inevitable and not the consequence of particular historical actors, classes, and events" (Lazarus-Black and Hirsch 1994, p. 7).

Applying a materialist interpretation and expanding the scope of hegemony to interstate relations, Wallerstein (1991) understands hegemony as referring to that situation in which the ongoing rivalry between so-called great powers is so unbalanced that one power can largely impose its rules and wishes (at the very least by effective veto power) in economic, military, diplomatic, and even cultural arenas (cited in Stiles and Akaha 1991, pp. 428–289). And international domination can be done by a powerful state either through market mechanism or coercive force associated with an empire (Wallerstein 1974). Robert Cox, the first to establish a crucial route to hegemony in international relations, sees hegemony as initially established by social forces occupying a leading role within a state but is projected on a world scale (Cox 1981, p. 139). In other words, hegemony in the global stage may be established within a state and gradually projected to the world to include other states. Hegemony in this sense involves the domination of one state–society complex—and in this case the United States—which becomes the center of the dominant mode of (capital) accumulation and is able to draw in other states and societies to participate in this accumulation (Saull 2012). And with the rise of globalization and informational capitalism, contemporary hegemony occurs not so much in economic and military fields but in the cultural realm of innovation and intellectual property (IP) using the cultural mechanism of law and jurisprudence to gain consent from the dominated economies.

2.2 U.S. Hegemony in Intellectual Property Trade

If the currency of the old capitalist social order is gold, the new currency of the new informational capitalism is said to be IP, that is, ownership of ideas, industrial designs, trademarks, copyright, and other creative products and services based on human creativity and innovation. As already mentioned in the previous chapter, "[c]reativity, in the form of ideas, innovations, and inventions, has replaced gold, colonies, and raw materials as the wealth of nations" (Warshofsky 1994). Innovation, both at the individual and group level, has been increasingly acknowledged by many as the true wealth of nations in the twenty-first century: "The creative economy has become a powerful transformative force in the world today and one of the most rapidly growing sectors of the world economy, not just in terms of income generation but also for job creation and export earnings" (UNESCO & UNDP, Creative Economy Report 2013, p. 15). A greater proportion of the world's intellectual and creative resources are now being invested in culture-based and IP-intensive industries. The concept of intellectual property which was used to be a specialist or an arcane subject has now moved center stage in the global economy (Fig. 2.1).

The American hegemony in IP trade did not arise instantly. It started gradually with the leading role of U.S. IP industries in creating a new IPR regime in the U.S. economy which soon projected on a worldwide scale in the 1980s with the opening of economies of developing countries through free trade and reduction and elimination of tariffs in the General Agreement on Tariffs and Trade (GATT), a multilateral agreement signed by 110 countries around the world. Countries who signed this agreement also agreed to the creation of the World Trade Organization (WTO) and to GATT's Trade-Related Aspects of Intellectual Property Rights agreement (TRIPS), a multilateral agreement which requires member countries to protect IP goods and services from counterfeiting and piracy. Historically, the United States was the first country to realize how greatly its economy depends on IP as a source of

Fig. 2.1 Creativity, in the form of ideas, innovations, and inventions, has replaced gold, colonies, and raw materials as the wealth of nations (Warshofsky 1994) (Photo: "Think Ideas Indicates Innovations Consider and Creativity" [Image courtesy of Stuart Miles at FreeDigitalPhotos.net])

national income and employment. Today, practically almost all sectors of the U.S. economy rely on some form of IP, because virtually "every industry either produces it or uses it."[1] Thus, as early as the 1970s when the world was reeling from OPEC's oil price increases, the United States first saw the need of a new foreign policy for IP, for the ownership of ideas that suit American interest (Warshofsky 1994). From the 1970s to the early 1990s, there was a widespread belief that the U.S. economy had declined and had been overtaken by Japan and that this decline can only be halted by a renewed emphasis on technological innovation to stimulate economic growth (Landes and Posner 2003, p. 2). The promotion and protection of American IP exports gradually emerged as the most viable response to this decline. Riker (2012) explained that there are strong indications that improvements in IPR protection in U.S. export markets could increase export revenues and income from direct investment abroad and increase royalties from licensing U.S. knowledge capital or from a combination of these three (p. 288). With this realization, the U.S. government shifted its economic focus from the traditional manufacturing and exportation of "hard" and "heavy" goods to "soft" and "liquid" goods and services of the creative economy which fit into the current globalization trends characterized by "liquidity" and mobility of things (Ritzer 2010). While China was busy converting its centrally planned economy into a market economy in the mid-1980s, the United States was preoccupied with harnessing its creative economy during this period, laying the foundation of a new economic infrastructure based on human innovation and IP.

To protect and accelerate the growth of this newfound "gold" in the U.S. economy, the government, influenced by the intense and sustained corporate lobbying of top American IP pharmaceutical multinationals, gave IP protection a special legislative push. Since the 1980s, the U.S. Congress introduced a series of legal reforms and innovations in IPR to curb piracy and counterfeiting at home and abroad. As a result, the profitability of American IP companies grew rapidly. Between 1987 and 1999, for instance, a period of only 12 years, the annual U.S. receipts from foreign IP trade rose from $10 billion to 36.5 billion. American exports in high-tech goods such as computers and electronic products amounted to $190 billion out of the total exports of $690 billion (28%) (Landes and Posner 2003, p. 3). The supremacy of IP in the U.S. economy became apparent when nearly 61% of American exports, $775 billion, come from IP-intensive industries in 2010.

The export of copyright-based industries such as films and computer software also increased to $89 billion in 2001. With sustained efforts of the U.S. government to protect the American IP goods and services from counterfeiting, the dramatic growth of IP trade at home and abroad continued to rise in the early 2000s (Landes and Posner 2003, p. 3). In 2010, the total merchandise exports of the U.S. IP-intensive industries have already reached a staggering $775 billion, accounting for 60.7 % of total U.S. merchandise exports and for 40.0 million direct and indirect jobs or 27.7 % of all jobs in the United States.[2] But in 2012, the IIPA estimated that the

[1] *Intellectual Property and the U.S. Economy: Industries in Focus* (March 2012), p. vi. Available at http://www.uspto.gov/sites/default/files/news/publications/IP_Report_March_2012.pdf

[2] *Intellectual Property and the U.S. Economy: Industries in Focus* (March 2012), p. viii. Available at http://www.uspto.gov/sites/default/files/news/publications/IP_Report_March_2012.pdf

value added by the core copyright industries to U.S. GDP exceeded $1 trillion dollars ($1015.6 billion) for the first time, accounting for 6.48 % of the U.S. economy, and the value added by the total copyright industries to GDP exceeded $1.7 trillion ($1765 billion), accounting for 11.25 % of the U.S. economy (Siwek 2012, p. 2).

In the realm of patents, the U.S. IP industries also showed dominance in the American economy. In patent medicine, four (7) out of the top ten (10) pharmaceutical companies in the world are American multinationals with Johnson & Johnson and Pfizer occupying the top spots with revenues of US$61.9 billion and US$50.01 billion, respectively.[3] In computer technology, the United States is overtaking other countries in terms of inventions in computer products and applications. The global leader in technology patent, the International Business Machines (IBM), for instance, has been a consistent number one patent creator in the world for a long time, amassing more U.S. patents than any other companies in the last 21 years. In 2013 alone, it created a total of 6809 patents, with more than 30 % of these coming from overseas.[4]

The significant contribution of the IP industries to the American economy has pushed the U.S. government to prioritize IPR protection at home and abroad in order to curb counterfeiting and piracy of American IP products and services. The strengthening of IPR protection abroad aims to build a global IP legal regime which makes it difficult for counterfeiters and infringers to hijack the exports of U.S. IP multinational companies (MNCs), the new key drivers of the American economy. The grand scheme of the United States includes the global institutionalization of the TRIPS and its own version of IPR protection which can dominate its top economic competitors and leading IP counterfeiters such as China, Brazil, India, Russia, and other piracy-laden ASEAN countries. To achieve this end without manifest opposition from developed and developing countries around the world, the United States has to use a consensual power judiciously in the diplomatic front through the cultural institution of law as a mechanism to shield its hegemonic agenda of dominating the global IP trade as well as to project an image that the American style of IPR protection serves the economic interest of all nations in the world.

2.3 Law as a Maker of Hegemony

All hegemonic relations are assumed to be based on domination and consensus through formulation and manipulation of existing rules. But domination cannot take place overtly without manifest resistance. Thus, in order to avoid open and active opposition, domination must get itself to be misrecognized. To achieve this, the effects of domination must always disguise themselves as moral relations (Mitchell 1990, p. 550). In the field of IP, "moral truths" on the sanctity of rights and private ownership, particularly on the rights of the author, inventor, and creator of IP goods,

[3] See "Top Ten Largest Pharmaceutical Companies in the World 2013" at http://www.toptenstip.com.

[4] See Barinka, "IBM Wins Most U.S. Patents for 21st Year in a Row" at http://www.bloomberg.com.

are vigorously portrayed by the dominant country such as the United States in its campaign against piracy to hide domination in the global IP trade arena. In this sense, the law becomes a perfect tool of misrecognition of IP domination by the leading state to pursue and hide its hegemonic agenda. The power of law to create a consensual view and to protect dominant ideologies makes it a powerful hegemonic tool for the IP leader like the United States to subtly impose its own version of the global IP trade and protection in the world (Fig. 2.2).

Since"[l]aw is all over" in society (Sarat 1990), it has the power to constitute hierarchies and relationships that are at the heart of the social fabric of society so that it catches people in ways that are "hardly noticed" (Yngvesson 1993, p. 120). Law also has the power to fix social relations and sideline other forms of knowledge (Smart 1989) which makes it a dominant tool of power. For critical legal scholars, law may appear from the outside as neutral and just, but from the inside its interest bends toward the lawmaker. And as part of the regulation system in society, law aims to fix and represent social reality in a stable and immutable way based on the interest of those who created them (Moore 1978, p. 40). Thus, every legal project is necessarily a social and political project. Peller (2011) argued that legal discourses are actually discourses of power. They contain the ideology of dominant groups in society. Seen from this perspective, the legal discourses on stricter IPR protection and the criminality of piracy are therefore discourses of power that reflect the interests of those who created them. The prominent position of law in the hierarchy of knowledge makes it a powerful hegemonic tool in gaining public consent and consensus without manifest coercion. The educative function of law and its role as a generator of social norms make it an effective tool for the leader in a hegemonic legal order to gain consent from the dominated without coercion or overt resistance. The advantage of law is that it can be both used coercively and persuasively (Cain in Sugarman (ed.) 1983, p. 101).

Fig. 2.2 Legal discourses are discourses of power (Photo: "Legal Gavel and Law Book" (Image courtesy of nirots at FreeDigitalPhotos.net))

For the United States, to maintain its leading role in the global IP trade and protect its interests from strong and overt opposition abroad, it has to create a consensus among nations through laws, legal discourses, contracts, and trade agreements to project to the world that "things are natural as they are" and that promoting and protecting IP against piracy also serve the interests of developing or non-IP-exporting countries. Sum (2003) argued that in the field of IP, global rules and networks are construed and interpreted around U.S. interests which can be considered hegemonic because they are dominant in their ability to provide material rewards and impose sanctions (including coercion) and, equally important, they are ideologically dominant. Through IPR laws in multilateral, regional, and bilateral agreements, the United States is surprisingly successful in portraying specific definitions of "intellectual property rights" and "creativity" as representing the general interests of developing countries and of the consuming public. Thus, hegemony in today's global IP order is the power to create consensual view through legal discourses of what is "just" and "natural" in the creative economy and to promote and protect, in a subtle way, the interest of the most powerful and leading nation in the IP trade.

2.3.1 The Role of NGOs and Top U.S. IP Companies

The establishment of U.S. IP hegemony in the world through law is not an instant and ready-made product created by the federal government alone but a gradual process which is shaped and directed by top American business nongovernment organizations (NGOs) and powerful U.S. multinational companies with specific interests in IPR protection. The fascination of the United States with legal discourses as an instrument of promoting IP hegemony abroad is precipitated by the intense lobbying of top IP business groups in the U.S. Congress for stricter laws against piracy. Prominent among them are the American film and pharmaceutical companies which saw the IP issue as an investment issue. These multinationals wanted to establish their production anywhere in the world and be assured that their intellectual property would be protected against piracy and counterfeiting (Braithwaite and Drahos 2000, p. 61). The top U.S. pharmaceutical companies led by Pfizer, for instance, needed a stronger IPR protection abroad to safeguard their expensive innovative research (R&D) which approximately costs 18 % of their drug sales (Maskus 2000, p. 53) (Fig. 2.3).

The U.S. copyright companies also needed a stronger IPR protection to defend their books, films, music, computer, and business software and computer applications against copyright piracy. These American companies are truly global in scope and thus vulnerable to counterfeiting abroad. With a weak IPR regime in the United States and overseas and the inability of the Paris Convention (an international treatise on protection of industrial property like patents of inventions) and Berne Convention (an international treatise on protection of literary and artistic works) to protect IP American interest abroad, the CEOs of these companies bonded together, shared resources, and stepped up their IP awareness campaign by highlighting heavy losses caused by piracy to convince the U.S. government to pass laws in the

Fig. 2.3 The campaign for a stricter IPR protection abroad was initiated by top U.S. pharmaceutical companies led by Pfizer (Photo: "3D Image Pharmaceutical Industry Issues Concept Word Cloud Back" (Images courtesy of David Castillo Dominici at FreeDigitalPhotos.net))

U.S. Congress which link American trade practices with IPR protection in order to promote their business interests. And these NGOs and top American companies are apparently successful in their campaign to influence IP legislation in the U.S. Congress to their favor (Braithwaite and Drahos 2000).

2.3.2 *Legal Tools for U.S. IP Hegemony*

After an intense campaign and lobbying of IP business groups led by top American pharmaceutical and copyright companies, the U.S. Congress finally enacted a series of IP laws and reformed judicial policies to strengthen IP protection at home and abroad against piracy. First of these laws is the overhaul of the American copyright law by passing the Copyright Act of 1976 which significantly lengthened the copyright term. This was followed by a law in 1982 which gave a monopoly of appeals in patent cases to the U.S. Court of Appeals for the Federal Circuit (Landes and Posner 2003, p. 2). And this legal reform continued in the 1990s with passage of the Visual Artists Rights Act, the Architectural Works Protection Act, the Sonny Bono Act, the Digital Millennium Copyright Act (DMCA), and other copyright statutes (Maskus 2000, p. 53, 406).

The U.S. legislature also passed a series of IP laws that protect American IP exports abroad against piracy. These statutes, envisioned and lobbied by top U.S. IP companies, now directly linked trade with IPR protection. In 1984, the U.S. Congress amended the Trade Act of 1974 to include IP in its Section 301 trade process. This was subsequently amended and called as the Omnibus Trade and Competitiveness Act of 1988. This time, it gave the U.S. President, through the United States Trade Representative (USTR), the power to impose trade sanctions to countries violating IPR laws. It also added more processes called "Regular 301," "Special 301," and "Super 301" that authorize the USTR "to identify countries, assess the level of abuse of US intellectual property interests, enter into negotiations to remedy the problems and ultimately, if this proved futile, to impose trade sanctions" (Braithwaite and Drahos 2000, p. 62). Of all these new IP laws which aimed to promote and protect American IP products in the United States and overseas, two statutes are said to stand out as the most potent legal tools of American hegemony in IP: Section 337 of the Tariff Act of 1930 and Section 301 of the Omnibus Trade and Competitive Act of 1988. Section 337 is domestically oriented and allows punitive action against imported products violating IPR regulations, while Special 301 is internationally oriented and allows the United States to unilaterally impose trade sanctions against countries engaging in piracy of American goods and services. Special 301 has also authorized the USTR to identify priority foreign countries which, according to the U.S. criteria, provide inadequate IPR protection and which cause the greatest adverse impact on U.S. right holders or products as well as to keep a Priority Watch List (PWL) and a Watch List (WL) of foreign countries engaging in piracy (Pugatch 2004, p. 66) (Fig. 2.4).

Section 301 of the U.S. Trade Act of 1988, therefore, appears to be the most effective tool of the United States in projecting its domestic IPR model worldwide, providing the basic standards of IPR protection around the globe, and thereby creating the American IP hegemony in the world. The provisions of this section became internationalized after the United States became successful in incorporating them in the General Agreement on Tariffs and Trade (GATT), particularly in the Trade-Related Aspects of Intellectual Property Rights (TRIPS) of this agreement, which was signed by 111 countries in Marrakesh, Uruguay, on April 15, 1994. This linking of IPR protection with international trade is basically a strategy crafted by the United States, prodded by its top pharmaceutical and copyright companies which allegedly lost billions of dollars abroad because of piracy and which had a strategic long-term commitment to doing business in developing countries (Braithwaite and Drahos 2000, pp. 60–61). Before the ratification of TRIPS, there was no uniform or common IPR protection standard in the world. Each country has its own system of IPR protection. And under the Paris and Berne Conventions' principle of national treatment, IPR protection given to non-nationals would be the same to that of the nation-

Fig. 2.4 The United States has to use the cultural mechanism of law to shield its hegemonic agenda in the global IP trade (Photo: "USA Flag Background with Fireworks" (Image courtesy of nirots at FreeDigitalPhotos.net))

als. But under TRIPS nations are compelled through WTO enforcement mechanisms to adopt certain IPR standards foreign to their local culture and legal system, standards which are largely patterned after the U.S. IPR protection system. "Thus there arises a fundamental conflict between the developed and developing world, since under TRIPS developing nations are increasingly being forced to accept the intellectual property laws of the West, if not their underlying philosophy" (Simons 1999, p. 63). On the part of the United States, a global IP trade without a uniform international IPR protection system is highly detrimental to its economic interest. The U.S. IP exports would be exposed to piracy without legal and judicial recourse to prosecute IPR violators. Thus, the United States uses the TRIPS and other legal mechanisms to achieve its hegemonic IP designs. It uses the TRIPS if a case can be resolved through the World Trade Organization (WTO) dispute settlement system. If not, then the United States would resort to its self-help legislative tool of the Special 301 provisions under the Trade Act to identify and initiate investigations against countries violating American IPR laws and take retaliatory actions such as economic sanctions or trade wars to curb piracy (Tian 2008, p. 230).

To institutionalize the TRIPS and the American-style IPR regime, the United States incorporated IPR protection in what Schott (2006) calls as the "three-dimensional" trade strategy—involving a mix of bilateral, regional, and multilateral negotiations in free trade agreements (FTAs)—in opening new markets for its exports, especially for U.S. IP products and services and ultimately in establishing its hegemonic role. These three types of FTAs are among the key hegemonic tools of the United States in the global stage to dominate the IP trade in the world. By signing these free trade agreements (FTAs), developing countries are subjected to the U.S. Special 301 provision which forces them to align their IP laws and judicial system with the TRIPS and American standards, thus enabling the United States to prosecute piracy and infringement cases more efficiently in legal forums. Free trade agreements (FTAs), which assume legal forms, are actually legal contracts which are binding to parties under international law. FTA disputes can then be brought to the World Trade Organization (WTO) for arbitration and resolution.

2.3.3 The Role of Multilateral and Regional Institutions

Multilateral and regional institutions are created through multilateral legal agreements or contracts forged by countries around the globe with the United States taking a dominant role. The regional and international multilateral institutions which are created by international law are said to be crucial to the maintenance of a global hegemony. The American IP hegemony is not only backed up by the powerful treaty of TRIPS and the institutionalization of WTO but also by the powerful multilateral and regional institutions dominated by the United States. The World Bank (WB), International Monetary Fund (IMF), and other regional development banks that promote TRIPS to developing countries are heavily influenced by the United States in their trade and political decisions. On the part of the United States, all multilateral institutions are seen as instruments of foreign policy which can be used in support of specific U.S. American aim and objective. The United States, being an economic superpower, is clearly the one nation which no multilateral institution can afford to ignore in the long run as it is one of the major contributors of the funds of these institutions. When the United States is actively forging international consensus, it can overwhelm other states that have taken on the role of swing or veto/blocking states (Braithwaite and Drahos 2000, p. 24).

The structure of the multilateral institutions is inspired by the joint-stock model of private capitalist corporations. Each member country's share of votes is weighted in accordance with the combined amount of capital it has paid in and is guaranteeing for (Bøås and Mcneill 2003, p. 17). Although these institutions are international in nature, the voting power would depend of the country's contribution to the general fund. Votes are, therefore, weighted according to the country's amount of shares. And in all these regional and multilateral institutions, the United States is said to be the number one shareholder. The voting of the United States in the World Bank (WB), for instance, is 16.14 % compared to the voting power of 7 % of Japan, the second highest contributor of the WB fund. Other top European countries such as Germany, France, and the United Kingdom only have 4 % voting power each. The United States also tops the voting power in the International Monetary Fund (IMF) with 17.11 % compared to 6.4 % of Japan, the next biggest contributor of the IMF fund (Bøås and McNeill 2003, pp. xi–xii).

The voting power of the United States in multilateral and regional networks has direct contribution to the maintenance of American hegemony in IP trade worldwide. The Advisory Committee for Trade Negotiation (ACTN), a powerful committee that gives the U.S. business sector direct input into the U.S. trade policy, for instance, recommended that "US Executive Directors to the International Monetary Fund, World Bank and regional development banks should, in exercising their voting power, examine the country's record on intellectual property protection" (Braithwaite and Drahos 2000, p. 62). Before a developing country can avail of any benefit or loan from these institutions, it has first to agree to comply to their conditions for IPR protection. Thus, the United States is utilizing these multilateral and regional institutions to pursue its hegemonic control in IP and to ensure that the U.S.-style IPR protection will be staged in the global arena and provide U.S. IP companies a legal infrastructure to counter counterfeiting and piracy.

2.3.4 Free Trade Agreements (FTAs) and IPR Protection

The United States does not only use the multilateral agreements and institutions to establish its IP hegemony in the world but also the various free trade agreements (FTAs) which are binding to parties under international law. Built around the basic framework of multilateral disciplines such as the World Trade Organization (WTO), FTAs can either be regional or bilateral (Brown and Stern 2011, p. 334). Regional FTAs (RTAs) are usually forged between countries of a particular region or trading block, while bilateral FTAs or BTAs are trading agreements entered into by two countries. In reality, around 80–90 % of these FTAs are bilateral and only 10 percent are RTAs: FTAs are predominantly bilateral in the international trade system rather than regional (Dent 2010, p. 50). Thus, to promote American leadership in IP, the U.S. government strategically uses these two types of FTAs as important IP hegemonic tools. By signing FTAs with the United States containing IPR protection clause, the countries involved are automatically subjected to the USTR's IPR monitoring and watch list systems and can be included in the yearly Special 301 watch list of piracy hotspots in the world if they fail to comply with the U.S. IPR demands. They are also under constant threat of losing their Generalized System of Preferences (GSPs) or other trading privileges with the United States if they fail to follow the USTR's progressive IPR recommendations against piracy.

Despite their rhetoric of promoting mutual development, trade agreements are usually shaped by political considerations rather than pure welfare estimations (Manoli 2013). Some scholars believe that FTAs undermine rather than promote the multilateral trading system envisioned by GATT. Through FTAs, contracting countries can pursue their own trading interests to the detriment of the multilateral trading system. Most FTAs are signed by countries based on their domestic economic and strategic motives rather than on their impact on the global trading system (Khatoon 2013). Thus, FTAs are more vulnerable to manipulation than multilateral agreements in international forums especially when entered into between powerful developed countries like the United States and developing countries. FTAs do not reflect a consensus of the interest of communities involved. Busaniche argued that negotiations are usually done in closed doors, with free assembled negotiating documents and zero public access to their proceedings and documents.[5] The United States prefers bilateral FTAs rather than regional or multilateral FTAs to achieve its myriad political, economic, and security interests (Schott 2006, p. 99) (Fig. 2.5).

The BTAs provide the United States an alternative mechanism to pursue its hegemonic designs in case a strong opposition arises in multilateral forums. Since the strengthening of IP protection engineered by the United States is increasingly contentious within multilateral forums as illustrated by the collapse of WTO Doha talks in 2006, the BTAs became a perfect tool for U.S. trade negotiators to deal with overt resistance (Morin 2006). As suggested by some theorists, bilateralism is often used by economically powerful states as their control over multilateral negotiation declines (e.g., Caparosa 1992; Yarbrough and Yarbrough 1992). What the United States cannot accomplish directly in multilateral forums with regard to IPR is usually pursued in BTAs using diplomatic and contractual maneuverings to achieve American trade objectives. The Bipartisan Trade Promotion Authority Act of 2002 (H.R. 3009) which outlines the authority of the USTR to conduct these FTAs specifically states that "any multilateral or bilateral trade agreement governing intellectual property rights that is entered into by the United States reflect a standard of protection similar to that found in United States law" (Krikorian and Szymkowiak 2007, pp. 388–393). In this sense, the model of IPR protection espoused by the U.S. government is not

[5] http://wealthofthecommons.org/essay/intellectual-property-rights-and-free-trade-agreements-never-ending-story

Fig. 2.5 The United States strategically uses free trade agreements (FTAs) to pursue its hegemonic agenda in the global IP trade (Photo: "Business Deal with Dollar" (Image courtesy of digitalart at FreeDigitalPhotos.net))

just based on TRIPS and other international IP conventions but on its own version of IPR protection which, of course, favors American IP interest.

The U.S. strategy of offering trading partners access to the U.S. market in BTAs is usually accompanied by political pressure to force these partners to pattern their IP regulatory measures from the American domestic political economy, thus reflecting the U.S. corporate interests (Dent 2010, p. 55). The objective of the United States in bilateral agreements is therefore to achieve a cumulative effect. By convincing more countries to accept its increasingly stringent IPR standards, it hopes to accrue a critical mass of support for its cause, thereby reinforcing its IP hegemony in the world (Krikorian and Szymkowiak 2007, p. 389).

2.4 Social Resistance and U.S. IP Hegemony

The American IP hegemony through legal discourses does not proceed without resistance from countries and groups who felt that the rules on the global IP trade are being imposed upon them. Resistance is a type of action which situates itself in relation to power. It exists side by side with power and domination (Sarat 1990, p. 246). If there is domination, there is also social resistance. Resistance is often understood as refusal and rejection against change, especially against imposed change (Brighenti 2011, pp. 57–58). Informational capitalism espoused by the Global North which aims to commodify the creative and cultural field does not proceed without social resistance from the marginalized countries. The IPR regime espoused by the United States and developed countries aims to privatize and commercialize ownership of creativity, invention, artistic works, trademarks, and other creative works. But this is in conflict with the general cultural understanding of the

Asians led by China and ASEAN countries which see creative and intellectual works as property of the commons and not just of individuals and groups. For Koreans, for instance, creativity such as inventions or artistic works is not generally considered as private property but as public goods. The Chinese too, with their strong Confucian tradition, also see inventions and creativity as public property which need to shared and enjoyed by all in the community (Warshofsky 1994).

The bottom line of the conflict is the incongruent cultural values and awareness between developed and developing countries on ownership of intellectual property: the Global North using a strict capitalist lens sees creative work as subject to private ownership and profit, while the Global South sees it primarily as part of communal ownership and subject to sharing. China and other Southeast Asian countries from the Global South view IPR as communal goods rather than private ownership. But the U.S.-inspired IPR system with a capitalist orientation aims to colonize the Global South's cultural understanding of IPR through legal discourses. By means of multilateralism, FTAs, and BTAs, the Global North led by the United States incorporates and imposes, in a subtle way, its own IPR law in trade provisions. The Global South and developing countries who are consumers of American and foreign IP products and services resist this form of legal colonization of their own cultural understanding of IP. Thus, some exploit the cracks and loopholes of the imposed American version of IPR legal system to express their opposition, oftentimes, in a more passive and covert way to protect their trade interest with the United States and its trading networks under the FTAs or GSP trade arrangements.

2.4.1 *Law as a Maker of Resistance*

Legal sociologists recognize that law is not only a maker of hegemony but also of social resistance. It is inherent in the nature of legal systems that they can never become fully coherent and consistent wholes which successfully regulate the entire fabric of social life. Thus, rule systems invariably include ambiguities, inconsistencies, gaps, and conflicts (Moore 1978, p. 3). A legal system can control a certain type of behavior but not the aggregate of behavior in society (Moore 1978, p. 30). Sociologists of law acknowledge that various legal systems can coexist in a given society. Legal pluralist theorists, in particular, identify two configurations of legal system coexisting in one state: the local legal systems and the state law (Guillet 1998, p. 44). Differing types of legal systems existing in a society often breed varying and conflicting legal cultures and contrasting attitudes and responses of people to law. The basic conflict lies in the underlying pattern and dynamics between the legal culture of lawyers and legal professionals or what Friedman (1975) calls as "internal legal culture" and the dominant legal culture of the lay or general public or which Friedman calls as the "external legal culture" (Fig. 2.6).

The U.S. lawyer–negotiators may be successful to some extent in their efforts to impose the American IP laws in the "internal legal culture" of the developing or IP-consuming countries through FTAs, but this does not mean immediate public acceptance by the "external legal culture" of people in the developing countries.

Fig. 2.6 Law is not only a maker of hegemony but also of social resistance. Resisters often use the same IP laws to challenge the U.S. IP hegemony (Photo: "The Law Book With Gavel" (Image courtesy of cooldesign at FreeDigitalPhotos.net))

Dominated groups, including government agencies, who felt marginalized by the new IP legal regime would always find ways to resist the official law, finding cracks and loopholes in the legal provisions to pursue their vested interests. Although the law aims to be "gapless" in its content and implementation, it cannot totally eliminate loopholes that allow social resistance of individuals and groups who oppose it. De Certeau argued that "people can resist the law by vigilantly making use of the cracks that particular conjunctions open in…proprietary powers…" (as cited in Sarat 1990, p. 347).

Socio-legal scholars often view the strategies of individuals as seldom (if ever) consistently committed to reliance on rule and other regularities. People seldom pattern their actions according to the official law. On the contrary, people oftentimes use the official law to their advantage. With the revitalization of legal anthropology, there is a growing realization that legal discourses are not only spaces of regulation, prohibition, and sanction but also spaces of resistance, possibility, and subversion. Thus, in understanding hegemony and resistance in relation to law, scholars have started to see law both as a maker of hegemony and social resistance. They view the law as providing both the means and forums for legitimizing and contesting dominant meanings and social hierarchies they support. Thus, even if the United States would be successful in establishing hegemonic control of the global IP trade and through TRIPS, FTAs, USTR, and other means, it is not insulated from strong criticism and social resistance from developing and IP-consuming countries. A bloc of developing countries led by India, for instance, "denounces the intellectual property system as a new form of colonial expense of the developing countries."[6] China and Southeast Asian countries such as the Philippines and Vietnam are among the resisters in the Asia Pacific region against the IPR protection directed by the United States through the USTR.

[6] Nathan Associates Inc. TCB Project (2003) "Intellectual Property and Developing Countries: An Overview," p. 1. https://www.hsdl.org/?view&did=446296

Resistance scholars often see power and resistance as forming a continuum. If one end of the continuum is hegemony, the other opposite end is social resistance. Hegemony and resistance are two opposite poles. In interstate relations, these two poles can refer to two superpowers or dominant states in contestation with each other, vying to control IP as the world's new prime asset in international trade. And in the current IP trade configuration, two dominant states emerged as top competitors: the United States assuming as the current hegemon or leader and China as the top resister or challenger using piracy and counterfeit trade as its main tools and weapons for resistance.

2.4.2 Piracy as Passive Resistance: The "Weapons of the Weak"

Legal pluralist scholars view the official law as only one of the many normative standards of behavior in society. There is a diversity of informal norms and customary laws that influence people's behavior. If the official law seriously conflicts with the preexisting legal culture of people, then it is more likely opposed and resisted by people. The American version of IPR legal protection as a new system—which basically contravenes the Asian concept of creative work as communal rather than privately owned—has not taken roots in the external legal cultures of Asians. Thus, resistance against this foreign and stricter IPR regime espoused by the United States can be expected from various levels and domains. With the aid of the Internet and latest Information Communication Technologies (ICTs), resistance could even be done more easily for people to circumvent the official law in the macro and micro levels.[7] In the Philippines, for instance, it is easier for illegal traders to evade detection from authorities with the use of mobile phones in optical disc piracy. The Internet and mobile technologies have given them anonymity and enriched communication network to circumvent the optical media law. Thus, the national governments of developing countries may appear agreeing publicly with the stricter IPR demands of the United States in the BTAs but may actually be resisting them covertly in the implementation of the IP laws in their respective IPR jurisdiction (Fig. 2.7).

The French philosopher Michel Foucault sees resistance as a multidimensional, multi-scale, and pervasive phenomenon. Thus, passive resistance against the stricter IPR protection system demanded by the USTR can take place both at the macro and micro levels in various forms. What IP-consuming and developing countries cannot demonstrate overtly against the American hegemony in IP is expressed covertly through passive resistance. James Scott (1987), in his book, *Weapons of the Weak*, emphasizes the importance of covert resistance in everyday struggles of the weak

[7] Overlooked in the current social resistance literature is the role of technology in the global and networked age. Since machines and technologies are more and more intertwined with humans, acts of resistance today are often mediated by technology and other material networks. Media piracy as an illegal form of resistance is highly mediated by information and communications technologies (ICTs).

Fig. 2.7 Passive resistance is the critique of power spoken by the weak behind the back of the dominant. Some optical media traders may appear doing legal business by fulfilling registration requirements but operate illegally by selling pirated discs (Photo: One of the many registered CD–DVD shops in Vietnam which are legally registered that sell pirated optical media discs [Image courtesy of the author])

against the powerful in daily life. Although Scott's resistance theory is originally applied to peasants' reaction to oppression, the current persistence of piracy in defiance of the TRIPS and IP laws can also be interpreted through the lens of this theory to account different infringing and nonconformist acts and attitudes as expressions of covert or passive resistance. Passive resistance constitutes what Scott calls as the "hidden script," i.e., "the critique of power spoken by the weak behind the back of the dominant" which can be consciously and unconsciously done by groups and individual actors (Scott 1990). When applied to IP, this can refer to what governments, agencies, communities, groups, and individuals of developing and non-IP-exporting countries secretly do outside the gaze of the USTR surveillance networks to express their growing resentment against the imposition of new IPR legal transplants modeled after the U.S. domestic laws that colonize their indigenous IP system and sideline their economic interests. The major problem with the USTR and IIPA'S approach of addressing the piracy problem is their heavy reliance on jurisprudence or the legal approach to understand and address the problem which oftentimes neglects the sociocultural underpinnings of piracy, particularly the dynamics of passive or covert social resistance to legal prescriptions. As already mentioned, law is just one of the many normative standards people can use to pattern their behavior. Other informal cultural standards also operate and sometimes in competition with the official law.

2.4.3 Overt or Active Resistant Acts and Strategies

The passage of TRIPS and the relative success of the United States to include its IP hegemonic designs in FTAs did not, however, deter countries and groups to find means to resist creatively this new mode of domination. While the United States uses the cultural mechanism of law as a means to hide its IP hegemony in the world, developing and IP-consuming countries also use this same mechanism plus other means of covert strategies to subvert this hegemony. The very IP laws that they oppose were the same laws that they use to resist IP hegemony both in the legal and nonlegal fields. Although sociologists of law acknowledged that law can be an instrument of hegemony, they also conceded that it can also be a powerful tool for resistance. E.P Thompson, for instance, argued that law is not only mystifying and faithfully working to the advantage of the class that implements it, but can also be an effective instrument for equalization (as cited in Gaines 2000, p. 7). Historically constructed and locally interpreted, the law can provide the means both for legitimizing and contesting dominant meanings and social hierarchies they support. Hirsch and Lazarus-Black (1994) explained that hegemony is an ongoing articulatory practice that is performatively enacted in juridical spaces where webs of dominant signification enmesh at one level even those who would resist at another. Hegemonic and oppositional strategies both constitute and configure each other (Coombe 1998, p. 26). Thus, the law as a discourse, process, and practice can be both a system of domination and social resistance.

Like any other official laws in contemporary state societies, the TRIPS, FTAs, and other IP laws used by the United States to pursue its hegemonic agenda bear loopholes, especially if transplanted to a foreign country with a different IP legal culture. The imposition of the U.S.-inspired IPR system in developing countries can create legal and cultural gaps that allow resistant actors and networks to question and challenge it. Legal pluralist scholars see the legal field in society as only one of the many normative fields that shape people's behavior and attitude toward the law. This pluralism can be internal or within one legal system or "external" or the ultimate plurality of laws in a given society (Griffiths 2002; Tamahana 2007). Plurality can also occur between the law and customs or informal normative systems (Moore 1978). This plurality when not well harmonized or networked to create a "gapless" legal system can result to loopholes either within a given legal order or between diverse laws from various legal systems which can become arenas of conflict and resistance. Despite various attempts of the United States and multilateral institutions to disregard legal pluralism in the current globalization process and proceed with their global IPR unification efforts, the empirical reality remains that legal gaps and diversity of IP customary laws exist in emerging economies of China and Southeast Asia, high-earning economies which try to adapt to the U.S.-prescribed IP trading system.

Overt legal resistance against American hegemony in the IP multilateral agreements is manifested in some public protests against stronger IPR protection prescribed by developed countries led by the United States. In the 1999 WTO meeting in Seattle, for instance, public resistance can be seen with demonstrations of civil society groups against the rigid IPR regime demanded by the United States and developed countries. In Doha, Qatar, this is also displayed by opposing groups and countries who showed displeasure with the United States and developed countries' rigid interpretation of TRIPS, particularly on patent medicines which can deprive the poor and developing countries of their licit access to cheap medicines against HIV. Countries which are subjected to the Special 301 of the USTR also show overt resistance on how the US handles IPR protection issues. Letters showing dissatisfaction on how the USTR implements the recommendations of the powerful IIPA with regard to the watch list system indicate overt resistance. Thailand, for instance, wrote a strong letter protesting the strict application of rules on patent medicines especially for HIV and why the country should be placed in the Priority Watch List despite the country's efforts to improve its IPR.[8] Countries in the watch lists also criticized strongly the USTR as inconsistent in applying trade rules and a biased judge in handling disputes with regard to Section 301. The USTR is said to be unilateral in interpreting trade rules and uses the negotiating style of the superpower. It is perceived as prosecutor, plea bargainer, judge, and executioner in trade disputes (Ryan 1995, pp. 5–6).

Overt resistance is also expressed overtly on the Internet. Popular websites being charged by top American IP companies for IPR violations manifest their resistance against a strong copyright system that stifles freedom on the Internet by using the very letter of the law to defend themselves in court. Although unsuccessful, the cyberlocking site *Hotfile,* for example, defends itself against an infringement lawsuit filed by the Motion Picture Association of America (MPAA) in court using the safe harbor provisions of the Digital Millennium Copyright Act as a defense. These provisions, *Hotfile* claimed, exempt online service providers from claims of copyright infringement made against them that result from the conduct of their customers. Thus, only the infringing customer, not the service provider's network, is liable for copyright infringement and monetary damages.[9]

Overt resistance can also be observed in some big infringing websites which continue to store and share copyrighted content in continued defiance against the USTR and IPR law despite warnings by the United States. These websites are usually found outside the jurisdictions of the U.S. courts, making it difficult for American stakeholders to file infringement cases and remove the sites and their infringement networks from the Internet. The pirate website *ThePirateBay.se*, for instance, was shut down in 2009 but is now resurrected and has constantly changed its server location to continue their infringing activities in open defiance to the United States' stricter IPR system. The infringing website *isohunt.to* is also being revived with a new domain name in a new country after being shut down by the MPAA last October 17, 2013 (Gil 2014). Changing location of servers and domains is an active resistant strategy to avoid law enforcement and to circumvent the copyright law. Without proper jurisdiction and extradition treaty, American stakeholders cannot initiate legal action and bring perpetrators to U.S. courts to face charges.

[8] https://www.wcl.american.edu/pijip/go/thainetwork2010

[9] See "MPAA Wins Hotfile Copyright Lawsuit" at http://deadline.com/2013/08/mpaa-wins-hotfile-copyright-infringement-suit-573949/.

Thus, the recourse of these stakeholders is to bring the cases to the IIPA which, in turn, will request the USTR to include mention in their Special 301 Annual Report and pressure the countries which host these infringing websites to remove them and take legal actions against the infringers. Most of these "defiant" websites are found in countries listed by the USTR as piracy hotspots in the world. Vietnam, for instance, has numerous pirate websites apparently facilitated by the resistant attitude of the government toward stricter IPR regime. Thus, Vietnam has been constantly pressured by the USTR and IIPA to shut down illegal websites using the IPR provisions of the U.S.–Vietnam BTA as a justification for the intervention.

Furthermore, active resistance can be observed in collective hacking which defies the Internet regulation of a country enforcing the IPR provision of their BTA. When the Anti-cybercrime Law was passed in the Philippine Congress, a group of hackers which identify themselves as Anonymous Philippines hacked various government sites as a sign of manifest resistance to the law. Singapore too, with a BTA with the United States, faced the same fate when it enacted a law which regulates the Internet.

Aside from collective acts of active resistance from governments, civil society groups, and big online groups against the stricter IPR regime created by the American hegemony, there is a whole range of small group and individual acts of active resistance on the web that show open defiance to the current IPR regime from an outright illegal downloading, peer-to-peer sharing, etc., to mere copying of a copyrighted logo or image from the Internet. For James Scott (1987), social resistance can emanate from below which can be both legal and illegal acts, and the perpetrator may not be aware that she/he is defying a social order by performing these resistant acts.

Active resistance can be identified and addressed by the USTR through its surveillance network. But passive or covert resistance against the American IP hegemony which is supported by the growing sophistication of technology is difficult to identify, monitor, and sanction given the inadequacy of jurisprudence and law enforcement system to deal with "cracks" and "loopholes" in the implementation of the IPR system. A strategic nonenforcement of the TRIPS and the American version of IPR regime—often influenced by the country's vested interests and bureaucratic corruption—by emerging economies and their law enforcement agencies is a form of passive resistance which is difficult to monitor and address even with the sophisticated surveillance network of the USTR and IIPA. Thus, media piracy in China and ASEAN countries as a form of passive resistance can be subtle and difficult to identify and regulate by authorities and stakeholders.

2.4.4 *Covert or Passive Resistant Acts and Strategies*

There is a whole range of passive resistant acts, from covert counterfeiting of IP trade secrets, strategic nonenforcement of the American-inspired copyright laws by governments, tolerance of corrupt practices of law enforcers, illegal downloading, and vending of pirated discs to illegal peer-to-peer sharing by individual Internet users. In Indonesia, for instance, infringers employ evasive behavior online to resist the copyright law such as switching online locations and website names to avoid detection as well as using other fraudulent practices such as using offshore servers (2014 IIPA Special 301 Report, p. 51). These types of covert infringing acts which are done at the backstage of IP negotiation process with the United States are the secret "Weapons of the Weak" (Scott 1987) of the IP-consuming and emerging countries to counter U.S. IP hegemony and the hegemonic IP prescriptions of the USTR. Passive resistance implies saying "yes" to the enforcement of the official IP laws in public stage or negotiation but allowing or tolerating various forms of counterfeiting and infringement at the backstage, away from the gaze and surveillance of the powerful USTR and its allied networks. Because of the threat of losing trade benefits with the United States in their FTAs, China and developing countries of the ASEAN cannot afford to engage in open defiance or active resistance against the USTR by directly challenging and opposing its IPR recommendations. To show their resentment and resistance, these countries, instead, employ indirect or passive resistance such as secretly engaging in counterfeiting activities, stealing trade secrets to achieve technology transfer, putting barriers to IP imports that compete local goods, allowing counterfeiting in their local economies to aid their informal or underground economies, or giving various excuses to the USTR for the delay of the implementation of its IPR recommendations to avoid losing trade benefits with the United States.

One specific overt resistant strategy is delaying tactics. Developing countries delay as much as possible the implementation of USTR's recommendations if they see it advantageous to their informal economy. This is sometimes caused by the government's strategy of not giving top priority to antipiracy initiatives—by not vigorously pursuing the prosecution of piracy cases, giving the necessary bureaucratic support, budget, personnel, and other equipment to the government's antipiracy agencies (2014 IIPA Special 301). The IIPA, for instance, lamented that Vietnam has only taken a few enforcement actions over the years. It has not resolved any piracy cases and has largely ignored concerns of the United States over onerous access restrictions (2013 IIPA Special 301 Report: Vietnam).

Allowing piracy and delaying the implementation of the annual recommendations of the USTR can be a strategic passive resistance on the part of some Asian governments in order to buy time and allow the covert technology transfer of American and foreign IP technologies to emerging economies such as China and the ASEAN. One major reason why emerging and developing countries resist a stricter IPR protection is the loss of access to new technologies and technology transfer. This is particularly true to patents of invention. Many developing countries favor unrestricted access to technology. Higher protection of IPR might preclude their access to new technology and innovation (Oyejide 1990, p. 441). History has shown that copying or imitating is the easiest way to advance technology in developing countries. By copying or pirating the superior technology of an industrial country, a less developed country can also attain industrial status. Japan and South Korea became industrialized by borrowing liberally from U.S. firms but barely paid compensation for designs and process technologies (Bello et al. 1996). With weaker IPR regimes before the advent of TRIPS and U.S. global IPR system, technology transfer (TT) became possible in less developed states. But with the current contemporary capitalism, IPR regimes are specifically designed to maintain unequal growth (Orsi and Coriat 2006). Thus, allowing a weak IPR protection to persist in their economies can be a strategic policy of IP-importing countries to allow the illegal transfer of IP technology as well as a mechanism to protect their local economies from unfair competition. China, for instance, has been accused by the United States of illegally copying its IP technology, digital spying, and stealing American IP trade secrets through its counterfeit computer software system and weak laws on trade secret protection to pirate U.S. technology and innovation. The most troubling development for the United States are the reports that actors affiliated with the Chinese government and the Chinese military have infiltrated the computer systems of U.S. companies inside and outside China, stealing terabytes of data, including the companies' intellectual property.[10] This strategy of copying or imitating U.S. IP technology and innovation, especially in the area of digital and communications media, has borne fruits as China is currently on top in IP imitation and innovation. In social media, for instance, China has its own version of the American Twitter called Weibo. China is now capable of producing high-tech computer and digital systems as well as high-tech gadgets such as smartphones, tablets, laptops, and computers. Top Chinese high-tech multinationals are said to have penetrated the U.S. market and have been listed in the U.S. stock exchange.

Related to this strategy is the tolerance of the government to local companies imitating indirectly IP products of American and foreign multinationals to attract more buyers for local goods rather than foreign products. In Vietnam, for example, individuals and companies apply for trademarks which are the same or confusingly similar marks which have been used for many years by foreign companies. Vietnamese companies, including state-owned companies, prefer to "imitate rather than innovate," copying the appearance of high-profile products manufactured by foreign products.[11] This strategy obviously aims to take advantage and free ride the popularity of trademarks of foreign products to expand the market share of local goods and services.

Another major resistant strategy is putting protectionist barriers to the U.S. and foreign IP exports which aim to access and capture local IP markets of developing countries. In response to the apparent intention of the United States and developed countries to control the huge Chinese market, for instance, the Chinese government, as a form of resistance, has put various market barriers making it difficult for American and IP-exporting countries to penetrate the local market. In the area of entertainment media like cinema, for instance, China has restricted the entry of American and foreign movies. It only allowed around 20 movies every year for public showing. It also blocked some American Internet companies such as Facebook and Twitter and instead allowed only Weibo, a hybrid Chinese social media microblogging site with a market penetration similar to that of Twitter.

---

[10] https://ustr.gov/sites/default/files/2014%20NTE%20Report%20on%20FTB%20China.pdf

[11] American Chamber of Commerce in Vietnam (2013). "Intellectual Property Rights in the Socialist Republic of Vietnam" p. 3. http://36mfjx1a0yt01ki78v3bb46n15gp.wpengine.netdna-cdn.com/wp-content/uploads/2013/04/130208-USTR_Special_301_Submission_VIETNAM.pdf

Another strategy of the Chinese government to resist the influx of U.S. and foreign goods and services to the Chinese market is to make it difficult for foreign multinational companies to do their daily operation in China, such as investigating foreign companies for any wrongdoing or corrupt practices in order to justify protectionist policies. The American multinational Apple, for instance, was forced to issue an apology for offering inadequate warranties.[12] Other piracy-laden countries in the ASEAN also employ this strategy of putting barriers in the local market to discourage the entry of American IP products and services. The IIPA, for example, opposed the implementation of Decision No. 20/2011/QD-TTg issued by the Vietnamese government in 2011 that jeopardized the business interest of foreign pay-TV operators who are required by this law, among others, to appoint and work through a locally registered landing agent to ensure their continued provision of services in Vietnam. For the IIPA, this type of regulation can expand censorship requirements and may lead to "editing" fees on international channels (2013 IIPA Special 301 Report, p. 296). In the Philippines, the IIPA identified five barriers which could discourage American and foreign copyright companies to penetrate the market: the (1) unreasonable taxes on motion picture businesses, (2) foreign ownership restrictions of media companies, (3) limitations on the ability of audiovisual content providers to enter into exclusive distribution agreements with local cable providers, (4) vague methods of valuation of customs duties for films, and (5) the potential introduction of restrictions on advertising by right holders on pay-TV channels (2014 IIPA Special 301, p. 202).

Developing countries take notice that their informal sectors which are great contributors to national income and employment generation would be better served without the stricter copyright protection imposed by the USTR. With poverty levels on the rise, developing countries are more concerned with the larger social agenda of development and quality of life for their citizens rather than abolishing the informal trade of media piracy, an informal business that provides employment for the poor and migrants and contributes to growth to their national economy. As discussed in Chap. 5, the informal and illegal vending of optical media discs provides jobs and alternative livelihood to the poor and socially discriminated migrants in the Philippines and Vietnam. In the absence of viable alternatives to replace the media piracy trade, the government could not immediately abolish piracy without absorbing the impact of greater unemployment and rise of criminality. At the peak of Quiapo's piracy business before its "closure" in 2011, some residents and retailers of pirated discs acknowledged, in an interview, that optical disc piracy has improved the economic status of the Muslim residents in the enclave and decreased petty crimes in the district as people became busy doing piracy trade in the area.

Covert resistance can also take place in enforcement actions. It is highly probable, for example, that the public burning and crushing of "confiscated CDs and DVDs" made by some government agencies in the presence of journalists and stakeholders were just for a show or publicity stunt to please the USTR and to camou-

[12] "China loses its allure" in The Economist (25 January 2014) at http://www.economist.com/news/leaders/21595001-life-getting-tougher-foreign-companies-those-want-stay-will-have-adjust-china

flage the real inept enforcement system that allows piracy. It is a common pattern for the police and law enforcers to document some of their achievements in front of the media reporters for purposes of accomplishment reports and enhancing the government image of its fight against piracy. The intention is not really to urgently put a stop of piracy but to impress the USTR, IIPA, and stakeholders that the government is doing something to fight piracy and, thus, the country must not be listed in or downgraded from the USTR's watch lists and be given better trading benefits with the United States.

Finally, passive resistance against a stricter IPR protection system can be manifested in the local governments' efforts to implement the IP laws and business procedures. The national government may have complied with the USTR's IP legislative recommendations, but the local government such as the provincial, district, city, or municipal governments can show resistance to this new setup. With strong personalism in the local culture, business deals are usually based on ongoing business relation or what is called as relational contracting rather than on official contract laws. The decision to cooperate in local business deals depends partly on repeated-game incentives and partly on suitably designed governance structures created by contracting parties rather than by the official regulatory structures (Mcmillan and Woodruff 1999, p. 3). With inconsistent and oftentimes conflicting provisions of the IP and copyright law and business procedures, local bureaucrats and law enforcers can always find ways to interpret and implement the official law and procedure based on the prevailing customs and informal normative standards to protect local trade interests and personal relations. If corruption is involved, the unscrupulous enforcers or regulators can cut corners to circumvent the law.[13] Very often, the local police are in cahoots with infringers in the illegal optical media business. In its February 8, 2013, report, for instance, the American Chamber of Commerce in Vietnam noted that authorities are often reluctant to enforce the copyright laws because of personal (but hidden) relationships with infringers and thus being "caught" remains unlikely in Vietnam.[14]

2.5 Asia Pacific: A Great Promise and Scourge for U.S. IP Hegemony

Forging FTAs with the largest and fastest-growing region in the world with a great potential as the leading U.S. overseas market can be a strategic move for the establishment of U.S. global IP hegemony. The Asia Pacific region as the largest and the fastest-growing economy in the world is, therefore, a very important economic

[13] Please see Chap. 6 of this book for a more detailed account on corruption and nonenforcement of optical media law in the Philippines and Vietnam.

[14] American Chamber of Commerce in Vietnam (2013). "Intellectual Property Rights in the Socialist Republic of Vietnam" p. 2. http://36mfjx1a0yt01ki78v3bb46n15gp.wpengine.netdna-cdn.com/wp-content/uploads/2013/04/130208-USTR_Special_301_Submission_VIETNAM.pdf

platform for the growth of the American IP hegemony in the current globalized economy. This region is dubbed as the new engine of global economic prosperity (Ming-Te and Tai Ting Liu 2011), hosting the fastest-growing East Asian economies of China, Taiwan, Japan, North and South Korea, and Mongolia as well as the vibrant Southeast Asian economies of Brunei, Burma (Myanmar), East Timor, Indonesia, Laos, Malaysia, Philippines, Singapore, Thailand, and Vietnam, all members of the Association of Southeast Asian Nations or ASEAN. The Asia Pacific region hosts nearly "60 % of the global GDP, the world's fastest-growing economies, half of the world's population, and an emerging class eager for American products and services."[15] For the United States, the Asia Pacific region will be the engine of global growth for the next decade with a profound impact on American IP companies. The U.S. Secretary of Commerce, Penny Pritzker, projected that by 2022, the Asia Pacific will be home to 54 % of the world's middle class and will account for 42 % of global middle class spending—the largest potential market for American IP goods and services. China alone has a vibrant middle class in this region that rose to 247 million or 18.2 % of the population and is expected to further increase to 607 million by 2020. At this point, its class spending will be on par with the United States after adjusting for inflation and purchasing power.[16]

With a vibrant and fast-rising middle class, Asia Pacific has a very dynamic media landscape and a high appetite for IP goods, particularly digital media, whose content and products are dominated by American copyright companies. The Asia Pacific region surpassed other regions such as Europe, for instance, in terms of television viewing and video consumption via the Internet or even through mobile phones. In 2013, it has the highest number of mobile-cellular subscriptions in the world with 3.5 billion out of 6.8 billion of the total subscribers. It ranks as the number one region in the world in terms of mobile broadband connection with 895 subscriptions.[17] Nielsen's global media consumption index also showed that Asia Pacific surpasses Europe and Western markets on television viewing and video consumption via Internet or mobiles. Being the fastest-growing economy in the world with a huge emerging class of digital media consumers hooked online, it is not surprising that the United States is eyeing the Asia Pacific region with special interest in order to expand its IP hegemonic presence in the world, more specifically in the area of copyright media. The region's huge and rising middle class which heavily consumes digital media can accelerate American copyright export in the coming years. Asia Pacific is, therefore, the "promised land" of the American digital and entertainment media.

---

[15] See "Commerce Secretary on U.S. Commitment to Asia-Pacific Region" at http://iipdigital.usembassy.gov/st/english/texttrans/2014/04/20140417297997.html#axzz3abdMbONe.

[16] "Spotlight on China: Building a Roadmap to Success in media and entertainment," p. 4 at http://www.ey.com/Publication/vwLUAssets/Media_and_Entertainment_-_Spotlight_on_China/$FILE/Spotlight_on_China.pdf

[17] International Telecommunication Union (ITU), "Measuring the Informational Society 2013" at https://www.itu.int/en/ITU-D/Statistics/Documents/publications/mis2013/MIS2013_without_Annex_4.pdf

2.5.1 *The Case of China and ASEAN*

China and the ASEAN countries, being the top emerging economies in the Asia Pacific, offer the greatest potential as a market for American IP exports, more specifically for U.S. digital media and services, giving the American copyright multinational corporations the widest and fastest-growing digital market in the world. If counterfeiting and media piracy of American products and services can be controlled by Chinese authorities, it is projected that China would become the largest market for U.S. digital exports. At present, China is rapidly becoming the world's largest digital media market. In 2016, it is predicted that China will overtake the Japanese market to become the largest entertainment and media market in the Asia Pacific region and rank number two in the world behind the United States.[18] Virtually every Chinese home has a television. And China's film sector has the second largest film market in the world after the United States and is predicted to overtake the U.S. box office by 2020. China also has the largest and fastest-growing Internet market for digital media in the world—the real significance to the American IP hegemony in copyright—from multimedia, music, and film to online gaming.[19] Although the Chinese Internet penetration is slower compared to the United States and developed countries, its potential is, however, staggering. At present, China already has the highest number of Internet users in the world and is expected to rise further with its more than 1.3 billion population. On February 3, 2015, China reported that it has 649 million Internet users, 47.9 % Internet penetration, and 85.8 % mobile Internet users.[20] With this rapidly increasing Internet users, plus the ongoing convergence of networks and the government's telecommunication infrastructure building which aim to combine telecom, broadcast, and Internet on a single platform to deliver voice, data, and video content, China's new digital and entertainment media is expected to reach unprecedented heights.[21] And if the United States can penetrate this huge digital media market in the near future and control China's digital piracy, American global IP hegemony, at least in the area of copyright, would then be fully realized given the significant size of the Chinese market. Thus, the United States, through the USTR, is zealously taking hegemonic steps to pressure China to agree to its own version of IPR protection in order to eventually dominate the giant Chinese digital and copyright market that includes music, films, software, online games, television programs, books, journals, and other digital media goods, services, and applications.

---

[18] "China-leading the race to digital media revenues in Asia-Pacific" at http://www.pwc.com/gx/en/global-entertainment-media-outlook/assets/china-summary.pdf

[19] "Spotlight on China: Building a Roadmap to Success in media and entertainment," p. 4 at http://www.ey.com/Publication/vwLUAssets/Media_and_Entertainment_-_Spotlight_on_China/$FILE/Spotlight_on_China.pdf

[20] https://translate.google.com/translate?sl=auto&tl=en&js=y&prev=_t&hl=en&ie=UTF-8&u=http%3A%2F%2Fwww.cac.gov.cn%2F2015-02%2F03%2Fc_1114237273.htm&edit-text=&act=url

[21] "Spotlight on China: Building a Roadmap to Success in media and entertainment," p. 4 at http://www.ey.com/Publication/vwLUAssets/Media_and_Entertainment_-_Spotlight_on_China/$FILE/Spotlight_on_China.pdf

Aside from China, the ASEAN economies too constitute a great promise for the American IP hegemony in digital media. The ASEAN is significant for the growth of the American IP hegemony in the Asia Pacific region. Besides its strategic military, security, and political importance to the U.S. interest, the ASEAN region is a dynamic and fast-growing economy which hosts nearly 600 million people and lies at the crossroads of huge markets, straddles critical shipping lanes, and controls substantial agricultural, mineral, and energy resources (Petri and Plummer 2014, p. 1). Above all, the ASEAN is a region which has a high demand for American digital media exports—thus a fertile ground for the establishment of the U.S. IP hegemony in Asia Pacific. Like China, the ASEAN is also a great promise as a market for American copyright goods and services. Vietnam, Indonesia, Malaysia, Thailand, the Philippines, Singapore, and other ASEAN countries manifest a growing appetite for digital and entertainment media which corresponds to the region's rising middle class and Internet users. The digital landscape is at a turning point for many consumers in the ASEAN as digital media is ingrained in their everyday lives with an Internet usage for digital and entertainment media which is even surpassing the time spent on traditional media such as television or print.[22] The Philippines, for instance, ranks as the number 2 user of Facebook, the top American social networking site with more than a billion users. Indonesia ranks fourth in the world among the top users of Facebook[23] and ranks fifth in Twitter, the top U.S. microblog site on the Internet.[24] A study by comScore in March 2013, for instance, showed that consumers of six ASEAN countries in the Asia Pacific, including the Philippines and Vietnam, used heavily digital and entertainment media such as music, movies, entertainment news, and television shows on the Internet. It also showed that over 620 million people in the region spent their time online, primarily consuming American digital and entertainment media content supplied by top U.S. Internet companies such as Google, Microsoft, and Yahoo. YouTube of Google emerged as the number 1 multimedia site of ASEAN countries.[25]

In summary, China and the ASEAN have shown the greatest promise for the establishment of U.S. IP hegemony in the Asia Pacific region, the main engine of the current global economy. With their rising middle class coupled with their largest and fastest-growing Internet connection and market for American digital and entertainment media, China and the ASEAN are the ideal regional ground for the United States to extend its IP hegemony and for the USTR's antipiracy surveillance system.

---

[22] Nielsen (2011), "The Digital Media Habits and Attitudes of Southeast Asian Consumers October 2011," pp. 2–3 at http://www.grahamhills.com/wp-content/uploads/2011/11/71370794-The-digital-media-and-habits-attitudes-of-South-East-Asian-Consumers.pdf

[23] http://www.statista.com/statistics/268136/top-15-countries-based-on-number-of-facebook-users/

[24] http://www.adweek.com/socialtimes/twitter-top-countries/468210

[25] comScore.com Media Metrix, March 2013 study, p. 41

2.5.2 Legal Tools to Combat Media Piracy in Asia Pacific

To achieve the great promise of the Asia Pacific region as the ideal market for U.S. IP exports and fertile ground for the establishment of American IP hegemony in the world, counterfeiting and piracy of U.S. and foreign IP must be monitored and controlled. Thus, the United States through the USTR has pressured piracy-laden countries of the Asia Pacific to reform their IPR protection system to curb counterfeiting, especially media piracy in the region. To achieve this, the United States took a series of legal steps through FTAs in the Asia Pacific Economic Cooperation (APEC) and through antipiracy prescriptions of the USTR to pressure the ASEAN countries to address the growing media piracy in the region. Through the U.S. influence, the Asia Pacific Economic Cooperation (APEC) created the Intellectual Property Rights Get-Together (IPR-GT) in 1996 which was subsequently renamed in 1997 as Intellectual Property Rights Experts' Group (IPEG) with a primary duty to ensure adequate protection, through legislative, administrative, and enforcement mechanisms, of intellectual rights in the Asia Pacific region based on the principles of WTO's TRIPS and other related agreements.[26] With regard to media piracy, APEC was able to produce two significant sets of guidelines to combat media piracy in the region: "Effective Practices for Addressing Unauthorized Camcording" and "Effective Practices for Regulations Related to Optical Disc Production."[27] The first one encourages APEC countries to pass laws against illegal recording of movies inside cinemas for film piracy, and the second one is intended to regulate optical disc plants in the region in order to prevent counterfeiting digital media products. Optical disc piracy of American music, software, games, and films using CDs and DVDs is rampant in the Asia Pacific region, particularly in China and Southeast Asian countries such as Malaysia, Thailand, Indonesia, Vietnam, and the Philippines. Illegal camcording, i.e., the unauthorized recording of foreign and local feature films inside movie houses and uploading and selling them as camcords on the Internet for peer-to-peer sharing or for illegal replication of pirated optical media discs and distribution in illegal CD–DVD shops and on the sidewalks of these countries, is rampant in these countries. For the United States, the passage of an anti-camcording legislation can be a deterrence against piracy of American movies which deprives the Motion Picture Association of America (MPAA) millions of dollars in sales and revenues. The passage of a law which also regulates and monitors optical disc plants is also very important for the United States in order to prevent the production and distribution of illegal disc containing American and foreign digital media.

In response to APEC's call against illegal camcording and after a long prodding of the USTR, the Philippines finally enacted the Anti-camcording Act of 2009 (R.A. 9995). Under this law, any person caught using or attempting to use an audiovisual

---

[26] See www.apec.org.

[27] The unauthorized recording of a feature film as it is shown in movie houses is known as *camcording* and resulting recording as *camcord*. The device used in camcording is called camcorder which includes video cameras, digital cameras, mobile phones, tablet, and other recording gadgets. Camcords are reproduced and distributed via camera and Internet file sharing and through sale of unlicensed optical discs (Koch et al. 2011, p. 1).

work in exhibition facility may be sentenced to imprisonment of 6 months and 1 day to 6 years and fined between US$1000 and 17,000.[28] But the directive in regulating optical disc plants remained unaddressed by the Philippine government. Other ASEAN piracy nations such as Thailand, Indonesia, Malaysia, and Vietnam have yet to enact appropriate laws regulating the production of optical discs and criminalizing camcording in movie houses despite the continuous pressure from the IIPA and the USTR.

2.5.3 Anti-online Piracy Regulations

The technological innovation and widespread adoption of the Internet around the globe posed major problems to the U.S. IP hegemony. "Copyright materials can be easily reproduced and cheaply transported in digital form all over the world via the Internet using any number of different protocols and distribution models."[29] And since the Internet cannot distinguish what is legal or illegal materials on its web and infringers can easily become anonymous and migrate outside national borders, regulating the Internet to curb media piracy has always been a major problem for the U.S. IP hegemony. With this realization, the USTR has been pressuring Asia Pacific countries to regulate not just camcording and optical disc plants but ultimately the Internet, the primary purveyor of infringing materials. This strategy corresponds with the changing media piracy landscape in China and the ASEAN in recent years where physical and optical disc piracy have been gradually replaced by online media piracy. The IIPA has observed that over the past several years, an increase in the severity of Internet piracy is accompanying increased Internet, broadband, and mobile connection and penetration. Optical disc piracy which uses CDs and DVDs has been gradually replaced by online media piracy spearheaded by the youth who has the strong inclination to use the latest technologies. Particularly noted in online piracy is the rising use of streaming, forum and blog, deep linking, peer-to-peer sharing (P2P), BitTorrent, and "one-click hosting" sites to infringe copyright in movies, music, software, and books and journals. "Mobile apps are also becoming a new platform for disseminating illegal content" (2014 IIPA, Special 301 Report, pp. 163–164). Internet piracy accompanies Internet penetration. And some of the emerging online piracy techniques include P2P file sharing services, BitTorrent file sharing, deep linking, blogs providing links to pirate materials, and cyberlockers which store infringing material by selling passwords for illegal access (2014 IIPA Special 301 Report, p. 201).

---

[28] See R.A. 9995 at http://www.lawphil.net/statutes/repacts/ra2010/ra_9995_2010.html.

[29] Ruggenar, C. (2011). Perspectives on Policy Responses to Online Copyright Responses: An Evolving Policy Landscape. WIPO, p. 3 at http://www.wipo.int/meetings/en/doc_details.jsp?doc_id=171017

2.5.4 Online Media Piracy in ASEAN Countries

The Internet is both an opportunity and a problem for the U.S. IP hegemony. As an opportunity, the Internet is the main platform for big and small American copyright industries which generate income and employment for the U.S. economy and help maintain the American economic leadership in the world. As a problem, the Internet is the main platform for counterfeiting and piracy. In optical media production and consumption, the web is the central platform for online and optical disc piracy. Copyright content is illegally uploaded, downloaded, and shared on the Internet. Master copies are also uploaded and downloaded from the Internet and are replicated in disc formats and sold in the illegal shops and stalls in piracy-laden emerging economies of the ASEAN. Online media piracy is the unintended effect of the growing Internet penetration and of the convergence of technologies. The Internet which is used to be connected only through cable wires in personal computers is now attached through wireless broadband to smartphones, iPods, tablets, laptops, and other high-tech gadgets. To curb online media piracy and assert the American hegemony in the region, the United States is now focusing on regulating the Internet in ASEAN piracy-laden countries through FTAs and GSPs to combat digital media piracy.

With the rising Internet connection and demand for digital media goods and services, the United States has noticed a dramatic increase of online piracy in ASEAN countries such as Thailand, Malaysia, the Philippines, and Vietnam. Thailand is the first ASEAN country to be placed in the USTR's Priority Watch List in 1989 and has a long history of copyright piracy. Lately, Thailand has one of the highest growth rates of online piracy in the region. In its 2014 Special 301 Annual Report, for instance, the IIPA alleged that the market for creative content in Thailand has deteriorated in recent years due mainly to piracy and lack of the needed IP legal reforms. With Thailand's increasing Internet connection, piracy (estimated 80 % of the Thai market) through online and mobile device (smartphone, tablet) has largely replaced physical piracy (2014 IIPA Special 301 Report, Thailand, p. 1). Because of this, the IIPA and USTR are pressuring Thailand to pass laws that regulate online piracy of digital media. But the Thai government has resisted this pressure and has not passed any law, as of date, which directly regulates the Internet to combat online media piracy.

Malaysia is another ASEAN country with a long history of media piracy in the USTR and IIPA's PWL and WL and with a rising online piracy. Although it has been removed from these lists, Malaysia continues to be in the forefront of optical media piracy. In fact, the IIPA recommended to the USTR to place Malaysia in the WL again because of the continuation of optical disc piracy. It noted that Malaysia remained a producer and supplier of pirated optical discs and lacked enforcement against licensed optical disc factories. It also observed an increase of vendors selling pirated discs. Thus, part of the priority actions requested by the IIPA in 2012 is to license all legitimate optical disc traders at "night" markets and to ban all sales of pirated discs in these areas (2011 IIPA Special 301 Report, pp. 201–202). Malaysia may have made significant progress in its fight against optical disc piracy, but it is struggling to fight online media piracy. With its impressive Internet penetration

(65.8 % of the population are Internet users) and broadband subscription (41.3 million mobile subscriptions or 100 % mobile penetration), Malaysia faces a serious online piracy challenge. The Malaysia Domestic Trade, Cooperatives and Consumerism Ministry and Malaysian police have been monitoring at least 30 suspected infringing websites that supply infringement material online (2014 IIPA Special 301 Report, p. 2). Despite the growing Internet piracy, Malaysia, as of date, has not enacted an Internet law to combat online piracy.

The Philippines, like Malaysia, has a long history in the USTR's watch list system due to optical disc piracy and, lately, due to growing online piracy of copyrighted materials. After years of IPR reform and struggle against optical disc piracy, the Philippines was finally removed from the USTR's watch lists in 2014. Despite this significant development, some antipiracy groups were not happy. The two U.S.-based IP lobby groups, the IIPA and International Anti-counterfeiting Coalition (IACC), have recommended that the Philippines must be retained in the Watch List of the USTR in 2014, instead of being removed from the watch list system altogether, because of the rising online trafficking of both counterfeit and pirated goods (De Vera 2014). Media piracy, therefore, has not waned but just migrated to the online platform with the rising Internet connections and the youth's increasing use of illegal digital media products and services. Although the Internet penetration in the Philippines is not as fast as Vietnam's, online piracy has been a growing concern of the USTR and IIPA. Optical disc piracy has slowly been eclipsed by online media piracy. And the Optical Media Board (OMB), the government's main antipiracy agency, can only regulate optical media production, conduct raids, and confiscate illegal discs, but it has no power and jurisdiction to curb online media piracy in mobile phones, computers, and other devices with Internet connection. Thus, the IIPA and USTR want the Philippine government to amend the current optical media law to empower the OMB to curb online piracy.

Unlike other ASEAN countries, the Philippines enacted an Internet law in 2013 to address online media piracy. After a long legislative debate, pressure from the USTR, and promise of U.S. military support for the country against China's incursion in West Philippine Sea, the Philippines finally enacted the Anti-cybercrime Law in 2013 despite strong resistance from Internet users and civil society groups. Although this law intends to fight cybercrime, some of its provisions are important for the United States in its fight against online media piracy. In recognition of this effort to pass a new Internet law, the Philippines was allegedly being removed from the USTR's piracy Watch List, just days before President Obama's visit to the Malacanang Palace last April 2014 despite the lack of solid empirical evidence which showed that media piracy has indeed declined in the country.

Finally, of all the ASEAN countries with high online media piracy, Vietnam poses a very serious threat to the American hegemony in the region. Being one of the fastest-growing Internet penetration in the world, ranking 18th in the world, eighth in Asia, and third in Southeast Asia with many Internet service providers and numerous pirate websites, Vietnam's online piracy on music, film, online games, and other digital media products and services is one of the fastest in the region, second only to China. The vast majority of the websites dealing with copyright content in Vietnam, for instance, are unlicensed. With regard to music, for example, the IIPA estimates that only 1 % of online music services offered by a few online operators are licensed. The digital media market is flooded with counterfeit copyright content. Only a very small percentage of this market is bought from licensed sites. "The rest are streaming and download sites (50 %), forums (21 %), video websites (17 %), search engines (8 %), deep linking, cyberlocker, and social network sites, all being employed to deliver unlicensed copyright content, including music, movies, entertainment and software, and published materials" (2013 IIPA Special 301 Report, p. 287). The rise of "notorious" infringing sites such as *nghenhac.info,vui.vn, Zing.vn, Socbay.com, Tamtay.cn, xemphimonlines.com, phimvang.org, xuongphim.com, viettorrent.vn, ephim24g.net*, and *phim.soha.vn* which seemed to be supported or tolerated by the Vietnamese government is now the major concern of the American hegemony in the communist state (2013 IIPA Special 301 Report). These infringing sites which disseminate largely American copyright materials are so popular that one time, the American embassy in Vietnam, as already mentioned, is forced to use a "Zingme" account of a top Vietnamese pirate site Zing.vn to reach out to young people in Vietnam (Brummit 2012).

Vietnam has been under intense pressure from the USTR to pass new laws to fight online media piracy. Online piracy is a growing problem in Vietnam. Experts indicate that up to "90 % of all digital content provided to users on the Internet in Vietnam such as music, movies, e-books, software, and mobile phone applications is pirated" (American Chamber of Commerce Vietnam 2013, p. 1). The pressure has probably moved Vietnam to curb online piracy. In 2014, Vietnam finally passed into law Decree 72 which aims to regulate the Internet and curb online piracy. The problem, however, is that this new Internet law appears to be regulating Internet freedom and dissent against the communist regime rather than curbing online media piracy. Thus, this new legislation is overshooting what is being recommended by the USTR and can be interpreted as a form of covert resistance to resist the U.S. IP hegemony.

2.6 China and ASEAN as a Scourge for American IP Hegemony

Of all economies in the Asia Pacific region, the United States has a specific focus on China and the Southeast Asian countries, particularly on the members of the ASEAN. China and the ASEAN constitute a new battleground for piracy which can make or break the American IP dominance in the region, specifically on digital and optical media. With China's strong and subtle resistance to the U.S. IP hegemony and wide trading connections with piracy-laden ASEAN countries, the U.S. economic and military presence in the Asia Pacific region, therefore, becomes a necessity to protect American interest. Thus, the Obama administration has given a priority to the "return to Asia" foreign policy to establish bilateral relations with ASEAN states and to counter China's growing economic and counterfeiting influence in the region and to monitor its infringing activities in ASEAN economies. For the United States, China and the ASEAN constitute a blessing and a curse for the American IP hegemony.

The economic and market network of China and the Southeast Asian countries does only constitute a great promise for the American IP goods and services but also a scourge and a counter-hegemony to the U.S. dominance in IP global trade. These fastest-growing economies with high Internet connection and rising appetite for IP are also leaders in counterfeiting and piracy of American digital goods and services. Except Singapore, China, Vietnam, Thailand, Indonesia, Malaysia, and the Philippines have long histories of counterfeiting and pirating American digital media, such as movies, music, computer and business software, video games, and other online digital media goods and services. They are also regularly listed in the Special 301 watch lists for being piracy hotspots in the world (Table 2.1).

If the United States, on one end of the continuum, is acting as the hegemonic power behind the current IP global trade and legal protection regime, together with Japan and European Union (EU), China is on the opposite end, acting as the counter-hegemonic power or the leading social resistance power against the United States, together with some ASEAN countries, India, Brazil, and Russia. These big emerging markets share a belief in their entitlement to a more influential role in world affairs (Hurrell 2006, p. 2). With high piracy levels and being piracy hotspots in the Asia Pacific region and regularly included in the Special 301 USTR watch lists, these economies are overtly and covertly opposing the current IP hegemonic regime of the United States and its allied trading partners. China, being a growing economic superpower and main challenger of the U.S. hegemonic position, is the leader of the current global piracy and the overall symbol of resistance of the non-IP-exporting and ASEAN developing countries against the strong IPR protection system demanded by the United States. China is not only the number one pirate producer and exporter of counterfeit goods and services around the world but also the leading trading partner of ASEAN countries with long histories in the piracy watch list system of the USTR such as Malaysia, Thailand, Indonesia, the Philippines, and Vietnam. While the United States leads in exporting genuine IP products and services around the globe, China leads in exporting counterfeit and fake goods and services to IP-consuming developing countries such as the Philippines and Vietnam. Counterfeit Chinese IP products such as bags, clothes, gadgets, and pirated DVDs

Table 2.1 Frequency of China and some ASEAN countries in USTR's Watch Lists[a]

Country	Frequency: Priority Watch List	Frequency: Watch List
China		
Indonesia	15	10
Malaysia	2	11
Philippines	6	19
Singapore		3
Thailand	13	10
Vietnam		16

[a]Based on author's personal count, data compiled from the USTR's Special 301 Annual Reports from 1989 to 2013

and CDs and their replicating technologies are exported to various countries around the world. The IP competition between the United States and China illustrates how the two powers of global trade interact in today's age of innovation and technology. Both parties are exchanging accusations of unfair trading practices. The United States, for instance, accused China of "dumping" products below their cost and failing to protect individual property rights. But China also accused the United States of "unfairly imposing tariffs on selected Chinese imports" (Greenberg 2012). The United States sees China as the "mastermind" of the global counterfeiting and piracy. But China sees the United States as the cunning global master who controls the IP trade in the world.

The social resistance of China and the ASEAN against stronger American-style IPR protection occurs both in legal and nonlegal arenas. In the legal arena, China contested much of the U.S. accusations and cases of piracy in the WTO, using law itself or the TRIPS provisions to oppose the hegemonic claims of the United States. It also uses a double-edge approach to IPR protection, issuing public statements acknowledging the TRIPS and the need of a stronger IP protection to combat piracy, but continues to use a soft-glove approach to piracy, especially with regard to theft of IP trade secrets of American multinationals, tolerating counterfeiting at home to allow locals to imitate American IP technology, putting barriers to American and foreign IP exports to prevent them from penetrating the local Chinese market, and allowing retail piracy to assist its huge informal or underground economy to benefit from the counterfeit trade. Oftentimes, China—as well as other piracy-laden countries—employs delaying tactics especially when confronted by the USTR on certain serious cases of piracy. It makes diplomatic promises to take some concrete steps to pass new legislations to address the piracy problem while making maneuvers to copy U.S. IP technology and to delay the implementation of USTR's recommendations.

In some cases, China engages in strategic nonenforcement by simply refusing to prosecute infringers despite clear evidence of piracy, baffling American IP stakeholders, lobby groups, and the USTR. The 2014 IIPA Special 301 Report has noted, for example, that the commitments made by China in the United States–China Joint Commission on Commerce and Trade (JCCT), the United States–China Strategic and Economic Dialogue (S&ED), and the United States–China Film Agreement remained unfulfilled, making full market access difficult for American and foreign companies. Film distribution of imported films also remains under the control of two state-owned enterprises (SOEs) despite the government's commitment to allow private Chinese enterprises to participate in film distribution (p. 22). Because of the tolerant attitude of the government toward piracy and counterfeiting, China remains a hub for the manufacturing and distribution of technologies and devices used around the world to circumvent access controls employed by copyright owners to manage access to their works and services. And the USTR and IIPA blame the Chinese government for refusing to file criminal charges against manufacturers and distributors of these circumvention technologies and devices. Finally, it is apparent that China tolerates piracy to protect its local economy. As part of its covert resistance, the Chinese government may agree to some U.S. IPR demands but becomes selective in implementing them at home in order to protect the local economy.

2.7 China: The Tie That Binds the Philippines and Vietnam to Piracy

The persistence of media piracy in the Philippines and Vietnam would not happen without an old mediating network which sustains it—China. China has a long trading history with ASEAN countries identified with piracy and counterfeiting such as the Philippines and Vietnam. This common preexisting trading network with China facilitates counterfeiting and piracy between China, the Philippines, and Vietnam, long before the U.S. IP hegemony came into the picture. This human and material network has its own dynamics and behavioral standards which tend to resist economic and cultural arenas which the TRIPS and U.S. IPR system aim to colonize. This preexisting network and trading relation makes it easier for China to export counterfeit goods, pirated discs, and illegal replicating technologies to the Philippines and Vietnam. China is the leading supplier of counterfeit discs and replicating technologies to these countries, and this has been consistently acknowledged by the USTR and IIPA in their yearly reports.

China is the tie that binds the Philippines and Vietnam to media piracy. Facilitating networks that relate media piracy of these countries to China did not happen just a decade ago when the digital technology became popular. The economic and cultural ties between China and some ASEAN countries like the Philippines and Vietnam have long been established by the enduring history of trading and cultural exchanges between these countries. Furthermore, the Philippines and Vietnam have dynamic communities or districts of ethnic Chinese traders—Binondo and Cholon, respectively—which serve as mediating networks which facilitate counterfeit trade with mainland China. Some ethnic Chinese traders in these districts often participate in the various aspects of the piracy trade. In the Philippines, for instance, Chinese traders provide paraphernalia or materials for packaging pirated DVDs to Quiapo optical disc producers. They also act as lenders of capital to optical disc piracy retails. The U.S. IP hegemony through USTR's recommendations could not just repress through the current IPR protection system the long cultural and trade ties between some piracy-laden countries and China without inviting social resistance from the local culture and from traders, unscrupulous law enforcers, and their allied networks who benefit from the piracy trade.

China's trade ties with the Philippines and Vietnam took root thousands of years ago. Records show that active and regular trade of the Philippines with China occurred as early as the tenth century which was transacted mainly through Champa (Vietnam) coast. Mai-i (Mindoro) traders later circumvented Vietnam and proceeded directly to China through Canton. China's occupation of Vietnam, on the other hand, dates back a thousand years ago between the Han conquest of Nam Viet in the second century BC and the reassertion of Vietnamese independence as Dai Viet in AD 967. Counterfeit informal trade in the Philippines and Vietnam did not just flourish during the contemporary period. Counterfeit goods were already traded even before the advent of digital products and services such as pirated CDs and DVDs.

Furthermore, the geographical network is also an important factor that connects China to Vietnam and the Philippines. On the one hand, Vietnam is physically closer to China. China shares borders with Vietnam and thus it is easier to transport counterfeit goods in a cross-border trade. Ecological theories note the social effect of ecological proximity to people's sociocultural and economic exchanges. By sharing common borders, China's connections with Vietnam can be considered in many ways a family affair, with all the closeness of shared values and bitterness of close rivals. No country in Southeast Asia is culturally closer to China than Vietnam (Lim 1999). Both countries are culturally aware of the cultural and trading ties that bind them together. These common ties facilitate the cross-border piracy trade. Moreover, the cities and district of Guangdong Province, the hotbed of counterfeiting and piracy, are relatively closer to the Vietnamese border. Owing to this geographical proximity as well as the lack of effective law enforcement, complicated terrain (mostly forests and sea), bureaucratic corruption, and smuggling, pirated goods and technologies can easily enter the Vietnamese border illegally. Moreover, through bribes and protection money that traders provide to corrupt Vietnamese and Chinese officials, the illegal cross-border delivery of pirated media and replicating machines to Vietnam can remain unnoticed by law enforcers in the borders. Bureaucratic corruption is high in Guangdong as well as in the Vietnamese borders. In 2003, for instance, Guangdong's people's court settled 950 corruption cases with 1895 people found guilty including 46 government officials (Lo 2009, p. 72).

The Philippines, on the other hand, may be thousands of miles away from China, but its cultural and trading history with Chinese traders dated back as early as the tenth century.[30] China is an old trading partner as well as a strong cultural influence for the Philippines before the Spaniards and the Americans colonized the archipelago. Records show that trading between the Philippines and China occurred as early as the tenth century which was transacted mainly through Champa (Vietnam) coast. Mai-i (Mindoro) traders later circumvented Vietnam and proceeded directly to China through Canton. Through a tribute mission, the Mai-i traders were able to secure blessing from the Chinese Emperor by gifting him with pearls, frankincense, myrrh, and colorful animals (Lim 1999). Centuries may have passed but this trading tradition and cultural network have not been broken but instead improved and even developed into a more sophisticated platform with the advent of new technologies and advanced communication and transportation networks.

[30] For a more detailed description of the Philippines–China trade, see Lim (1999). The Political Economy of Philippine-Chinese Relations. PASCN Discussion Paper No. 99–16 at http://pascn.pids.gov.ph/files/Discussions%20Papers/1999/pascndp9916.pdf.

2.8 Guangdong as Mediating Network for the Philippines and Vietnam

The Chinese provinces of Fujian and Guangdong have long been regarded as hotbeds for counterfeiting, pirating, and forgery. Guangdong is home to thousands of factories that produce legitimate and counterfeit products. A few years back when most pirated DVDs and CDs were directly imported from China, Guangdong has been regarded by law enforcers and some pirate producers in the Philippines as the main hub of optical disc piracy in China. Fujian is another province for counterfeiting, especially for forged securities, documents, and gift certificates. It has printing facilities that can expertly copy any coupon, certificate, voucher, and other documents. These two provinces symbolize China's piracy and counterfeiting activities. But the Guangdong Province is the mediating network which directly facilitates the importation of pirated discs, equipment, and replicating technologies to the Philippines and Vietnam. No less than the USTR and the IIPA recognize the role of Guangdong as the main source of counterfeit optical media discs and replicating technologies to piracy hotspots in the ASEAN such as the Philippines and Vietnam.

The most notorious cities and counterfeiting markets in Guangdong include the capital city Guangzhou, Shenzhen, Shantou, Chaoyang, and Jieyang and several markets in Baiyun District (2006 USTR Special 301, p. 21). Some key informants of the sociological studies on which this book is based identified Guangzhou as one of the top sources of pirated discs for the Philippines and Vietnam. This city is widely known as a major piracy hub in China and one major exporter of counterfeit discs. In 2007, for instance, Chinese officials confiscated 1.6 million worth of pirated DVDs, the largest antipiracy haul in Guangzhou, China.[31] Guangdong is regarded as a hotbed for counterfeiting and pirating. It is home to thousands of factories in China that produce counterfeit goods as well as legitimate ones.[32] It is often cited in Special 301 Annual Reports of the USTR as the hub of large-scale counterfeiting and the engine of export of pirated products for the Philippines, Vietnam, and other parts of the world. Chinese pirated discs and equipment usually originate from the illegal optical disc plants and warehouses in Guangdong Province. During the golden years of the Quiapo piracy network, when pirated discs were mostly imported from China, producers admitted that most of their counterfeit discs came from some secret warehouses in Guangzhou, Guangdong, China. With their contacts in Guangzhou, they were able to regularly purchase thousands of pirated discs of the latest foreign and

[31] One of the biggest cases involving pirated discs manufactured abroad and imported to China is Lin Yuehua's case. Lin is the boss of a CD piracy and smuggling operation, the largest one which has been so far uncovered in China. He and his 11 associates were sentenced to jail for life by an intermediate people's court in South China's Guangxi Zhuang Autonomous Region. The court said Lin and his men bought five advanced CD production lines worth more than US$ 10 million and established a company abroad in 2002, mass-producing pirate DVDs and VCDs. The gang then smuggled the pirated audio and video products into the Chinese mainland (Xinhua News Agency, November 24, 2006), retrieved from http://www.china.org.cn/english/China/190070.htm

[32] http://factsanddetails.com/china.php?itemid=356

American films and music and export them to the Philippines through customs brokers and corruption networks in airports and bureau of customs.

2.9 Summary

This chapter has provided a critical analysis and global context of the persistence of counterfeiting and media piracy in the Philippines and Vietnam using some sociological theories on power, law, hegemony, resistance, technology, and network. It situates the media piracy in the Philippines and Vietnam within the ongoing struggle of hegemony and social resistance of the global IP trade led by the United States and China and their allied networks. It pursues three major arguments:

First, it argued that piracy is primarily a form of social resistance, both active and passive, of IP-consuming countries led by China and ASEAN countries like the Philippines and Vietnam against the hegemonic power of the United States in the global IP trade. Realizing the crucial role of IP in the U.S. economy and the need to curb piracy at home and abroad, the United States designed a new economic order and global legal infrastructure that connects trading with the United States with IPR protection of U.S. IP exports abroad, utilizing U.S.-dominated multilateral institutions and trade agreements (FTAs) to realize this design. To hide its hegemonic design, the cultural mechanism of law as constituted in multilateral agreements, FTAs, RTAs, and BTAs became a potent tool of the United States to control the direction of the global IP trade and to project a message that IPR protection is for the good of all nations.

Second, law is not only a maker of hegemony but also of social resistance. Following the legal pluralist theory, the official law is only one of the many normative standards in society. Thus, it has cracks and loopholes where resistant parties can exploit and use to oppose hegemonic control. The IP regime which sees creative work as private property is basically patterned after the U.S. IPR system. This is met with resistance by the Global South which sees creative work and IP as communal rather than privately owned.

Finally, it argued that piracy in the Asia Pacific especially in the Philippines and Vietnam is a manifestation of resistance to the U.S. hegemonic design in the Asia Pacific region. In the current trade configuration, the Asia Pacific, which comprises China and the ASEAN countries such as the Philippines and Vietnam, is the most promising and fastest-growing economic region in the world particularly in terms of consumption and market of IP and digital goods and services. Hence, the U.S. IP hegemonic strategies are centered on the Asia Pacific region, pressuring piracy-laden countries such as China, the Philippines, and Vietnam through the USTR to force developing countries adopt legal measures to curb optical disc and online media piracy. But this approach does not proceed without passive resistance. China has a long cultural and trading history with its neighboring ASEAN countries such as the Philippines and Vietnam which facilitates the importation of counterfeit media goods, discs, and replicating technologies for media piracy. Finally, China's Guangdong Province which is known and recognized by the USTR and IIPA as the hub of global piracy and counterfeiting serves as the main source of counterfeit goods and technologies for piracy and the central mediating network that connects China with media piracy networks in the Philippines and Vietnam.

References

American Chamber of Commerce Vietnam (2013). Intellectual property rights in the socialist republic of Vietnam. February 8, 2013. www.amchamhanoi.com/wp-content/uploads/2014/.../special301old.pdf. Accessed 6 June 2015.

Bello, W. et al. (1996). *The anti-development state: The political economy of permanent crisis in the Philippines*. London: Zed Books.

Bøås, M., & McNeill, D. (2003). *Multilateral institutions: A critical introduction*. London: Pluto Press.

Bocock, R. (1986). *Hegemony*. New York: Tavistock Publications.

Braithwaite, J., & Drahos, P. (2000). *Global business regulation*. Cambridge, MA: Cambridge University Press.

Brighenti, A. (2011). Power, substraction and social transformation: Canetti and Foucault on the notion of resistance. *Distinktion: Scandinavian Journal of Social Theory, 12*(1), 57–78. Doi: 10.1080/1600910X.2011.549331.

Brown, A. G., & Stern, R. M. (2011). Free trade agreements and governance of the global trading system. *The World Economy*. Doi: 10.1111/j.1467-9701.2011.01333.x.

Brummitt, C. (2012). Online piracy a big problem in Vietnam. *Mercury News*. http://www.mercurynews.com/ci_21967091/online-piracy-big-problem-vietnam. Accessed 10 May 2014.

Cain, M. (1983). Gramci, the state, and the place of law. In D. Sugarman (Ed.), *Legality, ideology, and the state*. London: Academic Press.

Caparosa, J. (1992). International relations theory and bilateralism: The search for foundations. *International Organization, 46*, 599–632.

Castells, M. (2009). *The rise of the network society* (2nd ed.). Oxford: John Wiley-Blackwell.

Chirot, D. (1985). The rise of the west. *American Sociological Review, 50*, 181–195.

Collins, R. (1986). *Weberian sociological theory*. Cambridge: Cambridge University Press.

Coombe, R. (1998). *The cultural life of intellectual properties: Authorship, appropriation, and the law*. Durham: Duke University Press.

Cox, R. W. (1981). Social forces, states and world orders: Beyond international relations theory. *Millennium: Journal of International Studies, 10*(2), 126–155.

Dent, C. M. (2010). Free trade, more regulation? Commercial regulatory provisions in Asia-Pacific free trade agreements. *Competition and Change, 14*(1), 48–79.

De Vera, B. A. (2014). 2 US anti-piracy groups slams rising online piracy in PH. *Newsbytes Philippines*. http://www.newbytes.ph. Accessed 28 May 2014.

Frank, G. (1967). *Capitalism and the underdevelopment of Latin America*. New York Monthly Review Press.

Friedman, L. M. (1975). *The legal system: A social science perspective*. New York: Russell Sage Foundation.

Gaines, J. M. (2000). *Contested culture, the image, the voice, and the law*. London: University of North Carolina Press.

Giddens, A. (1984). *The constitution of society*. Cambridge: Polity.

Giddens, A. (1985). *The nation-state and violence: Volume two of a contemporary critique of historical materialism*. Cambridge: Polity.

Gil, P. (2014). The 30 best torrent download sites of 2014, where users go to find music and movie files. http://netforbeginners.about.com/od/peersharing/a/torrent_Search.htm. Accessed 22 May 2013.

Greenberg, M. R. (2012). Time for a China-U.S. free trade agreement. China does not have to invest here, but it is to America's advantage. *The Wall Street Journal*. http://online.wsj.com. Accessed 19 Apr 2014.
Griffiths, A. (2002). Legal pluralism. In R. Banakar & M. Travers (Eds.), *An introduction to law and social theory* (pp. 289–310). Oxford: Hart Publishing.
Guillet, D. (1998). Rethinking legal pluralism: Local law and state law in the evolution of water property rights in northwestern Spain. *Comparative Studies in Society and History, 40*(1), 42–70.
Hall, S. (1977). Culture, media and the ideological effect. In J. Curran et al. (Eds.), *Mass communication and society* (pp. 315–348); reprint, Beverly Hills: Sage Publications, 1952.
Hall, S. (1985). Authoritarian populism: A reply. *New Left Review, 151*(1), 115–124.
Hall, S., & Jefferson, T. (1976). *Resistance through rituals, youth subcultures in post-war Britain*. London: HarperCollins Academic.
Hurrell, A. (2006). Hegemony, liberalism and global order: What space for would-be great powers? *International Affairs, 82*(1), 1–19.
IIPA (2011). International intellectual property alliance 2011 special 301 report. www.iipa.com. Accessed 22 Nov 2014.
IIPA (2013). International intellectual property alliance 2011 special 301 report. www.iipa.com. Accessed 10 Feb 2014.
IIPA (2014). International intellectual property alliance 2011 special 301 report. www.iipa.com. Accessed 5 Jan 2015.
Khatoon, S. (2013). In defense of regionalism: The developing countries' perspective. *IUP Journal of International Relations*. April 2015 issue.
Koch, J., Smith, M., & Telang, R. (2011). *Camcording and film piracy in Asia-Pacific economic cooperation economies*. International Intellectual Property Institute (IIPI).
Krikorian, G. P., & Szymkowiak, D. M. (2007). Intellectual property rights in the making: The evolution of intellectual property provisions in US free trade agreements and access to medicine. *The Journal of World Intellectual Property, 10*(5), 388–418. Doi: 10.1111/j.1747-1796.2007.00328.x.
Landes, W. M., & Posner, R. A. (2003). *The economic structure of intellectual property rights*. Cambridge, MA: Harvard University Press.
Lazarus-Black, M., & Hirsch S. F. (Eds.). (1994). Introduction/performance and paradox: Exploring law's role in hegemony and resistance. In M. Lazarus-Black & S. F. Hirsch (Eds.), *Contested states: Law, hegemony, and resistance* (pp. 1–31). New York: Routledge.
Lim, B. (1999).*The political economy of Philippines-China relations*. PASCN Discussion Paper No. 99-16. http://pascn.pids.gov.ph/DiscList/d99/s99-16.pdf
Lo, S. S. (2009). *The politics of cross-border crime*. New York: M.E. Sharpe, Inc.
Manoli, P. (2013). Political economy aspects of deep and comprehensive free trade agreements. *Eastern Journal of European Studies, 4*(2), 51–73.
Maskus, K. E. (2000). *Intellectual property rights in the global economy*. Washington, DC: Institute for International Economics.
McMillan, J., & Woodruff, C. (1999). *Dispute prevention without courts in Vietnam*. San Diego: Graduate School of International Relations and Pacific Studies University of California. http://202.154.59.182/ejournal/files/Dispute%20Prevention%20without%20Courts%20in%20Vietnam%20John%20McMillan.pdf
Ming-Te, H. & Tai Ting Liu, T. (2011). Sino-U.S. Strategic competition in Southeast Asia: China's rise and U.S. foreign policy transformation since 9/11*. *Political Perspectives, 5*(3), 96–119. http://china.praguesummerschools.org/files/china/2china2012.pdf
Mitchell, T. (1990). Everyday metaphors of power. *Theory and Society, 19*, 545–577.
Moore, S. F. (1978). *Law as process: An anthropological approach*. London: Routledge & Kegan Paul.
Morin, J.-F. (2006). Tripping up TRIPS debates: IP and health in bilateral agreements. *International Journal of Intellectual Property Management, 1*(1–2), 37–53.

Nathan Associates Inc. (2003, December). *Intellectual property and developing countries: An overview*. Briefing Paper. https://www.hsdl.org/?view&did=446296

O'Conner, J. (1973). *The fiscal crisis of the state*. New York: St. Martha's Press.

Orsi, F., & Coriat, B. (2006). The new role and status of intellectual property rights in contemporary capitalism. *Competition & Change, 10*(2), 162–179. Doi: 10.1179/102452906X104222.

Oyejide, A. T. (1990). Africa and the Uruguay round. *The World Economy, 13*(3), 427–433.

Peller, G. (2011). History, identity, and alienation. *Connecticut Law Review, 43*(5). http://archive.connecticutlawreview.org/documents/Peller.pdf

Petri, P. A., &, Plummer, M. G. (2014). ASEAN centrality and the ASEAN-US economic relationship. *Policy Studies, 69*. http://www.eastwestcenter.org. Accessed 11 May 2014.

Pugatch, M. P. (2004). *The international political economy of intellectual property rights*. Cheltenham: Edward Elgar Publishing Limited.

Riker, D. (2012). Has special 301 promoted US manufacturing exports? *Review of International Economics, 20*(2), 288–298. Doi: 10.1111/j.1467-9396.2012.01022.x.

Ritzer, G. (2010). *Globalization: The essentials*. West Sussex: Wiley-Blackwell.

Ryan, M. (1995). *Playing by the rules: American trade power and diplomacy in the Pacific*. Washington, DC: Washington University Press.

Sarat, A. (1990). ". . . The law is all over": Power, resistance, and the legal consciousness of the poor. *Journal of Law and Humanities, 2*, 343–379.

Saull, R. (2012). Rethinking hegemony: Uneven development, historical blocs, and the world economic crisis. *International Studies Quarterly, 56*, 323–338.

Schott, J. (2006). Free trade agreements and US trade policy: A comparative analysis of US initiatives in Latin America, the Asia-Pacific region, and the Middle East and North Africa. *The International Trade Journal*, *20*(2), 95–138.

Scott, J. C. (1987). *Weapons of the weak: Everyday forms of peasant resistance*. New Haven: Yale University Press.

Scott, J. C. (1990). *Domination and the arts of resistance: Hidden transcripts*. New Haven: Yale University Press.

Simons, J. J. (1999) Cooperation and coercion: The protection of intellectual property in developing countries. *Bond Law Review, 11*(1), Article 5. http://epublications.bond.edu.au/blr/vol11/iss1/5. Accessed 4 Sept 2014.

Siwek, S. E. (2012). *Copyright industries in the U.S., the 2013 report*. International Intellectual Property Alliance (IIPA). http://www.iipa.com/pdf/2013_Copyright_Industries_Full_Report.PDF. Accessed 17 Jan 2015.

Smart, C. (1989). *Feminism and the power of law*. London: Routledge.

Stewart, A. (2001). *Theories of power and domination*. London: Sage Publication.

Stiles, K. W., & Akaha, T. (1991). *International political economy: A reader*. New York: HarperCollins.

Sum, N.-L. (2003). Informational capitalism and U. S. economic hegemony. *Critical Asian Studies, 35*(3). London: Routledge.

Tamahana, B. (2007). Understanding legal pluralism: Past to present, local to global. *Sydney Law Review. 29*, 600.

The Economist. (2014, January 25). China loses its allure. http://www.economist.com/news/leaders/21595001-life-getting-tougher-foreign-companies-those-want-stay-will-have-adjust-china. Accessed 25 May 2014.

Tian, D. (2008). The USTR special 301 reports: An analysis of the US hegemonic pressure upon the organizational change in China's IPR regime. *Chinese Journal of Communication, 1*(2), 224–241.

UNESCO & UNDP. (2013). *Creative economy report 2013 special edition: Widening local development pathways*. http://www.unesco.org/culture/pdf/creative-economy-report-2013.pdf. Accessed 4 Nov 2014.

USTR (2006). United States trade representative 2006 special 301 report. www.ustr.gov. Accessed 5 Feb 2014.

Wallerstein, E. (1974). *The modern world-system*, vol. II. Mercantilism and the consolidation of the European world-economy 1600–1750. New York: Academic Press.
Wallerstein, E. (1991). *Geopolitics and geocultures: Essays on the changing world systems.* Cambridge: Cambridge University Press.
Warshofsky, F. (1994). *Patent wars: The battle to own world's technology*. New York: Wiley.
Williams, R. (1973). Base and superstructure in Marxist cultural theory. *New Left Review, 82*, 3–16.
Yarbrough, B., & Yarbrough, R. (1992). *Cooperation and governance in international trade: The strategic organizational approach.* Princeton: Princeton University Press.
Yngvesson, B. (1993). *Virtuous citizens, disruptive subjects: Order and complaint in a New England court*. New York: Routledge.

Chapter 3
The Government's Attitude Toward the Informal Sector and Piracy

3.1 The Prevalence of the Informal Sector and Formalization

It is an undisputed reality that the informal sector is a growing and increasingly complex phenomenon in the economic, social, and political life of developing countries (Maldonando 1995). It is also an uncontested pattern that the growing informal sector in the developing countries of Southeast Asia is accompanied by a thriving optical media piracy trade in this sector. In their annual Special 301 Reports, the International Intellectual Property Alliance (IIPA), the umbrella organization of top US copyright industries, and United States Trade Representative (USTR) have often mentioned in their Priority Watch List (PWL) and Watch List (WL) of top violators of the intellectual property laws five (5) developing countries of Southeast Asia known for the illegal media piracy trade, namely, the Philippines, Thailand, Vietnam, Malaysia, and Indonesia. In their 2011 IIPA Special 301 Report, for instance, the Philippines, Indonesia, Vietnam, and Thailand are placed in the PWL and WL despite the modest efforts by their governments to combat piracy.[1] All these countries are known to have a high level of informality in their economies, with their governments either actively supporting the informal sector or tolerant of its growth and expansion. The informal sector comprises between 40 % and 80 % of the entire urban economy of these countries, and around 60 % of those working in nonagricultural sector are employed in the informal sector (ILO 2002 Report). One can, therefore, ask: Does the attitude of the government toward the informal sector has

[1] Although the Philippines was removed from the USTR's watch lists since 2014, doubts still linger whether media piracy has really waned as the IIPA still wants the country to remain in the lists due to continued copyright infringement in the country. Speculations abound which suggest that the removal of the Philippines from the lists has something to do with the signing of the Enhanced Defense Cooperation Agreement (EDCA) with the United States that allows joint military exercises between the two countries to counter China's excursion in the West Philippine Sea. Malaysia was removed from the lists, but Internet piracy still remains in the country according to the 2014 IIPA Special 301 Report. Indonesia and Thailand remained in the lists and Vietnam was placed in PWL for the first time after being in the WL for a long time (2014 IIPA Special 301 Report, Vietnam).

V.O. Ballano, *Sociological Perspectives on Media Piracy in the Philippines and Vietnam*, DOI 10.1007/978-981-287-922-6_3

something to do with the persistence of the illegal optical media trade in these Southeast Asian countries, particularly in the Philippines and Vietnam?

The informal sector is prevalent in Vietnam. In 2007, for instance, almost 11 million jobs out of a total of 46 million jobs are informal in the country. The majority of the domestic jobs are informal. In trade, an estimated 31 % of the total employment is informal. Although there are no current policies targeting the informal sector, the Vietnamese government with its new policy of *Doi Moi* (economic renovation) since the Sixth National Party Congress in December 1986 is apparently tolerating informal businesses as no current efforts have been exerted to formalize informal trading (Cling et al. 2010, pp. 6–10).[2]

The Philippines too has a strong informal sector in its economy. The National Statistics Office (NSO), for instance, reported that there were about 10.5 million informal sector operators in the Philippines in 2008. Because of its great contribution to the economy, the Philippine government has been supportive of this sector. In fact, over the past 20 years, the Philippine government has passed numerous laws and programs that directly or indirectly aim to improve the informal sector. Unfortunately, these efforts have not been sufficiently effective in providing more benefits to the poor traders nor have encourage them to formalize their businesses.

Because the informal sector reduces unemployment and contributes to poverty alleviation, the government tolerates it. Although governments in developing countries do not officially recognize the informal sector, they are under some pressure to formalize it (Rawaa 2013, p. 575). This is particularly true to piracy-laden members of the Association of the Southeast Asian Nations (ASEAN) whose governments are tolerant or supportive of the informal trading without much thought of its implication to the full formalization of the intellectual property rights (IPR) such as the optical media retail trade in their economies. Thus, the growth of the informal sector in an era of intellectual property (IP) and digital technology in ASEAN countries such as the Philippines and Vietnam is accompanied by a persistence of informal trading and media piracy. Singapore, which has the most underdeveloped informal sector in the ASEAN, does not have a problem of having open piracy hubs of pirated discs and other counterfeit products in its informal markets, while other countries like the Philippines and Vietnam whose thriving informal sector is relatively tolerated or even encouraged by the government and civil society groups are notoriously known for illegal optical media piracy markets.

Formalization of the informal sector can be generally understood as "the process whereby previously non-compliant enterprises become integrated into these formal or state-sanctioned institutions, such as property registries and tax-rolls" (Kenyon 2007, p. 3). Formalization process can, however, mean different things for various segments of the informal economy. To the policymakers, formalization means that informal enterprises should obtain a license, register their accounts, and pay taxes.

[2] *Doi Moi* is a major economic reform policy in Vietnam which aims to transform its economy from centrally planned economy to market economy. One important feature of this reform is the privatization of state-owned enterprises (SOEs) which encourages informal trading and small informal business.

To the self-employed traders, it requires paying the cost of entry into the formal sector and receiving benefits such as enforceable commercial contracts, legal ownership of their place of business and means of production, tax breaks and incentive packages to increase their competitiveness, membership in trade associations, and statutory social protection (Chen 2007, p. 11).

The formalization of intellectual property trade and the persistence of optical disc piracy have always been a major problem to many Southeast Asian countries. Being members of the World Trade Organization (WTO) and signatories of the Trade-Related Aspects of Intellectual Property Rights (TRIPS) agreement, they are at a dilemma on how to empower the informal sector and, at the same time, transplant the foreign IPR legal system into the local culture and prevent the intellectual property products from being peddled illegally by this sector. The full implementation of the IPR law is a prerequisite in establishing a free market digital economy in the world, particularly in piracy-laden countries of the Southeast Asian region. Formalization permits large organizations to achieve economies of scale and reduce uncertainty in economic transactions (Sutton et al. 1994, pp. 946–947). The United States, being the leading exporter of intellectual property products and services in the world, has required its trading partners to formalize the intellectual property trade in their respective economies under TRIPS and the Generalized System of Preferences (GSP). The Asia-Pacific Economic Cooperation (APEC), being a regional trading block highly influenced by the United States, has, in turn, placed IPR protection and abolishing piracy as two of its major trade agenda. Despite these efforts, the piracy trade in Southeast Asian countries such as the Philippines and Vietnam continues with impunity.

Although rarely mentioned in piracy studies and reports, the growth of the informal sector and the accompanying persistence of optical media piracy trade often pose a serious challenge to governments of piracy-laden countries of the ASEAN. Being signatories of the General Agreement on Tariffs and Trade (GATT) and its provisions on the Trade-Related Aspects of Intellectual Property Rights (TRIPS) agreement, they are in a dilemma on how to achieve high economic growth in their local economies and at the same time protect IPR products and services, particularly optical media goods, from being copied and sold illegally by local traders. What is common to all ASEAN countries with long histories in the IIPA and USTR's PWL and WL is the persistence of the informal sector in their urban economy which supports the illegal and informal optical media trade. It is undeniable that the growth of the informal sector in these countries is accompanied by a rise in illegal optical media trade. An average of about 40 % of the economies of the ASEAN is informal, and around 20 % engages in informal trading, including the informal retail trading or vending of optical media discs in urban centers.

Understanding the persistence of piracy trade in the context of the informal sector in developing countries is relatively absent in piracy research and investigation. The legal perspective which sees the persistence of optical media piracy in terms of absence and lack of effective copyright laws and law enforcement dominates most of the Special 301 Annual reports of the IIPA and the USTR. The bigger picture which includes other sociopolitical factors that support the persistence of piracy trade is often overlooked. In particular, the sociological perspective which aims to understand the growth of the counterfeit trade from a holistic and multicausal perspective is apparently absent in piracy debates and investigations.

One important area that is overlooked in media piracy research is the link between the persistence of the counterfeit trade and the government's support of informality and informal trading in the economies of developing countries in Southeast Asia. The informal optical media piracy trade thrives in a strong and growing informal economy. Thus, the efforts of the government and nongovernmental organizations and copyright companies to fight counterfeiting and media piracy must also include exploring ways in formalizing the informal sector, particularly informal trading, which seems to fuel the growth of optical media piracy trade.

3.2 Understanding the Nature of the Informal Sector

Defining and clarifying the nature of the informal sector must be undertaken before investigating its role in the persistence of the informal and illegal retail piracy trade. Analyzing the informal sector poses some problems to researchers, much more when it relates to the illegal and informal trading of optical media. One main obstacle in understanding the true nature of the informal sector is the uniformity of its definition and measurement. The term "informal sector" is often laced with various meanings and labels. It has been called by some authors as the irregular economy (Ferman and Ferman 1973), the subterranean economy (Gutmann 1977), the underground economy (Houston 1987; Simon and Witte 1982), the black economy (Dilnot and Morris 1981), and the informal economy (McCrohan and Smith 1986). The popular media labels the informal sector as invisible, hidden, submerged, shadow, irregular, nonofficial, unrecorded, and clandestine (Losby et al. 2002). Indeed, Kabra (1995) states that some 30 terms including the survival sector, nonstructured sector, and transitional activities have been and/or are currently used to describe the informal sector. The term has also changed over time in several dimensions (Bluch 2001). Defining and classifying what constitutes the informal sector is made difficult by the fact that those who define and construct taxonomies are themselves selecting criteria based on their own structural position and interests (Henry 1987). Recently, economists have started to recognize the heterogeneity of the informal sector owing to its various modes of production, although some of its common features can still be identified in this type of economy (Fields 2005; Rawaa 2013). In general terms, the informal sector can refer to the unregulated, nonformal portion of the market economy that produces goods and services for sale or for other forms of remuneration. Lagos (1995) defines it as a "group of activities which are illegal in the sense that they do not comply with economic regulations pertaining to fiscal, employment, health and other matters" (p. 112). The informal sector includes all economic activities of workers or by economic units that are—in law or practice—not covered or insufficiently covered by formal arrangements (Becker 2004, p. 11). The informal optical media piracy trade in the Philippines and Vietnam being illegal and beyond the regulation of the government aptly belongs to this sector.

3.2.1 *Measuring the Informal Sector*

Because of the crucial role played by the informal sector in developing countries, efforts have been made to measure and estimate the extent of the informal economy in the overall economy of the country in order to provide policymakers some guide in understanding the economic status of the nation. The Interregional Cooperation on the Measurement of Informal Sector and Informal Employment (ICMISIE) project estimates that the informal sector accounts for more than 50 % of nonagricultural employment and about 30 % of the nonagricultural Gross Domestic Product (GDP) in many countries (ibid.). One striking characteristic which separates the contemporary patterns of urbanization from the past in much of the developing world on the basis of the past experience of industrialized countries or of stereotypical models of urban industrialization is the emergence of the informal sector as a major characteristic of larger cities, taking on a complicated but, on balance, positive role in the process of economic development and demographic transition of a country (Hackenberg 1980, p. 391).

The main problem in measuring the informal sector is the diversity of definitions used by researchers. Most often, the measurement depends on the definition and methodology used by researchers who study it. As mentioned above, the term informal sector or informal economy has different definitions and perspectives and, thus, difficult to come up with one standard of measurement. In practice, the definition that is most useful depends on the policy concern that motivates analysis and data availability (e.g., Easton 2001; Feld and Schneider 2010). For instance, policymakers and researchers who approach the informal economy from a social protection perspective tend to focus on employment, where one or more of the legal requirements are not complied with (e.g., mandatory contributions to social security and pension schemes) (Andrews et al. 2011). Furthermore, methodologies used by researchers in measuring it also differ from one study to another as the economic activities of the informal sector vary according to their capital and labor intensiveness, the presence and absence of monetary exchange, and their scale of operations (Gaughan and Ferman 1987). To measure the size of the informal sector remains a serious challenge to researchers. It remains an inexact science, although a variety of approaches have been used by researchers to measure it (Losby et al. 2002).

Another reason why the measurement of the informal sector is problematic is that some units of the informal economy are characterized by high mobility and turnover, seasonality, and lack of recognizable features for identification and reluctance to share information. Thus, these units are often excluded in the sampling frame by establishment or enterprise surveys—although they may be covered by household surveys which do not include questions on production. The problem of mobility and reluctance of traders to share information apply to the illegal optical media trade. In the informal optical media retail trade, traders move from one place to another to sell pirated discs and to avoid arrest and confiscation of their pirated goods, thus making it difficult for government agencies to make a reliable count on the number of informal traders. And if they are part of the sampling frame, many would obviously refuse to share information about their personal background and knowledge on the illegal trade for fear of identification and arrest by authorities. Because of these problems, the illegal and informal vending optical media is often excluded from the regular survey system of National Statistics Offices (NSOs). Only special surveys intended solely to measure the informal sector statistics can achieve this purpose of collecting demographic data of illegal traders of the optical media piracy trade.[3] Even then, this task would still be difficult given the illegal nature of the trade and the involvement of unscrupulous law enforcers in the business. Because optical media piracy has been labeled by law as a crime, producers, retailers, and vendors would still be reluctant to share information in specialized surveys. Thus far, no reliable and formal surveys have been done yet to account the number of distributors, retailers, and producers of the optical media piracy trade. Like other illegal trade as drugs, gambling, smuggling, prostitution, etc., no official statistics and studies have been done to measure their activities and contribution to the national economy. Despite this difficulty, the fact remains that the underground and illegal economy such as optical media piracy trade plays an important role in providing informal employment to the poor and migrants in Southeast Asian countries, particularly in piracy-laden countries such as the Philippines and Vietnam.

3.2.2 *The Context: Prevalence of the Informal Sector in SEA*

Studies on the extent of the informal sector around the world are scarce. But economists, researchers, and policymakers believe that informality in the economies of the world is prevalent and massive. Since traders of counterfeit and fake retail goods belong to this sector which has a significant force in the world economy, antipiracy groups and stakeholders would face a difficult battle to formalize it. For illustrative purposes, the table below adopts Schneider's study (2010) on the informal sector of 162 countries from 1999 to 2007, bearing in mind some nuances of the term "shadow economy" from the more popular term "informal sector" or "informal economy," to illustrate the dominance of the shadow economy in the ASEAN region. Using Smith's (1994) definition, the study understands the shadow economy as "market-based production of goods and services, whether legal or illegal, that escapes detection in the official estimates of GDP" or "those economic activities and income derived from them that circumvent or otherwise avoid government regulation, taxation or observation" (cited in Schneider et al. 2010, p. 5). Using a Multiple Indicators Multiple Causes (MIMIC) model, a particular type of a structural equations model (SEM), Schneider and others analyzed and estimated the shadow economies of 162 countries around the world. Table 3.1 shows the extent and growth of the informal sector in Southeast Asian countries, including the ASEAN countries identified by the USTR and IIPA as hotspots of the informal and illegal trade of optical media piracy.

[3] "Measuring the informal sector" *ADB Regional Technical Assistance Report*. December 2007 at http://www.adb.org/sites/default/files/project-document/65472/41144-reg-tar.pdf

Table 3.1 The size of the informal economy of SEA countries by rank from 1999 to 2006

Rank	Country	Year									Country average
		1999	2000	2001	2002	2003	2004	2005	2006	2007	
1	Myanmar[a]	53.6	52.6	53.7	54.5	56.3	56.2	57.4	–	–	54.9
2	Thailand	51.8	52.6	52.8	53.8	55.1	55.8	56.4	56.9	57.2	54.7
3	Cambodia	49.8	50.1	50.6	50.2	51.0	51.4	52.4	53.4	54.2	50.9
4	Philippines	42.7	43.3	43.6	44.1	44.7	45.0	46.6	47.2	48.4	45.1
5	Laos	30.3	30.6	31.0	31.2	31.4	31.8	32.3	32.8	33.2	31.6
6	Brunei	30.8	31.1	31.2	32.0	32.3	31.0	30.4	31.4	31.0	31.3
6	Malaysia	30.1	31.1	30.6	30.7	31.0	31.4	31.7	32.2	32.6	31.3
7	Indonesia	19.1	19.4	19.4	19.5	19.7	20.0	20.2	20.5	20.9	19.9
8	Vietnam	15.4	15.6	15.7	15.9	16.0	16.1	16.5	16.6	16.8	16.1
9	Singapore	12.9	13.1	12.9	12.9	13.1	13.4	13.5	13.8	14.0	13.3

Source: Data are compiled from Appendix 4, Schneider et al. (2010). Shadow economies all over the world, new estimates for 162 countries from 1999 to 2007. Policy research working paper 5356, World Bank, p. 45. Available: elibrary.worldbank.org

[a]Data for 2006 and 2007 were not yet available

Looking at the estimates of the table above, one can notice that a greater part of the economy of Southeast Asian (SEA) countries, except Singapore, is informal. Although Myanmar has no data in 2006 and 2007, it ranks number 1 in the list with an average of 54.9 % of its economy belonging to the shadow economy. This is followed by Thailand, Cambodia, and the Philippines. This group of SEA countries does not only show high percentages but also consistent growth of informality through the years, from 1999 to 2007. A growing informality in the economy is also shown in Indonesia and Vietnam, although its scope is not as wide as those of other SEA countries. Laos, Brunei, and Malaysia have shown a moderate growth and size in their underground or shadow economy. But they did not show significant and consistent growth through the years compared to Myanmar, Thailand, Cambodia, and the Philippines.

Table 3.1 also showed that the piracy-laden countries of SEA which are consistently listed in the Priority Watch List and Watch List of the IIPA and USTR have a high percentage of informality in their economy: Thailand has the highest with 53.4 % followed by the Philippines with 44.7 % and Indonesia with 19.3 %. Malaysia which is also consistently listed in the Watch List in previous years but was removed in 2012 also has a high informal sector at 30.8 %. Vietnam, a fast-growing economy in Southeast Asia which is consistent in the Watch List for years and is now being listed in the Priority Watch List for the first time in 2014, has an average of 16.0 % in informal economy. And one can notice that since 1999, Vietnam's informal sector is steadily growing from 15.4 % in 1999 to 16.7 % in 2006. This can be attributed to the Vietnamese government's policy of privatizing state-owned enterprises and allowing private enterprises to grow.

3.2.3 The Informal Sector and Its Share in the GDP

The contribution of the informal sector to the economy is not only limited to the creation of jobs. It also contributes to the Gross Domestic Product (GDP) of the economy. Among the SEA countries identified of piracy, the share of the informal sector to the country's GDP is significant. Although not the most recent estimate, the table below somehow provides an insight on the importance of the informal sector to the GDP and overall economic growth of the ASEAN piracy-laden countries.

As shown in Table 3.2, Thailand which is consistently included in the Priority Watch List of the USTR and where retail piracy and informal piracy trading are popular has the highest level of informality (52.4 %) and share to the country's economy GDP (52.6 %) among ASEAN countries. This is followed by the Philippines with high informality at 42.9 % and its share to the country's GDP is also high at 43.4 %. Like Thailand, the Philippines is also regularly listed in the Priority Watch List of the USTR since 2001, although it has been downgraded at times to the Watch List and finally removed from both lists in 2014. The informality of Malaysia is also significant with more than one-third of its economy being informal. Its share of the country's GDP is pegged as high average at 31.1 %. Malaysia

Table 3.2 ASEAN countries and the estimated percentage of their informal sector and their contribution to the country's GDP

Country	Average percentage of informal economy (1999–2000)*	Percentage contribution to GDP (1999–2000)
Indonesia	19.45	19.4
Malaysia	30.95	31.1
Philippines	42.9	43.4
Singapore	13.1	13.1
Thailand	52.4	52.6
Vietnam	15.5	15.6

Source: Data are compiled from Friedrich Schneider (2002) "Size and Measurement of the Informal Economy in 110 Countries Around the World" (http://rru.worldbank.org).

is also consistently listed on the Watch List of the USTR because of rampant piracy activities. Although Malaysia was removed from these two piracy lists of the USTR in April 2012, informal trade of optical disc and online piracy remain significant in its informal sector. In its 2013 Special Annual Report, the IIPA observed that hard goods piracy and optical disc piracy trade in the informal markets continue despite the removal of Malaysia from the piracy lists. It is noted that the illegal manufacturing of discs by optical disc plants as well as the sale of pirated discs at certain urban "hotspots" and night markets (*pasar alam*) continues to flourish despite numerous raids by authorities (pp. 312–313). Indonesia has a lower informal sector in its economy (19.45 %), and its share to the country's GDP (19.4 %) is not that significant compared to other ASEAN countries such as the Philippines and Thailand. But Indonesia has a robust piracy trade in its informal sector and has produced more jobs to urban poor and migrants. In fact, Indonesia has always been listed in the Priority Watch List of the USTR since 2001. Finally, Vietnam, like Indonesia, has a low average percentage of informal sector (15.5 %), and its share to the GDP is only 15.6 %. But Vietnam's informal economy is fast growing with the ongoing privatization of the economy by the government, providing informality to thrive. In fact, it is common to see pirated discs and other products sold in shops or mobile vending stalls in major cities of Vietnam such as Hanoi, Danang, or Ho Chi Minh. If the informal and illegal piracy trade is intrinsically embedded in the informal economy of the developing countries of the ASEAN, providing the latter with the much needed job and GDP share, its abolition could not just be done without the government addressing the problem of unemployment and rural poverty that generally drive people to migrate to cities and join the illegal trade of piracy.

3.3 Informal Employment in SEA

To fully appreciate the connection of the importance of the informal economy to piracy-laden ASEAN countries and the persistence of the informal media piracy trade, one must also examine the role of the informal employment in the national economy of these countries. Having a large number of informal workers in the informal sector seems to be a permanent fixture in developing economies such as the Philippines and Vietnam where income and assets are not equitably distributed (Fig. 3.1).

The traditional labor market theory of Harris and Todaro (1954) and Lewis (1954) suggests that the growth of informal employment in developing countries in terms of labor is a transition between two sectors, the capitalist and the subsistence sector. It views the labor market as segmented into two: the formal and the informal employment. Those who cannot find jobs in the formal labor sector are forced to join the informal sector. This approach, therefore, treats the informal sector as the last source of employment.

To some extent, Todaro and Lewis' theory on informal employment can be applied to optical disc retail piracy trade in the Philippines and Vietnam, particularly to small retailers and informal workers in the piracy trade. Many poor migrants are forced to join the informal and illegal optical disc retail piracy business as mobile vendors of pirated discs or as informal employees or sales persons of some small- and medium-sized CD and DVD shops in the Philippines and Vietnam due to the lack of job opportunities in the formal sector. This is particularly true to many poor Maranao Muslim retailers and informal workers of medium- or large-sized optical disc piracy businesses who are forced to join the informal optical disc trade because of social discrimination and lack of formal jobs for Muslims in the Philippines. In Ho Chi Minh City, Vietnam, the informal media piracy trade is also the last resort

Fig. 3.1 The author posing with two migrant informal workers from the central region of Vietnam who are employed in a family-owned CD–DVD shop selling pirated discs (Image courtesy of the author)

for some poor and unemployed Vietnamese migrants from the middle and northern provinces of Vietnam who moved into the city in search for greener pastures.

Both in the Philippines and Vietnam, the informal sector remains as the last resort for migrants and the poor who cannot be absorbed in the formal sector. Some of those who cannot be employed in the formal sector join the informal sector for employment and micro trade. This is consistent with current socioeconomic patterns in developing countries which show that the informal sector employs between 35 % and 65 % of the labor force and produce 20–40 % of GDP (Chickering and Salahdine 1991, p. 3). If economic growth is not accompanied by improvement in employment levels and income distribution in developing countries, the informal sector is said to increase continuously. Both the Philippines and Vietnam experience modest and high economic growth in recent years, but rural poverty and social inequality in terms of income distribution remain high, pushing people to migrate from the impoverished provinces to the fast-growing urban centers and engage in nonagricultural informal jobs.

Estimates show that nonagricultural employment share of the informal workforce is 78 % in Africa, 57 % in Latin America and the Caribbean, and 45–85 % in Asia (Becker 2004, p. 3). Within Asia, a large group of developing countries with thriving informal sector and employment is found in Southeast Asia (SEA). This includes Brunei, Cambodia, East Timor, Indonesia, Laos, Malaysia, Myanmar, the Philippines, Thailand, and Vietnam. Except Singapore, SEA countries have a high level of informality and strong informal optical disc piracy trade in their economies. Physical piracy is common to these countries, and retailers and mobile vendors selling pirated discs in the sidewalks are a common sight in their urban economies. Many of those who joined in the informal optical media retail trade in the Philippines and Vietnam came from agricultural areas and who used to work in the farms. Some Muslim retailers in Quiapo Barter Trade Center Complex, for instance, were farm workers or poor farmers. Poverty, social discrimination of Muslims, and the ongoing war in the Muslim regions of Mindanao between government soldiers and Muslim rebels forced many Maranao and Maguindanao Muslims to migrate to Metro Manila and other cities and join the illegal optical disc piracy business as an alternative livelihood.[4] In Vietnam, massive poverty in the middle and northern regions of the country has forced some Vietnamese to migrate to Hanoi, Ho Chi Minh, and other major cities and enroll in the informal piracy business as informal workers and small traders.

3.3.1 The Participation of Migrants in the Optical Media Piracy Trade

One common factor which connects the Philippines and Vietnam to the persistence of optical media piracy is the growing informal sector and informal trading triggered by massive migration of people from rural areas to urban centers. Both the

[4] Please see Chap. 6 of this book for a more detailed discussion on the social forces that drive Muslims into the informal piracy trade.

Philippines and Vietnam have significant urban migration which resulted in an increased informal employment in the informal sector. In the Philippines, there is a direct relationship between migration and increased participation in the informal sector. An early study by Koo and Smith (1983) on migration and urban informal sector showed a strong connection between migration and increased employment and participation of migrants in various informal sectors in the cities including the informal and illegal trade of optical disc piracy.

There is a common pattern between the Philippines and Vietnam with regard to migration and participation of people in the informal optical media trade: people who join the optical media retail trade are primarily migrants who came from impoverished or war-torn regions. In the Philippines, migrants who dominate the optical disc piracy trade are the Maranao Muslim migrants from Mindanao. In Vietnam, the key traders of this type of informal business are Kinh migrants who came from impoverished provinces of the middle and northern provinces of Vietnam. In a study on the rural–urban migration in Vietnam, Cu Chi Loi (2005) identified that new migrants worked as factory workers, hired workers in shops, or as small traders or street vendors. The top priority of new migrants is to work in small and informal enterprises (25.14 %), joint ventures (14.31 %), and domestic private enterprises (10.29). They usually work in public sectors (a small percentage), as factory workers (60%), and as traders, small service providers, or street vendors (30 %) (Cu Chi Loi 2005, pp. 134–135). Small and mobile optical disc traders and informal workers of optical disc retail stores in Vietnam are migrants who belong to the last two categories: they work either as small traders or mobile vendors of pirated discs or informal workers in informal and semi-formal privately or family-owned optical media enterprises. The high population growth in the central and northern towns of Vietnam and the greater opportunities offered by the growing industrialization of Vietnamese cities are the common factors that pushed people away from their impoverished towns into major Vietnamese cities such as Hanoi and Ho Chi Minh. The government's *Doi Moi* (economic renovation) which aims to transform the national economy into a market economy which privatizes state-owned enterprises has encouraged more Vietnamese to engage in business and search for greener pastures in urban centers. The accession of Vietnam to the WTO and the restoration of its trade relations with the United States have resulted in the importation of more U.S. and foreign high-tech and copyright products and services, influx of digital technologies, popularity of technology trade such as mobile optical media vending, and establishment of CD–DVD shops. For migrants, the popularity of the optical disc trade implies more jobs and opportunities to engage in small mobile business. But for rich Vietnamese and traders, it implies more income and profits as the optical disc trade is a highly profitable business. According to informants, many migrants from distant and neighboring villages of Ho Chi Minh are actually lured by the opportunities offered by big cities such as Ho Chi Minh City, dreaming to engage in business as soon as they move into the city. Many poor Vietnamese from central and northern parts of Vietnam see Ho Chi Minh City as a sort of a "promised land" which can liberate them from poverty. This view is apparently true as Ho Chi Minh City has the highest in-migration in the country with 29 %, higher than the capital city Hanoi with only 11 % (Cu Chi Loi 2005, p. 16).

The Philippines seemed to share with Vietnam some similar push factors such as increasing population, rural poverty, and unemployment that drove people from the impoverished areas into cities and forced some of them to engage in the illegal optical media piracy trade in order to survive. In some cases, what differentiate Filipino traders from the Vietnamese are the following push factors: social discrimination and the ongoing conflict and war in Muslim areas in Mindanao where the main bulk of optical media traders come from. An earlier study by Koo and Smith (1983, p. 223) also indicated that Filipino migrants such as those who moved to Manila and secondary cities of Metro Manila joined the small trade sector and worked menial jobs as their means for survival and livelihood.

Unlike the Vietnamese piracy trade, the illegal optical disc business in the Philippines is dominated by Maranao Muslims, the largest Muslim group which is forced to migrate to Metro Manila and other major Philippine cities because of the displacement caused by the ongoing war in the Muslim areas of Mindanao and social discrimination of Muslims who are unfairly tagged by some print and broadcast media reports as terrorists, making it difficult for people with Muslim-sounding names such as the Maranaos to find jobs in the formal sector.[5]

As a whole, rural–urban migration plays an important role in bringing people into the informal sector and the informal optical disc retail piracy trade. Both Vietnam and the Philippines have high rural–urban migration which facilitates the participation of poor people in the informal sector and in the illegal piracy trade.

The informal optical media trade in some ASEAN countries, therefore, plays an important role in generating jobs and alternative livelihood for migrants who experienced poverty and conflict in the remote provinces of the Philippines and Vietnam. Although ASEAN countries do not have the same levels and modes of development, they do share one similarity—they have a wide and strong informal urban economy which absorbs people from impoverished or war-torn villages and rural areas. For these countries, such as the Philippines and Vietnam, the informal sector, which includes the informal and illegal optical media trade, contributes more than half of their total employment, thus a major generator of jobs and income.

3.4 The Government's Attitude Toward the Informal Sector

The development of the informal economy remains inherently linked to the state's regulatory intervention. All states intervene in the process of economic activities on the basis of a set of enforceable rules (Castells and Portes 1989). These rules determine who can participate in economic life, what kinds of economic activities can be undertaken, and how. The state intervention and degree of regulation, therefore,

[5] Please see Chap. 5 for a more detailed description on the social forces that push Maranao Muslims into the informal optical piracy trade.

structure the environment within which economic actors operate. The state through its political instrument, the government, determines what economic activities to be allowed, prohibited, and tolerated. In the case of IPR protection, the policy of the government in its fight against the informal optical media piracy is connected with its attitude toward the informal economy, known as the number one provider of informal jobs and a leading contributor to the nation's income in developing countries. If the government is serious and determined to formalize the informal and illegal piracy trade, the formalization process of businesses must be prioritized to encourage prospective media traders to achieve legality. There is a relationship between tolerating informality in the economy and the persistence of media piracy trade. If the informal traders do not have access to capital, the business requirements for registration and licensing are costly and complex, the enforcement of business regulation is weak, and the government is not determined to address these problems, informal trading such as the optical media trade could indeed prosper under this "friendly" environment.

One crucial factor which contributes to the persistence of optical media piracy in Southeast Asian countries, particularly in the Philippines and Vietnam, is the nonhostile attitude of the government toward the informal sector and informal trading. Government's attitude or tendency in the formulation of policies toward the informal sector can vary: It can be supportive, tolerant, or indifferent. Any of these attitudes can help the informal sector to grow to boost the local economy. A government's nonhostile attitude has a positive effect to the informal sector. It allows an unhampered growth of informality in trade and encourages informal trading and employment such as the illegal optical media trade to flourish at the expense of the full formalization of business in the local economy. Most governments of Southeast Asia view the informal sector as a major engine for economic growth; thus, they generally assume a nonhostile attitude toward it (Fig. 3.2).

Although considered as a separate and marginal economy by some economists, the role of the informal sector in the megacities of Southeast Asia is crucial. It is not only large, but also an important source of a wide range of products and services integral to urban economies. The informal sector fuels the economic growth of developing countries and plays a role in supporting business firms in the formal sector (Jamil 2013). It provides cheap products such as pirated discs as substitutes for more expensive genuine products in the formal sector.[6] It also provides cheap menial jobs and services to those who are employed in the formal sector. With this role, the informal sector, in effect, subsidizes the formal sector. It reduces production cost and increases the savings and earnings of the business firms in the formal sector and thus increases their capability for expansion (Karaos 1985). With these benefits, governments often take a supportive attitude toward the informal economy and tolerate its growth to propel the national economy to greater heights.

ASEAN countries which are often included in the USTR's Priority Watch List (PWL) and Watch List (WL) tend to encourage informal trading and employment in nonagricultural sector in urban centers to provide employment to their migrants and

[6] http://www.gdrc.org/informal/annex1.pdf

Fig. 3.2 Makeshift sidewalk stores and mobile vendors in an entrance of a government relocation in Rodriguez, Rizal. Sidewalk and mobile vending is a common site in the Philippine informal economy

urban poor. In Asia, the contribution of the informal sector to nonagricultural work in urban economy in employment generation is quite significant. No wonder the government continues to support this sector. This positive attitude of the SEA governments toward the informal sector can be reflected in the legislation and program that relate to the informal sector.

3.5 The Philippines' and Vietnam's Attitudes Toward Informality

The approach of the Philippines and Vietnam in regulating and creating laws for the informal sector seems to be contrasting, yet both yielding similar results—a steady growth of informality in the economy. On the one hand, Vietnam has manifested an indifference toward the informal sector. But it has acknowledged its important role implicitly, especially informal trade, by not aggressively suppressing it. In fact, the government's policy of *Doi Moi*, or economic renovation, has indirectly encouraged informality in the economy. With the introduction of numerous new laws to comply with international standards of the market economy and to open its economy to the world, loopholes are created which allow informality to influence the business regulation system. On the other hand the Philippines has shown a more positive attitude toward the informal sector and informal trading. The Philippine government has officially acknowledged the existence and contribution of the informal sector to the national economy and has openly introduced programs to encourage people to engage informal trade and employment. It has passed several legal measures and created programs to encourage people to join the informal economy. Although the enforcement of laws and programs that assist the informal sector is perceived to be weak, nonetheless, the informal sector continues to grow without serious government interference.

3.5.1 The Philippine Government

A presidential adviser for political affairs and a close friend of a Philippine President was photographed by a news reporter buying pirated DVDs worth more than 2000 pesos in a mall. He was allegedly a regular buyer of pirated discs of the said mall. Despite some calls for him to resign from his post, the Malacañang Palace, the seat power in the Philippines, only reprimanded him and issued a statement that he has not committed an illegal or criminal act since buying pirated discs is not punishable by law. When asked by media for the apparent inaction of the Malacañang Palace to the case, the President declared that the piracy issue was not his number one priority: "You know that we have so many problems. That DVD (issue) is kind of low on our [list of] priorities."[7]

This incident provided a glimpse of the Philippine government's low priority to copyright protection and its tolerant attitude toward piracy: despite its commitment to comply with TRIPS and other international copyright laws, power holders still do not consider IPR protection and enforcement worthy of government's attention and resources. The illegal optical disc piracy in the Philippines belongs to the informal sector. As an informal trade, it usually employs migrant Muslims who are victims of poverty and conflict between government soldiers and Muslim rebels in Mindanao.

The Philippines is one of the SEA governments that support small-sized enterprises and trade such as the informal optical media business in the informal sector. In fact, the Philippine government has officially recognized the existence and the significant role of the informal sector in the generation of output, employment, and income in the country. The acknowledgment of the contribution of the informal sector to the national economy is reflected in the Social Reform and Poverty Alleviation Act of 1997 (Republic Act 8425), the only piece of legislation that recognizes the existence of informal workers as one of the basic sectors (Casanova-Dorato 2010,

[7] http://newsinfo.inquirer.net/134309/aquino-on-llamas%E2%80%99-dvds-he-could%E2%80%99ve-been-just-passing-by

p. 4). Furthermore, the government officially approved the adoption of a standard conceptual and operational definition of the informal sector, largely culled from the prescribed international definition of the International Labor Organization (ILO), in order to identify it and to facilitate the collection of data about its activities (Pastrana 2009, p. 4). Through the National Statistical Coordination Board (NSCB) Resolution No. 15, Series of 2002, the Philippine government officially adopted the following definition of the informal sector:

> The informal sector consists of "units" engaged in the production of goods and services with the primary objective of generating employment and incomes to the persons concerned in order to earn a living.
>
> These units typically operate at a low level of organization, with little or no division between labour and capital as factors of production. It consists of household unincorporated enterprises that are market and non-market producers of goods as well as market producers of services.
>
> Labor relations, where they exist, are based on casual employment, kinship or personal and social relations rather than formal or contractual arrangements.[8]

The Philippine government did not only provide a standard definition of the informal sector, but it also undertook a series of survey to identify it. To understand its coverage, it commissioned the National Statistics Office (NSO) to conduct the first nationwide survey of the informal sector in April 2008—the 2008 Informal Sector Survey (ISS). And this survey showed that there were about 10.5 million informal sector operators in the Philippines, and about 9.1 million were self-employed and 1.3 million as employers (Pastrana 2009, p. 8). Then, it also authorized the Labor Force Survey (LFS) by the Department of Labor and Employment (DOLE) in April 2008 to determine the labor force of the informal sector. Results revealed that there were around 36.4 million people who worked in the informal sector, constituting around 30 % of the total labor force of the country.[9]

3.5.1.1 Government Policies and Issuances for the Informal Sector

Here are some of the Philippine government's legislations that show support for the informal sector:

1. *Republic Act (RA) 8425 or the Social Reform and Poverty Alleviation Act of 1997*. This law expressly recognizes the informal sector as one of the disadvantaged sectors in Philippine society. It also employs a multidimensional approach to poverty for the disadvantaged sectors and provides provision on social, economic, ecological, and governance reforms. In particular, it aims to protect workers in the informal sector and to provide microfinance to support small livelihood programs of the urban poor. It created the National Anti-Poverty

[8] http://www.nscb.gov.ph/resolutions/2002/15_1.asp

[9] http://www.bles.dole.gov.ph/

Commission under the Office of the President as a coordinating body to implement this law (Sections 4–5).

2. *Magna Carta of Women (RA 9710).* This law aims to promote the rights of women in the marginalized sector. This is considered a women's human rights law which seeks to eliminate gender-based discrimination in Philippine society. It guarantees the civil, political, and economic rights of women in the marginalized sector, who are workers of the informal sector.
3. *Magna Carta for Small Farmers (RA 7607).* This law was enacted in 1992. It aims to empower small farmers to form their own organizations and be represented in government agencies' board. It states that the government shall provide assistance to the small farmers especially in gaining access to obtaining, owning, or opening facilities necessary for pre- and postharvest activities. Small farmers are defined as those "natural persons dependent on small-scale subsistence farming as their primary source of income and whose sale, barter or exchange of agricultural products do not exceed a gross value of one hundred eighty thousand pesos (P180,000) per annum based on 1992 constant prices" (Section 4).
4. *Magna Carta for Small Enterprises (RA 6977 enacted in 1991 and amended by RA 8289 in 1997).* This law recognizes the potential of small- and medium-scale enterprises for more employment generation and economic growth of the country. It also recognizes the small informal enterprises' contribution as a self-sufficient industrial foundation for the country. Thus, the law aims to promote, support, strengthen, and encourage the growth and development of small- and medium-sized enterprises in all productive sectors of the economy (Section 1). This law also enjoins all government agencies having to do with small-sized enterprises to minimize procedural rules to encourage entrepreneurial spirit among the citizenry. This includes simplification in the act of registration, availment of financing, and accessing other government services and assistance (Section 5).
5. *Barangay Microbusiness Enterprises Act (RA 9178)* Republic Act No. 9178. This law is called Barangay Micro Business Enterprises (BMBEs) Act of 2002. This law defines micro business enterprise as any business entity or enterprise engaged in the production, processing, or manufacturing of products or commodities, including agro-processing, trading, and services, whose total assets including those arising from loans but exclusive of the land on which the particular business entity's office, plant, and equipment are situated shall not be more than three million pesos (P3,000,000).This law provides tax exemptions to small-sized enterprises, exemption from coverage of the minimum wage law, financing assistance from the government's Land Bank of the Philippines, technology transfer, production and management training, and marketing assistance. The Department of Trade and Industry is also mandated to create incentives to small-, medium-, and large-sized enterprises under this law.
6. *The Cooperative Code of the Philippines (RA 6938) as amended by the Cooperative of 2008 (RA 9520).* Under this law, cooperatives are small, autonomous, and registered associations of people who share common interests. Cooperatives enable small traders to form voluntary associations recognized by the government to increase their productivity. One important feature of coopera-

tives in the Philippines is that these associations are generally exempted from taxation.

7. *Executive Order 452 (1997)* providing for the guidelines that ensure the security of registered vendors in the workplace, among others. This law provides guidelines for the security and system of registration for all vendors nationwide. The guidelines shall cover vendors in all cities and municipalities throughout the country, whereby each city and municipality shall establish a system for registration and issuance of permit to vendors to protect their rights and the interest of consumers and the general public (Section 3). All concerned National Government Agencies shall provide the support necessary for the vendors' self-development into healthy, informed, environmentally aware, progressive, and productive citizens. The city or municipality, in consultation with vendors, the affected community, and other sectors or groups, shall identify and designate viable workplaces and design a system of assigning spaces to registered vendors (Section 4). Vendors shall be encouraged to organize themselves into associations reflective of their ideals and aspirations (Section 5). Laws on social development and protection which likewise applies to members of the informal sector such as the Social Security Act (RA 8282), National Health Insurance Act (RA 7875), and Technical Education and Skills Development Act (RA 7796) are meant to provide social benefits as well as technical training to the poor and informal workers to enhance their social welfare (Pastrana 2009).

3.5.2 The Vietnamese Government

The informal sector is predominant in Vietnam. In 2007, it accounted for almost 11 million of the country's 46 million jobs which represented nearly a quarter of all main jobs in the country and nearly half of nonfarm jobs (Cling et al. 2012, p. 1). Most employment (82 %) in Vietnam can, therefore, be defined as informal. Informal employment is widespread in the country. It is not just found in agriculture but also in domestic enterprises. In some industries such as construction, trade, and accommodation, most workers are informally employed (Cling et al. 2010, pp. 5–6).

Because informality supports and dominates the local economy in terms of jobs, the Vietnamese government, like the Philippines, also manifests supportive attitude toward the informal sector, although indirectly and, sometimes, ambivalent and inconstant (Cling et al. 2010). Vietnam defined the informal sector as "all private unincorporated enterprises that produce at least some of their goods and services for sale or barter, do not have a business license, and are engaged in nonagricultural activities" (MoLISA 2010; Arnold 2013, p. 473).

With its *Doi Moi* policy, the Vietnamese government and the Communist Party (VCP) acknowledged the importance of free enterprise and private employment to change Vietnam's economic structure from a socialist to a free market economy. Thus far, the government has not taken systematic steps to curtail the growth of the informal sector, particularly informal trade and microenterprises. Instead, it promulgated a new Enterprise Law in 2000 to create over 120,000 new enterprises in the country. With the introduction of economic reforms and privatizations of government-owned enterprises under *Doi Moi,* Vietnam's informal sector and informal trade have grown tremendously. But to what extent they have fully formalized small- and medium-sized enterprises remains unclear. The current size in the distribution of enterprises does not seem to indicate that the government's legalization program has resulted in the formalization of many informal trading and growth of many small businesses into large firms. In Vietnam, the private sector is almost entirely associated with small- and micro-sized enterprises. The medium-sized enterprises are very narrow and almost missing in the distribution structure, the larger ones are mainly state-owned enterprises (SOEs), and foreign-owned enterprises are prominent (Hakkala and Kokko 2007, p. 1), suggesting that many small businesses in the informal economy have not grown into large business firms and have remain informal. And if they have been formalized in the sense that they are registered, informality remains an important component in their business operations such in the case of registered CD–DVD shops operating informally by selling counterfeit optical media discs.

3.5.2.1 Doi Moi and the Turning Point of the Informal Sector in Vietnam

Vietnam shifted to a free market economy with *Doi Moi* in 1986 and moved away from socialist economic policies, realizing that centralized planning of the economy in Hanoi has disastrous effects to the economy. In the late 1980s, Vietnam faced a formidable economic challenge: a high inflation rate, a persistent budget imbalance, a heavy dependence on imports and foreign assistance, and an international economic embargo resulting from its occupation of Kampuchea (Szalontai 2008, p. 201).

During the Sixth Party Congress in 1986, the National Assembly adopted a new Five-Year Plan that advocates reforms and dismantles existing economic management in order to encourage initiatives in the production and trade (Williams 1992, p. 46). This is the dawn of *Doi Moi*, or economic renovation, in Vietnam. This new program represents a sustained attack on the old model of centrally planned economy and a new thrust toward liberalization and free market economy. *Doi Moi* aims to improve lagging productivity, to raise living standards, and to curb rapid inflation, which reached almost 500 % a year in the mid-1980s. It also aims to increase foreign investment and to establish a multisectoral economy driven by private enterprises under the supervision of a communist government (Freeman 1996, p. 1).

The *Doi Moi* was not the beginning of informal sector in Vietnam but its turning point. There was already a large informal sector which was composed mostly of family-oriented commercial and peasant enterprises, financiers, currency traders, and smugglers that operated outside the control of the communist government during the decade after the Vietnam War (Freeman 1996, p. 1). But *Doi Moi* spurred growth in this sector after 1986. With a sharp reduction of internal trade barriers, liberalization of foreign trade, withdrawal of state subsidies, and high unemployment caused by retrenchment in government bureaucracy, more people started to engage in informal trading. Thus, the informal sector of the economy suddenly opened up, and small-scale private enterprises began to flourish in towns. During the first 6 months of 1987 alone, for instance, some 3000 private shops were opened in Ho Chi Minh City, employing around 30,000 workers (ibid., p. 50). Informal traders flock the streets of Hanoi and Ho Chi Minh, as well as the rice fields of the Mekong Delta (Williams 1992, pp. 50–58). Today, informal trade represents the second largest informal industry in Vietnam which eats up 31 % of the total informal employment of the country at the national level (Cling et al. 2010, p. 16).

Although the Vietnamese government supported full formalization and development of small private enterprises, following the introduction of an SME Decree in 2001, it has no official policy supporting the growth of small private firms into larger ones (Hakkala and Kokko 2007, p. 2). It does not officially recognize the existence and contribution of the informal sector to the national wealth and has been busy reforming the formal sector toward the market economy. It has not introduced incentives and stricter regulation and enforcement mechanism to discourage traders to go informal in their business and employment. It instituted, instead, a series of policies consistent with its *Doi Moi* program which inadvertently encourages people to join the informal sector. With the government's strong privatization drive during the early 1990s, for instance, the exodus of employees from the state sector to the informal sector continued throughout Vietnam. The "managerial apparatus streamlining" (*tinh giam bo may quan ly*) during the late 1980s after *Doi Moi* in 1986 and the drive of many people to leave an inefficient bureaucracy in search of new entrepreneurial opportunities are important reasons of this exodus of workers to the informal sector. It is estimated that during this period more than 700,000 were made redundant workers by the government and were retrenched. And out of this number, around 70 % started working in the non-state sector by creating small-sized enterprises or being employed by small business owners (Le and Rondinelli 1993, p. 9). This retrenchment of government workers continued in 2005–2006 with the equitization drive by the government to further privatize the state-controlled economy. An additional 100,400 workers were laid off in state-owned enterprises (SOEs). Again, the great majority of this is said to have joined the informal sector partly owing to age limits set for those who enter the formal sector. The narrowing down of land allocation for agriculture in favor of urbanization and industrialization by the government is another instance which also forced people to join the informal sector. Between 2000 and 2006, for instance, about 2.6 million farmers lost their jobs and joined the informal economy as informal workers (Van 2008, pp. 215–216). Thus, Vietnam's efforts of renovating the economy into a more formalized and market-driven economy through *Doi Moi* have led to the unintended effect of driving more people into the informal sector and informal employment. During this transition, the government has no choice but to allow informality to flourish and to pass a series of legislations to redirect it to *Doi Moi*'s main goal of establishing a market economy under a communist rule.

Despite the difference in sociohistorical context and approach in supporting the informal sector, both the Philippines and Vietnam, nevertheless, share similar structural feature with regard to the formalization of business which encourages informality in their local economies. Both countries have complex, costly, and time-consuming requirements in doing formal business which discourage people to legalize their informal trade. The Philippines and Vietnam are among the economies which ranked very low with regard to the level of ease in doing formal business in the country. Both countries have high legal and bureaucratic burdens in opening and maintaining a legitimate business and thus encourage people to join the informal economy. Based on the World Bank (WB) and International Finance Corporation (IFC) study entitled "Doing Business 2015," the Philippines[10] only ranked 95th and Vietnam[11] ranked 78th among the 189 economies measured.

The Vietnamese government, bent in regulating and reforming the centrally planned socialist economy into a free market economy, issues numerous and evolving laws and imposes heavy bureaucratic requirements with high compliance cost to directly control and supervise state-owned enterprises (SOEs) and privately owned business firms in the formal sector. As a result of this complexity of laws and costly bureaucratic requirements plus the perceived lack of effective law enforcement on the part of the government, more and more people are said to be driven to the informal sector. In some ways, people exploit the cracks and loopholes created by the overlapping, numerous, and, at times, unenforceable laws to engage in informality in business. The case of legitimate and registered shops selling pirated discs in Ho Chi Minh City is an example of informality in formal business establishments in spite of the numerous decrees and IP laws against copyright piracy.

3.5.2.2 Legislations Affecting Vietnam's Informal Sector

Most business laws today in Vietnam were enacted after *Do Moi* in 1986 and were designed to establish a free market economy. To establish the right mix of building a capitalist market controlled by a communist regime, Vietnam's legal system is constantly evolving and business laws and regulations become unstable and unpredictable. Although it aims to regulate and formalize the economy, *Doi Moi* actually encourages informality with its thrust to privatize business and legalize informal trade and employment. With the rapid change in legislation, informality enters into the unstable system through loopholes in the legal system and instability in law enforcement. In Vietnam, overlapping laws, conflicting legal interpretation, and styles of law enforcement are common as the country undergoes a transition toward a market economy. The government, for instance, issued more than 70 legal documents since 2000, some seeming to contradict the spirit of the basic Enterprise Law through the reintroduction of licenses, capital requirements, and other limits to the marketplace entry (Tenev et al. 2003).

The major problem in the formalization and privatization program of the Vietnamese government is that no single measure exists to gauge and monitor the

[10] http://www.doingbusiness.org/data/exploreeconomies/philippines

[11] http://www.doingbusiness.org/data/exploreeconomies/vietnam/

level of regulatory activity and its impact on business. This is compounded by the fact that the country is just beginning to establish a legal framework to establish the market economy. Thus, the level and intensity of legal and regulatory activity are bound to be high (Tenev et al. 2003, p. 7). But the bureaucracy which implements this business regulation, especially in the lower level, remains unprepared to respond to the contingencies of legal reforms. In this case, the growth of the informal economy can be attributed to the overregulation and instability of laws after *Doi Moi* that encourages people to go informal in business and employment. In a way, the government's reform agenda and policies unintendedly encourage informality and informal jobs in the local economy, providing a friendly environment for the informal and illegal optical media retail piracy to thrive in Vietnam.

In Vietnam, there are currently no policies targeting the informal sector (Cling et al. 2010, p. 35). But there are some laws that indirectly favor the informal sector. Vietnam has created an adequate legal framework and conditions for securing basic rights for informal laborers. Below are some of the decrees and laws which were enacted after *Doi Moi* that seemed to benefit the informal sector and encourage small and informal trading such the piracy retail trade to grow in Vietnam.[12]

1. *Revised 1992 Constitution*. The revised 1992 Constitution of Vietnam has legalized the market economy concept, ensuring that any Vietnamese had the right to engage in entrepreneurial activities. This revision of the constitution which provides a legal framework for the privatization of state-owned enterprises (SOEs) and the creation of private businesses has somehow inspired people to engage in informal trade and employment.
2. *Labor Code of 1994*. The labor code of Vietnam was promulgated in 1994 consistent with the 1992 Constitution. This has been amended several times, but the basic purpose of the code remains the same: it defines the rights and obligations of workers and employers; it establishes the labor standards and principles to be used in order to manage labor and help boost production. Although the code is primarily intended for formal establishments, its labor regulations are generally seen to include workers in the informal sector.
3. *Enactment in 2000 of the 1999 Enterprise Law*. The Enterprise Law abolished 150 types of business licenses, shortened the legal process of establishing an enterprise from an average of 90 days to about 15, and significantly reduced registration costs (Tenev et al. 2003). This simplification encourages people in the informal sector to engage in small-sized enterprises or trade. They are encouraged to register and thus attain legality. The main problem, however, is how they maintain legality. With bureaucratic corruption, traders can always bribe inspectors and economic police to circumvent the laws. This is what happened in optical media retail piracy. It is easier for traders to open a CD–DVD shop and register it. But it is difficult for government regulators to ensure that

[12] See "Research of Informal Employment in Vietnam: Current Situation and Solutions," pp. 9–15 at http://www.ilo.org/wcmsp5/groups/public/DOUBLEHYPHEN-asia/DOUBLEHYPHEN-ro-bangkok/DOUBLEHYPHEN-ilo-hanoi/documents/publication/wcms_171762.pdf.

legality of the business is maintained due to corruption and overlapping of laws and jurisdictions of government agencies.

4. *Decree No. 90/2002/2001/CP-ND of 2001*. This decree was passed supporting small- and medium-sized enterprises and introduced substantial legal reforms allowing for important restructuring in business licensing procedures which, in turn, helped many new enterprises to become established.[13] This decree revised the definition from previous documents and decrees regarding small- and medium-sized enterprises in Vietnam. Under this decree, small- and medium-sized enterprises are those independent business and production establishments that have registered their business under the current legislation, have the registered capital of less than VND 10 billion [approximately US$670,000], or have the average number of annual employees of less than 300 (Socialist Republic of Vietnam, p. 2.). In Vietnam, there is a continuing lack of distinction as what constitutes a small- or a medium-sized enterprise. Freeman (1996) identified some common characteristics of small characteristics of small-sized enterprises operating in the Vietnamese context, including their small-scale, individual, or family operation: lack of standardized production, failure to conform with government labor, licensing or taxation laws, strongly competitive nature, and impermanence (Freeman 1996, p. 180). Under this description, the optical media trade can qualify as small- and medium-sized enterprises. Except the mobile vendors, CD–DVD shops in Vietnam are registered as small- and medium-sized enterprises. The small ones are usually the family or household businesses while the medium firms can be corporations. This decree encourages small traders to register their informal trade and thus achieve legality, but because of problems of law enforcement and corruption, they oftentimes operate informally.
5. *The Cooperative Law of 2003*. This law was enacted in November 26, 2003, to encourage traders to join cooperatives and to participate in forms of insurance. Under this law, the government shall not interfere in the internal management of cooperatives. It also recognized the basic contents of the official recognition of the organization of cooperatives as businesses in general.

3.6 Vietnam and the Philippines on Legality and Informality

Much of the literature perceived informality as an involuntary condition brought about by excessive regulation and weakness of the legal system. And regulatory burden, judicial inefficiency, and limited access to financing are commonly cited as constraints which determine a firm's decision to operate informally (Dabla-Norris and Inchauste 2008). The business environment of the country, therefore, matters in determining the nature and size of the cost advantages of informality. The higher the regulatory burdens of being formal, the higher are the savings from informality.

[13] sme.com.vn, 2003

This cost–benefit calculation affects the size of the informal sector as higher savings from being informal draw more firms to informality, resulting in a bigger informal sector (Djankov et al. 2002; Schneider and Enste 2000). The regulatory burdens are not the only factor that motivates traders to go informal. It also includes the government's capacity to enforce these burdens. If traders perceive that their informal firm's chances of getting caught for not complying with laws and regulations are low, then they would rather prefer to operate informally to minimize expenses and increase savings.

Both Vietnam and the Philippines encounter serious problems in formalizing business owing to numerous and oftentimes conflicting business laws and regulations and weak enforcement system. The main difference it seems is that the Philippines appears to be slow and consistent in its attitude of helping the informal sector, at least on paper, whereas Vietnam appears to have created more bureaucratic loopholes that allow the informal sector to flourish with its determination to reform the economy from a centrally planned system to a capitalist market economy. The Vietnamese government does not also introduce repressive laws which curtail the growth to the informal sector.

The Philippines, on the one hand, has supportive laws and programs for the informal sector but faces some serious problems in enforcing them. Vietnam, on the other hand, lacks direct supportive laws for the informal sector, but its drive to constantly revise and create numerous business laws and requirements to comply with market standards recommended by the WTO, United States, and USTR has inadvertently encouraged people to join the informal sector. Vietnam as a transition economy has undergone a constant legal transformation that greatly contributes to the growth of the informal economy.

The growth of informality in the Philippines and Vietnam is both fueled by complex and numerous legal and bureaucratic requirements that drive start-up or small entrepreneurs to join the informal sector. Informality in the Vietnamese economy is basically driven by cracks in the legal and enforcement system owing to constant revision of laws and conflicting interpretation in the various levels of regulatory bodies from the district to the national government. Based on 2015 World Bank study on the ease of doing business, Vietnam still ranked low despite making significant steps in simplifying business requirements.[14]

This seems to be the case on why informal traders of the Philippines and Vietnam prefer to go informal and illegal in their optical media trade. The regulatory requirements for going formal in business operations in these countries are burdensome, time consuming, and costly, and thus traders prefer to operate informally. And since the enforcement of copyright laws in these countries is weak and often negotiated, traders are encouraged to remain illegal in their business operations. The government's capacity to enforce regulations also matters in the assessment of the cost of regulatory obligations firms face. An informal firm's chances of getting caught for

[14] http://www.doingbusiness.org/data/exploreeconomies/vietnam/

not complying with laws and regulations are a direct function of the government's capacity to enforce the law.

3.7 Employment in the Piracy Trade as Informal and Illegal

The type of work and employment status offered by the optical media piracy business in the Philippines and Vietnam differ from the more common types of micro business in the informal sector. It is not only informal in a sense that it is unregistered and operating outside the law but also illegal by its very nature. Informal employment has many forms. Thus, defining what constitute informal work is crucial in determining the nature of employment in the optical media piracy business.

One way of defining informal employment is by examining its characteristics based on legality and illegality. The United States Labor Department (USLD), for instance, differentiates legal from illegal labor in the underground economy. Legal labor generates income from goods and services whose sale or exchange is not prohibited by law. Although the appropriate reporting requirement to a taxing or regulatory authority may not be fulfilled, the income generated from the economic activities is legal. Illegal labor generates income from activities that are illegal themselves. By the very nature of the entrepreneurial activities, illegally sourced income of illegal labor is not recorded in official statistics (1992, p. 2). Like illegal gambling, smuggling, or loan sharking, labor and income from optical media piracy trade are illegal as the sale of pirated discs is illegal in itself as defined by copyright law. The sale of street food and legitimate products such as bottled drinks or snacks in the sidewalks is illegal in a sense that the seller is violating some noncriminal zoning laws and not because she/he is vending illegal goods. The legality and illegality of informal labor would, therefore, depend on the type of economic activity done in the informal sector. The sale of food, clothing, or health products as legal commodities, for instance, may originate from both legal and illegal production arrangements. If these are produced by legitimate manufacturers but sold in illegal spaces such as sidewalks, the informal activity is illegal only because it violates some noncriminal rule or law such as not filing taxes and adhering to labor laws or violation of zoning ordinance. But if the products or services sold such as illegal drugs, fake bags, and gadgets or beauty products are illegal, then the income generated from selling this type of goods is considered intrinsically illegal and usually excluded from official statistics (Losby et al. 2002, p. 5). The informal employment in optical media piracy business in the Philippines and Vietnam is not only informal but also illegal in terms of retail venue and the nature of the product sold in retail outlets.

The sale of pirated optical media discs on sidewalks and other public places is doubly illegal and thus much more likely excluded from any official labor statistics.[15] Despite its illegality, the optical media piracy is considered part of the infor-

[15] This explains why there are no official records on the number and profile of illegal vendors and informal workers of the piracy trade that exist.

mal employment of the informal urban economy. The ILO broadly defines informal employment which can include the illegal optical media retail trade as follows: “Informal employment is the sum of employment in the informal sector and informal employment found outside the formal sector.” This conceptual definition has been used by the ILO Department of Statistics in providing technical assistance to countries doing national surveys on the informal sector (ILO Department of Statistics, June 2012).

3.8 Formality and Illegality in the Optical Disc Piracy Trade

Informality can assume several forms as illustrated in the optical media retail business in the Philippines and Vietnam. It can be overt, in a sense that a trade can altogether operate outside the law by operating illegally and selling illegal items or products in illegal spaces. It can also be covert or hidden in a sense that a business can appear legitimate, registered, and compliant with some regulatory requirements but operate informally by engaging in illegal activities outside the official regulatory framework of the government.

To simplify the classification and analysis of the extent of the formalization status and legality of the various forms of optical media businesses in the Philippines and Vietnam, the following schema will be used (Fig. 3.3).

In this diagram, the full formal business establishments are those which comply completely with all the legal and bureaucratic requirements for registration and licensing of the government and do business within the prescribed rules of operation officially set by the regulators and maintain them in their daily business operations. The partially formal or informal businesses are those which completely comply with all the business requirements of the government to start the business such as registration and licensing but fail to comply completely and consistently with the prescribed legal modes of business operation or partially comply with the entrance requirements of the business and with legal modes of business operation and thus partially complying the entire obligations for the full formalization of the business. This type of business circumvents some rules of registration or licensing and operates in some illegal or informal activities such as engaging in the illegal sale of counterfeit items instead of the genuine ones, cheating the government of taxes, and other forms of illegal acts (Fig. 3.4).

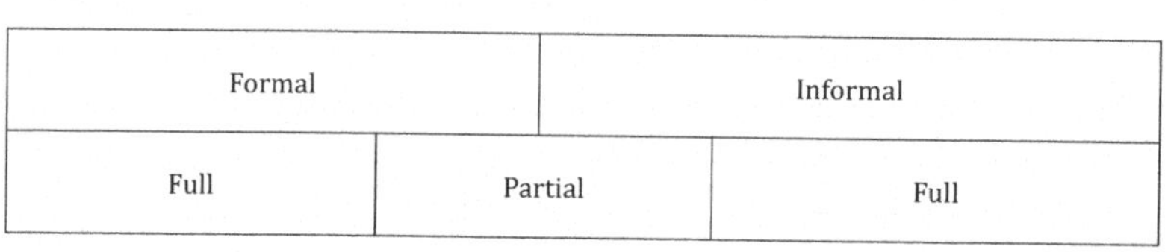

Fig. 3.3 Levels of formality and informality in business (Image courtesy of the author)

Fig. 3.4 The CD–DVD section of one popular super mall in Quezon City, Philippines, showing all original media products can be an example of full formalization of IP business from registration to daily operation (Image courtesy of the author)

The partially formal or informal trade can also be subdivided into a partially low formal business or partially high informal business and partially high informal business or partially low formal trade. Those firms which only have few violations of the official business regulations can be considered a partially high formal business firm or a partially low informal trade. But those with many illegalities can be considered a partially low formal business or partially high informal business.

The completely informal can also be subdivided into two types, depending on the extent of the illegal nature of the business and whether or not they gravely jeopardize public safety, welfare, morals, or health. This can either be completely informal but patently criminal in nature or completely informal but patently entrepreneurial in essence. Smuggling, sale of dangerous drugs, and human trafficking belong to the first type, but selling pirated discs by the poor in sidewalks can be completely informal and illegal but patently entrepreneurial in spirit. Although the goods are illegal and the occupation of public space is also illegal, the effect does not gravely jeopardize the public—although it deprives stakeholders some income, and the motive behind it is to earn income for poor families.

The categories in the schema must be considered ideal types rather than empirical categories as deviation from official rules is inevitable in social life and oftentimes remains unnoticed by authorities. Even big corporations which appear completely formal and legal in their business operation can commit covert illegal acts or corporate crimes hidden from public view.

The ideal type of formalization the USTR and IIPA demanded from developing countries such as the Philippines and Vietnam is full formalization in all aspects and types of manufacturing, mastering, distributing, and retailing of optical or digital media products and services which must be done strictly in accordance to official business and copyright laws and government regulations. This type of formalization may be applicable to developed countries with a high level of formality in their economies but not with developing and emerging economies in SEA like the Philippines and Vietnam whose local economies are largely influenced by the informal sector and informal business practices. A large-scale formalization of business, including that of optical media business, therefore, presupposes a high level of industrialization, stability of business laws, and strong legal framework and law enforcement.

3.8.1 Full Formality in Big CD–DVD Retail Outlets

Full formality in optical media trade, whether in production, distribution, or retail where all business operations are strictly done in accordance to law, is the ideal business model demanded by the United States and the USTR from the Philippines and Vietnam.

Although progress has been made to formalize some aspects of the optical media business, the Vietnamese market continues to remain largely pirate and informal. It is very rare, if not absent, to see optical media firms such as CD–DVD shops operating completely formal in their operations. What is common in Vietnam are partially formal firms: optical media stores which are registered in the district or local government and compliant with some legal requirements such as paying taxes, issuing sales invoice, or allowing inspections required by the local government, but operate informally by selling pirated or counterfeit optical discs. In the author's visits with various CD–DVD shops in the Ho Chi Minh City (HCMC) during his fieldwork, he never saw a registered shop selling all genuine optical media discs sold to its customers. There is apparently no full formalization of the optical media retail business in Vietnam. It is not surprising then that in 2014, the USTR elevated Vietnam, for the first time, from WL to PWL to indicate the growing threat of piracy in the Vietnamese market (2014 USTR Special 301 Report) (Fig. 3.5).

Vietnam's case seems to be in contrast with the Philippines. Although the Philippine market for optical media is dominated by informality and piracy, it has a small segment of fully formalized CD–DVD retail shops which fully follow the government requirements for registration, taxation, and operation. Most of these are business firms with big capital and usually have a chain of CD–DVD retail outlets and usually found in legal establishments such as those found in the major malls (e.g., SM, Robinsons, or Ayala Malls) and large shopping centers or grocery markets (e.g., Rustan's Shopwise). These retail stores sell all genuine optical media

Fig. 3.5 Partial Formality: A registered family-owned CD–DVD shop in Vietnam selling pirated CDs and DVDs (Image courtesy of the author)

Fig. 3.6 Genuine CDs and DVDs for sale inside a big fully formalized bookstore in the Philippines (Image courtesy of the author)

goods with all the necessary government stickers, sales invoice, and verification codes or holograms. Like any formal establishments in the country, companies which own these retail stores regularly pay government taxes and are subject to regular government inspections (Fig. 3.6).

3.8.2 Partial Formality or Informality in Registered CD–DVD Shops

Optical media business can be partially formal or informal if some of the legal requirements for entering and achieving legality as set by law and government regulation are not being satisfied by business media owners or traders. They may comply with some but not all the requirements in establishing or maintaining an optical media business. There is gradation in this type of formalization. The partial compliance may have to do with other legal requirements but not directly connected with the nature of the business. Strictly speaking, this type of legal compliance is very minimal, and the business operation can be considered strictly informal. A classical example for this in optical disc retail piracy is when a trader or retailer of optical discs secured a business permit and complies with the local government's requirement for retail business, let us say, for setting up a variety store (*sari-sari*) or dry goods but sells all pirated CDs, DVDs, or other digital products not authorized by the business license. This is one common type of retail piracy stores in the Philippines found in the Quiapo Barter Trade Center piracy hub in Manila. Most of the retail shops had business permits from the city hall for the retail of variety of goods but not for optical discs. The law requires that optical media retailers must first get a license and registration from the Optical Media Board (OMB) before they can sell genuine discs (Fig. 3.7).

Others stores in the Philippines resort to mixing to hide their informality. They get a local license for their retail stores and mix their legal goods with some pirated CDs and DVDs. One retail store, for instance, in the province of Rizal, sells not only a variety of fruits for which it is licensed but also some pirated discs. In another case, a retailer rents his retail space legally in a big grocery center in Quezon City, Philippines, displaying his business license which authorized him to sell mobile phones and accessories, but he also sells some pirated DVDs to his customers (Figs. 3.8 and 3.9).

The case of retail piracy in registered CD–DVD shops in Vietnam is quite different from the Philippines with regard to partial formality. The shops are registered and authorized by the district or local government to sell genuine optical media discs but sells almost all pirated CDs and DVDs. There may be a few original discs, but they are mainly used for display purposes for law enforcers or inspectors. The big stores even issue sales invoice and follow government regulations, but the goods they sell are fake and illegal.

Fig. 3.7 Author inspecting a display rack full of nicely packed CD and DVD cases (they can be mistaken as genuine!) of high-quality copies of pirated films and music in a medium-sized registered CD–DVD store in Vietnam (Image courtesy of the author)

Fig. 3.8 Pirated DVDs and CDs sold with other items in a rented shop in a Philippine public market (Image courtesy of the author)

Fig. 3.9 Mixing Strategy: A retailer in a legal stall inside a big grocery center in the Philippines sells some pirated DVDs from Quiapo Barter Trade Center in Manila together with the legal items sold in his store—souvenir items and electronic gadgets. Mixing illegal discs with legal goods is a common tactic in retail piracy trade to avoid law enforcement (Image courtesy of the author)

3.8.3 Full Informality in Mobile or Sidewalk Vending

In the Philippines, informality in optical media trade, particularly retail business, is largely overt and can be altogether informal and illegal if the trader decides not to register the business and sell illegal and pirated discs from illegal source in a prohibited public space. In Metro Manila and nearby provinces, the operators of this type of business are usually the poor migrant Muslims who are either Maranao or Maguindanao traders—although poor Christians also joined the trade in network with Muslim traders—who came from Mindanao and settled in major cities in the Philippines and engaged in illegal mobile vending of pirated DVDs and CDs in public spaces such as in sidewalks, kiosks, or parking lots. Newcomers with less capital usually prefer to sell pirated discs by walking door to door or by offering to whoever people they meet in the street using backpacks to carry their stocks. The Philippine government has laws and ordinances banning the illegal use of sidewalks. But implementing them proved difficult as some unscrupulous law enforcers allowed illegal vending in exchange of a regular bribe (*tong*) or "protection money" which can either be given by the vendor to the enforcer in a daily, weekly, or monthly basis or "as the need arises" (Fig. 3.10).

Fig. 3.10 A sidewalk retailer in the Philippines selling pirated CDs and DVDs at night in a makeshift stall occupying public space. This is an all-informal and illegal enterprise and the retailer admitted giving regular protection money to the local police (Image courtesy of the author)

In Vietnam, particularly in Ho Chi Minh City (HCMC), only a few mobile traders can now be found in the streets probably owing to a stricter state regulation against illegal vending. The areas which used to be full of sidewalk vendors of pirated discs were nowhere to be found during a search for mobile vendors of DVDs in Ho Chi Minh in a fieldwork. What was found on the streets in some districts of the city were few mobile Vietnamese vendors using push carts to sell pirated CDs and DVDS to pedestrians as shown in the picture below. Most sellers of this kind are poor Vietnamese migrants who come from either the middle or northern part of Vietnam.

One mobile trader interviewed in Ho Chi Minh during the fieldwork is a young male migrant from the northern part of Vietnam. He said that life in his province is difficult. He came to Ho Chi Minh by train to find a job. He said his older brother first came to the city and worked as a factory worker. Then two younger brothers followed him and also worked as factory workers. He was the last of the siblings to migrate to the city. With the help of his brothers, he was able to start his mobile piracy retail business using a push cart to sell DVD/CD discs. He said he bought the discs from a nearby illegal factory at 5,000 Vietnamese Dong per DVD disc and sells it at 10,000 Dong or at 100 % profit. He said he uses the pushcart since it is easier for him to run away from the police to avoid confiscation of his discs.

3.9 Piracy as a Source of Informal Employment

The leading generator of jobs in developing ASEAN countries identified as piracy hotspots is the informal sector. The 2011 Global Employment Trends report revealed that the main market challenge in the South Asian region is not unemployment but the persistence of low-productivity, low-paying jobs which are mostly found in the informal sectors. In fact, the employment rate in South Asia is estimated to have been just 3.6 % in 2011, down from 3.8 % a year before. Furthermore, the report indicated that there is a structural transformation in the region with a trend of declining agriculture and increase in industry and service jobs in urban centers. There is an accelerating movement of poor people out of agriculture into more productive jobs in the nonfarm sector (ILO 2012 Global Employment Trends p. 69). And those who moved out from rural areas and left their agricultural jobs are assumed to have joined the urban informal sectors for livelihood. In the Philippines, many Maranao Muslims who left their farms in the rural areas of Mindanao because of the ongoing war between the government forces and some Muslim rebels joined the informal sector and are employed in informal jobs such as street vending of pirated DVDs and CDs. Mobile vendors of pirated DVDs and CDs in Ho Chi Minh City—as already mentioned—are usually poor migrants who came poor provinces of Vietnam. The urban informal sector is the number one provider of informal jobs to many poor migrants in the Philippines and Vietnam.

3.9.1 Informal Employment Structure in the Optical Disc Piracy Trade

The growing popularity of measuring the informal sector in terms of labor employment (labor approach) rather than in terms of production units has shifted the focus of research on measuring informalization of the economy. Anthropologists and sociologists focused their definition on the cash and noncash exchanges between and within households to emphasize the role of the informal economy as a household economic strategy or as a source of community cohesion (Losby et al. 2002, p. 6).

The estimates of informal employment in developing countries have changed through the years. The informal employment figures in the Philippines, for example, which are based on the 2005 labor force survey, had increased to as high as 76.34 % or 24.6 million of the country's total employed, an increase of several percentage points from previous estimates (National Labor Force Survey 2005). This rise in informal sector employment is accompanied by an alarming decrease in the ranks of formal workers.

Browmik (2005) identifies two categories of people who are forced to join the informal sector. The first category is low-skilled rural migrants who are forced to join the informal sector in the city because of poverty in the villages or rural areas. The second are those who were working in the formal sector but were forced to join the informal sector due to closures of several industries for a variety of reasons such outsourcing of work, mergers of some of the corporations, downsizing of production units, etc. The first category is usually found in countries with weak industrial base and urban workforce, while the second category is usually located in industrial and developed countries. Those who engage in the informal trade of optical media piracy trade in the Philippines and Vietnam predominantly belong to the first category. They are mostly rural migrants who were driven out from their villages because of poverty and peace and order problems in the countryside. In the

Philippines, the optical media traders are mostly Maranao Muslim migrants who were driven out from their homeland and livelihood because of poverty, war in Muslim Mindanao, and social discrimination which prevent Muslims to join the formal sector. In Vietnam, rural poverty is a major force which forced some Vietnamese from the northern and central towns of Vietnam to migrate to bigger cities such as Ho Chi Minh City and join the optical disc retail trade. The following are the different types of traders and informal workers in the optical disc piracy trade in the Philippines and Vietnam:

A. *Producer–supplier*: This person owns an illegal duplication and manufacturing of pirated discs and employs relative and/or nonrelative but co-ethnic workers. Not all producers of pirated discs are wholly self-employed. Some work full time in the illegal trade by overseeing its daily operations. But others work full time in government agencies and manage their business through the use of the mobile phones and other high-tech gadgets with Internet connection.

   1. *Full-time self-employed*: This producer works as full-time entrepreneur of illegal pirated optical media. He personally supervises the various production stages of his informal business.
   2. *Part-time self-employed*: This producer has full-time formal job usually in the government or private sector and manages his media piracy business through mobile phones. In the Philippines, this trader is usually educated and some are even law graduates or lawyers working as directors in government agencies.

B. *Retailer*: This person is a self-employed trader who buys their pirated discs from distributors and sell them in his/her rented store, shop, or mobile outlet. This is usually found in the Philippines. In Vietnam, especially in Ho Chi Minh, some retailers buy directly their discs from illegal optical disc factories.

   1. *Complete piracy retailer*: This full-time retailer does not sell other non-media products but all pirated media goods such as CDs and DVDs.
   2. *Partial piracy retailer*: A partial piracy retailer sells other non-media goods such as electronic products or even agricultural products such as fruits or vegetables. Stores which sell legitimate computer products but also sell pirated software illegally can also be considered as partial retailer of pirated media. This type of retailer resorts to mixing of legal and illegal goods to avoid detection from law enforcers.

C. *Mobile vendor*: Browmik (2005) broadly defines a street vendor as a person who offers goods for sale to the public without having a permanent built-up structure from which to sell. Street vendors may be stationary or mobile. A stationary vendor is one who occupies space on the pavements or other public/private spaces. A mobile is one who moves from place to place by carrying their wares on push carts or in baskets on their heads (Browmik 2005, p. 2256).

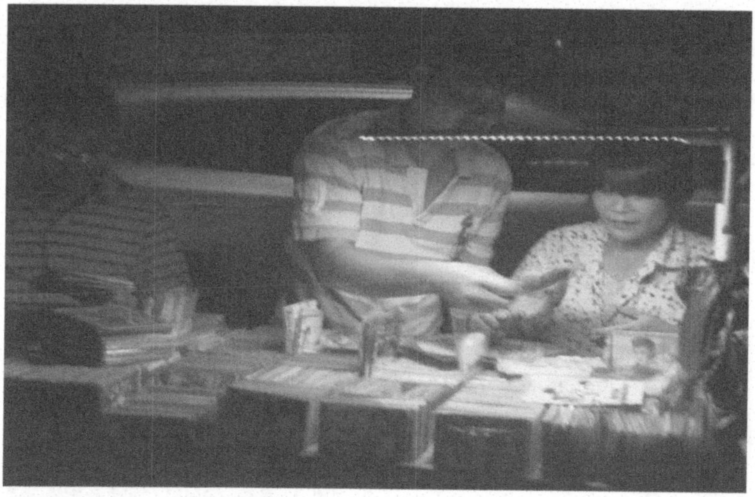

Fig. 3.11 Customers searching for their favorite movie titles and songs in a mobile stall selling pirated CDs and DVDs at night in a sidewalk of a major road in Vietnam (Image courtesy of the author)

1. *Street vendor*: This vendor usually occupies the sidewalk with a makeshift stall to sell pirated discs. Depending on the law enforcement in the area, she/he usually stations regularly in the same vending area.
2. *Backpacker*: This mobile vendor usually has a backpack full of pirated discs. He moves around from house to house to sell pirated discs or offers it to whoever he meets on the street or public place.
3. *Car/van retailer*: This vendor usually parks his car or van in parks or other crowded public places and open its luggage compartment full of pirated discs in order to display and sell them to people nearby. This type of retailers are particularly found in the Philippines.
4. *Pushcart retailer*: This retailer is common in Vietnam, especially in Ho Chi Minh City. This trader is usually self-employed. He uses a push cart to sell pirated discs in some crowded city streets which are less visible to the local police. The pushcart allows the retailer to move around to avoid arrest and confiscation of their discs (Fig. 3.11).

D. *Supplier*: This trader provides paraphernalia such as plastic covers, casing, blank discs, printing materials, disc cases, etc., for the production of pirated discs. In the Philippines, most suppliers are Chinese.
E. *Loader*: This self-employed trader transports boxes of DVDs and CDs from the producer's manufacturing site to the airport for a fee. He is also responsible for bribing the authorities and some corrupt airport and airline personnel to avoid confiscation or seizure of the discs.
F. *Distributor*: This self-employed trader serves as the middleman between the producer and retailer. He buys pirated discs in large quantity and wholesale

Fig. 3.12 A CD–DVD shop worker arranging pirated discs and cases in a big registered CD–DVD store in Vietnam (Image courtesy of the author)

price directly from the producers and sells them to various retailers at a higher price. With the use of transport vehicles such as a closed van, he distributes the discs from one retailer to another.

G. *Salesperson*: This person is an informal employee of a self-employed retailer and who is in charge of the daily sales of the retail outlet. She/he can be a member of the family such as the wife or children, a relative, or someone who is usually personally known by the owner or a co-ethnic of the owner. Only non-members of the immediate family are usually paid on a regular or seasonal basis by the owner. Salespersons in big registered CD–DVD shops in Vietnam are usually employed as formal employees.
H. *Shop worker*: This person can either be a family member or a hired employee who does various works inside the manufacturing or retail shop such as arranging, packaging, or preparing the boxes of discs for loading and distribution (Fig. 3.12).

3.9.2 Summary

This chapter explored the connection between the positive attitude of the government toward the informal sector and employment and the persistence of the optical media trade. It was shown that the positive attitude of the government as manifested in the type of legislation and program toward the informal sector and informal employment has contributed to the persistence of the optical media trade in the piracy-laden countries of Southeast Asia, particularly in the Philippines and Vietnam. The informal sector of the developing countries in Southeast Asia constitutes a bigger share in the income generation for the national economy. The Philippines and Vietnam have shown positive attitude toward the informal sector, although the former is not direct and overt compared to the latter. Moreover, the Philippines has directly acknowledged the contribution of the informal sector to the national economy and thus included it in its national reform agenda. The informal sector contributes a bigger percentage to the country's GDP and is the major generator of jobs and national income.

References

Andrews, D., Caldera Sánchez, A., & Johansson, Å. (2011). *Towards a better understanding of the informal economy*. OECD Economics Department Working Papers, No. 873, OECD Publishing. http://dx.doi.org/10.1787/5kgb1mf88x28-en

Arnold, D. (2013). Social margins and precarious work in Vietnam. *American Behavioral Scientist, 57*(4), 468–487. Doi: 10.1177/0002764212466245.

Becker, K. (2004). *The informal economy: Fact finding study*. Stockholm: SIDA.

Bluch, N. (2001). *The informal sector revisited: A synthesis across space and time*. Social protection discussion series, World Bank. http://siteresources.worldbank.org/SOCIALPROTECTION/Resources/SP-Discussion-papers/Labor-Market-DP/0119.pdf

Browmik, S. (2005). Street vendors in Asia: A review. *Economic and Political Weekly, 40*(22–23), 2256–2264.

Casanova-Dorato, F. (2010, March). *Informal economy budget analysis in Philippines and Quezon City*. WEIGO Working Paper No. 12. http://www.inclusivecities.org/wp-content/uploads/2012/07/Casanova-Dorotan_WIEGO_WP12.pdf. Accessed 20 May 2015.

Castells, M., & Portes, A. (1989). World underneath: The origins, dynamics and effects of the informal economy. In A. Portes, M. Castells, & L. A. Benton (Eds.), *The informal economy: Studies in advanced and less developed countries*, Baltimore: The Johns Hopkins University Press.

Chen, M. A. (2007). *Rethinking the informal sector: linkages with the formal economy and formal regulatory environment*. DESA Working Paper No. 46. ST/ESA/2007/DWP/46. http://www.un.org/esa/desa/papers/2007/wp46_2007.pdf. Accessed 5 Apr 2014.

Chickering, A., & Salahdine, M. (1991), Introduction. In A. Chickeringa & M. Salahdine (Eds.), *The silent revolution*. San Francisco: International Center for Economic Growth.

Cling, J. P., Razafindrakoto, M., Roubaud, F. (2010). The informal sector in Vietnam, study for the ILO. http://www.tamdaoconf.com/tamdao/wp-content/uploads/downloads/2010/08/DIAL-ILO-Study-informal-Vietnam-2010.pdf. Accessed 3 May 2014.

Cling, J. P., Razafindrakoto, M., & Roubaud, F. (2012). Explanatory factors behind formalizing non-farm household businesses in Vietnam. www.dial.ird.fr/.../DT+2012-20+Cling+–+Razafindrakoto+–+Roubaud.pdf

Cu Chi Loi. (2005). Rural to urban migration in Viet Nam. http://www.ide.go.jp/English /Publish/Download/Asedp/pdf/071_7.pdf

Dabla-Norris, E., & Inchauste, G. (2008). Informality and regulations: What drives the growth of firms? *IMF Staff Papers, 55*(1). International Monetary Fund. http://www.Imf.org

Dilnot, A., & Morris, C. (1981). What do we know about the black economy in the United Kingdom? *Fiscal Studies, 2*, 163–179.

Djankov, S., et al. (2002). The regulation of entry. *The Quarterly Journal of Economics, CXVII*(1), 1–37.
Easton, S. (2001). *The size of the underground economy: A review of the estimates*. Mimeo: Simon Fraser University.
Feld, L. P., & Schneider, F. (2010). Survey on the shadow economy and undeclared earnings in OECD countries. *German Economic Review, 11*(2), 109–149.
Ferman, P., & Ferman, L. (1973). The structural underpinning of the irregular economy. *Poverty and Human Resources Abstracts, 8*, 3–17.
Fields, G. (2005). *A guide to multisector market models, social protection*. Discussion Paper No. 0505, World Bank. http://siteresources.worldbank.org/SOCIALPROTECTION/Resources/SP-Discussion-papers/Labor-Market-DP/0505.pdf
Freeman, D. B. (1996). Doi Moi policy and the small-enterprise boom in Ho Chi Minh city, Vietnam. *The Geographical Review, 86*. http://www.questia.com/googleScholar.qst?docId=5001643249.
Gaughan, J., & Ferman, L.A. (1987). Toward an understanding of the informal economy. *ANNALS, AAPSS, 493*, 15–25.
Gutmann, P. (1977). The subterranean economy. *Financial Analysis Journal, 33*, 24–27.
Hackenberg, R. A. (1980). New patterns of urbanization in Southeast Asia: An assessment. *Population and Development Review*, *6*(3), 391–419. Doi: 10.2307/1972408.
Hakkala, K., & Kokko, A. (2007). The state and the private sector in Vietnam. Working Paper 236. http://www.swopec.hhs.se/eijswp/papers/eijswp0236.Pdf
Harris, J. R., & Todaro, M. P. (1970). Migration, unemployment and development: A two-sector analysis. *American Economic Review, 60*(1), 126–142.
Henry, S. (1987). The political economy of informal economies. *ANNALS, AAPSS*, *493*, 137–153.
Houston, J. (1987). The underground economy: A troubling issue for policymakers. *Business Review Federal Reserve Bank of Philadelphia*, *1987*, 3–12.
ILO. (2002). *Women and men in the informal sector: A statistical picture*. Geneva: Employment Sector. http://onlinewomeninpolitics.org/beijing12/womenmen.pdf. Accessed 8 Feb 2014.
Jamil, S. (2013, January) *Connecting the dots: The urban informal sector and climate vulnerabilities in Southeast Asian megacities*. NTS Alert No. AL13-01. http://www.rsis.edu.sg/nts/html-newsletter/alert/nts-alert-1301.html
Kabra, K. N. (1995). The informal sector: A reappraisal. *Journal of Contemporary Asia*, *25*(2), 197–232.
Karaos, A. (1985). Manila urban poor: Dimensions of marginality and powers. *Pulso, 1*(3), 241–252.
Kenyon, T. (2007). A framework for thinking about enterprise formalization policies in developing countries. World Bank Policy Research Working Paper No. 4235. http://www.papers.ssrn.com/sol3/papers.cfm?abstract_id=988845. Accessed 7 Jan 2014.
Koo, H., & Smith, P. C. (1983). Migration, the urban informal sector, and earnings in the Philippines. *The Sociological Quarterly*, *24*(2), 219–232.
Lagos, R. A. (1995). Formalizing the informal sector: Costs and barriers. *Development and Change*, *26*(1), 111–131.
Lewis, A. (1954). Economic development with unlimited supplies of labor. *Manchester School*, *22*, 139–191.
Le, N. N. & Rondinelli, D. (1993). Small business development and economic transformation in Vietnam. *Journal of Asian Business*, *9*, 1–23.
Losby, J. L. et al. (2002). *Informal economy literature review*. ISED/Aspen institute. http://www.kingslow-assoc.com/images/Informal_Economy_Lit_Review.pdf
Maldonando, C. (1995). The informal sector: Legalization or laissez-faire? *International Labour Review*, *134*(6), 705–728.

MoLISA (2010).Vietnam employment trends 2010. Ministry of Labor Invalids and Social Affairs (MoLISA). Jan 2011. http://www.ilo.org/hanoi/Whatwedo/Publications/WCMS_151318/lang--en/index.htm. Accessed 4 July 2015.

McCrohan, K., & Smith, J. (1986). A consumer expenditure approach to estimating the size of the underground economy. *Journal of Marketing*, *50*, 48–60.

Pastrana, C. S. (2009). The informal sector and the non-Regular employment in the Philippines. http://www.adbi.org/files/2009.12.15.cpp.sess2.3.pastrana.paper.non.regular.employment.philippines.pdf

Rawaa, H. (2013). Heterogeneity in the Egyptian informal labour market: Choice or obligation? ftp://mse.univ-paris1.fr/pub/mse/CES2013/13032.pdf. Accessed 5 June 2015.

Schneider, F. (2002) Size and measurement of the informal economy in 110 countries around the world. http://rru.worldbank.org

Schneider, F., Buehn, A., Montenegro, C. E. (2010). *Shadow economies all over the world, new estimates for 162 countries from 1999 to 2007*. Policy research working paper 5356, July 2010, the World Bank. elibrary.worldbank.org

Schneider, F., & Enste, D. H. (2000). Shadow economies: Size, causes and consequences. *Journal of Economic Literature*, *38*(1), 77–114.

Simon, C., & Witte, A. (1982). *Beating the system: The underground economy*. Boston: Auburn House Publishing Company.

Smith, P. (1994). Assessing the size of the underground economy: The Statistics Canada perspectives. Canadian Economic Observer, Catalogue No.: 11-010, 3.16-33, at 3.18.Spiro, Peter, S. (1993). Evidence of a post-GST increase in the underground economy. *Canadian Tax Journal/ Revue Fiscale Canadienne*, *41*(2), 247–258.

Sutton, J., et al. (1994). The legalization of the workplace. *The American Journal of Sociology*, *99*(4), 944–971.

Szalontai, B. (2008). The diplomacy of economic reform in Vietnam: The genesis of Doi Moi, 1986–1989. *Journal of Asiatic Studies (Korea University, Asiatic Research Center)*, *51*(2), 199–252.

Tenev, S. et al. (2003). *Informality and the playing field in Vietnam's business sector*. Washington, DC: IFC, World Bank, and MPDF. www.ifc.org/wps/connect/9 aae680047ad-b52f9311f7752622ff02/VN-informality-playing field-VN.pdf

Tokman, V. E. (2007, June). *Modernizing the informal sector*. DESA Working Paper No. 42, ST/ESA/2007/DWP/42. http://www.un.org/esa/desa/papers/2007/w42_2007.Pdf. Accessed 5 Feb 2014.

Van, T. H. (2008). Viet Nam. *Asian Law Review 2008*. http://apirnet.ilo.org/resources/Asian-labour-law-review-2008-vietnam. Accessed 20 May 2015.

Williams, M. C. (1992). *Vietnam at the crossroads*. New York: The Royal Institute of Internal Affairs, Council of Foreign Relations Press.

Chapter 4
Obstacles in Formalizing the Optical Media Trade

4.1 Understanding Formalization of Business

Formalization of business can be generally understood as "the process whereby previously noncompliant enterprises become integrated into these formal or state-sanctioned institutions, such as property registries and tax-rolls" (Kenyon 2007, p. 3). The process of formalization of business enterprises has two interrelated dimensions—achieving legality and retaining legality. In achieving legality, obstacles may occur in the various legal requirements of the government that discourage people in registering and licensing their business, while in maintaining legality, problems can consist of business firms' lack of consistency in paying taxes and complying with government regulations. Lagos (1995) in his study on the barriers and cost of formalizing the informal sector in eight Latin American countries, for instance, also showed that the process of formalization of microenterprise comprises two distinct but related aspects: achieving legality, i.e., being part of regulated and formal economy, and retaining legality. In both aspects, financial, legal, and bureaucratic burdens can hinder the legalization of informal trade such as the optical media retail piracy trade.

The formalization of microbusiness enterprise such as retail trading needs further distinction to relate it to the current problems of legalizing the informal optical disc trade in the Philippines and Vietnam. In this case, Amin's (2009) distinction between two types of entrepreneurs is relevant. The first type of entrepreneur, according to him, is the necessity entrepreneur (equivalently, necessity firm) who started (or took over) a business because he/she cannot find a necessary job. In contrast, an opportunity entrepreneur (equivalently, opportunity firm) is one who started (or took over) a business to take advantage of a business opportunity (Amin 2009, p. 1). The informal optical media trade in the Philippines and Vietnam can be classified under these two types of entrepreneurs. The necessity traders, which make up the main bulk of piracy traders in the Philippines, are the poor retailers and hawkers of pirated discs who can be found in sidewalks, kiosks, and stalls, are mostly

V.O. Ballano, *Sociological Perspectives on Media Piracy in the Philippines and Vietnam*, DOI 10.1007/978-981-287-922-6_4

self-employed, and are forced to join the illegal trade because they cannot find jobs in the formal sector either because of high level of unemployment or the entry requirements are difficult for applicants to comply. These poor necessity entrepreneurs are less likely to go legal in their small trade.

The opportunity traders are usually the big-time legal and illegal producers–suppliers, distributors, and retailers of media discs in the Philippines and Vietnam. It is not difficult to see that this latter type of traders or business firms are more capable and would more likely to legalize or maintain full legality if the business regulatory environment becomes efficient and friendly. The necessity might also be convinced to formalize their small trade if the government assists them through the formalization process by simplifying the procedures and providing them with the necessary assistance programs to help them access capital for their microbusiness. Interviews with some informal vendors of optical discs in the Philippines, for instance, revealed that they are willing to go legal as they are tired of raids and confiscations by law enforcers and paying bribes to corrupt authorities to protect their illegal goods. They said that all that they want is a livelihood which can support their families. But they do not know how their illegal vending of discs can become legal without the government's assistance. The main obstacle, they said, is apparently poverty and regulatory burdens imposed to those who want to enter the formal optical media business. Being new to the city, the poor, migrant, and less literate small retailers said that they cannot obviously afford and comply with the business requirements for legalization.

4.1.1 Formalization and the Law

Achieving full formalization of business, especially with regard to informal media trade, has something to do with the legal system and culture. If business and optical media laws are comprehensive and culturally responsive to cover contingencies or what Weber calls as "gapless" laws, achieving and maintaining legality of the optical media business would not be that difficult. Law as one important normative apparatus of society has peculiar power of fixing social and business arrangements in society; thus, the copyright laws in WIPO treaties, TRIPS, and local legislations against piracy would have been sufficient to secure compliance. Carol Smart (1989) argued that the law has hegemonic power which can sideline other forms of knowledge in society. Legal pronouncement by the court can silence competing nonlegal knowledge or interpretation. Despite this enormous power, the official law is not, however, the only normative standard in society. There are other social fields or what Sally Moore (1978) calls as "semi-autonomous fields," i.e., the various formal and informal normative standards operating between the state law and empirical reality that compete the official law. If the official law is incomplete, incoherent, overlapping, and evolving, then other normative fields can challenge and oppose it and create various loopholes and unintended effects, making it complex and difficult for the official law and its enforcement systems to formalize and regulate business.

Enforcing copyright business laws and governing optical media trade are often difficult to undertake when they contravene the local customary laws on creative works. This is even more difficult in transitioning and emerging economies like Vietnam where the legal system is still unstable and where new IP laws and multilateral agreements such as the TRIPS and other international treatises on copyright conflict with the local legal culture. Moreover, laws have difficulty achieving their intended effects when they are incomplete and constantly evolving and overlapping as illustrated by the piecemeal construction of new copyright laws such as that of Vietnam, conflicting interpretation through various levels of government bureaucracy and selective law enforcement by authorities. Oftentimes, ambiguities and complexities in legal interpretation and implementation can encourage nonlegal normative fields or informal norms to challenge the official law as well as enable some unscrupulous law enforcers and business regulators to engage in corruption and red tape.

The Philippines and Vietnam need to reform their existing IPR systems and harmonize them with the foreign international IP standards which are largely patterned after the US IPR regime. But since no two legal systems are similar and compatible, cracks and loopholes in the new mixed legal system can arise. Overlapping of laws can create loopholes which pose serious challenge to government regulators on how to reconcile them. Overlapping or inconsistent laws can create ambiguity in legal interpretation and, thus, can give state regulators more discretionary powers on how to implement them. And this can lead to more bureaucratic burdens and red tape in formalizing business enterprises since additional unofficial interpretation and procedures maybe added by bureaucrats to reconcile conflicting laws.

4.1.2 The Overall Regulatory Environment and Formalization

The overall regulatory environment affects the process of formalization of business in a particular country. Optical disc trade in the Philippines and Vietnam mainly operates informally and illegally. In the Philippines, only a few registered firms operate formally in the country selling genuine media discs, and they are mostly found in malls and shopping centers; the rest are informal and illegal traders selling counterfeit discs in sidewalks, rented stalls, kiosks, and other public places. In Vietnam, almost all optical disc businesses operate informally; around 90 % of counterfeit discs are sold in registered CD–DVD shops and bookstores, and around 10 % are sold on sidewalks through mobile vending. A closer look at these optical disc firms and shops reveals a serious problem of truly achieving legality or/and maintaining legality in their business operations. Both aspects point to regulatory problems in attaining full formalization of their businesses. Thus, many optical disc traders prefer to do business informally.

Much of the literature on business development perceived informality as an involuntary condition brought about by excessive regulation and weakness of the legal system. And regulatory burden, judicial inefficiency, and limited access to financing are commonly cited as constraints which determine a firm's decision to operate informally (Dabla-Norris and Inchauste 2008). The business environment of the country, therefore, matters in determining the nature and size of the cost advantages of informality. The higher the regulatory burdens of being formal, the higher are the savings from informality. The prospect of higher savings draws more firms and traders to operate informally, resulting in a bigger informal sector (Djankov et al. 2002; Schneider 2000). And a growing informal sector can be a major threat to the full formalization of businesses and their competitiveness in the country. The growing informality in trading is, therefore, tied with the regulatory burdens imposed by the government. Lowering these burdens can be a key toward a greater formalization of business enterprises and toward leveling the playing field in the market for various types of trade in emerging economies.

One major reason why traders and business firms in the informal sector prefer to go informal is the costly, time-consuming, and complex legal and bureaucratic requirements in legalizing and maintaining the legality of their business enterprise. Building a dynamic model of the informal sector, Braun and Loayza (1994) argued that the informal sector exists when overregulation (high tax rates and a high cost for entering the formal sector) is coupled with an inefficient and corrupt system of compliance control. The regulatory burdens and the government's capacity to enforce these burdens are important factors that motivate traders to go informal. If traders' perceive that going informal enables them to save time, money, and effort and that the chances of getting caught for not complying with the prescribed laws and regulations are low, then they would more likely prefer to operate informally and illegally (Braun and Loayza 1994, p. 2). And this seems to be the case of the informal traders of optical media piracy of SEA countries, particularly those in the Philippines and Vietnam who prefer to go informal and illegal in their business operations. The regulatory obligations to formalize business enterprises in these countries are burdensome, time consuming, and costly. With the government's weak capacity to enforce business regulations, people are encouraged to go informal in business operations. This is particularly applicable in formalizing and maintaining a legitimate optical media production and retail business. Many SEA governments demand from business applicants burdensome requirements that encourage people to go informal rather than legal in their trade.

A closer look at the regulatory requirements to start a new business and maintain legal operation in SEA countries reveals some patterns of difficulties for traders to legalize their business enterprise. Thus, the problem of persistence of the optical disc trade in developing countries must also be seen within the context of this rigid business regulatory structure of the government as well as the capacity and readiness of informal traders to join the ranks of formal business firms. The degree of ease in achieving and maintaining legality in business enterprises in SEA countries can be a key toward achieving a higher degree of formalization in optical media trade. SEA countries which have been included in the Priority Watch List (PWL) and Watch List (WL) of the USTR are also economies which ranked low in the ease of doing business in the World Bank (WB) and the International Finance Corporation (IFC) annual business surveys. Although the Doing Business surveys may not directly relate to the ease of doing the informal business of optical media piracy as it assumes, among others, that the business is a limited liability company; located in the largest business city, with 10–50 employees; and conducts general commercial or industrial activities, they, nevertheless, provide an overview of the business requirements and bureaucratic burdens traders would face in formalizing their business in a specific country. The ease of legalizing a business depends chiefly on the overall regulatory environment of doing business in a particular jurisdiction.

4.2 Legal and Judicial Obstacles of Formalization

4.2.1 Deficient Copyright Laws

One major obstacle toward the full formalization of optical or digital media business in the Philippines and Vietnam is the lack of the necessary copyright laws which support the type of IPR regime demanded by the USTR and IIPA. The fact that copyright laws that govern optical media trade work well in developed countries like the United States does not necessarily mean that they would also be responsive to protect IP interests in developing countries like the Philippines and Vietnam. Due to social resistance, piracy-laden countries take a reactive rather than proactive stance with regard to copyright legislation. Like other SEA countries in the watch lists of the USTR, the Philippines and Vietnam usually only enact copyright laws to control piracy when pressured and threatened with trade sanctions by the United States under the Generalized System of Preferences (GSP) arrangement or Free Trade Agreement (FTA). Because of this resistant attitude, the copyright legal systems of these countries remain deficient of the necessary laws based on international standards and TRIPS-inspired legislation. Their local copyright legal systems therefore remain dominated by customary copyright laws which are prone to counterfeiting and piracy.

When foreign laws are transplanted in a piecemeal manner into emerging markets such as those of the Philippines and Vietnam where the national economy is still in the process of transition, developing countries' cooperation and compliance with international copyright standards demanded by the USTR could not be expected to yield immediate results. Moreover, numerous contingencies and legal gaps would arise from this highly deficient copyright legal system, resulting in more informalities for copyright business which can invite resisters and counterfeiters to exploit the system.

Since the USTR is demanding a stricter US-inspired IPR regime which is complex for IP-consuming economies and constantly evolving owing to technology advancement, developing countries like the Philippines and Vietnam would find it difficult to catch up with the legislative demands of the USTR and IIPA. Altering local laws implies altering existing economic and social relations. And this would not be easy as any new legislation could face resistance from people and even law enforcers if it contravenes customary laws. Some local policemen in the Philippines, for instance, are hesitant to arrest the poor mobile vendors and confiscate their illegal discs because of "awa" (mercy) because they view the sidewalk vending of optical media, particularly by poor Muslims, as "paghahanap-buhay ng mahihirap nating mga kapatid na Muslim" (a means of livelihood of our poor Muslim brothers) rather than a criminal act as defined by the Optical Media Law of 2003.[1]

The USTR and the IIPA have been recommending to the Philippines and Vietnam numerous legislative and administrative actions to address the deficiency of the US-inspired copyright laws in the local legal system to curb piracy. In copyright protection, the USTR and the IIPA recommend the following actions to improve copyright protection in the Philippines: (1) modernize laws to deal with infringements; (2) amend Optical Media Act to include CD-R burning, mobile device piracy, "media box" piracy, and border enforcement; and (3) implement Republic Act 9184 (an act providing for the modernization and regulation of the procurement activities of the government and for other purposes) (IIPA 2014 Special 301: The Philippines, pp. 199–200). For Vietnam, they recommended the following for 2014: (1) issue implementing guidelines for the revised Criminal Code, (2) make necessary changes to Vietnam's laws and implementing decrees in full compliance with bilateral trade agreement (BTA) with the United States and with other international obligations, (3) join the WIPO Copyright Treaty (WCT) and WIPO Performances and Phonograms Treaty (WPPT), (4) clarify that Decree No. 85 measures imposing onerous collective management do not apply to foreign collective management organizations (CMOs) or to the administration of foreign rights, and (4) adopt an anti-camcording legislation (IIPA 2014 Special 301 Report: Vietnam, p. 77).

4.2.2 Weak Judicial System on Intellectual Property

The Philippines and Vietnam are not only lacking the necessary copyright laws to imitate the US and international IPR protection system but also a responsive judicial system that is ready to handle and prosecute IPR violations. In both countries, prosecutors and judges are not well trained to process IP cases in addition to the lack of remedial and administrative IPR rules and procedures in court. Since legal IP trade is a new development to countries such as Vietnam and the Philippines which are used to counterfeiting and copyright infringement, the government has not yet exerted more efforts to reform the judicial system. At present, only few lawyers and judges specialize in IP cases and very few cases filed in court resulted in convictions. One reason for this is prevalence of amicable settlement (*areglo*) in resolving optical disc piracy cases and the leniency of the police with regard to IPR violations especially if they involve the poor and Muslim migrant retailers. In the Philippines, retail optical disc piracy involving vendors of pirated discs rarely reach prosecution stage as relatives of the vendors arrested would usually approach the police and reach an amicable settlement. Corruption is another reason why IP cases do not prosper in court. Law enforcers who received regular protection money from illegal

[1] Based on interviews with two policemen and OMB chair on the attitude of policemen toward illegal sidewalk vending in the Philippines

IP traders usually do not apprehend real culprits but only traders who do not provide the bribe demanded by these enforcers.[2] In a culture where personalism is strong, legal cases often end up in amicable settlement between violators and law enforcers. Oftentimes, the offenders and local police are familiar or socially related with one another. Some Muslim policemen assigned in police stations near the Muslim-dominated Quiapo Barter Trade piracy market are socially connected with optical disc piracy traders by common religious affiliation. Thus, when Muslim vendors are arrested for illegal vending of pirated discs, local Muslim leaders or relatives of the vendors would usually approach these Muslim police to intervene for the release of the vendors. In Vietnam, local police are also familiar and related with traders by friendship or consanguinity with the owners and managers of CD–DVD shops selling pirated discs. Thus, arrests and prosecutions rarely happen and cases often end up in amicable settlement and giving of bribes.

The IIPA and the USTR have long noticed this scarcity of cases filed in courts and convictions involving copyright infringement. In Vietnam, to IIPA's knowledge, no criminal copyright infringement case has ever been brought to courts. And for IIPA, the main reason for this is the government's great reluctance to file criminal remedies to even the most serious cases of infringement. Other reasons include complex procedures, delays, and a lack of certainty as to the expected outcome (2014 IIPA Special 301 Report, p. 80). The IIPA recommends the building of IP expertise in the judicial system as part of its overall judicial reforms. Training should be provided to police and prosecutors as they play a very important role in bringing a criminal offense case to the courts (2012 IIPA Special 301 Report, p. 279).

Like Vietnam, the Philippines is also slow to prosecute and file criminal cases against violators of copyright and optical media law. The government is not also determined to address the prevalence of amicable settlement in IP cases, corruption, and upgrading the IP capability of Philippine courts. But it has made some progress lately with some cases being filed in court and resulted few convictions and with some reforms to upgrade the IP capability of Philippine courts.

4.2.3 *Problems in Law Enforcement*

The formalization of IP business, particularly that of the optical media business, requires a more comprehensive, well-funded, and graft-free law enforcement system. But this seems to be not the case in the Philippines and Vietnam.

[2] Raids against traders of pirated discs in the Philippines and Vietnam are often aimed against those who do not pay the bribe or regular protection money demanded by law enforcers. Please see Chap. 6 of this book for a detailed description on bribery and corruption in the optical media trade.

4.2.3.1 Philippines

The Philippine law enforcement system seems to be ready to combat media piracy. Under the present setup, the Intellectual Property Office (IPO) is the overall government agency which oversees all IPR protection system in the country. The three enforcing arms of the IPO include the Philippine National Police (PNP), the National Bureau of Investigation, and the Optical Media Board (OMB). On paper, the law enforcement system against piracy seems to be in order. But empirical reality shows otherwise.

With regard to enforcing the law against media piracy, one major problem faced by the OMB in the Philippines is the low budget or annual appropriation set aside by the national government to combat optical media infringement. The low annual budget is a perennial problem in the OMB. The agency cannot hire new personnel and agents or buy new and necessary equipment to monitor and apprehend infringers and finance massive raids intelligence operations due of lack of funds.[3] Moreover, the agency is not graft-free. It is also accused of corrupt practices involving agents and even OMB chairs. One OMB chair and four other OMB officials were charged with graft by the Ombudsman, the Philippines' constitutional anti-graft body, because of "neglect of duty" for the alleged illegal release of boxes of confiscated DVDs from the OMB compound.[4] Allegations and rumors are also ripe that some agents who received bribes from illegal traders leaked information through texts in cell phones of an impending raid and seizure operation of the OMB. This is the reason, according to an OMB Chair in an interview, why cell phones of operatives are confiscated and the location of raids is only announced to agents just moments before the OMB team leaves for the operation to avoid leak of information and corruption. Finally, the OMB jurisdiction has no jurisdiction on online piracy which is rising with the advent of the Internet, computers, tablets, iPads mobile phones, and other high-tech gadgets with Internet connection. The optical media law in the Philippines only authorizes the OMB to apprehend illegal trade of optical discs in CD, DVD, Blu-ray, and other formats but not online infringement such as peer-to-peer (P2P) sharing, cyberlocker, deeplinking, and other types of Internet media piracy. This is the reason why the USTR and IIPA in their 2014 Special 301 reports want the Philippine government to amend the current optical media law to include Internet media piracy.

---

[3] For a more detailed discussion, please read http://www.wikileaks.org/plusd/cables/06MANILA3805_a.html.

[4] Please see: "Ronnie Ricketts and 4 others suspended by Ombudsman for 'neglect of duty' at http://entertainment.inquirer.net/151606/ronnie-ricketts-4-others-suspended-by-ombudsman-for-neglect-of-duty. For an earlier and more detailed allegation of corruption at the OMB, see Ducky Paredes: "Trouble at OMB" at http://www.duckyparedes.com/blogs/2012/02/20/trouble-at-omb/.

4.2.3.2 Vietnam

The main stumbling with regard to law enforcement against media piracy in Vietnam is the government's lack of determination to fight copyright infringement. Although it recognized, for instance, the existence of hard goods piracy, it did not devote more resources and take immediate action to curb it. The Vietnamese Customs, according to the IIPA, does not also intercept infringing imports like high-quality CD–DVD imports from China despite proper documentation on hard goods piracy (IIPA 2014 Special 301 Report, p. 80). In its recommendation to the USTR to elevate Vietnam to the PWL, the IIPA blamed the resistance and unwillingness of the Vietnamese government to seriously take actions against piracy. It remained unwilling to mete out deterrent administrative fines, to file criminal action against infringers, and to remove onerous market access barriers to allow legitimate foreign exports to enter the country. The IIPA lamented that the "Vietnamese government has long recognized the increasing sophistication of piracy and its violations to copyright laws, but its actions have not been commensurate with that acknowledgement" (IIPA 2014 Special 301, p. 78). Thus, government's resistance and inaction remain as the main barrier in law enforcement and formalization of optical media business in Vietnam.

Because of this strategic inaction, the Vietnamese government has not been acting swiftly and decisively to delineate the jurisdiction of enforcing agencies to avoid overlapping of functions and empower Vietnam's drive against copyright piracy. In Vietnam, there are various enforcement bodies tasked by law to address IPR infringement problems. These include the Ministry of Information and Communication (MIC), Ministry of Science and Technology Inspectorate (MST), the Ministry of Culture, Sports and Tourism Inspectorate (MCST), the Ministry of Industry and Trade's Market Management Bureau, the Ministry of Public Security's Economic Police, the Ministry of Finance Customs Office, and the People's Court (Civil Court). As a result of this overlapping jurisdictions, there are no clear-cut lines of responsibility among these agencies.[5] There is also a lack of clear guidelines with regard to the coordination of these various government agencies on enforcement action against piracy. The IIPA often complained of this jurisdictional overlap among various enforcement agencies in Vietnam which weakens the country's campaign against infringement. Moreover, it also noticed that Vietnam's enforcement agencies receive low budget from the government which further incapacitates the country's antipiracy drive against copyright infringers. Finally, Vietnam's enforcement agencies against piracy, like the Philippines, are also plagued with corruption.

---

[5] Doing Business in Vietnam: 2013 Country Commercial Guide for U.S. Companies, p. 20 at http://export.gov/vietnam/build/groups/public/@eg_vn/documents/webcontent/eg_vn_063160.pdf

4.3 Bureaucratic Obstacles

As already mentioned, the growth of informality in optical media business in the Philippines and Vietnam is both fueled by complex and numerous legal and bureaucratic requirements that drive entrepreneurs to the informal sector. Informality in the Philippine and Vietnamese economy is basically driven by the constant revision of laws, overregulation of the economy, and complex, expensive, and time-consuming bureaucratic requirements in doing business in the country. Both Vietnam and the Philippines have some serious problems with regard to numerous laws and requirements in formalizing business.

The main difference of the two countries seems to that the Philippines may appear slow and consistent in its attitude in helping the informal sector, at least in paper, whereas Vietnam appears to be busy revising economic laws to privatize the state-controlled economy to comply foreign demands to transform the local economy into a capitalist market economy, which inadvertently left the informal sector to flourish. The Philippines has supportive laws and programs for the informal sector but faces some serious problems in enforcing them. Vietnam, on the other hand, lacks supportive legislations for the informal sector, but its drive to constantly revise and create numerous business laws and requirements to comply with market standards has inadvertently encouraged people to join the informal sector. Vietnam as a transition economy has undergone some sort of constant legal transformation that greatly contributes to the growth of the informal economy. The problem with Vietnam is that there is no single measure to gauge and monitor the level of regulatory activity and its impact on business. This is aggravated by the fact that the country is just beginning to establish a legal framework and a set of rules that can accommodate the market economy. Therefore, the level and intensity of legal and regulatory activity are bound to be high (Tenev et al. 2003 , p. 7). The growth of the informal economy in Vietnam can largely be attributed to this overregulation of the economy by the government that encourages people to go informal in business and employment.

4.3.1 Red Tape

Research and theory have been inconsistent and ambiguous on the nature of "red tape." But there is understanding that red tape has something to do with excessive or meaningless paperwork (Bennett and Johnson 1979); a high degree of formalization and constraint (Hall 1968); unnecessary rules, procedures, and regulations; inefficiency; unjustifiable delays; and, as a result from all this, frustration and vexation (Bozeman 1993, p. 273). Rosenfeld (1984) defines red tape as the sum of government guidelines, procedures, and forms that are perceived as excessive, unwieldy, or pointless in relation to official decisions and policy (as cited in Bozeman 1993,

Table 4.1 Starting a business in Singapore, Philippines, and Vietnam by number of procedures, time, cost, and paid-in capital

	Singapore	Philippines[a]	Vietnam
World Rank	(1)	(138)	(99)
Procedures (number)	3	16	10
Time (days)	3	36	34
Cost (% of income per capita)	0.6	18.1	8.7
Paid-in min. capital (% of income per capita)	0.0	4.8	0.0

Source: Data are compiled from 2013 IFC-WB Doing Business Report
[a]In this report, the Philippines has actually lowered its overall ranking compared to last year, from rank 136 in 2012 to rank 138 in 2013

p. 276). Theories abound why red tape exists in government regulation. But one popular theory sees the concern of government to create check and balance in the regulation process in order to avoid corruption and deviation from official law as causing red tape.

Red tape is one of the more serious bureaucratic obstacles in addition to legal obstacles in the full formalization of business in the local economy. With numerous unnecessary paper works, bureaucratic requirements and procedures, and unexplained delays in securing business registration, licenses, and permits as well as compliance with the yearly requirements and inspections to maintain legality in business, traders or entrepreneurs would be discouraged and prefer to go informal and illegal in their business operations. The Philippines and Vietnam are two Southeast Asian countries listed in 2013 IFC-WB Report on the ease of doing business as among the economies with burdensome regulations, which can mean that traders especially the poorer ones in these countries would more likely go informal to start and maintain their business. Out of 185 economies surveyed, the Philippines is ranked 138, while Vietnam is on the 99th, both were very far in rank from a fellow Southeast Asian country, Singapore, which got the number one spot as the country with the most conducive regulatory environment for starting and operating formal business.

Table 4.1 showed that starting a formal business in the Philippines and Vietnam is complex, time consuming, and expensive. Compared to Singapore which ranks number one in the ease of starting a formal business, the Philippines ranked 138th and Vietnam 99th of the 185 economies included in the international survey. It also showed that Singapore only has three steps in starting a business, while the Philippines has 16 and Vietnam has 10. In Singapore, it takes only 3 days to complete the registration and completion of the business requirements of a new business, while in the Philippines and Vietnam, it needs 36 and 34 days, respectively, to complete the process. Singapore uses online transaction to speed up the registration of new business. Vietnam and the Philippines are still in the process of improving its online registration process.

Table 4.2 Comparing the Philippines and Vietnam on ease of doing business

	Country	
	Philippines	Vietnam
World Rank	158	109
Indicator		
Procedures (number)	16	10
Time (days)	36	34
Cost (% of income per capita)	18.1	8.7
Paid-in minimum capital (% of income per capita)	4.8	0.0

Source: Data are compiled from 2013 IFC-WB Doing Business Report

4.3.2 Complex and Time-Consuming Business Requirements

The Philippines and Vietnam are two Southeast Asian countries listed in 2013 IFC-WB Report on the ease of doing business as among the economies with burdensome regulations.

As shown on Table 4.2, the Philippines and Vietnam have both earned a lower overall rank in the 2013 World Bank and International Financial Corporations' annual report on business regulation entitled *Doing Business 2013: Smarter Regulations for Small and Medium-Size Enterprises.* With regard to the level of ease in starting and registering a new business in the country, the Philippines got an overall rank of 158 out of the 185 economies included in the survey, while Vietnam got a rank of 109. This means that it is more difficult to start a new business in the Philippines than in Vietnam, particularly in terms of the number of procedures, time, cost, and paid-in minimum capital. It takes 16 procedures to register a new business in the Philippines while only 10 in Vietnam. It takes around 36 days to finish the entire registration process in the Philippines but only 34 days in Vietnam. A prospective company or trader spends more money to pay for the cost of the entire registration process, around 18.1 % of income per capita, while only 9.7 % in Vietnam. Entrepreneurs in the Philippines are also required a paid-in minimum capital of 4.8 %, while those in Vietnam, traders pay nothing.

Vietnam is well ahead of the Philippines with regard to the regulatory reforms of its local business. The entry of foreign business firms especially with regard to retail business remains difficult though. The regulatory environment favors local firms which make them more competitive against foreign counterparts. It has implemented a total of 18 institutional or regulatory reforms, in 8 of 10 areas of business regulation measured by the annual Doing Business report of the World Bank (WB) and International Finance Corporation (IFC) over the past 8 years. In its 2013 report the World Bank and the IFC found out that between June 2011 and June 2012, Vietnam improved its business environment through a regulatory reform that makes it easier for local firms to start a business. The most recent reform is to allow Vietnamese companies to use self-printed value-added tax invoices. Having shorter and easier procedures to start a business is not an assurance that full formalization can easily be achieved. The main problem in the formalization of retail business in Vietnam is maintaining legality. With the government's *Doi Moi*, all new private business firms are required to register. The government has substantially reduced the steps and expenses in registering new firms. The main problem, however, is how the government can consistently monitor and regulate the daily operation of the registered business firms.

The Philippines, on the other, has lagged behind in terms of easing the regulatory burdens on formalizing new businesses—although, lately, it has done efforts to short-cut the registration process of businesses by using online transaction.

Generally, it is difficult to achieve legality but easier to maintain it in the Philippines. This is opposite to Vietnam's case where it is easy to achieve legality but difficult to maintain legality. This seems to be the reason why the bulk of CDs and DVDs in Vietnam are counterfeit and sold in registered CD–DVD shops, while in the Philippines the bulk of pirated discs are found in mobile stalls on sidewalks and in rented shops and stores which are either unregistered or registered by the local government but for legal products and not for vending counterfeit discs.

In the Philippines, it is difficult, costly, and time consuming to register a new business, especially for a small sole proprietorship media trade. To open a new small retail store of CDs and DVDs, the prospective trader has to undergo twice the complexity, cost, and delay of obtaining a business registration compared to an ordinary non-disc store such as a small sari-sari, or variety, store. Aside from obtaining a business permit in the local city or municipal hall office, the owner further needs to register the business again and obtain licenses from the Optical Media Board (OMB) and pay another round of fees. And because the Philippines is weak in e-government or using the Internet for government transactions, the whole process of registering and licensing involves physical presence, sometimes lining up in the city or municipal halls for a longer period, unless one pays a fixer to expedite the whole process of getting a business permit, license, and other requirements. Only rich traders and big companies with lawyers who are tasked to handle these matters would most likely not feel the inconvenience, complexity, and cost in achieving legality for their optical disc business. But this is another story for the self-employed, less literate, poor, and migrant traders who only just want to earn a living to support their families in an alienating city. Without the support and viable alternative supported by the government, poor traders would just forego all these requirements and immediately start a small retail business through mobile or illegal vending than complying with all these numerous and costly legal and bureaucratic obligations.

The good news in the Philippine case is that once the new business has been registered and licensed, maintaining legality and semblance of stability is assured, although there are still some problems in the regulation system.

The case of Vietnam seems the opposite. It is easier to open and start a retail optical trade for Vietnamese in Vietnam but difficult to maintain its legality. Some owners of CD–DVD shops in Ho Chi Minh admitted that it is easy to start an optical retail business in Vietnam. The requirements and steps are easy and the cost of processing them is less expensive. But to maintain legality and comply with government's regulation is difficult because of corruption and weak government monitoring, and thus some resort later into illegality and informality in their business dealings. With weak government law enforcement, many registered firms such as CD–DVD shops can easily circumvent the law and sell counterfeit items.

4.4 Opening an Optical Media Business in the Philippines

Starting a new business in the Philippines is generally difficult, expensive, and time consuming. This is particularly true to optical media business. A prospective trader is expected to deal with two major sets of complex and expensive processes to be able to operate a retail shop for CDs and DVDs. First, the trader or firm has to follow the usual complex process of registering the new business with the local government business licensing office. And he/she is also expected to complete the licensing and registering requirements of the Optical Media Board (OMB) for his/her CD/DVD operations which entails extra work, time, and expenses. Once a prospective trader finds a suitable place to rent for his/her CD–DVD shop, he/she then proceeds to register with at least four (4) major government agencies and comply with numerous requirements:

A. *General registration requirements:*[6]

1. Department of Trade and Industry
   - 1.1 Come up with three business names.
   - 1.2 Search DTI's website to see if there are similar existing registered firms.
   - 1.3 If business name is available, fill out Business Name (BN) application form.
   - 1.4 Submit BN application form to DTI office/branch.
   - 1.5 Wait for DTI certification of registration.
2. Local government units where the business is located
   - 2.1 Barangay
     - 2.1.2 Barangay where the business is located to secure and fill out application form.
     - 2.1.3 Submit completed form together with the DTI business registration certificate.
   - 2.2 Valid proof of address
   - 2.3 Mayor's Office
3. Bureau of Internal Revenue (BIR)
4. If with employees, register with the following agencies:

[6] Compiled from Philippine government websites

   4.1 Social Security System
   4.2 Philippine Health and Insurance System
   4.3 Home Development Mutual Fund (Pag-IBIG)

5. Optical Media Board (OMB)

B. *Additional requirements: OMB's requirements for registration and licensing for sole proprietorship (Per MC 2012-001 effective October 4, 2012, OMB's Website):*

General requirements:

1. Letter of application addressed to the chairman
2. Duly filled out and notarized application form
3. Two (2) pieces latest 2×2 signed photo of the applicant
4. Picture of the establishment's façade with permanent signboard
5. Comprehensive location sketch of the establishment
6. Floor plan of the establishment
7. Tax Identification Number (TIN) of the business establishment
8. Contract from source of rights and/or suppliers
9. Special power of attorney, if needed
10. Certificate of business name from the Department of Trade and Industry (DTI)
11. National Bureau of Investigation (NBI) clearance

Licensing requirements (for local licensee):

1. Contract from the producer of the film/source of rights (foreign film)
2. Certificate of Ownership (local films)
3. Notarized Affidavit of Undertaking
4. Replicating permit prior to replication/duplication of product
5. Name of authorized replicator
6. Import/export permit prior to importation or exportation of the product

Duplicator (CD-burning services):

1. Software inventory audit per computer unit
2. List of machines/equipment (CD writer)—make/model/serial no.

Replicator:

1. Certified list of machine with serial no., brand name, type of machine, and no. of units
2. Photo of interior or reproduction site showing the machine/s setup
3. Flow of program or production for VCD/DVD replication/mastering process (from raw material to finished product
4. Certificate of SID Code from Philips International
5. Notice of Allocation of SID Code from Optical Media Board

Film transfer:

1. Certified list of equipments with serial no., brand name, type of machine, no. of units
2. Photo of interior showing the duplication site
3. Flow of production for duplication
4. Notarized Affidavit of Undertaking
5. Certified list of clients for duplication

All these monetary and documentary requirements can easily discourage small informal traders to register their business and go legal in their business transactions. Starting a registered CD–DVD retail business is already expensive and complex, much more if a trader wants to engage in manufacturing, production, mastering, or distributing genuine CDs and DVDs of digital media such as songs or feature films. The exportation and licensing of replicating machines abroad could also be highly expensive and tedious. This time, the trader needs to deal with corrupt customs officials aside from paying the necessary taxes at the Bureau of Customs (BOC). The Philippine BOC is consistently regarded as one of the most corrupt government agencies in the country. In this case, opening a legitimate optical media business whether production, distribution, or retail is only appropriate for big businesses or corporations which have huge capital or resources to register and comply to the numerous and expensive entry requirements as well as to pay bribes to unscrupulous law enforcers and government regulators and not for small entrepreneurs. Thus, the majority of Maranao Muslim traders of pirated CDs and DVDS who are migrant and poor could not afford to legalize their mobile or sidewalk vending and would not have any chance to legalize their trade. Thus, one can see in the Philippines two groups of optical media traders: the big ones whose business is fully formalized and the small ones in rented shops, mobile, and makeshift stalls whose business is fully informal and illegal.

4.5 Starting a New Optical Media Business in Vietnam

Vietnam's case with regard to formalizing business, particularly the digital or optical media trade, is quite different from the Philippines. Unlike in the Philippines, starting a new business in Vietnam is much easier, faster, and cheaper and favorable to small- and medium-sized firms of Vietnamese traders. The application process is done online and the steps are fewer compared to the Philippines. Since the enactment of the Enterprise Law in 2000, business registration process in Vietnam has tremendously become easier and thus encouraged many traders to register their businesses. A sample in a survey in 2005, for instance, showed that it took business firms 50 days (or around 23 days for those using a service provider) to complete the whole registration and formation process, from applying for a registration certificate to being issued their first "red invoice" book for VAT purposes (Freeman et al. 2005, p. vi). But at present the process is much shorter. Starting and registering a new business in Vietnam, as reported by the 2013 World Bank-IFC report on the ease of doing business, would now take only 34 days (WB-IFC 2013). And this is basically for new big business firms in Vietnam. For small business such as sole proprietorship or retail business owned by Vietnamese, this process of formalization is much easier and faster. With the government determined to use the Internet to simplify and expedite the process through online transaction, business registration is expected to be much faster and cost efficient for big and small business firms in the near future. At present, however, it is still difficult for foreigners to start an optical media business in Vietnam. They need to partner with local Vietnamese traders and comply with the government's numerous requirement to engage in media business in Vietnam.

4.5.1 Opening an Optical Disc Shop in Vietnam

Opening an optical media business for foreigners is difficult because of the many bureaucratic barriers and requirements set by the government for foreign investors. But for the Vietnamese traders, opening a retail business such as a DVD shop is relatively easy. Some owners of CD–DVD shops in HCMC when interviewed said that opening and registering an optical disc shop is relatively easy and less time consuming. With the current state's drive of simplifying business procedures and requirements, traders who want to open and register a new business can expect fewer hurdles with the government's *Doi Moi* policy. Today, a business registration requires fewer procedures, lesser cost, and shorter period to acquire a license and registration compared to the pre-*Doi Moi* era. Based on our interviews and observations, opening and registering a CD–DVD shop in HCMC for Vietnamese traders seem to be fast and easy. With the government's ongoing computerization of business transactions, much of the procedures are done online. One important initial step before one applies a registration certificate is to find a suitable place to establish the retail shop. If the applicant does not own the place, he/she can look for a strategic place to rent. Once he/she has a lease agreement with the owner, the prospective trader usually undergoes the following steps[7]:

1. Download the business registration form from the Internet.
2. Prepare the following requirements:

   (a) Fully accomplished registration application form
   (b) Identification Card
   (c) Capital/financial requirement
   (d) Machines for checking quality of discs (usually a big TV, CD–DVD player, and a good sound system)
   (e) Guarantee from economy department of the district

[7] This list of requirements was given by a Vietnamese key informant which he said was based on a government website and interview.

   (f) Contracts of employment
   (g) Tax requirements (license tax, VAT, income tax)

3. Submit form and documents to local service of planning and investment agency.
4. Apply a special license for the optical media operation at the local agency of the Ministry of Culture, Tourism, Information and Sports (MCST).

Owing to the government efforts to streamline the procedures in opening a business, the steps in securing business license became fewer and less expensive for new traders of optical media. But this does not mean that full formalization of retail businesses has been achieved in Vietnam. Achieving legality in optical media business may be easy, but maintaining legality is the major problem in optical disc retail business. The regulatory environment of a country is not only influenced by policy or the content of regulatory regimes but also by the discretionary power of bureaucrats entrusted with the application of rules and regulations (Duvanova 2014, p. 2). Thus, corruption and discretion of regulators on how and when to apply the rules enter into the picture. Because of bureaucratic corruption, regulation of business operations after the firm has been set up is not consistently pursued to maintain legality. Thus, when representatives from the government or economic police inspects CD–DVD shops, bribe is often given to them so they would not report violations of license and business registration.

The bureaucratic hurdles after registration are more difficult in Vietnam than in the Philippines. To overcome this, traders resort to shortcuts which entail corruption to shorten the process and minimize time and expenses. The end product is partial formalization in which digital media firms are externally and initially formal but performs a lot of informality in their daily business operations.

4.6 Regulation and Formalization of Technologies for Media Piracy

The most difficult hurdle to formalize the optical and digital media is regulating and legalizing technologies, particularly replicating, copying, and sharing technologies used offline and online. In today's global age, technology is fast evolving and improving that regulation, legislation, and law enforcement to control and curb any form of counterfeiting, piracy, and other illegal activities can hardly catch up with its development. Moreover, with the growing capacity of technology to merge networks, the illegal has become so intimately connected with the legal in the cyberspace that when authorities run after the criminal and illegal, the legal and legitimate are affected. Oftentimes the illegal rides on the legal and the legal, at times, use the illegal to gain more profit. Some peer-to-peer networks, for instance, allow the sharing of copyrighted digital media materials in the Internet to attract more users and advertisers.

Hard goods piracy also thrives in using legal technologies for illegal purposes. Mobile phones, for example, are used by producers to get orders from distributors of pirated discs for the provinces in the Philippines. The automated teller machine (ATM) technology in the banking system is also utilized for payoffs of bribe or regular protection money to corrupt law enforcers. Media piracy is also using copying machines or burners which are legal and sold in legal computer stores. This merging of the legal and illegal made more intimate by technology challenges policymakers and law enforcers to craft enforcement guidelines which can distinguish and separate the illegal from the legal and the genuine from the counterfeit.

Finally, one major factor why the importation of illegal replicating equipment and technologies for piracy occurs despite strict laws and rules on smuggling is corruption. The Philippines and Vietnam have high corruption index based on surveys of Transparency International (TI). The nonenforcement of custom laws and corruption in the Bureau of Customs of these countries have always been cited by the USTR and IIPA as a reason why replicating technologies enter the country from China. Another reason is the deceptive strategies used by legal importers of replicating technologies for piracy to avoid law enforcement. Legal importers, according to informants, declare the replicating machines at the customs as legal but will be used for illegal purposes. Once these technologies entered the country, owners or importers would secretly use them for counterfeiting and copyright infringement.

4.6.1 Regulating the Internet Against Piracy

The Internet technology has been the primary purveyor of counterfeiting of copyrighted materials since the disc has been invented to copy optical media. Producers use it for the preproduction and production stages of their business. The Internet is an indispensable technology to download or get materials for illegal replication. Oftentimes, the master copy of the movie and music to be copied in the discs for retail piracy originates from the Internet. The Internet is the main source of information of an upcoming or latest movie, music, or software to be copied and marketed by the producer. It is also a source of information about the latest computer software, computer application, replicating equipment, and paraphernalia to be used for piracy production as well as the design of the cover and label for the pirated discs. The use of discs for optical media content can be a temporary form of media piracy more prevalent in developing countries with lower broadband and Internet penetration. But as Internet connection and computer literacy increase in a developing country, optical disc piracy would most likely wane and be replaced by online piracy. Online piracy of optical media is faster, more convenient, and cheaper than buying a disc in a CD–DVD shop. Users can easily download and share copyright materials by just a touch on the screen or click of the mouse. This pattern can be noticed both in the Philippines and Vietnam with the increase of online piracy lately. The increase of purchase of laptops, personal computers, smartphones, tablets, and other gadgets with Internet connections in HCMC is accompanied by a decrease of sidewalk and mobile vendors of pirated discs in the city and sale of DVD players and discs. Another indicative pattern is the increase of piracy websites and illegal downloading and sharing of copyrighted materials as pointed out by a more recent USTR annual report (e.g., 2012, 2013). In Vietnam, media piracy has shifted to a new phase and has become more online and Internet based. The Philippines too seems to follow this pattern of going online in infringing activities but slower compared to Vietnam because of its slow Internet connection and penetration.

The main issue with regard to eliminating online media piracy is this: To what extent the Internet technology can be regulated to minimize or eradicate digital media piracy? Behind Internet's operation are big business interests led by the top U.S. multinational tech giants such as Microsoft, Apple, Google, Facebook, Yahoo, etc., and billions of users around the world. To regulate the Internet to curtail copyright piracy is to invite social resistance from various business interest groups and social networks of users who benefit from its openness and flexibility. The fate of two anti-online piracy bills in the U.S. Congress, known as PIPA (Protect Intellectual Property Act) in the Senate and SOPA (Stop Online Piracy Act) in the House of Representatives, is an example of various vested interests who oppose any form of Internet regulation. Internet regulation legislation has been a top agenda of entertainment and pharmaceutical companies, publishers, and other copyright industry groups which lost sales and revenues in the United States and abroad due to online piracy. But Internet giants such as Goggle, Twitter, Facebook, and Wikipedia and other interest groups protested these two bills. Protests of thousands of users and various business groups who depend on the Internet for their business, use, and consumption blanketed the Internet resulting in the postponement of the vote for the bills and the subsequent abandonment.[8] The simultaneous blacking out of popular websites by their administrators as a form of protest and resistance helped increase public awareness of and opposition to the two bills (Kelly et al. 2012). In the Philippines, the latest episode of hacking of government websites by a group called Anonymous Collective in response to Singapore's new Internet licensing framework that regulates the Web is another example of public and corporate resistance against the regulation of the Internet.

4.6.2 Internet Regulation in the Philippines and Vietnam

The Philippine and Vietnamese governments have contrasting policy with regard to restrictions and regulations of the Internet. Based on the 2012 survey, the Philippines has been listed as one of the freest countries in terms of Internet freedom, while Vietnam is one of the most restrictive countries which censor the use of the Internet especially for political or anti government propaganda.

Before the passage of the Anti-Cybercrime Law, the Philippines is one of the top countries which respect Internet freedom as shown below (Table 4.3).

[8] "SOPA, PIPA anti-online piracy bills halted by U.S. Congress after Wikipedia protest" at http://business.financialpost.com/fp-tech-desk/u-s-congress-pulls-sopa-legislation?__lsa=8f93-8629

Table 4.3 Comparing Internet regulation in the Philippines and Vietnam

Country	Internet control				
	Notable political blocking	New law/ regulation increasing censorship or punishment	Blogger/ICT user arrested for political or social writing	Blogger/ICT physically attacked or killed (including in custody)	Technical attacks against government critics
Philippines					
Vietnam	X	X	X	X	X

Source: Data are compiled from Freedom on the Net 2012

The table shows that the Philippines is much more free from government control in terms of Internet use compared to Vietnam based on the five areas identified by the Freedom on the Net 2012 study. Vietnam as a communist and one-party system is against any attack or criticism against the established government posted on the Internet. Thus, it filters and blocks any posting or comment by any blogger or ICT user which can undermine the ruling party and the government. It passed new laws that increase censorship or punishment against anyone who put the government in a bad light. Anyone who criticizes the government can suffer harassment or end up in prison as noted by the study.

Although Vietnam is one of the restrictive countries with regard to the Internet, its control is basically political in nature and directed only to any political opposition to the current regime. It is, however, liberal to any online activity that tends to achieve its economic goal of promoting Vietnamese productivity and achieving higher economic growth. In fact, the government through the Ministry of Information and Communication (MIC) plans to install Internet connection throughout Vietnam, especially in remote and isolated places in order to improve the productivity of the entire country. Thus, Vietnam is against any use of the Internet for political attacks against the regime but tolerant to any online activity that uplifts the economy of the country in accordance with the *Doi Moi* policy of the government. Optical media piracy, whether online or in sidewalks or registered shops, has undeniably helped improve the productivity, income, and life of Vietnamese in the informal sector. As already mentioned, optical disc piracy provides recent Vietnamese migrants alternative livelihood to support their families. It also provides traders with registered CD–DVD shops higher profit margins and ordinary buyers of pirated discs with some savings which they can use to buy food for their families.

4.7 Harmonizing ICT and Copyright Business Interests

Optical media piracy can be the unintended consequence of the ongoing competition between technology manufacturers and service providers of the Internet and its allied mediating technologies against copyright industries which provide content of these technologies. Many of these are mostly American information technology

(IT) and telecommunication multinational corporations with manufacturing plants and subsidiaries abroad which compete for greater sales with other local and foreign firms in the digital markets of IP-consuming countries such as the Philippines and Vietnam. The technologies sold by these companies such as computer hardware and software are the very same technologies used by users and counterfeiters for illegal downloading, sharing, and reproduction of optical media for piracy trade. Exporters of these products led by the United States cannot just impose restrictions on the exportation of American non-copyright high-tech products that can be used for media piracy as these are the major drivers of US exports in their sectors, providing employment and revenues to the US economy. The U.S. government cannot just control Internet use and connection and the sale of computers, mobile phones, replicating machines, DVD and Blu-ray duplicators, burners, or computer software which are often used for illegal downloading, copying, or converting files as they are also legitimately sold by top US IT or ICT companies in developing countries. ICT-exporting countries such as the United States would then ensure that trade barriers in the exportation and sale of these high-tech technologies abroad are minimized or removed. In Vietnam, for instance, the United States introduced provisions in the BTA to open the Vietnamese economy to the entry and sale of American ICT as well as copyright products and services. Vietnam's accession to the WTO which was sponsored by the United States has further paved the way to a more liberal trade policies between the two countries that facilitate the importation of ICT to the communist state at the expense, at times, of copyright technologies which are exposed to counterfeiting and media piracy given the weak IPR protection system in developing countries (Fig. 4.1).

4.8 Summary

This chapter identified some major legal and bureaucratic obstacles in the formalization of the optical media business in the Philippines and Vietnam. The overall regulatory environment of a country affects the formalization of business. Deficient copyright laws due to the slow transplantation of foreign- and American-inspired laws demanded by the USTR can create loopholes which can result in piracy and informality. Moreover, these foreign laws often contravene the customary IP laws in developing countries such the Philippines and Vietnam, creating local resistance against compliance with foreign IPR system and formalization. Regulatory burdens or the complex, time-consuming, and costly requirements in achieving legality through registration and maintaining legality by following the bureaucratic requirements after registration can discourage traders to formalize their business. Both the Philippines and Vietnam scored lower rankings on the ease of doing business compared to Singapore and other advanced economies. Achieving legality in the Philippines is easier than maintaining legality. Opening a new business, particularly an optical retail business in the Philippines, is tedious, expensive, and time-consuming, favorable to big corporations than to the many poor and migrant

Fig. 4.1 An electronics store in Ho Chi Minh City selling some latest models of American mobile phones and accessories (Image courtesy of the author)

retailers of pirated discs. But once legality is achieved through registration and licensing, the monitoring and government business regulation is relatively more efficient in the Philippines compared to Vietnam. Vietnam has lesser requirements, and online transaction is encouraged in opening a new optical media store and thus easier to achieve legality. Maintaining legality, however, is more difficult in Vietnam as government monitoring and law enforcement is weak and laden with corruption. Finally, the regulation of technologies for piracy, especially the Internet, is also difficult to achieve due to strong resistance of consumers and of the various legal and illegal businesses dependent on a freer Web. Legality and illegality have become more intimately connected by technological advancement. The very technologies used for legal consumption and trade are also used for counterfeiting and copyright infringement. This necessitates dialogue between top US hardware and software technology multinational companies and top copyright multinaltional firms to delineate and harmonize business interest to better combat media piracy.

References

Amin, M. (2009). Necessity vs. opportunity entrepreneurs in the informal sector (short note), Mimeograph. http://works.bepress.com/mohammad_amin/. Accessed 4 July 2015.

Bennett, J. R., & Johnson, M. H. (1979). Paperwork and bureaucracy. *Economic Inquiry, 17*, 435–451.

Bozeman, B. (1993). A theory of government "Red tape". *Journal of Public Administration Research and Theory, Inc*. Public Management Research Association. J-PART, *3*(3), 273–303. http://www.jstor.org/stable/1181785. Accessed 4 Feb 2013.

Braun, J., & Loayza, N. V. (1994). *Taxation, public services, and the informal sector in a model of endogenous growth*. Policy Research Working Paper 1334, World Bank, Washington, DC.

Dabla-Norris, E., & Inchauste, G. (2008). Informality and regulations: What drives the growth of firms? *IMF Staff Papers, 55*(1). International Monetary Fund. http://www.imf.org

Djankov, S. et al. (2002). The regulation of entry. *The Quarterly Journal of Economics*, *CXVII*(1), 1–37.

Duvanova, D. (2014). British Journal of Political Science/*FirstView* Article/March 2014, pp. 1–24. Doi: 10.1017/S0007123411000457, Published online: 05 Jan 2012.

Freeman, N., et al. (2005). Beyond the headline numbers: Business registration and start up in Vietnam. IFC, MPDF (Mekong private sector development facility), PSDP, (20), 2005.

IIPA (2014). International intellectual property alliance 2014 special 301 report.

International Finance Corporation & World Bank. (2013). Doing business, measuring business regulations. http://www.doingbusiness

Kelly, S., Cook, S., & Truong, M. (Eds.) (2012). *Freedom the Net 2012, A global Assessment of internet and digital media*. Freedom House. http://www.freedomhouse.org/sites/default/files/resources/FOTN%202012%20Summary%20of%20Findings.pdf. Accessed 2 Feb 2014.

Kenyon, T. (2007). *A framework for thinking about enterprise formalization policies in developing countries*. World Bank Policy Research Working Paper No. 4235. http://papers.ssrn.com/sol3/papers.cfm?abstract_id=988845

Lagos, R. A. (1995). Formalizing the informal sector: Costs and barriers. *Development and Change. 26*(1), 111–131.

Moore, S. F. (1978). *Law as process: An anthropological approach*. London: Routledge & Kegan Paul.

Rosefeld, R. A. (1984). An expression and application of Kaufman's model of red tape: The case of community's development to block grants. *Western Political Quarterly*, *37*, 603–620.

Smart, C. (1989). *Feminism and the power of law*. London: Routledge.

Tenev, S. et al. (2003). Informality and the playing field in Vietnam's business sector. Washington, DC: IFC, World Bank, and MPDF. www.ifc.org/wps/connect/9 aae680047ad-b52f9311f7752622ff02/VN-informality-playing field-VN.pdf

WB-IFC (2013). Doing business, measuring business regulations. World Bank and International Finance Corporation. http://www.doingbusiness. Accessed 2 May 2014.

Chapter 5
Social and Technological Forces Supporting Piracy

5.1 The General Profile of the Piracy Traders

In the Philippines, the optical media piracy trade is dominated and controlled by a minority ethnic group—the Maranaos—while in Vietnam, it is controlled by a majority ethnic group—the Vietnamese or Kinh. Both groups are generally socialized in trading and have strong trade connections inside and outside their respective countries. Given the illegal nature of this trade, these groups are in a better position compared to other ethnic groups in the country to engage in illegal trade. Although only comprising a small minority in the Philippines, the Maranaos are the biggest group of Muslims in the Philippines in terms of population. And the Maranaos as Muslims are also generally stereotyped by a great majority of the Christian population (55 %) in the Philippines as belligerent, prone to violence, and, therefore, dangerous according to 2006 Pulse Asia nationwide survey. With this negative image, Christians would not be surprised if some Muslims would engage in a dangerous and illegal undertaking such as counterfeiting and piracy. The case of the Kiln or Vietnamese traders is quite different with regard to their involvement and leadership in the counterfeit or media piracy trade. The Kiln traders belong to the majority ethnic group in Vietnam who controls formal and informal trading in the country. According to informants, one cannot engage on lucrative trade, especially if it is illegal and if she/he does not speak Vietnamese. Vietnamese is the language of traders in Vietnam. Moreover, Kiln traders have strong formal and informal networks with fellow traders and government bureaucrats and law enforcers to engage in the informal business of optical media piracy.

What is common to both traders in the Philippines and Vietnam is their partnership and alliance with ethnic Chinese traders in the country who serve as a mediating network that links Filipino and Vietnamese piracy producers, distributors, and retailers with the piracy network in mainland China, the counterfeit and piracy capital of the world and the number one exporter of counterfeit goods and piracy replication technologies in the world.

V.O. Ballano, *Sociological Perspectives on Media Piracy in the Philippines and Vietnam*, DOI 10.1007/978-981-287-922-6_5

5.1.1 The Producers–Suppliers

As already mentioned, the leaders of the informal optical media trade in the Philippines are Maranao Muslims, while in Vietnam, the leaders are the Kiln. These two ethnic groups, though different in their political and social status in society, possess what it takes to engage in illegal trade such as the optical media piracy. These groups can be considered as "ethnic mafias." Ethnic resources such as common heritage and language, kinship ties, as well as their long experience in informal and counterfeit business enable piracy traders to pursue their business despite its illegality.

Contrary to many media reports, the direct producers–suppliers of pirated optical media discs in the Philippines and Vietnam are not really the gun-toting criminal syndicates or extremist groups portrayed in the mass media or movies who kill people who try to block their way. Neither are they extremist Muslim groups who control the illegal trade to finance terrorism as portrayed by some U.S. military or antipiracy organizations, nor do they belong to the Chinese or Hong Kong triads. Those who control the illegal optical media piracy are "ethnic mafias" rather than an organized group of criminals. In the Philippines, those who control the optical piracy trade are migrant Maranao Muslims who have strong and cohesive networks of relatives in the Quiapo Barter Trade Center Complex (QBTCC) and who became rich through long years of hard work and participation in informal trading in the area. Because of their growing wealth and affiliation with some top fellow Muslim politicians, they have slowly established strong political connection and social network in the government. According to key informants, some of these producers–suppliers are educated Muslims who even occupy some top government posts. Some are former commanders of a Moro armed group who surrendered to the government and were given amnesty and appointed in government by a former Philippine president as a gesture of peace and reconciliation for Muslims in Mindanao in the 1990s.

Producers are generally based in Quiapo, since the center of operations for optical disc piracy is best suited in a strategic urban center like Manila, although some have urban residence in Metro Manila and provincial residence in Lanao. According to a Muslim community organizer, rich producers in the enclave are not ostentatious of their wealth and affleunt lifestyle. Since the trade is labeled by law as illegal, they prefer to be anonymous in their business and social activities. Since the informal optical media duplication business requires a big capital, producers are said to be silent millionaires who have powerful connections in the government and law enforcement agencies.

In Vietnam, the producers, distributors, and big retailers of pirated optical media discs are Vietnamese or Kiln who possess strong connections with some top government bureaucrats and law enforcers in the country. Vietnamese traders are in the best position to engage in the piracy trade than the minority ethnic groups in Vietnam. The minority groups live in remote and mountainous areas in Vietnam.

The Chinese traders in the Philippines and Vietnam serve as the intermediary network that connects both countries to the mainland China, the global hub of piracy goods in the world. The local Chinese traders generally do not directly involve themselves in the direct distribution and retail of pirated optical media in the country. They usually act as middlemen between traders–suppliers in mainland China and Maranao traders in Manila. The foreign Chinese traders act as suppliers of high-quality pirated optical media discs, technology, and replicating equipment and manpower to operate an illegal optical disc factory. The local Chinese traders can also act as suppliers of raw materials and paraphernalia for manufacturing and packaging of pirated optical media discs. If foreign traders do operate directly in the manufacturing of illegal optical disc plants, they oftentimes partner with local traders who know the business environment and law enforcement system in the country. Both the Philippines and Vietnam have established colonies of Chinese traders: Binondo in the Philippines and Cholon in Vietnam's Chinatown in Ho Chi Minh City which act as intermediaries between the mainland China and the local underground economy.

The United States Trade Representative (USTR) office and the International Intellectual Property Alliance (IIPA) have consistently placed China as the largest exporter of illegal replicating technologies and pirated goods such as counterfeit optical media containing copyrighted film, music, computer, and business software. Leading in the USTR and IIPA Special 301 Priority Watch List and Watch List are Southeast Asian countries such as the Philippines and Vietnam which have historical ties and trade relations with China. Vietnam shares borders with China and has a long history of trading partnership with the country. The Philippines may be far away from China, but its trade ties with the country started as early as the tenth century when the first Filipino traders, the Mindoro traders, first established trading relations with the Chinese Emperor in mainland China before the Spanish colonization in the late sixteenth century. During this same era, the Philippines had also started establishing trade connections with Vietnam which was known then as Champa. In short, there were already preexisting trading structures and relations between China, the Philippines, and Vietnam which were long been established in the past which serve as the fertile ground for the informal and counterfeit trade to flourish in the local economy.

5.1.2 The Sellers

As already mentioned, the optical disc piracy trade in the Quiapo Barter Trade Center in Manila and its distribution networks is primarily a Maranao Muslim trade. The author's informal survey in the area and interviews with key informants revealed that around 90 % of the sellers in Quiapo are Maranao Muslims and only around 10 % are Maguindanao Muslims and Christians. Christian traders and retailers buy pirated discs and goods from the Maranao producers and distributors. Outside the Quiapo piracy hub, the sellers may not be Maranaos. In one municipality far from Quiapo, for instance, the distributors and retailers are Maguindanao Muslims and a few from other Muslim groups.

There are two major classifications of sellers in Quiapo with regard to legality, regardless of the quantity of illegal discs they sell. The first group of sellers are those who occupy legal spaces or who sell in rented space or stalls. The second group are the ambulant vendors who occupy the sidewalks of Quiapo illegally. Those who occupy legal spaces are mostly former members of the defunct Rajah Sulaiman Traders' Association, an association of Muslim traders which was given a legal personality by virtue of a law transforming Quiapo into a barter center. Because of the rapid expansion of the optical disc piracy trade, other sellers started to lease private retail spaces within the association's vending area. These sellers who occupy legal spaces do not usually experience harassment from the local police. But the ambulant vendors are regularly harassed by the law enforcers especially if they do not pay the regular "tong" (bribe). Since they sell illegal goods in illegal spaces, they are expected by some unscrupulous police to pay a daily protection money or a monthly bribe—if Maranaos—through their leaders in Maranao Muslim associations called "agamas" in the area.

The hawkers or sidewalk vendors are usually selling counterfeit discs and goods in makeshift stalls along the streets of Quiapo. They generally sell fewer discs compared to those in legal spaces. They are the most harassed group of sellers as they are illegally squatting on public spaces as well as selling illegal goods.

5.2 The Piracy Traders in the Philippines

The Maranao Muslims are said to control the optical media piracy trade in the Philippines. The word "Maranao" which means "people of the lake" are one of the major Muslim ethnolinguistic groups in Mindanao. Their territory straddles the modern-day provinces of Lanao de Norte, Lanao del Sur, and Misamis Oriental, in northwestern Mindanao, some 7000 km south of Manila. They are concentrated in Lanao del Sur which comprises an estimated 91.5 % of the province's population. In Lanao de Norte, they constitute 36 % of its population (Gonzales 1999, p. 95).

Historically, it was during the American period that Maranao Muslims began visiting Manila. American programs, education, training, political development, and some degree of tolerance to Islam encouraged the Muslims to visit Manila and for the first time became legislators (Casambre 1969). While in Manila, some Maranao students, politicians, and delegates visited the Quiapo Muslim enclave from time to time while studying or working in the legislative department. Despite this development, anti-Muslim policies continued after the American period and pushed the Maranaos from self-sufficiency to impoverishment. In Lanao del Sur, for instance, where the Maranao population is concentrated, 63.9 % of the population live below the poverty line. Of the 37 towns in the province, 32 are classified as sixth-class municipalities, reflecting low tax revenues and poor facilities (Gonzales 1999, p. 95). According to key informants, poverty and the lingering war in Lanao between government troops and Muslim secessionist groups during the Marcos era became a major push factor which drove Maranao Muslims to Manila, particularly to the Quiapo Barter Trade Center Complex (QBTCC), to engage in informal trade as an alternative livelihood. Through hard work and solidarity with other Muslim traders, they gradually control the informal trade of optical disc piracy in the area.

The Maranao control of the optical disc trade network in Quiapo did not happen instantly. According to informants, the Maranao traders started as the leading informal traders of legal goods in the area. They even founded the Rajah Sulaiman Traders' Association in 1979. When the Quiapo enclave was designated as a barter zone, that is, an area where barter goods are exempt from taxes or custom duties by virtue of Presidential Decree 93 issued by President Marcos, the Maranaos intensified their sale of imported merchandise in the trade center (Hassan 1983, p. 83). But toward the latter part of the 1990s, according to informants, with the advent of movies in Betamax and VHS formats and thereafter followed by the VCD format which was fueled by the popularity of video recorders and players in the local market, the Maranaos started mixing their legal goods with counterfeit videos in the Quiapo Barter Trade Center area. With the advent of digital technology and the rising demand for pirated discs in the late 1990s, the Maranaos started concentrating on selling pirated CD and VCD discs and replicating some of their copyrighted content using digital copiers and burners to supplement their imported discs. Then, the Maranao traders expanded their informal business operations and started to improve the quality of their pirated discs by buying sophisticated computer disc duplicators and printers abroad or in big computer establishments in the country.

The Maranaos, according to informants, are basically socialized as informal traders. They travel a lot to engage in trade not only within the country but also in neighboring Muslim-dominated countries to buy and sell dry goods. They travel to nearby Southeast Asian (SEA) countries with fellow Muslim traders to import merchandise items such as cigarettes, clothes, carpets, and counterfeit goods and sell them in the Philippines, particularly in the Quiapo Barter Trade Center. Because of their travels and acquaintances with other Muslim traders abroad as well as acquaintances with other Muslims in their yearly pilgrimage to Mecca, some Maranao traders of Quiapo were able to establish contacts with other Muslim merchants in Southeast Asia, especially those in Malaysia and Indonesia, two known exporters and distributors of counterfeit goods and optical media discs in the late 1990s and early 2000s.

At the core of the Quiapo piracy network are the few rich Maranao families who are said to control the lucrative and illegal business from preproduction to postproduction. They also control the distributorship of pirated discs inside and outside the barter trade center, including its nationwide marketing network. Outside the core are other Muslim traders especially Maguindanao traders who participate covertly in the distribution networks of the business through some of the local Muslim associations in local government units. At the periphery of the network are Christian retailers who have relatives and contacts with Muslims in the piracy business. Informants estimated that around 80 % of the optical media piracy trade is controlled by Maranao and Maguindanao Muslims and around 20 % by Christians. Most Christian retailers have relatives who have intermarried with Muslim traders and thus became involved in the informal trade. But with high profit offered by the piracy retail trade, more Christian informal retailers who have no direct relatives with Muslim traders joined the trade, purchasing their pirated discs and goods directly from Muslim traders in Quiapo Barter Trade Center Complex (Fig. 5.1).

Fig. 5.1 Some of the pirated DVDs and CDs sold in many stalls inside a compound in Quiapo Barter Trade Center Complex (QBTCC) after the area was ordered closed by Mayor Lim and the OMB in 2011. Many stores in QBTCC continued to sell pirated discs to retailers and direct buyers after the closure but with CCTV cameras and security guards to prevent law enforcers from entering the clandestine compounds in the area (Image courtesy of the author)

5.3 The Piracy Traders in Vietnam

Like the Philippines, Vietnam is also a multicultural country. The Vietnamese government classifies people into 54 ethnic groups based on language, territories, lifestyle, and cultural heritage. These ethnic groups can be divided into two major groups: the ethnic majorities and ethnic minorities. The ethnic majorities are concentrated in inland deltas and coastal areas. They have political and economic power and are generally richer than minority groups, with easy access to infrastructure, health services, and education. The most dominant ethnic majority group is called "Viet" or "Kinh," which constitutes 86 % of the population of about 84 million. This is followed by the "Hoa" or Chinese (Imai and Gaiha 2007, p. 3). Being the most influential ethnic groups, the Viets and the Chinese are in the best position to engage in formal and informal trade in Vietnam. According to informants, one must know the Vietnamese language to engage in business in Vietnam. It is an important business and cultural tool for those who want to engage in trade in a country dominated by Kiln. The minority ethnic groups which are found in the remote areas of Vietnam speak languages not comprehensible to Vietnamese traders.

The optical disc traders in Vietnam belong to the ethnic Chinese and Kiln who are familiar with the general business environment of the country. The big optical disc traders are top manufacturers or owners of factories of pirated discs who are often in network with big-time counterfeit Chinese traders. These people usually have strong connections in the government bureaucracy and with the underworld of the *Giang ho* groups operating in illegal and protection rackets in the districts. They are followed in the business hierarchy by the big distributors who sell pirated discs in boxes to CD – DVD shops as well as to small retailers. According to informants, there is one area or street in Ho Chi Minh City which is lined up with CD–DVD distribution outlets, similar to the Quiapo piracy network, which sell pirated discs in boxes to those who ordered them in advance. Through mobile phones, owners of CD–DVD retail stores are able to order new titles from the distributors and pick the discs from this area.

The largest group of Kiln optical media traders in Vietnam are the retailers. They are the owners of big CD–DVD shops or small, family-owned CD–DVD shops. Big retailers hire employees, while small retailers usually have family members as salespersons or employees. With the current policy of the government to formalize business and simplify registration of businesses, CD–DVD shops in Vietnam are registered but operate informally by selling pirated discs. The poorest group of pirated disc retailers in Vietnam is the migrant Kiln traders who engage in sidewalk and mobile vending of CDs and DVDs in some roads in Ho Chi Minh, Hanoi, and other big cities. The number of sidewalk vendors has significantly decreased with the issuance of a government decree banning sidewalk vending in certain districts and thoroughfares of Vietnam. In one of the author's tours and observational studies in Ho Chi Minh City, his guide and informant was surprised that the sidewalks which used to be full of vendors of pirated discs were no longer there. According to this guide, the absence of semi-mobile vendors in some roads of the city is probably due to a series of laws and decrees enacted by the government to clear the sidewalks of obstacles. To reclaim the sidewalk for pedestrians, especially for tourists, and to improve city aestheticism, the capital city Hanoi banned street vendors from 62 streets within its inner city in 2008. Similarly, Ho Chi Minh City also implemented a law (Decision 74) requiring licenses for all temporary uses of the sidewalk (Sung 2011, pp. 11–12). Hanoi's resolution 02/2008/QD UBND2008 effectively bans street vendors from a total of 62 selected streets and 48 public spaces in Hanoi (Turner and Schoenberger 2012, p. 3). On top of Hanoi and Ho Chi Minh's ordinances against sidewalk vending, Prime Minister Nguyen Tan Dung issued a decree dated March 16, 2007 (Decree No 39/2007/NĐ-CP), which requires street vendors, small merchants, shoeshine boys, barbers, and lottery sellers to register for a license and prohibits them to run their business at historical, cultural, or religious sites, state offices, diplomatic corps, international organizations, international border gates, airports, railway stations, bus stations, schools, hospitals, and pavements (Vietnam News 2007). Piracy retailers who obviously sell illegal goods were greatly affected by these decrees which require licenses for small businesses and prohibit the use of sidewalks and other public places for vending. This is one main reason why semi mobile vendors are scarce in Ho Chi Minh City and other major Vietnamese cities. Many have become mobile retailers, constantly moving from one place to another to avoid law enforcers, either by personally offering pirated discs to tourists and pedestrians or using mobile vending pushcarts or motorbikes to peddle their pirated goods to people on the streets.

5.4 Factors Fueling the Piracy Trade in the Philippines

The relational approach of the actor–network theory (ANT) sees the social structure in terms of heterogeneous networks of human and nonhuman actors interacting with the various social forces and intermediaries that constitute a social reality. By thinking in terms of network, ANT gets rid of the tyranny of distance or proximity: elements which are close when disconnected may be infinitely remote depending on circumstances. Similarly, elements which appear as infinitely distant or unconnected are in fact close when their connections are analyzed and brought back into the picture (Latour 1996). The current enforcement approach of the government and antipiracy lobbying groups with regard to the persistence of media piracy often overlooks the socioeconomic forces which drive people to engage in the illegal optical disc trade. Applying the relational approach of ANT, what seems to be irrelevant in understanding the persistence of media piracy becomes relevant when one considers the interconnection and significance of some macro and micro forces which sustain it. Thus, what is going on in the poor provinces in the Philippines and Vietnam can be relevant in understanding the persistence of the optical media trade in urban centers. Beyond the popular view that the sale of illegal optical discs continues because of their cheap price, this section examines how some macro forces or the main "push" and "pull" drive people in the Philippines and Vietnamese to engage and persist in the illegal optical media piracy.

5.4.1 Push Factors of Optical Disc Piracy

The great majority of people who engage in illegal and informal business of counterfeit CDs and DVDs in the Philippines are neither armed criminals nor members of extremist groups but poor Maranao Muslim migrants. Many studies suggest that people who lack resources and social connections in the city usually resort to informal business as a means of livelihood. Some studies indicate that migrants in urban areas can be characterized by higher labor force participation rates, lower unemployment rates, and a higher participation in the informal sector than urban natives (e.g., Castañeda 1993; Leibovich 1996). The underground economy which does not follow the usual legal requirements and procedures provides migrant entrepreneurs the cheapest way to start a livelihood in an alienating environment of the city.

According to key informants, there is a positive correlation between the increase of Maranao migrants' engagement in optical disc piracy in Quiapo, Metro Manila, and other parts of the country with the unstable peace and the deteriorating peace and order situation in Muslim Mindanao. The increase of Maranao in-migration due to war in Mindanao has also considerably risen the number of retailers and distributors of optical discs in the country. The counterfeit optical media business—being easy and cheap to establish with its distribution and production being controlled by fellow Maranaos—is, thus far, the most convenient livelihood to new Maranao migrants according to informants. With the aid of relatives and co-ethics who are already connected with the piracy business network, a neophyte migrant trader can easily begin his/her own retail network with a very minimal capital.

Key informants cite four major factors which pushed the Maranaos and other Muslims groups to leave Mindanao and join the informal and illegal business of selling counterfeit CDs and DVDs. In general, what drives thousands of Maranao Muslims and their allied Maguindanao traders to engage in optical disc media piracy are the adverse economic, social, and political conditions in a Christian-dominated country like the Philippines. The push factors include (1) the precarious peace and order in the Autonomous Region of Muslim Mindanao (ARMM); (2) the massive poverty and the continuing armed conflict between the secessionist groups and Armed Forces of the Philippines (AFP); (3) the social discrimination and anti-Muslim bias in Philippine society, a major noneconomic spillover of the Mindanao war and of the prevailing campaign against terrorism sponsored by the United States; as well as (4) the exclusion of Muslims in business law as well as the complex, time-consuming, and expensive legal requirements in starting a legitimate optical media trade in the country. This section will illustrate how these factors facilitate the enrollment and participation of the Maranao Muslims in the illegal and informal business of producing, distributing, and selling of counterfeit CDs and DVDs in the Philippines.

5.4.1.1 Migration and Conflict in Muslim Mindanao

While it is true that the search for "greener pastures" to escape poverty is a primary factor in Maranao Muslim migration, it is also equally certain that many were driven out of Lanao because of the precarious peace and order situation in the province. The war in Mindanao, often mentioned by key informants of the study, is a primary push factor that forces the Maranaos of Lanao Province and other Maranao-dominated towns and cities to leave their hometowns and migrate to Metro Manila and other urban centers in the Philippines. Says Maranao writer Busan-Yao:

> The conflict in Muslim Mindanao, particularly in Lanao del Sur, spans decades, even centuries, and is complex, deeply rooted and multifaceted. Its long history has brought tremendous economic losses, displacement, pain, humiliation and deep trauma to those affected. And more than the economic costs which are so high that they have affected the entire Philippines, it is the social costs that have almost systematically destroyed the lives of the people directly affected—the Moros. (Busran-Yao 2006, p. 1)

The migration of Muslims from Southern Mindanao to various parts in the Philippines can be traced back to the American period. Adverse government policies which allowed the migrant Christians to take over the ancestral lands of the Muslims in Mindanao forced Moros to leave their homeland and migrate to other places. The first wave of massive migration of Muslims, particularly involving Maranaos, occurred between 1972 and 1976, during the martial law years in the country, with the precarious peace and order in Lanao (Matuan 1983). During this period, Nur

Misuari's Moro National Liberation Front (MNLF) and Bangsamoro Army became the biggest threats to national security. The MNLF attacked Marawi City shortly after martial law was declared and Muslim separatism spread to other parts of the Mindanao–Sulu–Palawan region (Hernandez 2006, p. 3). The war between Muslim separatists and government forces had displaced many Muslims from their ancestral lands and eventually forced them to live as migrants in urban centers.

This continuous displacement of people came as a result of bombing and armed conflict between the Muslim secessionist groups and government soldiers. Its increase over time coincides with the declaration of an all-out war waged by the Philippine government against Muslim rebels. In August 2008, the total number of people displaced in conflict areas of Mindanao, for instance, reached 452,258, 85 % of which are Muslim, as a result of President Estrada's "all-out-war" policy against the Moro Islamic Liberation Front (MILF) rebels. Though this number had subsided to 44,532 in 2004, it nevertheless started to rise from 2005 up to the present with government's renewed efforts to subdue these rebels.[1] With the breakdown of the memorandum of agreement (MOA) between the Moro Islamic Liberation Front (MILF) and Philippine government on the issue of ancestral land in 2008, intense fighting between the MILF, led by Commander Bravo and government soldiers in the Autonomous Region of Muslim Mindanao (ARMM), displaced an estimated 296,000 people. The numbers are still increasing. Clearly, the struggle of Muslims including Maranaos in Mindanao is embedded in the overall struggle of the Moros against government policies and anti-Muslim programs. This Moro struggle has a long historical root that traces back to the Spanish and American colonialists' efforts to subjugate the Muslims into their fold with the aid of Christian Filipino allies (Busran-Yao 2006, p. 2).

The Maranao Muslims, the key traders of the informal trade of optical media in the Philippines, are the leading Muslim group in this displacement process. The 2005 Philippine Human Development Report shows that Lanao, the main hometown province of the Maranaos, is among the Muslim provinces most affected by the ongoing conflict between the government and Moro rebels. The Mindanao conflict has continually displaced thousands of Maranaos from their hometowns. The spillover of the conflict is manifested in the number of Maranaos who now live in diasporas throughout the country. In 2005 alone, thousands of Maranao fled Lanao and migrated to various regions of the country to escape the horrors of war between the MILF and the government soldiers. The Maranao, or "people of the Lake (i.e., *ranao*)," comprise the largest Muslim group who live in the plains around Lake Lanao. They are among the most devout and most traditional of the Muslim groups (PHDR 2005, p. 20). Though some of them travel around the country and neighboring Southeast Asian countries to engage in trade, they are basically described as extremely clannish and family-centered Muslims, and thus many tended to view migration to distant places as disruptive of family ties and relationships.

[1] http://www.internaldisplacement.org/8025708F004CE90B/(httpCountrySummaries)02AFE7CCBB2E41D6C12574A5002DFAF3?OpenDocument&count=10000

The reluctance of the Maranao Muslims to leave their homeland was, however, overcome by some inevitable "push" factors that forced them and other Muslims to migrate as far as the National Capital Region (NCR). One of such factors was the loss of livelihood caused by the constant bombardment between government soldiers and Muslim separatists in Muslim areas. The deteriorating peace and order situation in Muslim Mindanao, particularly that of Lanao, forced the Maranaos to migrate to Luzon and the Visayas to avoid the war and to search for better economic opportunities. In 1984, for instance, the estimated number of Maranao migrants in Manila alone was between 30,000 and 35,000. After the Marcos years, the Maranaos moving to Manila continued to increase. Though there were efforts during the Aquino and Ramos administrations to minimize military offensives and extend amnesty to separatists to avoid further exodus of Muslims in search for temporary shelters in urban centers (Hernandez 2006, pp. 4–5), the all-out-war policy of Presidents Estrada and Arroyo against MILF and MNLF has, however, reversed this trend and thus resumed the mass in-migration of Maranaos and other Muslims to other parts of the country. This diaspora has swelled the Maranao and Muslim populations of urban centers in Metro Manila, Baguio City, Cavite Province, and Palawan. In 2005, the number of Maranao migrants throughout the country reached to almost two million, of which 83, 831 are found in Metro Manila (PHDR 2005). A considerable percentage of this Maranao population in the NCR and Manila are found in Culiat, Quezon City, San Miguel, and Quiapo.

The Quiapo Barter Trade Center Complex, the hub of the optical disc piracy business in the Philippines, became the main destination for migrant Maranaos who wish to join the informal optical media retail piracy trade while in Metro Manila. Although there are no reliable census data, key informants of the study estimated that around 90 % of the Muslim population in the area are Maranao who are mostly engaged in optical disc piracy. The link between migration and ongoing war in Mindanao is direct: the more the war in Mindanao is intensified, the more Maranaos leave their farms and homes and migrate to the NCR or Metro Manila and more likely to engage in the informal optical media trade. The informal business of selling and retailing optical media discs has become the most convenient means of livelihood for Maranao Muslim migrants enrolled in the Quiapo piracy network. The armed conflict in Mindanao has, therefore, driven many Maranao Muslims into the informal sector as illustrated by one story of a Muslim youth recounting his life before and after the war in 2000:

> Before the war of 2000, we had a fairly decent life. My parents could send us to school. The war changed everything—we had to leave our home to live in an evacuation center, my father's health deteriorated, our property had to be sold little by little to meet basic needs, and school became unaffordable. Two of my sisters became sidewalk vendors and I became a motorcycle driver. I still do not have a regular source of income.[2]

[2] Excerpt from an individual interview at http://www.internal-displacement.org/8025708F004CE90B/(httpDocuments)/2CE5CACB40B55CD1C1257288004C3B25/$file/WP35_Web.pdf0

The unstable peace and order in conflict areas has disrupted the livelihood of Muslims in the area. Nasser Dimalidseg, one villager, illustrates vividly the effect of war on the livelihood of Muslims:

> Evacuating and conflict is very tiring. Whenever new armed groups enter our communities, tensions immediately mount. The community becomes unstable even if violent confrontations do not occur yet. We are always in a constant state of alertness and our deep fright prevents us from engaging in farming or other forms of livelihood. How can we sustain any economic activity? They always barge into our communities when it's harvest season. At any rate, gunfire exchange soon erupts and we are forced to leave everything. (World Bank 2003, p. 8)

The war is an important contributory cause of poverty in Muslim region aside from the apparent neglect of the government to uplift the economic life of the Muslims in Mindanao. Poverty, in turn, also contributes to the continuation of the war. Some Moros joined the secessionist movement and fight the government because of poverty and government indifference to the economic situation of the Muslims. The story of a 10-year-old Muslim girl illustrates how the war in Mindanao has dispersed Muslim families and forced some of them to work as informal vendors:

> The war wrecked our home. My father abandoned us in the evacuation center. My mother worked in the market as tobacco vendor. My eldest brother was forced to work hard labor and then as street vendor in Manila. (Busran-Yao 2006, p. 5)

One Maranao informal vendor named Omar Pacasum, 18, revealed that he came to Manila to escape the war in Mindanao. He left Marawi City to get away from the fighting between government troops and rebels seeking to establish an Islamic state in Mindanao, the Southern Philippine region.[3]

The displacement caused by the war in Mindanao has prepared Muslims and Maranaos to migrate elsewhere rather than return to their place of origin after evacuation. One social assessment report on the displaced Muslims in Mindanao sponsored by the World Bank revealed that many of the Muslims who fled their homes and stayed in evacuation centers did not want to return to their place of origin (World Bank 2003). Instead, they migrate to other regions of the country and some joined the illegal informal sector to survive in the city.

5.4.1.2 Poverty in Autonomous Region of Muslim Mindanao

The poor economic condition of Muslim areas in Mindanao is another factor that drives Maranao Muslims out of Mindanao and pushes them to join the informal and illegal optical media piracy trade. The Autonomous Region of Muslim Mindanao (ARMM) which includes the provinces of Maguindanao, Basilan, Sulu, Tawi-Tawi, and Lanao are the poorest regions in the Philippines. In terms of poverty incidence, this region has the highest level of poverty incidence; has a poverty incidence of 62.9 % compared to the national poverty incidence, nearly twice the national

[3] http://www.worldmission.ph/MARCH06/Migration%of%20of%20Muslims.htm

poverty incidence of 34 %; and ranks last or 16th out of the 16 regions (World Bank 2003). Other human indicators of human development in ARMM, particularly areas occupied by Maranaos, were also very low in the study. In terms of income, life expectancy, mortality, and enrollment rate, the ARMM is way below the national average and occupying the bottom of the regional rankings. In particular, Marawi, the capital city of Lanao and the hometown of the Maranaos, is one of the poorest cities in the Philippines. In escape to poverty, Maranaos migrated to urban centers particularly to Metro Manila and joined the informal sector. And many enrolled themselves in the informal and illegal optical disc trade.

Aina, a 30-year-old mother of four children and a Maranao street peddler, for instance, explained that hunger compelled her family to move to Manila from Marawi City, Lanao del Sur Province, some 820 km southeast of Manila. In Marawi, they subsisted on bananas, as well as cassava and other root crops, between rice and corn harvests. At the same market, Asgar, also 30, was selling music and video compact discs. He came to Manila from Iligan City, Lanao del Norte Province, about 25 km north of Marawi. He said that working at the Tandang Sora Market enables him to send money home to his parents.[4]

In Quiapo Barter Trade Center piracy complex, similar sentiments were revealed by some Maranao traders. They said that they were forced to migrate to Manila and sell illegal discs in the enclave because they could not find a formal employment in their hometown in Mindanao. Myrma, 20 years old, for instance, who finished 2 years in high school, said that she became a vendor of counterfeit discs in Manila because she could not land a formal job to support her family in the province:

> Wala na kasi akong mapasukan na trabaho, kapit sa patalim na lang. Kahit alam kung illegal ang tinitinda namin, pero wala akong magawa… kailangan kong kumita.
>
> ("I can't find a job, that's why I just hold on to anything to survive. Even if I know that what we sell is illegal, we cannot do anything about it…I have to earn a living").

Ali, 15 years old, another disc vendor in the barter trade center in Quiapo before it was closed by Mayor Lim, also said that he migrated to Metro Manila a few months ago from Marawi to escape the economic hardship in his hometown. He said it was difficult for him to find a good job in Marawi to support his family. There were not many jobs available for him in the city especially for the youth. So he decided to migrate to Manila and became a vendor of pirated discs with the help of his relatives in Quiapo to support his poor parents and siblings.

5.4.1.3 Anti-Muslim Bias and Social Discrimination

Aside from armed conflict in Mindanao and poverty in the ARMM, key informants of the study also revealed that the prevailing anti-Muslim bias of Christians has also influenced the Muslim participation in the optical disc piracy trade network. This deep-seated bias of Christians against Muslims which is an old issue is the

---

[4] http://www.worldmission.ph/MARCH06/Migration%20%20Muslims.htm

consequence of the failed attempt of the Spanish conquistadors to Christianize and subdue the Muslims in Mindanao during the eighteenth century that resulted in the raiding of the Visayan Christian missions and the enslaving of the newly baptized Christians by Muslims as a retaliation against the Spaniards. The ongoing armed conflict in Mindanao has renewed and even intensified this bias. Beyond the ARMM boundaries, discrimination and exclusion in job hiring, school admission, and house leasing are just few instances (Latiph 2007) that confront Muslims, and Maranaos in particular, in their daily lives that narrow their economic opportunities in the Christian-dominated Philippine society. The 2006 nationwide survey of Pulse Asia [2006, p. xiv] reinforces this when it found that "a considerable percentage of Filipinos (33–39 %) are biased against Muslims."

Indeed, having a Muslim-sounding name can be a source of problems for Muslims in the Philippines. According to the 2006 Pulse Asia survey, the randomly selected respondents were asked to choose between two persons said to be alike in all other relevant aspects, but with one having a Christian name and the other having a Muslim-sounding name. The results showed that respondents were more likely to accept applicants with Christian-sounding names as their male boarder, female domestic helper, and male worker than those with Muslim-sounding names. Greater percentages of those aged 55 years or over tended to choose the person with Christian name than those below 35 years of age. Interestingly, less than 10 % in Luzon would choose the person with Muslim-sounding name as their boarder, domestic helper, and worker.

According to some Maranao informants in the study, their Muslim names became a hindrance when they applied for formal jobs. Hiring officers upon learning their Muslim identity usually reject their applications. One retailer said that he was forced to lie and changed his Muslim name to a Christian one just to be accepted in a job in the Province of Cavite. This predicament is also experienced by some Maranaos in Culiat, Quezon City, according to a study by De Quiros and Gonzales (2002). Respondent Maranaos claimed that when people in charge of hiring learned that they were Muslims, they would usually tell the applicants that they will have to wait for the company to call them and they never do (De Quiros and Gonzales 2002, p. 18).

Some of the optical disc traders in the Quiapo Barter Trade piracy complex also experienced this prevailing anti-Muslim bias. In the enclave, 90 % of the 27 optical disc retailers interviewed have not finished high school nor have they finished college. The lack of educational attainment is already a barrier for them to land in formal jobs. But having a Muslim doubles this barrier. One Muslim leader, for example, recalled in an interview by the author how his son was rejected in a job application in a mall in Manila just because of his Muslim-sounding name.

Muslim professionals are not spared from this discrimination. One professor narrated:

> My colleague was invited by the UN to present a paper at a UN forum on indigenous peoples in New York. He was barred entry in California because his name is[Muslim-sounding]. (PHDR 2005, p. 53)

Another professional had a different complaint:

> I earn more than P20,000 and a member of my staff earns P14,000. When we both applied for a loan, hers was approved, mine was rejected. I asked the management, "Why are you doing this, when in fact, I am the one signing because as her department head." (PHDR 2005, p. 53)

Muslim women are also not spared from social discrimination. The mere use of the headscarf provoked discrimination. One Muslim woman revealed her experience:

> I used to wear my veil. I always brought my laptop with me and I was always stopped at airports and asked me to open my laptop. Once I tried asking a male colleague to bring my laptop, and no one asked him to open it. (PHDR 2005)

Another Muslim woman recounted her experience of discrimination in Manila:

> My husband and I were waiting for a taxi in Manila and no one would stop. My husband told me to remove my veil. So I had to take off my veil simply because we could not ride a taxi. (PHDR 2005)

This social discrimination of Muslims in Philippine society is also partly caused by the current campaign of the United States, and endorsed by the Philippine government, against terrorism. The "terrorist tag" hounds Filipino Muslims, making it difficult for them to enter the formal sector or participate without bias in the business market. Some informants confirmed this assessment. A trader in Quiapo said that the war against terrorism launched by President George Bush Jr. after the September 11 attack in the United States has exposed Muslims to unjust labeling as terrorists. Whenever something is wrong with Philippine society, the Muslims are often targeted as the usual suspects, laments one Muslim Filipino legislator. Thus, after the September 11 attack in the United States, Muslims around the world have more often than not become targets of profiling and indiscriminate accusations by state authorities and mass media as terrorists and troublemakers. In a nationwide survey conducted by Pulse Asia last March 2006 with 1200 randomly selected respondents, many Filipino Christians think that Muslims are prone to run amok or violence (55 %), while a plurality believe that Muslims are probably terrorists or extremists. Abu Sayyaf (30 %) and Muslims (27 %) are the most oft-cited groups associated with terrorism.

After the September 11, 2001, terrorist attack in New York, Muslims around the world and in the Philippines, in particular, were not only blamed for terrorism but also for the proliferation of illegal optical media discs. The passage of the optical media law upon the instigation of the United States to pattern the local copyright law after the Trade-Related Aspects of Intellectual Property Rights (TRIPS) of the General Agreement on Tariffs and Trade (GATT) under the auspices of the World Trade Organization (WTO) did not, however, lead to the intended democratization of the benefits of a stronger intellectual property protection to stakeholders, consumers, as well as the poor. On the contrary, the updating of the local copyright law and the enactment of the Optical Media Act of 2003 has reinforced the labeling of the Muslims as terrorists and the Maranao Muslims who run the informal optical disc trade in the country as financiers of terrorism. According to an Interpol report prepared for the House Committee on International Relations of the U.S. Congress, intellectual property crimes such as piracy are a growing resource for terrorist groups.[5] This unfounded allegation linking the informal optical media trade to terrorism has intensified anti-American sentiment of the Muslims. According to some Muslim retailers at the QBTCC, the law against "piracy" is created by the Americans, particularly by President Bush, to further oppress the Muslims. Moreover, it has accentuated the distrust of Christians toward Muslims.

A nationwide survey by Pulse Asia in 2006 showed that the mass media (TV, radio, and newspapers) is the main source of Christian Filipinos' knowledge about Muslims, with the television as the foremost source of information (78 %), followed by radio (48 %) and newspapers (29 %). Only 14 % of the responses mentioned that they know about Muslims through personal encounter and interaction. And since media reporting tends to be selective and more often reported from a Christian point of view, one can expect that the knowledge Christians get from media reporting would most likely be incomplete and to some extent biased against Muslims.

One story that illustrates this misconception of Christians about Muslims owing to the lack of personal encounters with them comes from a high-ranking official of a prestigious Mindanao University:

> I was once part of a batch picked to undergo training in Australia, I was told my name was erased, but the phrase Moro Nationalist could be read clearly beside it. (PHDR 2005, p. 53)

The same official once signed a contract with a manager of Pepsi or Coca-Cola in GenSan. The manager met the college dean of education and he said, "You know I met your chancellor, and it's the first time I met a public official who's not crooked. But I find that hard to accept because he's a Muslim, and how come he's not corrupt?" (PHDR 2005, p. 53).

A community organizer in the Quiapo Muslim enclave said that the knowledge of Christians about Muslims originates from biased reports of the media rather than from actual personal experience and interaction with Muslims. For him, most Muslims are good and generous. In fact, he feels more secure and protected when he is among Muslims inside in the enclave. One key informant of the study narrated to the author that one Muslim leader in the Quiapo Muslim enclave hired a Christian domestic helper. And the house helper was said to have been surprised when she knew that her generous employer who extended financial help to her relatives during an emergency despite the fact that she was a Christian is a Muslim. Indeed, her employment in a Muslim home in the enclave made her realize for the first time that Muslims are not really bad as portrayed or implied in many mass media reports.

---

[5] http://www.allbusiness.com/retail-trade/miscellaneous-retail-retail-stores-not/4368051-1.html

5.5 Informal Trading and Overcoming Discrimination

Economists and social scientists differentiate two segments of the urban labor market: the government-regulated "formal sector" which requires a higher level of formal schooling and which consists of the more or less permanently employed in private or public agencies and the "informal sector" which includes a wide variety of activities that are small scale and labor-intensive, with workers who have little formal education and who generally engage in simple manufacturing and processing, services, and retail trade. These activities and enterprises are minimally regulated by the government (Karaos 1985).

As already mentioned in Chap.3, the International Labor Organization defines the informal sector as consisting of "small-scale, self-employed activities (with or without hired workers), typically at a low level of organization and technology, with the primary objective of generating employment and incomes. The activities are usually conducted without proper recognition from the authorities, and escape the attention of the administrative machinery responsible for enforcing laws and regulations."[6] The informal sector therefore generally operates outside the provisions of the law on doing business. It does not pay taxes directly to the government and other registrations and licenses to the national and local government.

The optical disc trade in the enclave generally belongs to the informal sector. The majority of the retailers and distributors of optical discs prefer to operate informally, hiring co-ethics and relatives as workers with generally little formal education and operating with no government licenses and regulations for their sale, distribution, and reproduction of copyrighted optical media and paraphernalia. By going informal and illegal, traders and migrants save a lot of money, effort, and time in rebuilding their lives in the city as an alternative livelihood and passive resistance against social discrimination that denies them of entry to formal jobs and escape from their poverty-stricken and war-torn hometowns in Mindanao.

The anti-Muslim bias has negative consequences to the participation of Muslims in the market and formal employment. Thus, the engagement of some Muslims in the informal optical media trade can also be seen as a strategy to overcome discriminatory employment structure and market or what James Scott (1987) calls as "weapons of the weak." Many retailers interviewed for this study indicated that the informal piracy trade is one of the more convenient means to get a job and livelihood. With their low educational attainment and the prevailing anti-Muslim bias, traders find that looking for a formal job is indeed difficult. A few revealed that their attempts to secure formal jobs proved futile as their Muslim-sounding names became the obvious obstacle. One said that he applied for a construction job, but because of his Muslim name, he was immediately rejected. Instead, he joined the optical disc retail business of his relatives to earn an income.

A study by De Quiros and Gonzales (2002) confirms that majority of Muslims resort to trading (i.e., become vendors in makeshift stalls or locations) because it is

[6] http://www.ilo.org/public/english/region/asro/bangkok/feature/inf_sect.htm

very hard to get a job, especially in the private sector (p. 19). Overall, the Maranao respondents of this study in Metro Manila said that Muslims are having a harder time in finding jobs than the general public. As they say, "yung mga hindi nagtitinda noon (sa Lanao), pagdating dito marunong na" ("those who were not selling before (in Lanao) automatically learn how to sell and trade upon coming to Manila") (De Quiros and Gonzales 2002, p. 19).

The Maranao optical disc traders of Quiapo share this view that informal vending is an alternative means to survive in a discriminatory job market outside their province in Lanao. According to a Muslim leader, a new vendor of pirated discs only needs a few hundred pesos to start his retailing business and livelihood. By buying a few discs from fellow Muslim distributors, new entrepreneurs can start their optical media business informally by selling VCDs or DVDs personally or directly to people with almost 50 % assured profit. Being self-employed, they are spared from the difficulties of applying for a formal job in the city. They also need not pretend to be Christians in order to be employed formally.

5.6 Factors Facilitating the Piracy Trade in Vietnam

While most forces which facilitate optical media piracy in the Philippines are more of push factors that drive Maranao Filipino traders to engage in the infringement trade, the social forces that encourage the piracy trade in Vietnam are more of pull factors that lure Vietnamese and Chinese traders into the informal and illegal copyright business. Unlike Filipino piracy traders who are poor, displaced by war, and forced by circumstance to engage in the illegal business to survive in urban centers, the Vietnamese traders are generally in duress to engage in the illegal trade of piracy for subsistence purposes. Those who engage in piracy for subsistence are only the migrant sidewalk vendors who peddle pirated discs to survive in Vietnamese cities. Vietnamese traders belong to the majority groups—the Kiln and Hoa who are relatively well-off and experienced traders in the country. Thus, while the main motive for the great majority traders in the Philippines is subsistence or earning a livelihood despite all odds, the primary motive among the Vietnamese traders is more on profit and the promise of higher return of investment (ROI) offered by the piracy trade. The Vietnamese traders, especially the owners of CD–DVD shops who belong to the top ethnic groups, enjoy a relatively "friendly" and peaceful environment to engage and maintain their counterfeit business.

5.6.1 The Informal Sector in Vietnam

Like the Philippines, Vietnam also has a high and vibrant informal sector, informal employment, as well as a thriving optical media piracy trade. The issue of migration is also relevant in accounting its significant increase of informal workers and traders joining the informal and illegal piracy trade.

According to Cling et al. (2010), 82 % of employment in Vietnam can be defined as informal. Workers can be found in the informal and "formal sectors." At the national level, manufacturing and construction is the largest informal economy (43 % of total employment, followed by trade at 31 % and services at 26 %). If the self-employed (own-account workers and employers) were classified as informal, informal work would constitute 86 % of the total employment in Vietnam.

A defining aspect of Vietnam's economic development is large-scale rural–urban migration. A significant proportion of migrants are employed in the industry, a driving force of Vietnam's postsocialist transition and integration into the global economy (Arnold 2013, p. 469).

Prior to 2007, statistical information on the informal economy is scarce in Vietnam. A brief review of the literature reveals that studies in the past on the informal sector are based on ad hoc partial surveys that cover only a few hundred businesses concentrated in certain sectors and provinces that differ on the study in question (Giang and Thu 1999; Dang Doanh and Minh Tu 1997; Jensen and Peppard 2003; Tenev et al. 2003; Bernabe and Krstic 2005; Taussig and Hang 2004). None of these studies investigated the informal sector based on a broader perspective using the international definition of the ILO.

The first comprehensive studies that examined the informal sector in Vietnam took place in 2007 with the Labor Force Survey (LFS2007) and the Household Business and Informal Sector Survey (HB&IS 2007/2008), both conducted in Hanoi and Ho Chi Minh City (HCMC). The LFS2007 survey showed that the informal sector accounts for almost 11 million jobs out of a total of 46 million in Vietnam, representing nearly a quarter of all main occupations (23.5 %), with nearly half of nonfarm work found in the informal sector or 12.4 million jobs if main and secondary jobs are added. The HB&IS survey also revealed that there are 8.4 million informal household businesses in Vietnam, of which 7.4 million are held by a head of the household (HB) in their main job and 1 million in their second job (Cling et al. 2012, p. 16).

Although Vietnam is the only Southeast Asian country that did not go into recession in 2009, all macroeconomic indicators showed that the yearly growth of the country is affected by the crisis. The GDP slowed down from 8.5 in 2007 to 6.3 in 2008 and then 5.3 in 2009 before recovering to 6.5 in 2010. A study sponsored by GSO-ISSS/IRD-DIAL in 2010 on the informal sector in Hanoi and Ho Chi Minh City showed that the employment growth in the informal sector has been increased by the 2008–2009 economic crisis. Between 2007 and 2009, the number of jobs in the informal sector increased by 56,000 in Hanoi (+6 %) and by 2,006,000 in HCMC (+19 %). The diminution of the rate of formalization of household-based (HB) businesses also indicated a growing informalization of the economy due to the crisis. The formal HB in Hanoi in 2009 is 15.2 % compared to 19.5 % in 2007. In HCMC, the decrease is even greater, from 25.4 % in 2007 to 17.6 % in 2009 (GSO-ISSS-DIAL 2010, pp. 3–4).

5.6.1.1 Tracing the Development of Vietnam's Informal Sector

Vietnam's economy has two different structures since communism was established in the country. The northern part is essentially socialist in structure with communist leaders being stationed in Hanoi. The richer southern part which is more agricultural and closely linked to Chinese borders is basically a free market system. Saigon, later renamed Ho Chi Minh City (HCMC), became its center for free enterprise trade. After the French were defeated in 1954, the colonial apparatus was removed, and the noncommunist Republic of South Vietnam was established with Saigon and its Chinatown, Cholon, as the administrative, industrial, and commercial hub of the country. By being a client state of the United States and with the presence of almost half a million U.S. and allied servicemen during the Vietnam War, free market capitalism and petty enterprise further flourished in the South. Market capitalism, particularly petty trading in the informal sector, did not halt with the occupation of the South by the communists in April 1973 and the renaming of Saigon–Cholon in honor of the revolutionary leader and hero of the North, Ho Chi Minh. The economic policies and enforcement apparatus of the communists were aimed at the medium-sized and large-scale private sector and not the petty-enterprise sector. The strict application of Stalinist ideology by General Secretary Le Duan from 1960 until 1986 with the introduction of a series of heavy-handed decrees and hard-line economic policies is said to have brought the economy to a halt: elimination or confiscation of formal-sector private enterprises, stringent control of finance and banking, and, in some areas, rapid, forced collectivization of agriculture. These draconian measures, however, actually laid the groundwork for the informal sector to survive and even expand before the *Doi Moi* policy was introduced in 1986 (Freeman 1996).

5.6.1.2 Doi Moi and the Turning Point of the Informal Sector

Vietnam shifted to a free market economy and moved away from socialist economic policies, realizing that centralized planning of the economy in Hanoi has disastrous effects to the economy. In the late 1980s, Vietnam faced a formidable economic challenge: a high inflation rate, a persistent budget imbalance, a heavy dependence on imports and foreign assistance, and an international economic embargo resulting from its occupation of Kampuchea (Szalontai 2008, p. 201).

During the Sixth National Party Congress in 1986, the National Assembly adopted a new Five-Year Plan that advocates reforms and dismantles existing economic management in order to encourage initiatives in production and trade (Williams 1992, p. 46). This is the dawn of *Doi Moi* or economic renovation in Vietnam. This new program represents a sustained attack on the old model of centrally planned economy and a new thrust toward liberalization and free market economy. The main objectives of *Doi Moi* are to improve productivity, raise living standards, and curb rapid inflation, which reached almost 500 % a year in the mid-1980s. It aimed to reestablish a multisector economy driven by private enterprise under government supervision and to increase foreign investment, curtailed during the United Nations embargo after Vietnam invaded Cambodia in 1978–1979 (Freeman 1996, p. 1).

The *Doi Moi* was not the beginning of informal sector in Vietnam but its turning point. The informal sector in Vietnam originated from a large shadow economy that operated outside the control of the communist government during the decade after the Vietnam War. This was composed mainly of unregulated, often family-oriented commercial and peasant enterprises, financiers, currency traders, and smugglers. This sector provided vital goods and services that sustained Vietnam during the exceptionally bleak years between 1975 and 1986 (Freeman 1996). The *Doi Moi* has spurred growth of the informal sector. With a sharp reduction of internal trade barriers, liberalization of foreign trade, withdrawal of state subsidies, and a high unemployment caused by retrenchment in government bureaucracy (around 50 % of the cadre jobs in cooperatives and collectives were sacrificed) (Williams 1992, p. 50), more and more people start to engage in informal trading. Thus, the informal sector of the economy suddenly opened up. Small-scale private enterprises began to flourish in towns. During the first 6 months of 1987 alone, for instance, some 3000 private shops were opened in Ho Chi Minh City, employing around 30,000 workers. Informal traders flock the streets of Hanoi, Ho Chi Minh, as well as the rice fields of the Mekong Delta (Williams 1992, p. 58). Today, informal trade represents the second largest informal industry in Vietnam which eats up 31 % of the total informal employment of the country at the national level (Cling et al. 2010, p. 16).

The introduction of technology trade that laid the ground for the informal optical media trading can be traced to the enactment of a new foreign investment code in December 1987. This new law allowed both joint and wholly owned foreign ventures. It allowed foreigners to hold management posts and repatriation of profits, and above all, it identified high-technology industries as one of the several priority areas for foreign investment (Williams, 1992, p. 51). The introduction of high technologies such as ICTs had laid the ground for the advent of the digital media trade in Vietnam including the informal and illegal optical disc piracy business. It also attracted Vietnamese from the poor towns of Central and Northern Vietnam to migrate to cities and join the informal media trade.

5.6.1.3 Rural–Urban Migration and Participation in the Informal Sector

Vietnam's industrialization has been taking place for the past decade. This resulted in an increasing number of enterprises around cities and creation of dynamic economic zones in different parts of the country and a high demand for labor force in urban areas. In contrast, the rural areas have become less dynamic and now are confronting the imbalance between human resources and land as a consequence of high population growth in the past decades. Thus, more farmers find themselves unemployed and underemployed with the standards of living deteriorating. With a high demand for urban labor and prospect of earning in the cities owing to industrialization, these people migrate to cities, and thus rural–urban migration in Vietnam has been steadily increasing year after year. Cities like Hanoi and Ho Chi Minh and some emerging economic centers have become magnets, pulling people from rural areas to work and settle in urban centers (Cu 2005).

5.6.1.4 Lure of Profits: High Profitability in the Piracy Trade

The illegal optical media trade is twice profitable compared to other legitimate and other small trade in the Philippines and Vietnam. Since the production cost of the illegal discs is much lower, the price of counterfeit CDs and DVDs is also lower than the original ones. The pirated version is always 8 to 10 times lower than the original copy. And traders, whether producers, distributors, or retailers, usually earn 100 % profit. In retail, for instance, informants said that retailers sell their discs twice the price of the buying price. In the Philippines, for instance, one pirated disc (one title only) usually sells around 30 pesos (less than a U.S. dollar). But the buying of this disc is only P15 for retailers. In Vietnam, one retailer said that he bought his discs for 5 Dong each and sells it for 10 Dong, earning 100 % income.

Although both traders in the Philippines and Vietnam experience a high margin of profit, not all, however, have the same motivation why they joined this illegal trade. More than 90 % of traders in the Philippines engage in piracy primarily for survival purposes, especially for the great majority of small retailers, while those in Vietnam, especially for owners of CD–DVD shops, are basically for profit. The majority of piracy retailers in Vietnam are relatively affluent compared to their Philippine counterparts. They either own or rent the store space for their CD–DVD shops, but in the Philippines, the majority of retailers are poor mobile or sidewalk vendors who use makeshift stalls to sell pirated discs.

5.7 Technological Networks for Piracy

The informal optical media trade is a digital and complex form of deviance which cannot be done without the indispensible cooperation of information and computer technologies. The access of the traders to the latest technology makes unauthorized reproduction and distribution of copyrighted optical media easier and faster. Technologies used for the informal trade can mediate actors or networks of actors with divergent viewpoints. They can act as an interface among bounded social worlds—allowing for the productive communication between these distinct social worlds (Strauss 1978, 1984; Star 1989). Technology, therefore, in this sense is a "boundary breaker" (Green 2001) that allows divergent networks to communicate and to merge.

One major boundary breaker in the informal optical disc trade that acts as an interface between legal and illegal networks and allows them to engage in productive communication is the Internet. The Internet links various legal networks with the illegal network of the trade. Through the Internet and cyberspace, the producers can have access to legal networks that display and sell the latest models of replicating machines or high-speed computers for the informal trade. According to the Optical Media Board or OMB and key informants, these computers are advertised on the Internet and can be imported legally. Through the computer screen, they can order the latest versions of computer software and hardware and pay electronically and legally through money transfer technologies. Lately, according to one producer–distributor, these high-speed computer burners for replication can be legally bought in big malls in Metro Manila.

Furthermore, the Internet also allows producers to have access to the world of Hollywood as well as foreign and local movies. With just a click of the mouse or a touch of the screen, they are updated on the latest upcoming films not yet released in the film market and shown in movie houses. From an array of new films advertised on the Internet screen, they can choose the titles they want to reproduce illegally. The display of these new and unreleased films on the Internet by major film companies and distributors is legal as this is part of their marketing strategy. They offer customers the chance to see upcoming films in the market.

5.7.1 Stages in Optical Disc Piracy

Although piracy in the Quiapo Barter Trade Center Complex area is an open network and is constantly adapting to changes in technology, environment, and copyright law, it, nevertheless, has identifiable stages. The description of these stages below was largely based on piracy operations before the QBTCC was ordered closed in 2011. This section just aimed to show the complexity of the piracy production and distribution system in the Philippines and the crucial role of technology in accomplishing and maintaining the illegal trade. Three major phases can be identified as follows:

5.7.1.1 The Preproduction Stage

For traders who engage in optical disc piracy, preproduction begins with the selection of titles of movies or other copyrighted materials to be pirated and ends with the overall estimate of the total number of copies of pirated discs to be distributed in the local and provincial market.

Selection of Titles

Several considerations are taken by the producer before selecting movie titles for informal trade. First, the title to be reproduced must have a “box office” appeal. The optical media traders, like any other entrepreneurs, think of higher return of investment. Thus, only potential blockbuster movies or popular songs that promise higher sales are normally included in the production list. Second, the kind of titles to be copied must exclude the type of films informally agreed upon by Quiapo producers and the OMB to be excluded in the trade. This covers Filipino movie titles which are currently shown in movie houses, especially those of the Metro Manila Film Festival (MMFF). To promote Filipino movies and resuscitate the dying Philippine film industry, producers and the authorities are said to agree implicitly, according to informants, to exclude Filipino movies, at least for the first 2 or 3 weeks before their release, from the producer's list. This was confirmed by the author's *suki* ("regular seller") in Quiapo when he inquired if he could buy a pirated copy of a Filipino film currently shown in Metro Manila cinemas. The retailer mentioned without elaborating that they don't sell pirated copies of Filipino movies currently shown in cinemas. A month later when the author asked two sellers in a provincial piracy outlet that bought pirated boxes of counterfeit discs from Quiapo if he could buy Filipino films of Metro Manila Film Festival currently shown in Philippine cinemas, they frankly replied that the OMB chair disallowed them to sell counterfeit copies if they were currently shown in the movie houses. They informed that author that they could only secure pirated copies after the New Year, i.e., around 2 weeks after their showing in the cinemas which is usually done within 2 weeks after Christmas. They also implied that the copies were already available but could not be released yet by local producers.

In the case of pirating Filipino movies, pirate producers can only copy Filipino films, the Metro Manila Film Festival films, after their showing in movie houses. This informal agreement between the OMB and Quiapo producers was said to be the main reason why the local film industry has shown a remarkable turnaround in 2006. In an accomplishment report (January–December 2006) made by the Film Development Council of the Philippines, [t]he box office revenues of local films grew by 40 % to 1.437 billion in 2006 from P1.025 billion in 2005. This was the first year in the last 7 years that local films' box office revenues have grown.

Assuming that the usual piracy processes are followed and all the technologies for the reproduction of the master copies are in the right place, the first step that the producer would usually do is to select music or movie titles from the Internet. Using the search engines, they would choose from the advertised titles of Hollywood or foreign movies. Then they would, through mobile phones, call their contacts through mobile phones in neighboring Asian countries like Malaysia, Indonesia, or China to check if disc copies of the "master copy" of the titles were available for purchase. Later, they became dependent on the Internet in securing master copies. There are two things for the local producer to consider here: if the movie has been released earlier in these countries, a legal copy of it can easily be obtained by the contact and purchased by the producer to be copied in Quiapo. Usually, foreign movies are released earlier in other Asian countries like Malaysia than in the Philippines according to an informant. But if the movie had not yet been released in the United States or anywhere in the world, the master copy is secured by the contact through an illegal source and sold at a higher price. According to the OMB, the price of a master copy ranges from twenty to thirty thousand pesos

(P20,000–P30,000). Informants said that these copies are usually leaked to interested individuals during the postproduction or editing of the film. *Time Magazine*, for example, had published an article suggesting that sometimes illegal copies of Hollywood movies can leak to outsiders through advanced copies given to jurors of the Oscars. According to OMB in an interview, Filipino movies shown in movie houses can be pirated with the use of high-tech cell phones and other gadgets through illegal camcording. To avoid detection inside the movie house, pirates usually form a group of 2 to 4 people to view simultaneously the same movie in different areas inside the movie house, and each member copies a portion of the movie and then connects these major portions of the movies afterward to produce a master copy. With the advent of high-tech smart phones and cameras, illegal camcording can now be done using one gadget with lookouts assisting the recording pirate. At times, cameramen or other postproduction technicians can secure illegal and advanced copies of Filipino movies and sell them to producers of illegal optical disc (OD) plants in the country or to the producers in the Quiapo piracy hub.

Old movies which can be reproduced into various collections in DVD formats can be downloaded directly from the Internet for free including their downloading software. Pornographic materials are also included in the informal optical media trade. The producers can easily get some "master copies" from the Internet. Foreign sex videos or adult films can be downloaded for free from the Internet. Others can only be viewed and downloaded with the use of specialized software after paying electronically on the Internet through international credit cards. To secure copies of the latest pornographic materials for pirate production, a producer can become a member of these pornographic sites and pay the required fee in dollars via credit cards. With regard to music, Internet sites are also available where producers can download for free and create their own collections of various music to be sold in Quiapo and other sidewalk stalls in the country. Peer-to-peer sharing sites are common sources for pirated music. The downloading software to download music is available for free or for sale.

Procurement of the "Master Copy"

Payment follows after the contact and the producer have made a deal with regard to master copies. After the payment is remitted, the master copy is done through modern technology. Sources say that payments are usually done through legitimate money transfer firms. After the payment is remitted, the master copy is sent by the contact to the designated address of the producer–supplier in the enclave. To avoid detection, the "master copy" is usually sent with other goods or items through the international airport and sent through a broker directly to the production site. It is also sent with other items through a legitimate courier directly to the Quiapo Barter Trade Center Complex by the contact of the producer working in the firm. With the popularity of online piracy, transactions and payments can also be done through the Internet. The torrent sites and peer-to-peer sharing sites are also utilized by producers lately to secure master copies of films to be pirated.

Taking of Orders from Distributors

Upon receiving the master copy, the producer usually calls or texts the major distributors in the provinces and in the metropolis through his mobile phone to receive orders. Each order normally consists of thousands of copies. The distribution network of the Quiapo Barter Trade Center Complex (QBTCC) piracy trade is said to be nationwide in jurisdiction according to informants. Orders come from different parts of the country. The distributors in the provinces are given priority over the local distributors in the enclave and its nearby suburbs. They are usually identified by the producer–supplier according to the name of the province, suggesting its nationwide distribution system. Since time is of the essence in this type of business, producers get the orders first from these distributors, because aside from their distance and thus longer time of shipment, there is always the danger that some of these distributors, because of delay, may order from other producers in the QBTCC. The producer usually knows the estimated number of copies of the local consumption in Quiapo and in Metro Manila. Because of proximity, he may not worry much about taking the orders of these distributors. Quiapo and Metro Manila do not require elaborate shipment networks to make sure the discs arrived quickly and safely. The regional and provincial orders, however, pose a challenge for a producer. Besides problems of delay and higher probability of confiscation of the orders by law enforcers, he has to deal with the "loader" or the person who is in charge of loading the boxes of pirated discs safely from QBTCC to the designated plane in the domestic airport. The loader gets a commission, thus increasing the price per disc.

5.7.1.2 The Production Stage

Production Outside the Enclave

The production of pirated discs for nationwide distribution in the Philippines has three major sources indicating how wide the piracy network can be: (1) those discs which are produced in other countries and are imported and shipped to the enclave, (2) those discs of Filipino movies which are produced by local plants in the Philippines, and (3) those discs which are locally produced by Muslim producers with the use of high-tech computers or burners in the enclave. DVD discs, according to one producer, which carry a collection of 12 films or more in one disc (e.g., 12 in 1 or 24 in 1), or high-quality discs are usually imported from China. And since China is tolerant of piracy, many imported pirated discs which are replicated by highly advanced replicating machines originate from this country. A collection disc, containing numerous titles, requires a very advanced replicating technology and local producers are not yet capable for this. Besides, this type of technology, according to informants, requires millions of capital and a bigger location. This assessment was confirmed by the OMB chair in an interview. Local producers, according to him, use only high-tech burners for replication but are not capable of operating an optical disc (OD) plant within the barter trade center complex. However, the producers "burn" the imported discs from China or other countries to meet the demands of the local market.

According to informants, most of the imported high-quality DVDs come from China. With their contacts in China, producers can choose a variety of movie titles in clandestine warehouses. Then a broker, hired by the Quiapo producer, would be responsible for shipping the purchased discs illegally to the international airport and loading them on the airline through contacts in their illegal airport network. When they reach Manila, another broker belonging to their illegal network in the airport would be responsible to deliver them directly to QBTCC. These are all done by brokers for a fee from the Quiapo importer–supplier.

In its 2007 Special 301 Annual Report, the International Intellectual Property Alliance (IIPA) confirmed this capacity of the piracy network of China to export to foreign countries like the Philippines. It is believed that there were approximately 92 optical disc plants in China, with 1482 total line bringing total disc capacity of 5.187 billion discs of high quality per year. It is also alleged that, in 2006, infringing product from China was found in nearly every major market in the world such as Germany, Italy, Australia, Norway, Belgium, Canada, Mexico, the United States, Russia, the United Kingdom, the Netherlands, Israel, Paraguay, Lithuania, Singapore, Taiwan, the Philippines, Indonesia, Vietnam, Hong Kong, Malaysia, Thailand, Chile, New Zealand, and South Africa (IIPA 2007 Special 301 Report: People's Republic of China, p. 99).

Digital counterfeit discs containing English movies come mainly from China, but discs containing Filipino movies are also said to be produced in the country but outside the enclave in Quiapo. They are said to be replicated by local plants owned by a powerful non-Muslim network with strong a political connection in Malacañang. The author's key informant, a supplier of discs in the QBTCC for nationwide distribution, was apparently very much convinced of this idea. Besides, a IIPA 2007 Special 301 report on the Philippines confirmed his allegation by hinting that there were indeed illegal machinery and optical disc (OD) plants operating in the Philippines. In 2006, it is believed that there was at least one unlicensed plant that remains in operation in the Philippines. It is also suspected that the replicating machines confiscated by authorities were used for piracy. For example, two machines from one of the closed plants remained in circulation despite the plant having been ordered to return the machines by the court (IIPA 2007 Special 301 Report: Philippines, p. 375).

Production Inside the Enclave

Fake DVD discs containing single English films are usually produced in the enclave. After the preproduction stage or after the producer has a complete picture of the total copies to be produced for each title, he then proceeds to the production stage. This stage has two steps: the actual copying of the "master copy" into pirated discs and packaging of these discs.

Before the "master copy" can be reproduced into thousands of copies to be sold in distribution outlets, a heterogeneous network of people and paraphernalia or equipment are needed by the producer. This includes the replicating machines, stamping machines, blank discs (CDs, CD-Rs, DVDs, DVD-Rs), labels, plastics, covers, cases for the discs, and so on. This also includes people assigned to act as operators or supervisors of these replicating and stamping machines, suppliers for blank discs, and workers who will assemble or pack the discs with their labels and cases in boxes.

Legal and illegal networks converge in the informal optical disc trade contributing its persistence. The replicating machines and CD or DVD computer duplicators are legal, purchased by the producer abroad or in local megamalls. Replicating machines which consist of high-speed computer disc duplicators are advertised in many Internet sites which anyone can purchase easily. The OMB acknowledges that these duplicators can be imported and sold legally. Though they can be bought legally by the producers through their credit cards or money transfers, they cannot be lawfully exported to the Philippines, especially if these are used commercially on copyrighted materials without the necessary license or permit from the OMB. Thus, bribery of some unscrupulous personnel, contacts in the customs, airport authorities, and airline personnel is a common practice by pirate producers. Producers, through their representatives, can pick up their high-speed disc duplicators, mixed with their other legal imported goods, undetected. Cell phone calls enable this transaction to occur between producers and their networks in the customs. Smaller or not so advanced duplicators can be bought legally in megamalls in Metro Manila.

The stamping machines are also legally available, as well as blank discs, labels, and cases. Usually some naturalized Chinese or Filipino–Chinese businessmen from Binondo or the Divisoria area serve as legitimate suppliers of these discs, plastics, labels, casings, and other paraphernalia for optical disc piracy. Their delivery trucks can be seen transporting these materials to the enclave during the day. Most of the materials used in the informal trade during the production stage are all legal. What is illegal is the content of the disc copied from the master copy that is reproduced from the copyrighted original as well as the labels or covers which are reproduced without permission. From the producer's and seller's point of view, the piracy trade is not completely an illegal activity since not all aspects of the business are illegal. The machines, software for duplication and copying, and the materials for the informal business are bought lawfully from legitimate sources. Moreover, the technological tools for communication such as cell phones and personal computers as well as television sets and players to test pirated discs for customers by sellers are also legal.

5.7.1.3 The Postproduction Stage

The postproduction is basically a public relations stage. To make sure that the ordered discs reach their destinations and are received by distributors without delay and confiscations by law enforcers, producers, using their mobile phones and personal assistants, usually contact their networks in the law enforcement agencies for protection. This includes the giving of regular protection money to the police commander and other government agents who may confiscate the discs after they are packed for distribution. The breakdown of coordination or networking between producers and law enforcers can lead to interception and confiscation of packed pirated discs in the pier or airport. For instance, last September, the PNP Aviation Security confiscated 27 packed boxes of pirated discs ready for shipment to Palawan, Bacolod, Davao, and other places throughout the country (*PS Ngayon*, September 10, 2007, p. 10).

5.7.2 Two Major Technologies for the Piracy Trade

5.7.2.1 The Internet Technology

While cell phones have easily blended into the daily routine of Filipinos in general, the Internet remains less accessible because of economic and technical reasons. But Internet access is readily available in cities and the youth have learned quickly how to navigate the cyberworld (Pertierra 2006, p. 3). With the advent of the broadband technology in the computer landscape in the Philippines, one can easily access the Internet at a cheaper price in one's cell phones as well as in one's personal computers and portable laptops. The Quiapo enclave has welcomed this intrusion and modernizing effect of the Internet technology into their social and economic way of life. The traders in the enclave primarily use the Internet in the preproduction and production stages of their optical disc business. The Internet allows traders to know potential blockbuster or upcoming Hollywood movies which they can reproduce for their business.

The Internet has also expanded the social networks of the traders and introduced them to intermediary non-Muslim networks which are necessary to their business.

The digital networks made possible by the Internet are encouraging new forms of individualism and cosmopolitanism among Muslim traders in QBTCC. Strangers are increasingly entering networks of intimacy hitherto limited to kin and close friends. These extended networks require individualizing responses and broaden outlooks, leading to more cosmopolitanism (Pertierra 2006, p. 4).

With the Internet, the traders and suppliers can align themselves with other legal economic networks (e.g., network of suppliers of replicating machines, computers, software), thus merging the legal and the illegal aspects of the informal optical media trade. The Internet blurs the distinction between the legality and illegality of the informal optical media business. When enclave traders buy replicating equipment and paraphernalia for piracy as legally advertised on the Internet, they have made the illegal nature of the informal optical media business look legal.

5.7.2.2 The Mobile Phone Technology

Another important technological landscape that sustains the informal optical media business in QBTCC is the mobile phone. The world has become smaller and networked because of the Internet and mobile phones. The revolution brought about by the new digital technology is said to have moved to the next stage: the Internet is now being installed on mobile phone devices. Though 7000 million people are online worldwide, this is nothing compared with the 2.1 billion people with cell phones. Rich Templeton, CEO of Texas Instruments, a leading maker of chips for mobile phones, predicts that four billion people will have mobile phones by 2010. And this has become a reality. Cell or mobile phones replace local experiences of time and place through their transformations into a series of digital electronic data.[7] They dissolve the dialectic between private–public, kin–stranger, and local–global into the virtual world of electronic impulses (Pertierra et al. 2002, p. 47).

The cell phone is the latest and most widely used of the new communications technology. Initially, they were only available to the rich, but lately, cheaper models have made their use accessible to many Filipinos. Cellular phones were introduced to the Philippines in 1994 when Smart and Globe started supplying cellular service. With a strong demand for communication lines, subscribers climbed steadily. After a year, Smart had 120,378 subscribers, and by 1997 its subscribers had climbed dramatically to 623,075, giving it a 46 % share of the cellular phone market. Globe, on the other hand, had increased its subscriber base in 1997 from 50,697 to 104,345—a rise of 106 % (Pertierra et al. 2002, p. 35).

With the phenomenal drop of prices of cell phones owing to steep competition between manufacturing companies, mobile phone ownership increased impressively. Merrill Lynch, for instance, reports that for the first quarter of 2001, there were approximately 7.2 million cell phone subscribers in the Philippines: 2.9 million (40.6 %) of them were held by Globe, 3.4 million (48.5 %) by Smart Communications, and 788, 000 (10.9 %) by Pilipino Telephone Corp. (Smart's sister company) (Pertierra et al. 2002, p. 88).

Cell phone service and ownership is concentrated in urban centers. High usage in texting and calls is particularly noted in large cities of Luzon, particularly in the National Capital Region and Metro Manila, including the City of Manila where QBTCC is located. Cell phones are sold in the barter trade center complex. With their relatives and co-ethnics in Virra Mall in Greenhills, a mall well known for cell phone retailing business, Quiapo barter traders can easily buy and sell cheaper mobile phones for their personal and business purposes. For the optical media producers and sellers, cell phones are very important technological tools that can connect them in the electronic space and protect their privacy and anonymity in the illegal piracy trade. During the author's visits in the enclave, he often observed sellers using mobile phones for their business operations. These cell phones are used to make inquiries on stocks and the availability of new disc titles from retailers

---

[7] http://web.ebscohost.com/ehost/delivery?vid=10&hid=108(&sid=fdf11375-5eOf-4d5a-aa64f-afe55c6ae973%sessionnmgr/08

to suppliers or vice versa or between producers and distributors. In one condominium he visited, he saw a resident–trader going in and out of her condo unit and texting on her cell phone. Later, he saw a teenager talking to her and receiving from her a box of "pirated" discs. According to one distributor, the cell phone makes their business easy to operate since they don't have to travel or use landline phones for transactions. Through this technology, the producers can easily take orders from provincial distributors. It also enables the traders to supervise their informal business without leaving their workplace or home. It makes transactions fast and anonymous. With just the touch of a finger, the traders can make a text or call and become connected in seconds with their business networks.

Cell phones are also indispensible tools in connecting the optical media network with the law enforcement network. The leaking of information on impending raids by some law enforcers and their agents aligned to the network is usually done by means of texting by mobile phones. With this electronic warning, producers and sellers are forewarned of the raid and thus have time to temporarily close their stores or to hide their equipment and stock. It is for this reason that the OMB chair revealed in a television interview that he requires the OMB raiding team to temporarily surrender their cell phones to him before revealing the time and place of the raid (interview with OMB chair in "The Buzz," Dec. 9, 2007). This strategy is not, however, reliable as agents can always borrow another cell phone or maintain another device secretly or buy another unit and SIM card—given the oversupply and falling prices of cell phones and their accessories—in order to text or call producers or sellers. The IIPA's 2007 Special 301 Report on the Philippine counterfeiting identifies the mobile phone as the source of leaks of information on raids and as one of the irregularities in the enforcement system in the fight against "piracy." Texting by cell phones is the major means of leaking information on impending raids from government agents to the traders. No less than the OMB chair acknowledges the power of cellular texting in providing the traders with tips on seizures and raids from corrupt enforcement agents.

5.8 Social Networks Supporting the Piracy Trade

5.8.1 Kinship Network in Piracy

One feature that persists in Muslim society despite the growing urbanization and modernization of Philippine society is the political structure of the *agama*. Highly aligned with the kinship system, this political structure is largely composed of networks of relatives who are either related to the head, the *datu*, or to the sultan by consanguinity or affinity. A Muslim *agama* is a kinship-based principality composed of about two dozen families headed by the *datu* as a political and religious leader (Bauzon 1991). It is the intermarriage between Muslim families that is largely responsible for the formation of the *datu* structure or sultanate in Muslim society.

The Maranao as the largest Muslim group in the Philippines also follows this political structure but with peculiar characteristics. Its political leadership is not territorial in nature but kinship based. In Maranao society, families and their relatives follow the leadership of their associations of kins and not the state's formal *barangay* leader. Muslims and relatives in the Quiapo Barter Trade Center Complex follow this kinship-based clustering of families and relatives in the enclave.

To know why the informal piracy network in QBTCC is cohesive implies an understanding of Maranao's kinship structure. Though Muslim Filipinos share similarities with regard to the kinship system, the Maranaos have a unique pattern that differentiates them from other Muslim groups. Maranao society, for example, consists of local communities, called *agamas*, which are nonlineal descent groups. Within the *agama* are a variety of units defined primarily by kinship. The *agama* is a small unit of the Maranao social organization where people relate themselves to each other under the traditional bond of kinship (Saber in Gowing 1988, p. 88). It is a community of persons who share a lineage or set of lineages rather than a place or territory (Saber and Madele 1975, p. 78).

Membership in *agamas* is based not on territorial residence but on lineage. "One may reside in the territory of an *agama* without membership in the *agama* and without a voice in the affairs of that *agama*." Membership in lineages is inherited bilaterally so each person belongs to a variety of lineages. Thus, a Maranao can belong to different agamas because of this bilateralism in kinship. Through ancestry, kinship and the offices in an *agama* provide Maranao Muslims the only roles for carrying out cooperative and collective action (Saber and Madele 1975, pp. 78–79). Even the most marginal Maranaos cannot identify themselves or pattern their relationships outside of these traditional social arrangements.

5.8.1.1 The Maranao Kinship System

The intimacy of relatives among the Maranaos in Quiapo can be manifested by their kinship organizations. While the Maranao kinship organizations in the enclave may not be exactly similar to the traditional *agamas* found in Lanao, other informal Maranao associations exist based on bilateral kinship ties. According to informants, for example, each building or condominium in the barter complex is socially organized based on kinship. Any Maranao, according to one *alim* or Muslim scholar, can organize his migrant or resident relatives in the enclave into an association. Usually, a Maranao who has a higher social status in the community can informally recruit his relatives from either his mother or father's side. Once organized, the members start to share resources to build their residential building in the enclave while the members pay their monthly rent to the association. The proceeds of the rent can either go to a common fund for the association or can be used for a good cause in Mindanao. In one association, for instance, the proceeds from the rent go to the support of a Maranao college in Lanao providing tertiary education to poor Muslims.

Through the informal optical media trade, some of the associations in the area were able to build their own commercial and residential buildings. In one Maranao condominium that the author visited, the head of the association, who is also a religious leader of the enclave, oversees the welfare of the lessees and members of the group. Though Maranao leader is not directly involved in piracy, many members of his association and residents of the condo engage in the optical disc piracy business. Stocks of piracy paraphernalia and boxes of pirated discs—some of which are stored inside their residential unit—are conspicuous in every floor of the building. An outsider who enters the building is usually asked about his purpose and who is the person he or she wishes to see. Since all of the residents in every condominium or building in the enclave are relatives by consanguinity or affinity, an outsider can easily be identified. The residents themselves serve as lookouts for government agents who may pose in the condominium as visitors or customers. Kinship in this sense has protected piracy from intrusion of outside networks. It is a source of social capital used and turned illegal by piracy operators to prevent law enforcement to intrude into the criminal network.

5.8.1.2 Kinship and Retail Piracy

When the average customer enters the Quiapo enclave to buy pirated discs, one will notice that the stalls or stores are often manned by family members and their relatives. In one stall that the author sometimes visits for discs that contain live concerts of popular American singers, he saw a mother entertaining his queries while she was attending to the needs of her 2-year-old son and her baby. When the titles he was inquiring were not available in their stall, her husband went to their relatives' stalls to inquire if these titles were available.

In interviews, some retailers revealed that the clustering of sellers in the area was based on kinship ties. To foster trust and collective support in the retail business, sellers usually position their stalls and stores adjacent to one another. If one seller lacks the title requested by a buyer, he or she would normally borrow from his/her neighboring relative sellers. And if necessary, a relative would volunteer to look for the requested title from other cluster of retailers with kinship links with them. More often, cell phones are used either by texting or calling to inquire from their relatives about the availability of titles. Since Maranaos and other Muslim groups selling counterfeit discs practice bilateral kinship ties, various clusters of sellers, together with their relative distributors and producers in the enclave, are in one way or another relatives by consanguinity or affinity. These heterogeneous and overlapping kinship clusters of sellers, distributors, and producers contribute to the maintenance of the illegal trade.

With this setup comes mutual support within the same networks of producer and his distributors and retailers. In terms of stocks, one retailer or distributor can lend stocks to others within the network. The producer also supports new retailers or distributors within his network. The producer gives logistics support to his distributor or retailer and even skills if the latter decides to become a producer himself and start his own network. According to one producer–supplier, a retailer who becomes successful in the business can ask permission from his relative producer to start his own network. The relative producer would normally support his relative's decision. Though stiff competition among producers and their networks within the enclave exists, a high degree of mutual support to promote the overall welfare of the business also thrives. Besides belonging to one ethnic network and being related by kinship, top producers, suppliers, and distributors, when faced with a common threat against the illegal business, would usually transcend their cultural differences to protect the piracy network. Proof of this is the collective effort of producers to monitor their ranks against violations of their informal agreement with the OMB regarding pirating local movies during the Metro Manila Film Festival. If they do not cooperate, everyone in the network would suffer the consequences of continuous raids by the OMB.

5.8.1.3 Kinship and Sponsorship in the Informal Business

Kinship networks play an important role in sponsoring new members in the informal optical media business in the Philippines. Maranao producers recruit retailers, distributors, and employees for their business from their pool of fellow Maranao relatives in the area or in Mindanao. Because of the illegal nature of the business, producers find trust and protection against raids by law enforcers and mutual support from their own relatives by consanguinity and affinity.

Table 5.1, based on an informal count by the author in the area, shows how kinship is salient in sponsoring new sellers of pirated discs in the enclave. The retailers in the enclave are largely recruited by their relatives. Around 10 % of the retailers in Quiapo are Christian, but most of them are either recruited by their Muslim relatives or friends in the area. These Christians belong to the so-called marginal Maranao or half Maranaos or Christians who have intermarried Maranao Muslims. They usually come from Mindanao and have migrated to Quiapo to join their relatives in search of greener pastures. Many of them are poor and poorly educated. In interviews, they said that they migrated to Quiapo with their relatives and engaged in retail piracy because they could not find jobs in the city ("walang mapasukang trabaho").

Table 5.1 shows that 20 of 27 sellers interviewed mentioned that they were sponsored by their relatives in joining the optical disc retail piracy. Only 7 of 27 say that their Muslim friends introduced them to the illegal retail business. Moreover, 22 retailers have relatives in Quiapo, while only 5 of 27 do not have kin in the enclave.

Table 5.1 The sponsors and relatives of selected piracy retailers in QBTCC

Type of retailers	Type of sponsor		Relatives in QBTCC	
	Relative	Muslim friend	With	Without
Muslims (N=18)	16	2	16	2
Christians (N=9)	4	5	6	3
Total	*20*	7	22	5

Source: Author's survey

Interviews with these 5 retailers revealed that even though they do not have relatives in the area, they, nevertheless, have Muslim friends that introduced them to the piracy business.

The important role of kinship and friendship in patronizing the retail business in the Quiapo enclave is also confirmed by another parallel sociological study by Azanza (1994) on the Muslim ambulant vendors in the area. The study showed that the entry of new vendors in the enclave is facilitated primarily by relatives (42 %), followed by friends (34 %), neighbor/townmate (20 %), and comember in religion (4 %) (Azanza 1994, p. 99).

How important to the optical disc piracy is the sponsorship system by kinship?

Given the illegal nature of the trade, sponsorship is important to ensure trust and security from the new players who were enrolled and aligned with the piracy network. The new traders are bound to protect the business secrets from outsiders. The sponsors would introduce these neophytes to old members of the trade and to fellow retailers and distributors in the area and assure them that they are not government agents and that their interests, if they are Christians, are aligned with the piracy trade interests.

Sponsorship is also essential to avoid harassment from other sellers and by arresting officers. It also serves as a means to mold the camaraderie between the old and the new vendors and distributors. For Muslims, it is usually the community leader or a relative of high social rank who introduces the newcomer to the community. Sometimes, this leader refers them to a more established distributor or retailer who could act as sponsor. According to informants, a sponsor is important to introduce neophytes to the clusters of sellers in the area as well as to the Muslim community and also teach them some secrets of the trade. The sponsor teaches the newcomer the essential practices of retail piracy, the warning signals on impending arrival of arresting officer or raids, pricing of products, techniques to entice more customers, where and how to get tips on raids, and so on.

5.8.1.4 Kinship and Surveillance

The kinship network does not only facilitate retailing, but it also provides protection against law enforcement. Based on an interview with the OMB chairman, the agency normally sends agents to QBTCC to gather information and to map out the areas to be raided before it applies for search warrants in the courts. Some relatives of Muslim retailers and distributors act as lookouts and security agents against law enforcers and spies who may pose as buyers to gather intelligence data. Thus, unknown to buyers, Muslim lookouts, who are relatives of the traders, are strategically positioned in the enclave to monitor people coming and in and out of the QBTCC to protect their informal business. These lookouts can be very inquisitive and sometimes threatening to people whom they suspect to be gathering information against them. This was confirmed during the preliminary phase of this research when the author's research assistants were followed, interrogated, and threatened by these lookouts. Some of his interviewers were even told that they could not leave the area alive if they continue their data gathering. Another incident, recounted by an informant, confirmed this surveillance against people perceived to be government agents: he said that a buyer got into trouble with the Muslim traders in QBTCC when the latter took pictures of the stalls and stores of pirated discs in the area without proper authorization from Muslim traders and leaders.

As mentioned above, these informal security agents or lookouts are relatives of the traders in the area. They act as coordinators with regard to tips and raids. According to informants, these coordinators use their cell phones to inform the producers, retailers, and distributors of an impending raid by the police, OMB, and other law enforcers. The tips may come from different sources—some said they get them from the customers themselves, and others mentioned they receive the tips from producers or major distributors, Chinese suppliers, from their "moles" or informers in the OMB, or from the local policemen who get daily protection money from the sellers. These tips give the sellers time to hide their new stocks of pirated discs within the area, usually in their residential homes or in other remote places within or outside the enclave. If the impending raid is orchestrated or mutually agreed upon by the law enforcers and sellers or producers to allow the former to present a good accomplishment report, the old stocks or titles of pirated discs mixed with a few new titles are usually prepared by sellers and distributors to be confiscated. This is what traders call as *paglilinis ng basura* ("cleaning of garbage"), as with the old pirated discs, old replicating machines, or burners being placed in a conspicuous place in their stores or stall waiting to be confiscated.

If the raid is unannounced or no tip was provided—by producers, distributors, or law enforcers enrolled in the piracy network—these lookouts quickly text or call their counterparts to inform them which side of the enclave the raid started. If the surprise raid begins at the right side of the enclave, for instance, the coordinators or lookouts there would inform their counterparts at the left side or the other portion of the enclave in order that the sellers there can run, close their shops or stalls, and hide their discs or burners.

In addition to the coordinating and monitoring functions, the coordinators or informal security agents in the enclave also provide protection to buyers against snatchers, holdup men, and other street crimes. According to informants, the Muslim entrepreneurs want to assure buyers that they are safe to do business inside the enclave. This is to ensure the continuous patronage of regular customers or buyers (*suki*) of their counterfeit goods. In Hassan's (1983) study, these plainclothes security agents who are relatives of the sellers are even registered as security personnel in the barangay hall and are known by the local police.

5.8.1.5 Kinship and Its Deterrence to Law Enforcement

Kinship ties also provide cover for the identity of sellers who have been arrested in a raid. According to an informant and community organizer of the enclave, Muslims in the metropolis, because of their strong drive for survival, are fond of using fictitious names or misleading information when confronted by law enforcers. They can then count on relatives to withhold giving the correct information to these enforcers. For instance, a Muslim may introduce himself to the police as Hadji Bedol but in the next encounter will change his name or address. This difficulty of verifying the identity of sellers involved in piracy as well as ascertaining whether they are really sellers or mere paid helpers or workers in the area is one reason why cases against the enclave traders do not prosper in court. The powerful support and deception strategies of traders and their relatives hinder the gathering of evidence for prosecution of piracy cases.

It is also through kinship ties that most cases of piracy are amicably settled. When a seller is arrested in the police station, the relatives, together with their leaders or a representative of the Office of Muslim Affairs (OMA), would come to their rescue and negotiate with the police for their release. According to informants, the police are normally lenient with regard to piracy cases when compared to other cases such as drugs. They are aware that these Muslim vendors are poor and earn little from their business. So far, according to the OMB, a total of 97 cases of piracy have been lodged against Quiapo piracy traders but none as of 2011 has been convicted of violating the optical media law as retailers and producers of optical disc piracy. Part of the problem, according to OMB chairman, is that it is not the OMB who is the complainant of these cases but the stakeholders or owners of the copyright. The OMB's role is only to provide the stakeholders with evidence and technical assistance to win the case. But for the meantime while the cases are filed in court, the relatives of the arrested disc retailers and their community leaders negotiate with the police to settle the case out of court.

In the QBTCC, there are two police substations. One substation is very close to the Golden Mosque and to the Muslim residential area, and the other is located near the vending area. In one of the author's visits to the substation near the Golden Mosque, he saw some Muslims entering and leaving the substation, while others were only sitting and casually talking with the some policemen, giving the impression that these Muslims and policemen were familiar with one another. One Manila policeman said that some policemen assigned in police stations near the enclave are Muslims. These informal ties reinforced by common religious identity can explain why cases against Muslim traders can be easily settled amicably before they are filed in court. When one Muslim vendor is arrested because of piracy, his or her relatives through *agamas* would rush to the vendor's rescue and use their informal connections with the local police to be able to release him/her amicably. In some situations, cases can easily be dismissed especially if the arrested sellers or distributors are relatives of some powerful Maranao producers or politicians because of the latter's government connections and power over law enforcement agencies. The regular protection money given to some law enforcers also weakens the government prosecution against the informal piracy trade.

5.8.2 *Ethnic Network in Piracy*

5.8.2.1 Defining Ethnicity

Ethnicity refers to "a people presumed to belong to the same society and who share the same culture and, especially, the same language" (Barfield 1997, p. 152). The most common characteristics distinguishing various ethnic groups are ancestry, a sense of history, religion, and language. For Banton (1967), ethnicity refers to relationships between groups whose members consider themselves distinctive. For Schaefer (2005, p. 253), "An ethnic group, unlike a racial group, is set apart from others because of its national origin or distinctive cultural patterns." Ethnic groups in closely knit residential neighborhoods (Bowles and Gintis 2004) not only achieve higher levels of cooperation but also engage in exclusionary practices toward outsiders. In an ethnic entrepreneurial neighborhood, people come to recognize each other as part of the same community by defining them as sharing similar location, circumstances, and biographies (Bertaux 1997; Bertaux-Wiame 1981; Salaff et al. 2002). Ethnic entrepreneurs then who form one closely knit community mobilize social capital through their ethnic social networks. Entrepreneurs from a similar ethnic background will get easier access to business networks in the enclave compared to outsiders. They will also be in an advantageous position to exploit ethnic networks for greater profits (Salaff et al. 2002).

Ethnic networks link producers, distributors, and consumers vertically and horizontally to enhance the social "embeddedness" of economic transactions (Granovetter 1985). In a closely knit urban entrepreneurial community, they provide problem-solving capacities. Among them are the powerful contractual enforcement mechanisms made possible by small-scale interactions, notably effective punishing of those who fail to keep promises, facilitated by close social ties, frequent and variegated interactions, and the availability of low-cost information concerning one's trading partners. This problem-solving capacity allows networks to counteract the restricted gains from trade and maintain their operations smoothly (Bowles and Gintis 2004, p. 3).

In the QBTCC, ethnicity has provided informal problem-solving mechanisms to maintain order and smoothen the operation of the illegal business. Ethnic ties between producers, distributors, and retailers, for instance, can bring about a level of trust and reciprocity that facilitates the economic transactions of the informal optical disc business in the area. Though Maranao suppliers or retailers compete with one another to increase sales, for example, there is an assurance and trust between themselves as members of the same ethnic group that one group will not recruit the pool of regular customers from the other group. According to informants, the Maranao retailer, for instance, should wait for the customer of another retailer to visit his stall and buy his discs and should not actively recruit the buyer of another retailer to purchase his disc. The same informal norm applies to producers and distributors with regard to their pool of regular customers. Doing so would mean loss of sales and profit as well as social honor for Maranaos. And if this is not settled amicably through their local leaders and the damage is serious, the aggrieved and his family can resort to vendetta against the offender and his family, one that results in a long-standing feud between two families. In other words, the ethnic dynamism and informal social control mechanism of the Maranaos called the *rido* or revenge against somebody who causes dishonor against fellow Maranaos has become a deterrence against rule breaking within the illegal business trade. Other Muslim ethnic groups in the enclave know the Maranao custom of the *rido* and participate in the illegal trade with full cognizance of this Maranao norm.

Ethnicity can also be the reason why different groups help each other in the trade. One retailer can lend his/her discs if another runs out of stock. Or a Maranao retailer can settle on a consignment arrangement—that she/he gets the stocks first and pays after they are sold—from a Maranao producer if she/he loses his/her stocks or capital in an unanticipated raid. Since the retailer is a co-ethnic and part of the business network, the producer accepts this type of arrangement. Moreover, the dominant Maranao ethnic system among traders has also made the network more cohesive and resistant against any form of intrusion from outsiders, especially from law enforcers.

5.8.2.2 Ethnic Business Relations

Ethnic entrepreneurship can typically give rise to complex economic relations. Proprietors use the norms of the ethnic group to run their business. The employer–employee bond is culturally based. Employees with inside language abilities and other cultural traits are in demand (Fong 2001). And since culture is a "taken-for-granted" framework, jobs are often governed by particularistic rules that everyone knows. The hiring contract, the code of conduct, and the management of the informal trade are based on culture. Owners hire or work with those whom they have real or symbolic ties. They limit business access to those with the coveted ethnic background (Salaff et al. 2002). Downplaying social class interest, employers plead that departing from statutory protection helps all parties. In the Quiapo piracy trade, the employer–employee relationship between the producer and his employees is basically guided by the norms of culture and ethnicity. The rich producers or suppliers would normally hire workers and recruit retailers and distributors from his co-ethnics in Mindanao. The assumption of loyalty toward masters usually emanates from ethnic ties. This bond is one reason why retailers, employees, and distributors are cohesive under one producer in one piracy.

Ethnicity can also be the reason why different groups help each other in the trade. One retailer can lend his discs if another runs out of supply of pirated CDs and DVDs. Or a Maranao retailer can settle on a consignment arrangement—that she/he gets the stocks first and pays after they are sold—from a Maranao producer if she/he loses his/her stocks or capital in an unanticipated raid. Since the retailer is a co-ethnic and part of the business network, the producer accepts this type of arrangement. Ethnic network, thus, links producers, distributors, and consumers vertically and horizontally to enhance the social "embeddedness" of economic transactions (Granovetter 1985; Portes and Sensenbrenner 1993). In a closely knit urban entrepreneurial community like QBTCC, this network can also provide problem-solving capacities. Among them are the powerful contractual enforcement mechanisms made possible by small-scale interactions, notably effective punishing of those who fail to keep promises, facilitated by close social ties, frequent and variegated interactions, and the availability of low-cost information concerning one's trading partners. This problem-solving capacity allows networks to counteract the restricted gains from trade and maintain their operations smoothly (Bowles and Gintis 2004, p. 3).

5.8.2.3 The Maranao Rido

One important function of ethnicity aside from recruitment, trust, and cooperation in business operation in optical disc piracy is the use of ethnic dispute resolution to ensure compliance of parties to informal and illegal business transactions in piracy trade contracts. To maintain the informal optical media trade, the most effective and oftentimes violent form of dispute settlement, especially when official law enforcers cannot punish violators, is the application of the Maranao cultural mechanism called "rido." *Rido*, which means "feud," refers not to the dispute itself but, more accurately, to the traditional Moro mode of "dispute settlement." It is synonymous to tribal war. "When a complainant declares a *rido* against an enemy, oppressor or criminal, the complainant's family is mobilized to exact revenge from, or even things up, this enemy" (Gonzales 1999, p. 88). *Rido* is practiced by Maranaos who possess a reputation as being a dangerous group of Muslims. According to a Maguindanao Muslim leader, the Maranaos are very protective of their honor (*maratabat*) compared to other Muslim groups. That is why *rido* is widely practiced among the Maranaos to resolve serious disputes, more than the Tausugs, Maguindanaos, or other Muslim groups.

Of all the Muslim ethnolinguistic groups in the Philippines, the Maranaos are the only Muslims who place a high premium on titles, ranks, sense of honor, status, and respect or the so-called maratabat. *Maratabat* is the ethnic foundation of *rido* or revenge against an enemy. The Maranao *maratabat* is always fearful of being shamed by someone outside the family. When an outsider offends a family member, the *maratabat* of the entire family is involved (Gowing 1979, pp. 98–99). When this happens, even to a degree which a non-Muslim might regard as trivial, retribution is demanded and can easily take violent forms (Baradas 1977). In the informal piracy business, Maranao Muslims are conscious of their primary role and leadership in the business and are always protective of their economic interests. The key Maranao producers, distributors, and retailers are aware of how the illegal trade has advanced their wealth, status, and honor in the community. Thus, any serious infraction of contractual relations and informal norms of piracy can lead to *rido* against the offender and oftentimes lead to killing.

The *rido* (vendetta) is a major deterrent to any major infraction of informal rules of the informal optical disc business. Since the informal optical disc trade is illegal, legal contracts are unenforceable and void under Philippine law. This is the reason why operators in the enclave cannot double-cross their peers in business contracts nor can they violate the code of silence of the illegal trade and report trade secrets to authorities. Furthermore, a trader cannot divulge secrets of the illegal trade to outsiders, thus making the trade network "impenetrable" to law enforcement. Any individual who betrays the community by leaking information to law enforcers about the illegal trade exposes himself or herself to the informal sanction of *rido* or retribution from the key piracy operators. *Rido* can also take place among producers. A producer who recruits distributors and retailers from another producer can also lead to *rido*, especially if the terms of the amicable settlement are not met. The decrease of the pool of distributors and customers as well as the diminution of business can cause shame or dishonor to the *maratabat* of the producer's family. Moreover, any form of dishonesty and nonperformance of informal business agreements may lead to extrajudicial killing through the institution of *rido*.

One producer–supplier illustrates how the Maranao informal norm of *maratabat* and *rido* actually works in the piracy business. This illustration is based on actual events. According to him, producers and distributors in the enclave usually have regular loaders who deliver the discs from the enclave to the airlines that will ship them to their provincial destinations. As regular customers, producers know the commission or fee per delivery of these loaders. One day, a newcomer or loader started receiving deliveries at a lower rate and successfully enticed the regular distributors or producers of another loader to use his services. This practice led to a loss of earning and an offense against the *maratabat* or honor of the original loader. According to him, a *rido* took place between them. An attempt to amicably settle the conflict by their Muslim leaders proved futile, as this was considered a serious offense of the *maratabat* in Maranao culture.

The application of the Maranao *maratabat* or *rido*, according to informants, applies particularly among Maranaos or with other Muslim groups and not so much between Muslims and Christians. When in conflict, the Christians usually go to the police or court, and this stops the series of revenge or *rido* between them and their families. Yet the fear of *rido* from the key players of the informal optical media trade is what informally binds contractual relations done within the enclave and its outside networks. Any serious violations of contracts are resolved by piracy operators outside the judicial system. This is because informal contracts in the informal trade are illegal. And illegal contracts are null and void because they are contrary to law according to the Civil Code of the Philippines.

In sum, the *maratabat* and *rido* are the most powerful factors in traditional Maranao social control that maintain peace and order in the Quiapo enclave and facilitate the persistence of the informal piracy trade in the QBTCC, as well as contribute to the "invincibility" of the piracy trade against law enforcement.

5.8.2.4 Ethnicity and the Culture of Resistance in Piracy

An illegal network like the informal optical media trade can be coordinated and structured in some sense: community members, guided by their culture of resistance (i.e., ideology, history, and local social structure), can unite to oppose a common competitor in the use of their resources. Such an expression of solidarity can translate into what Peluso (1994) calls a "culture of conspiracy" where people and communities experiencing similar issues are drawn to the community's struggle to fight contested set of laws.

Ethnicity plays an important role in this culture of conspiracy against the law. It harmonizes the seemingly chaotic and discordant processes of everyday forms of opposition to the law: "Similarities in status, attitudes, beliefs, and behavior facilitate the formation of intimate (or consensual) relationships among incumbents of social positions." Ethnicity is likewise a social force that strengthens urban social networks of marginalized individuals (Laumann 1973, p. 5). This collective feeling and identity of belonging to community that shares a language, religion, race, and ancestral homeland (Yinger 1985, p. 159) is what empowers rule breakers to invert the terms of the oppressive discourse or what Castells calls "the exclusion of excluders by the excluded" (Castells 1997, p. 9).

For QBTCC Muslim traders, the imposition of copyright laws to criminalize their informal business is seen as another American strategy, with the cooperation of the national government, to further deprive them of economic opportunities already denied to them by mainstream society. One Muslim voiced his opposition to the link made between the informal trade and terrorism. For him, the informal optical media business of some Muslims is not financing terrorism. This is only a justification of the former U.S. President George Bush Jr. to oppress Muslims around the world. For him, the Muslims are only earning a living in optical disc trading. For retailers, the optical discs that they sell are not stolen but bought from suppliers or producers. They said that the informal trade is the only decent way of earning a living because the government has neglected them. They do not care much whether what they sell is illegal or not. Some even agree to legalize their retail piracy if the government would help them. All that they need from the government is a decent livelihood for their families.

This feeling of being oppressed and discriminated as an ethnic and religious group by the mainstream Philippine society and by the United States is another factor that binds traders together, particularly those in Quiapo, and nurtures a "culture of resistance" that enables them to fight against any other form of social exclusion and harassment. As one retailer says,

> Tutol kami sa gusto ng gobyerno na ihinto ang pagtitinda ng pirated. Maraming mga Muslim na naging milyunaryo dahil sa mga panindang ito, kaya pinagtyatyagaan naming ito kahit alam naming iligal (sic).
>
> (We are against the government's drive to stop the vending of pirated discs. Many Muslims became millionaires because of these goods, that's why we still continue vending them even if we know that it is illegal).

One reason why this type of illegal trade continues, according to some retailers, is the unity and collective resistance of the various ethnic groups in the QBTCC enclave against those who attempt to stop their sale of counterfeit discs. Enclave traders say that this work is the best alternative at the moment in their fight against poverty. This can also be seen in their collective effort to resist any form of raid against their retailing business. This "conspiracy" can be manifested in their coordination to anticipate tips of impending raids, in sharing information through cell phones on the progress of an ongoing trade, in the norm of secrecy that prevents sensitive information to be leaked to outsiders, and, above all, in the joint efforts of some QBTCC associations to put up regular protection money for law enforcers in order to maintain the business. Their sense of belonging to one history, religion, cultural heritage, and language and their feeling of being socially excluded from the Christian-dominated society are two important factors that fuel the fire of collective resistance against discrimination and the anti-copyright infringement drive of the government.

5.8.2.5 The Power of Language

One powerful ethnic resource used by the Maranaos in actual business operation and to protect the illegal trade of optical disc piracy business from law enforcement is the Maranao language. Language is the window of culture. Unless one knows the language, it is difficult to penetrate the way of life of a particular group of people. The Maranao language is a complex language which is only spoken by Muslims living in the provinces of Lanao, Iligan, and other Maranao areas in Mindanao. The only group of Filipinos who can understand the language is the Maguindanao Muslims who are said to be "cousins" in cultural heritage with the Maranaos and who also participate in the optical disc trades. In QBTCC, language is a primary tool used by producers, distributors, and retailers against raids and law enforcement. To protect the secrecy of the informal business, traders switch language from Tagalog to Maranao when talking to their fellow traders on sensitive matters regarding the piracy business in the presence of non-Muslim customers or outsiders. This is also true during raids. The law enforcers who are usually Christians and who do not know Maranao cannot understand the retailers and traders when they arrived in the area as traders and their friends and relatives would normally switch their language when police or government agents serve a warrant or conduct a raid. During search, law enforcers cannot understand what traders and residents are talking about in their presence. They cannot also ascertain whether the Maranao traders or resident in QBTCC are giving them reliable information during legitimate search for counterfeit discs and replicating machines. Likewise, the police cannot verify whether a retailer who pretends to be a mere paid worker when caught vending counterfeit discs during a raid is telling the truth. She/he can always inform Muslim bystanders in Maranao to lie in order for him/her to avoid arrest.

5.8.3 Religious Network in Piracy

Many piracy investigations overlooked the importance of religious network as a possible cultural force which can sustain the informal optical media trade in the Philippines. Common religious affiliation can be used by people to overcome social and economic discrimination in Philippine society. Just like any other members of any church or religious group such the Catholic Church, *Iglesia ni Cristo*, Baptist Church, or *El Shaddai*, religious solidarity or the sense of "we" or "communitas" brought about by common religious affiliation can sometimes be tapped by people as a social resource to pursue common interest. The exclusive hiring of people belonging to the same religion in a business firm as practiced by some members of the *Iglesia ni Cristo* in the Philippines is an example on how common religious affiliation can be used to control material resource and to exclude outsiders. When faced with social exclusion and survival, religious affiliation can somehow be an effective network for poor people and migrants to mobilize in order to pursue and maintain an informal trade in the underground economy. Some authors suggest that common religious affiliation can be tapped by people to overcome differences and pursue common goals. Gowing and McAmis (1974), for instance, note that common religious identity among Muslims promotes brotherhood:

> [t]he Muslim Filipinos may seem to be hopelessly divided among themselves, but outside observers will never understand the reality…that despite their differences, the Muslims regard themselves regard one another as brothers in the Faith of Islam. (Gowing and McAmis 1974, p. x)

They are aware that their religion is distinct from the religions of other Filipinos and that despite their differences in ethnic background, Muslims all belong to one religious group. They recognize each other as members of a wider community that transcends linguistic, racial, tribal, and national boundaries (Majul 1985, p. 14). According to Majul (1985), Muslims pray together, within or outside their communities, and regardless of the degree of their participation in national or civic affairs, or in other institutions and associations, the major source of their identity is religion. Religious identity brings together different Muslim groups in a feeling of oneness in religion (Isidro and Mamitua 1968, p. 19).

Despite cultural diversity, all Muslims in the QBTCC, just like their fellow Muslims in the country and around the world, recognize the paramount importance of religion to their identity and sense of solidarity as one religious community. This is not to deny that Muslims, like Christians, have fought and killed one another. In the informal optical disc business in Quiapo, for instance, betrayal or disloyalty of one retailer or distributor against his/her producer can lead to Muslims killing fellow Muslims. An informal norm states that a distributor or retailer must procure his supply from his original producer or supplier. They are not allowed to transfer to another producer to continue their business. They may start their own informal trade network recruiting their relatives as distributors, workers, and retailers, but they are not allowed to recruit from an existing pool of retailers or distributors controlled by a particular producer. Doing this, according to informants, can lead to

Muslim traders killing fellow Muslim traders. Despite personal conflicts, Muslims help one another as brothers just as Christians are considered as members of the one body of Christ.

Some informants suggest that the concept of "umma" or brotherhood may probably have something to do with Muslim traders protecting fellow Muslim traders from law enforcement. The Arabic word *umma* or *ummah* comes from a word that simply means "people." This is used in several senses in the Qu'ran but always indicates a group of people who are a part of a divine plan and salvation. The term "Muslim world" refers to the vast expanse of geography populated by the adherents of the Islamic religion who, by virtue of their common faith, collectively form the *ummah*. Because of diverse cultural backgrounds, various Muslim groups around the world may be different from one another, "but through membership in the *ummah*, their membership is subordinated to the broader Islamic notion of nationhood based on ideals of unity, justice, and equality" (Bauzon 1991, p. 52). Despite cultural differences, "[a]ll Muslims" regardless of their moral life are "brothers." Their brotherhood ideally means that every Muslim shares the pains and happiness of every other Muslim (Isidro and Mamitua 1968, p. 19).

The concept of unity under one *ummah* contributes to the cohesiveness of the network of Muslim traders and residents in QBTCC and other Muslim areas. This sense of brotherhood among Maranao Muslim traders and their alliances under one common religious affiliation contributes to the maintenance of the informal optical media business in the area. Common religious affiliation oftentimes prevents people from betraying fellow believers even if illegal acts have been committed. It can serve to block the leakage of information about the informal trade in the case of the piracy trade. It can also exclude those who are not enrolled or aligned in the business network. Thus, if policemen, for instance, serve a search warrant from the court to search for counterfeit discs and replicating machines, the traders' neighborhood in the enclave whose members share a similar religious affiliation would normally deny that there are such owners mentioned in the warrant. These authorities are considered outsiders and are therefore denied of vital information that concerns their neighbors. This is also the reason why raiding agents cannot double-check the veracity of the retailers or distributors caught selling counterfeit discs. More often these vendors pose as helpers of the real piracy retailers or producers and thus can be exempt from criminal liability. Even bystanders during raids who are also comembers in the QBTCC worshipping community tend to protect their fellow brothers and sisters who are piracy traders in front of hostile law enforcers.

With the frequent religious rituals and activities and the religious solidarity it engenders, traders and enclave residents in QBTCC help protect informal traders with their underground business from the intrusion of law enforcement. Getting sensitive inside information about the production and distribution system of the informal trade in the area is, therefore, difficult for outsiders and law enforcers who do not have the similar religious affiliation. Even non-traders in the enclave protect fellow believers/traders with regard to the counterfeiting business. This protection is primarily based on religious solidarity in the Muslim enclave that promote the economic welfare of many Muslims and even Christians who are involved in the informal optical media trade in the Philippines.

5.9 Summary

This chapter has illustrated that the illegal traders in the Philippines and Vietnam are not really the gun-toting crime syndicates or organized criminals who finance terrorism from the sales of pirated CDs, DVDs, and other counterfeit goods as what some mass media, government, or intelligence reports would like to portray as the cause of persistence of the illegal piracy trade. The traders belong to a certain entrepreneurial ethnic group who controls the piracy trade in their own country. In the Philippines, the traders who control the optical disc piracy belong to the minority Muslim ethnic group called Maranaos, while in Vietnam, the operators belong to the majority ethnic group called Kiln. Both types of traders are in alliance with ethnic Chinese traders in their own country who usually act as suppliers and intermediaries between local traders and top Chinese piracy suppliers from the mainland China.

The illegal trade of optical disc piracy persists in the Philippines and Vietnam because of some major "push" and "pull" factors which drive or attract people into the informal trade. In the Philippines, the urban migration caused by adverse socio-economic situations such as displacement caused by the ongoing war between government forces and Muslim rebel groups, chronic poverty in ARMM due to government neglect and profiling of Muslims as terrorists in mass media, as well as the social discrimination of Muslims in Philippine society which makes it difficult for Muslims to be employed in the formal sector are among the major macro forces which drive Maranao Muslim migrants to engage in the illegal optical disc business in Quiapo and other urban centers in the country. In Vietnam, opening of more trading opportunities facilitated by the *Doi Moi* (renovation) economic policy of the Vietnamese government, the lure of higher profits in optical disc piracy trade, and the ease of registering and maintaining CD–DVD shops are among the major forces which influence Kiln traders to engage in the piracy trade.

This chapter has also illustrated that the persistence of the optical disc piracy trade in the Philippines is facilitated by technological and social networks which enable traders to engage in illegal piracy business. Piracy is highly mediated by technology. Optical disc piracy's preproduction, production, and postproduction stages would not be possible without the indispensable role of the ICT technologies such as the cell phone and the Internet. Technologies create networks which connect and align illegal traders with other piracy networks and unscrupulous law enforcers for protection money using the ATM technology as well as to maintain the informal trade. Piracy also tapped social networks to pursue illegal transactions and protect the illegal trade system from intrusion of outsiders and law enforcers. The bilateral kinship network of the Maranaos is utilized as a social resource in the informal disc trade to recruit new retailers and informal workers and to promote trust and cooperation in the piracy business enterprise and to protect trade secret from outsiders. Ethnic Maranao network based on common language and cultural heritage is also used as another resource to assure fulfillment of illegal contractual duties in the piracy trade. The Maranao “rido” (family feud or vendetta) and “maratabat” (honor) become powerful enforcement tools to ensure compliance of parties to illegal contractual obligations in the piracy business and to avoid law enforcement and raids. The Maranao language is also another powerful tool used by Maranao traders against arrests, raids, or confiscations of discs. Finally, the common religious affiliation of the Maranao traders as Muslims has unintendedly helped the maintenance of the piracy trade. The Muslim concept of “ummah” or brotherhood has created religious solidarity among Muslim traders in QTCC which further protected the trade from betrayal, identity of traders during raids, and revelation of the illegal trade operations to non-Muslim outsiders and law enforcers. The optical media piracy persists in the Philippines and Vietnam not just because the copyright laws and the law enforcement are weak but because there are strong technological and social networks that support and maintain its illegal operations.

References

Arnold, D. (2013). Social margins and precarious work in Vietnam. *American Behavioral Scientist, 57*(4), 468–487. Doi: 10.1177/0002764212466245.

Azanza, P. A. (1994). *The subculture of ambulant vendors in Quiapo: A sociological analysis*. Unpublished master’s thesis in Sociology, Department of Sociology, University of the Philippines.

Banton, M. (1967). *Race relations*. New York: Basic Books.

Baradas, D. (1977). Maranao law: A study of conflict and its resolution in a multicentric power system. *Mindanao Journal III, 3–4*(January–June), 187–196.

Barfield, T. (Ed.). (1997). *The dictionary of anthropology*. New York: Blackwell Publishers.

Bauzon, K. E. (1991). *Liberalism and the quest for Islamic identity in the Philippines*. Quezon City: ADMU Press.

Bernabe, S., & Krstic, G. (2005). *Labor productivity and access to market matters for pro-poor growth, the 1990s in Burkina Faso and Vietnam, operationalising pro-poor growth study*. Washington, DC: World Bank.

Bertaux, D. (1997). Transmission in extreme situations: Russian families expropriated by the October revolution. In D. Bertaux & P. Thompson (Eds.), *Pathways to social class* (pp. 230–258). Oxford: Oxford University Press.

Bertaux-Wiame, I. (1981). The life-history approach to the study of internal migration. In D. Bertaux (Ed.), *Biography and society* (pp. 249–265). Thousand Oaks: Sage.

Bowles, S., & Gintis, H. (2004). Persistent parochialism: Trust and exclusion in ethnic network. *Journal of Economic Behavior & Organization, 55*, 1–23.

Busran-Yao, J. (2006). Policy notes, PIDS no. 2005–05 (April 2006).

Casambre, N. J. (1969). The response to Harrison’s administration in the Philippines, 1913–21. *Asian Studies [Manila], 7*(2), 156–170.

Castañeda, W. (1993). Patrones de Migracion hacia Barranquilla, Cali, Medellin y Santafe de Bogota. *Revista Coyuntura Social*, 9, Noviembre.

Castells, M. (1997). *The information age, economy, society and culture, Volume II, The power of identity*. Oxford: Blackwell Publishing Ltd.

Cling, J. P., Razafindrakoto, M., Roubaud, F. (2010). The informal sector in Vietnam, study for the ILO. http://www.tamdaoconf.com/tamdao/wp-content/uploads/downloads/2010/08/DIAL-ILO-Study-informal-Vietnam-2010.pdf. Accessed 3 May 2014.

Cling, J. P., Razafindrakoto, M., Roubaud, F. (2012). Explanatory factors behind formalizing non-farm household businesses in Vietnam. www.dial.ird.fr/…/DT+2012-20+Cling+–+Razafindrakoto+–+Roubaud.pd. Accessed 20 June 2013.

Cu, C. L. (2005). Rural to urban migration in Vietnam. http://www.ide-jetro.jp/English/Publish/Download/Asedp/pdf/071_7.pdf. Accessed 24 Jan 2015.

Dang Doanh, L., & Minh Tu, P. (1997). *The informal sector: International experiences and Vietnam in the economic transition period*. Hanoi: National Political Publishing House.

De Soto, H. (1989). *The other path: The economic answer to terrorism*. New York: Perseus Books.

Gonzales, F. L. (1999). Sultans of a violent land. In E. Guttierrz et al. (Ed.), *Rebels, warlords and Ulama: A reader on Muslim separatism and the war in southern Philippines*. Quezon City: University of the Philippines Press.

De Quiros, E. F., & Gonzales, F. G. (2002). Excluding Muslim Filipinos: A study on exclusionary processes on Maranao Muslims in Salam compound. http://www.docstoc.com/docs/55726988/EXCLUDING-MUSLIM-FILIPINOS-A-STUDY-ON-EXCLUSIONARY-PROCESSES-ON

Fong, T. (2001). A new and dynamic community: The case of Monterey Park, California. In M. Lopez-Garza & D. R. Diaz (Eds.) *Asian and Latin immigrants in a restructuring economy: The metamorphosis of Southern California* (pp. 313–333). Stanford: Stanford University Press.

Freeman, D. B. (1996). Doi Moi policy and the small-enterprise boom in Ho Chi Minh City, Vietnam. *The Geographical Review, 86*. http://www.questia.com/googleScholar.qst?docId=5001643249

Gowing, P., & McAmis, R. (Eds.). (1974). *The Muslim Filipinos*. Manila: Solidaridad Publishing House.

Gowing, P. (1979). *Muslim Filipinos—Heritage and horizon*. Quezon City: New Day Publishers.

Gowing, P. (Ed.). (1988). *Understanding Islam and Muslims in the Philippines*. Detroit: Cellar Book Shop.

Granovetter, M. (1985). Economic action and social structure: The problem of embeddedness. *American Journal of Sociology, 91*, 481–510.

Green, L. (2001). *Communication, technology and society*. London: Sage Publications.

GSO/IRD-DIAL (2010). Dynamics of the informal sector in Hanoi and Ho Chi Minh City 2007–2009: Main findings of the household business & informal sector survey (HB&IS). GSO/IRD-DIAL project. www.colloques.tamdaoconf.com. Accessed 10 Feb 2014.

Hassan, S. (1983). *Social networks of Muslim Filipino in Quiapo, Philippines*. Unpublished dissertation in anthropology, Department of Anthropology, University of the Philippines, Diliman, Quezon City.

Hernandez, C. (2006). The AFP's institutional response to armed conflict: A continuing quest for the right approach. Policy notes. Philippine Institute for Development Studies (PIDS). No. 2006–02 (March 2006). http://www.hdn.org.ph. Accessed 20 Dec 2014.

Imai, K., & Gaiha, R. (2007). Poverty, inequality and ethnic minorities in Vietnam. Policy Research Working Paper 6114, Washington, DC: The World Bank.

Isidro, A., & Mamitua, S. (Eds.). (1968). *Muslim Philippines*. Marawi: Mindanao State University.

Jensen, R., & Peppard, D. M. (2003). Hanoi's informal sector and the Vietnamese economy: A case study of roving street vendors. *Journal of Asian and African Studies, 38*(1), 71–84.

Karaos, A. M. (1985). Manila's urban poor dimensions of marginality and power. *Pulso, 1*(3), 241–252.

Latiph, A. (2007). Development dichotomy in Mindanao. http://pspa.ph/files/PSPA2014/Latiph%20Acram_Development%20Dichotomy%20in%20Mindanao%28doc%29.pdf

Latour, B. (1996). *Aramis, or the love of technology*. Cambridge, MA: Harvard University Press.

Laumann, E. O. (1973). *Bonds of pluralism: The forms and substance of urban social networks*. New York: Wiley.

Leibovich, J. (1996). La Migracion Interna en Colombia. Un Modelo Explicativo del proceso de asimilacion. *Revista Planeacion y Desarollo, 27*(4), Octubre–Diciembre.

Majul, C. A. (1985). *The contemporary Muslim movement in the Philippines*. Berkeley: Mizan Press.

Matuan, M. I. (1983). The Maranao migrants in Metro manila. MA thesis, San Carlos University. A version was published in *Dansalan Quarterly*, *4*(2): 1985.

Peluso, N. L. (1994). *Rich forests, poor people: Resource control and resistance in Java*. Berkeley: University of California Press.

Pertierra, R., et al. (2002). *TXT-ING SELVES, cellphones and Philippine modernity*. Malate: De la Salle University Press, Inc.

Pertierra, R. (2006). *Transforming technologies: Altered selves*. Malate: De la Salle University Press, Inc.

PHDR (2005). Philippine human development report 2005. Peace, human security and human development in the Philippines. 2nd Edition. Human Development Network. www.hdr.undp.org. Accessed 20 Apr 2014.

Portes, A., & Sensenbrenner, J. (1993). Embeddedness and immigration: Notes on the social determinants of economic action. *American Journal of Sociology*, *98,* 1320–1350.

PS Ngayon (2007). Pilipino Star Ngayon Newspaper, September 10, 2007 issue. www.Philstar.com. Accessed 22 Sept 2013.

Pulse Asia (2006). Ulat ng Bayan Survey, October 21–November 8, 2006/Philippines. Final report for the human development network. www.hdn.org.ph. Accessed 7 May 2015.

Saber, A. & Madele, A. (Eds.). (1975). *The Maranao*. Manila: Solidaridad Publishing House.

Salaff, J. W. et al. (2002). Ethnic entrepreneurship, social networks, and the enclave. http://www.chass.utoronto.ca/~agreve/Salaff-Greve-Wong-Xu.pdf

Schaefer, R. (2005). *Sociology, 10th international edition*. New York: McGraw-Hill Education.

Scott, J. C. (1987). *Weapons of the weak: Everyday forms of peasant resistance*. New Haven: Yale University Press.

Strauss, A. (1978). A social world perspective. In N. Denzin (Ed.) *Studies in symbolic interaction 4* (pp. 171–128). Greenwich: JAI Press.

Strauss, A. (1984). Social worlds and their segmentation processes. In N. Denzin (Ed.) *Studies in symbolic interaction 5* (pp. 123–139). Greenwich: JAI Press.

Szalontai, B. (2008). The diplomacy of economic reform in Vietnam: The genesis of Doi Moi, 1986–1989. *Journal of Asiatic Studies* (Korea University, Asiatic Research Center), *51*(2), 199–252.

Taussig, M., & Thi Thu Hang, P. (2004). *Private enterprise formality and the role of local governance. ADB making markets work better for the poor*, Discussion paper 02. Hanoi: Asian Development Bank.

Tenev, S. et al. (2003). Informality and the playing field in Vietnam's business sector. Washington, DC: IFC/World Bank/MPDF. www.ifc.org/wps/connect/9aae680047adb52f9311f7752622ff02/VN-informality-playing field-VN.pdf. Accessed 2 July 2015.

Thu Giang, V., & Thi Thu, T. (1999). *Women labour in the informal sector in Hanoi—Real situation and choices*. Hanoi: National Economic University.

Turner, S., & Schoenberger, L. (2012). Street vendor livelihoods and everyday politics in Hanoi, Vietnam: The seeds of a diverse economy? *Urban Studies, 49*(5), 1027–1044.

Salaff, J. W. (2002). Structural barriers and the job hunt for professional PRC migrants in Canada. *The International Journal of Human Resource Management*, *13*, 450–464.

Star, S. L. (1989). The structure of ill-structure solutions: Boundary objects and heterogeneous distributed problem solving. In M. N. Huhns & I. Gasser (Eds.), *Distributed artificial intelligence* (Vol. 2, pp. 37–54). London: Pitman.

Sung, C. (2011). *Drawing the line: Spatial street vendor management in Ho Chi Minh City*. M.A. thesis, Massachusetts Institute of Technology. http://dspace.mit.edu/98E80CA3-F429-43D4-9F6D-8CBE5A89127C/FinalDownload/DownloadId-68473C8D7EADEC6D43F19A2E91CE7494/98E80CA3-F429-43D4-9F6D-8CBE5A89127C/bitstream/handle/1721.1/67241/759124561.pdf?sequence=1. Accessed 1 Aug 2014.

Vietnam News. (2007, March 26). Street vendors must obtain licenses, Government in action. http://vietnamnews.vn/politics-laws/law-justice/163114/street-vendors-must-obtain-licences.html. Accessed 18 Sept 2014.

Williams, M. C. (1992). *Vietnam at the crossroads*. New York: The Royal Institute of Internal Affairs, Council of Foreign Relations Press.

Yinger, J. M. (1985). Ethnicity and social change: The interaction of structural, cultural, and personality factors. *Ethnic and Racial Studies*, *6*(4), 395–409.

World Bank. (2003). *Human development for peace and prosperity in autonomous region in Muslim Mindanao,* also cited in Jasmin Busran-Yao, Policy Notes, PIDS No. 2005-05 (April 2006).

Chapter 6
Corruption and the Nonenforcement of the Optical Media Law

6.1 Law Enforcement and Corruption in Sociology

What constitutes law remains a continuing debate among sociologists. But one thing is certain for sociologists of law: there is no legal order if the law is not effectively enforced. Max Weber was the first to point out the necessity of a "gapless" law where the law is enforced in all its dimensions by a specialized staff to ensure coercion, sanction, and deterrence, against anyone who intends to violate the law. In short, law enforcement is an essential element in defining law. And this all depends on the people behind the law who are tasked by the state to interpret and implement the official law. Law enforcement implies power and discretion of officers of the law. Thus state functionaries such as judges, government regulators, and police officers have the discretion to interpret the official law and to determine how and when to apply it on actual social situations.

The discretionary power of law enforcers has often been cited in criminology and sociology research as a problem area in law enforcement. Gary Marx (1981), for instance, argues that crime or illegality does not always stem from the absence of social control. On the contrary, situations exist where the presence of social control contributes to, or even generates, criminal behavior. Law enforcers who have discretion can implement the substantive law different from the official one. Ironically, the presence of law enforcement can, in some cases, permit crime through (1) escalation (by taking enforcement action, authorities unintentionally encourage rule breaking), (2) nonenforcement (by strategically taking no enforcement action, authorities intentionally permit rule breaking), and (3) covert facilitation (by taking hidden deceptive enforcement action, authorities intentionally encourage rule breaking). Of these three types, Marx acknowledges that nonenforcement is the most difficult form to identify empirically. As a strategy, it is often illegal and hidden. Nonenforcement may literally involve taking no enforcement action, or simply passing on information regarding police and criminal activities. And most often monetary and bureaucratic corruption influences the discretionary powers of public

V.O. Ballano, *Sociological Perspectives on Media Piracy in the Philippines and Vietnam*, DOI 10.1007/978-981-287-922-6_6

officer or agency in deciding what course of action to take among many possible choices in implementing the law. Thus unscrupulous law enforcers who participate in illegal optical disc piracy trade strategically decide not to take enforcement action against it in exchange of monetary and non-monetary gifts.

Corruption and the nonenforcement of copyright laws are often alluded to in some piracy reports and investigations as causing the persistence of the illegal trade of optical disc piracy in Southeast Asia. But a sociological analysis of monetary and bureaucratic corruption showing the collusion patterns between law enforcers, traders, and government business regulators in the piracy trade is apparently missing in copyright infringement literature. This reflects the apparent absence of sociology in corruption debates (Hodgkinson 1997; Jong-Sung and Khagram 2005; Khondker 2006), much more in the area of intellectual property rights (IPR) infringement. Corruption, being a difficult and complex concept, is often avoided by sociologists. Most literature on corruption is not produced by sociologists but by political scientists and economists, with a small contribution from business ethics (Aguilera and Vadera 2007, p. 431). But the magnitude of the effect of corruption to the developing economies, particularly those in Southeast Asia, is too great to be ignored which prompted some sociologists to investigate it seriously. Professor Syed Hussein Alatas pioneered the sociological study of corruption. His four books on sociology of corruption were the first to do a systematic sociological analysis on the nature of corruption as well as its effects to the economy (Alatas 1968, 1977, 1990, 1999). A few followed this path such as Paravala's (1993) study on the elite construction of corruption in India, Deflem's (1995) conception of corruption using Habermas' theory of communicative action, Jonathan Hyslop's (2005) analysis of political corruption in South Africa, and Sten Widmalm's (2008) book on the complex relationship between corruption, decentralization, and social capital. Despite these efforts, sociological studies on corruption have not developed into a specialized field that includes investigations of current trade issues such as corruption in intellectual property rights infringement, particularly in the illegal copyright business. Most literature written on piracy is more prescriptive and theoretical in approach rather than empirical and sociological and focused on the relationship between corruption and law.

One of the difficulties of studying corruption in sociology or in any other discipline lies in its definition. There are as many definitions of corruption as there are many academic disciplines. And almost everyone who writes about it tries to define it (Jain 2001, p. 104). There is no agreement among scholars on the definition of corruption. Definitions vary depending on the scholar's theoretical leaning and academic training. What is common, however, among corruption scholars is the tendency to define corruption in terms of acts rather than in terms of networks and social relations. Narrow definitions of corruption see corruption as "corruptive activities" or deeds which are just morally corrupt (Johnston 1994). There is a consensus among scholars that corruption refers to acts in which the power of the public office is used for personal gain in a manner that contravenes the rules of the game (Jain 2001, p. 73). But some scholars argue that corruption is a broader phenomenon, or rather a hardly definable set of phenomena (The Hungarian Gallup Institute

1999, p. 1). Sociologists, in particular, view corruption as a problem in social structure and social relations rather than a problem of moral defect of individuals and groups in society. Most corruption cases, particularly in piracy trade, are relational and networked, based on longer reciprocal social relations—as one trader would say "You scratch my back and I'll scratch yours"—rather than on aggregate episodic encounters. The widespread and persistent production and sale of counterfeit discs imply some sustained corrupt relations and bribery where some sectors of the law enforcement system have been dominated by illegal groups, rather than aggregate corrupt acts. Thus the definition of the sociologist Mathieu Deflem (1995) on corruption, and one which will be applied in this chapter, is relevant in the sociological analysis of corruption and nonenforcement of the optical media law. For him, corruption is the "colonization of social relations in which two or more actors undertake an exchange relation by way of a successful transfer of the steering-media of money or power, thereby sidestepping the legally prescribed procedure to regulate the relation" (Deflem 1995, p. 1). Corruption can either be monetary or bureaucratic. Monetary corruption is the exchange relation between two or more actors which is carried out by way of a transfer of money, while a bureaucratic corruption is carried out by a transfer of power. These two types of corruption intertwined to sustain the illegal trade of optical disc piracy in the Philippines and Vietnam.

6.2 Understanding the Nonenforcement of the Optical Media Law

One morning, while the author was doing an observational research in Quiapo Barter Trade Center Complex before it was closed in 2011, he saw three policemen standing at the corner of a major street looking as if they seriously examined the movements of people in the area and ready to arrest anyone who violates the law. Ironically, behind them were hundreds of retailers selling counterfeit discs. Instead of arresting these traders and confiscating their illegal goods, these policemen preferred to ignore them, pretending as if nothing illegal was happening in their midst. A similar incident also happened in Vietnam. During his recent observational research of CD–DVD shops in Ho Chi Minh, Vietnam, he visited one big registered CD–DVD shop in the city, and to his surprise, he saw various kinds of pirated discs openly displayed and sold to customers. And from a distance, he also saw some local policemen patrolling the area. Yet he did not see any serious concern from these law enforcers to inspect the shop, confiscate the counterfeit discs, and arrest the people behind the illegal trade (Fig. 6.1).

The aggressiveness of the retailers and traders who sell counterfeit discs openly in the makeshift stalls in the sidewalks, rented stalls in the Philippines, as well as in registered CD–DVD shops in Vietnam has often baffled many people, including stakeholders, media practitioners, government regulators, and the general public. Many wonder why such open sale of counterfeit optical media continues despite explicit prohibition and criminalization of this activity by the copyright law. This is

Fig. 6.1 One of the popular registered CD–DVD shops selling pirated discs in Vietnam (Image courtesy of the author)

even more surprising to non-Vietnamese observers to see counterfeit copies of original music and film discs displayed and sold publicly in registered stores in Vietnam, particularly in Ho Chi Minh City. This phenomenon of legal CD–DVD stores selling pirated discs is unheard of in the Philippines. Normally, illegal discs are sold in illegal outlets and the legal ones in the registered establishments. But Vietnam has shown a special case where the legal and illegal are openly and directly mixed up in the business operations of its optical media trade. CD–DVD stores are overtly legal as the establishments are registered and regulated by the government, but they are also illegal as they engage in the sale of illegal products. So how does one account this overt selling and marketing of pirated discs in the Philippines and Vietnam?

One explanation to account this open selling of counterfeit discs in the Philippines is allegedly the difficulty of law enforcers, particularly the local police, in distinguishing the genuine discs from illegal ones. They hesitate to confiscate at once counterfeit copies sold on sidewalks for fear of being charged in court by sellers for robbery and illegal seizure. Another reason, according to some informants, is that only the designated government agencies against piracy such as the Optical Media Board (OMB) or the Ministry of Information and Communication (MIC) have the expertise and direct mandate to identify and confiscate fake media discs. Other law enforcement agencies must first coordinate with theses agencies before initiating enforcement action. By law, they said, policemen cannot unilaterally decide to arrest vendors and confiscate their discs without the explicit authorization from these agencies. But do these explanations accurately account for the open and persistent sale of pirated discs in the Philippines? Or these are just justifications to hide corruption and the involvement of some law enforcers in this type of trade?

By mere appearance, one can easily detect whether a disc is original or fake. In the Philippines, the counterfeit ones are usually wrapped with hard covers and plastics and not placed in CD or DVD cases as this can add more cost to the already cheap discs. Original copies bear original holograms and logos of stakeholders and Movie and Television Review and Classification Board's (MTRCB) classification which are not usually found in pirated ones. In Vietnam, original CDs and DVDs bear the green government sticker at the back of the CD or DVD case label. Moreover, because of the strict separation with regard to the venue of sale between the legal and illegal, original discs are sold in registered and licensed CD–DVD stores in legitimate malls, bookstores, shopping centers, and other legitimate business establishment, while fake discs are purchased in mobile or makeshift stalls in public spaces such sidewalks or kiosks and in rented stores or shops with no OMB license. Thus, one can easily distinguish the original discs from the pirated ones by mere appearance and location of the store where the discs are purchased. In Vietnam, it is easy to distinguish the original disc from the pirated one by inspecting the CD or DVD cover whether it contains the ministry's sticker or not. But distinguishing a genuine copy from a pirated one seems not an issue for Vietnamese. Everyone seems not interested to know the difference as almost all or around 99 % of the optical media discs sold in Vietnamese CD–DVD shops, bookstores, and mobile stores are counterfeit copies or pirated discs. During the author's visits, only a few big CD–DVD shops displayed some original cases of CDs and DVDs. But they seemed to be for display purposes only as key informants said that the salesperson at the cashier usually offers to the customer a clear digital copy, instead of the original one, at a price usually 10 times cheaper than the genuine copy. In a big CD–DVD shop in Ho Chi Minh, for instance, an original DVD costs around 120,000 Vietnamese Dong (VND) while a clear illegal copy costs only around 10,000–12,000 VND (Figs. 6.2 and 6.3).

Thus, if one takes a closer and critical look at the aggressiveness of retail traders in the Philippines and Vietnam to openly sell counterfeit discs beyond mass media reports, he/she can discover a different story. According to some informants with an inside knowledge of the trade, it is not the law enforcer's lack of technical knowledge or legal jurisdiction to seize counterfeit optical discs and to arrest illegal vendors that prevents law enforcement. Rather, it is the "colonization" or the influence of the informal trade network over the law enforcement agencies of the government, more specifically on the local police in the Philippines and Vietnam. The local police who are supposed to be the first line of defense in law enforcement against illegality take no enforcement actions against piracy as some of their ranks are involved in corruption and protection rackets, at times in coordination with gangsters especially in Vietnam, that allow illegal traders to pursue their counterfeit business. It is well known that some police personnel sometimes underenforce the law. This is the reason why some laws are more enforced than others (Brown 1991, p. 285). Police discretion or the ability of the police officer or agency to make

Fig. 6.2 This picture shows a pirated (*left*) and an original CD (*right*) disc displayed together in a big bookstore in Ho Chi Minh City. The original disc bears the green government control sticker at the bottom of the right side of the case, while the pirated one has none (Image courtesy of the author)

Fig. 6.3 Samples of pirated Chinese, Korean, and Vietnamese movies and TV shows sold in Ho Chi Minh CD–DVD shops (Image courtesy of the author)

choices among possible courses of action is said to play a crucial role in cases of this type of selective enforcement. Police and law enforcers who engage in illegal protection rackets become blind to illegal businesses they "protect." In an interview with a Muslim leader of the piracy trade in a Philippine province who also heads the local Muslim association in the area, the police chief is said to have a regular contact with him. When the author asked one policeman who is a close relative of his wife to arrange an interview with this leader, this police commander summoned the latter to his office and asked him to accommodate him. The author found this ironic and indicative of the illegal alliance between the police and the optical media traders: a law enforcer summoning rather than arresting a rule breaker to speak about his experience on law breaking is highly irregular!

6.3 Corruption and Media Piracy in SEA

The role of corruption in the persistence of the illegal trade of optical disc piracy is often presumed to exist rather than documented and analyzed sociologically in piracy reports. Since corruption is often covert and hidden from the public eye, piracy investigations tend to sideline this problem and instead focus on the deficient legal and judicial systems of developing countries to search for causes on the persistence of media counterfeiting. And yet the connection between corruption and the endurance of optical media piracy trade in Southeast Asia seems apparent to be ignored. On a first glance, it is evident that the Southeast Asian (SEA) countries which are often mentioned in the USTR and IIPA Special 301 reports as piracy hot spots in the world are also corrupt countries in the corruption index of the global anti-corruption coalition Transparency International (TI).[1] The Philippines and Vietnam, in particular, are among the SEA countries which are not only frequently cited in the piracy watch lists of the USTR but also in the TI's list of most corrupt countries in the world. In TI's corruption perception index, a country which obtains a score of below 50 in its annual surveys is considered having a serious problem in corruption. Table 6.1 shows that the SEA countries in the USTR's Priority Watch List and Watch List are also countries with low scores and thus facing serious corruption problem.

Singapore, Brunei, Malaysia, Thailand, the Philippines, Indonesia, and Vietnam are the only SEA countries which are cited in the USTR's Special 301 piracy watch lists from 1989 to 2015. Singapore with a very high score (84) in TI's corruption index is the cleanest country in SEA with an overall rank of 7. It is only listed in the WL three times (1989–1991) and has long been removed from this list since 1991. Singapore is followed by Brunei Darussalam, a new entrant in the watch lists with a score of 55 and a world rank of 46 in terms of corruption index. So far, Singapore and Brunei were the only SEA countries with less frequency in the USTR watch lists. The rest of the SEA countries cited in the USTR watch lists such as Malaysia,

[1] http://www.transparency.org

Table 6.1 2014 corruption indices of Southeast Asian countries appearing in USTR special 301 reports (1989–2015) by score and world rank and type of USTR list

			Frequency in USTR piracy reports (1989–2015)[b]	
Country	Score	World rank	Priority watch list (PWL)	Watch list (WL)
Singapore	84	7		3
Brunei	55	46[a]		4
Malaysia	49	54[a]	2	11
Thailand	38	85	15	10
Philippines	38	85	6	19
Indonesia	34	107	17	10
Vietnam	31	119	2	16

Sources: Data are compiled from 2015 Corruption Index, Transparency International, USTR Special 301 Reports from 1989 to 2015

[a]2013 data, no 2014 data available yet online as of June 23, 1015

[b]Based on the author's personal count of the listings

Thailand, the Philippines, Indonesia, and Vietnam have lower scores and world ranks in corruption index and higher frequencies in the piracy watch lists. In particular, the Philippines and Vietnam, together with Indonesia, are SEA countries with higher frequencies in USTR's watch lists but with high corruption rates. The Philippines has been listed six times in the PWL and as high as 19 times in the WL since the creation of these lists by the USTR in 1989. Although downgraded from PWL to WL in 2013 and removed from the lists altogether in 2014 and 2015, media piracy in the Philippines remained high. Vietnam was upgraded by the USTR in 2014 from WL to PWL for the first time after being listed in WL for 16 consecutive years from 1997 up to 2013. Warnings of the USTR against piracy in these countries have been strong and consistent. Despite these warnings and government efforts to curb piracy, the Philippines and Vietnam remained de facto as two of the top piracy sites in the world, particularly with regard to illegal replication and widespread sale of illegal CDs and DVDs containing copyrighted music, film, and computer software. There is a connection between the persistence of media piracy in these SEA countries and level of corruption index. Countries with high corruption indices are more likely to support the illegal optical media trade than those with low indices.

6.4 The Nonenforcement of the Optical Media Law

The threat of economic sanctions under the Generalized System of Preferences (GSP) trade arrangement and bilateral trade agreements with the United States as well as the constant warnings from the USTR have influenced the Philippine and Vietnamese governments to take some major steps to protect intellectual property from counterfeiting. In the field of optical media, both governments have responded to the call of the United States to update their copyright laws in accordance with international standards. Thus, in 2004, the Philippines approved the passage of the Optical Media Act of 2004. Under this law, any person or group who engages in mastering, manufacture, replication, importation, or exportation of optical media without the necessary licenses from the Optical Media Board (OMB) shall be punished with an imprisonment of at least 3 years but not more than 6 years and a fine of not less than five hundred thousand pesos (Php 500,000.00) but not exceeding one million five hundred thousand pesos (Php 1,500,000.00). Vietnam too updated its copyright law and amended its Intellectual Property Code to impose heavier administrative sanctions to those who commit copyright infringement. Under Article 214 of Law No. 36/2009 of Vietnam, any organization or individual who commit infringement, such as optical disc piracy, is compelled to discontinue the act and shall be penalized by administrative sanctions such as caution, fine, and confiscation of the counterfeit goods, raw materials, and means for trading counterfeit goods or suspension of the business activities in domains where infringement is committed. In addition, the violators are compelled to destroy the counterfeit goods, material, and means for infringement or transport them out of Vietnamese territory. Both laws expressly prohibit the mastering, manufacturing, and sale of copyrighted optical media discs containing original music, film, and business software and imposed stiff sanctions against violators.

The Optical Media Act has been an effective law since 2004 in the Philippines, and the amended provision of the Intellectual Property Code of Vietnam against infringement has been implemented since 2010, and yet copyright piracy of optical media continues to thrive with impunity in these two Southeast Asian countries. In the Philippines, open piracy or the illegal sale of pirated CDs and DVDs in rented shops and in makeshift stalls remains a popular sight in many sidewalks and rented stalls in Metro Manila as well as in many major cities in the country, despite the "closure" of the alleged central hub of pirated discs in the country last July 2011—the Quiapo Barter Trade piracy center in Manila. In Vietnam, counterfeit discs are sold openly in many registered CD–DVD shops in Ho Chi Minh, Hanoi, and other big cities in the communist state. Thus one wonders: How is law enforcement against piracy done in the Philippines and Vietnam? Why is the law not effectively enforced? To what extent bribery and corruption play an important role in this non-enforcement of the optical media law in these two countries?

6.5 Corruption and Illegal Business Protection System

One major reason why the optical media law is not properly enforced and the production and sale of illegal media discs continue in the Philippines and Vietnam is that some illegal groups protect traders and retailers against arrest and confiscation of counterfeit discs for violating the law. By giving a bribe and forming an illegal partnership with the local police and their allied networks, illegal entrepreneurs such as piracy traders receive security and immunity from legal sanction and prosecution. Benefits traders can get from this informal business protection outweigh the cost of the bribe. Thus corruption is not generally perceived as particularly destructive, and bribes are seen more as a customary business practice rather than illegal acts. Oftentimes, organized crimes such as gangs participate in this illegal business protection system. Although organized crime and corruption are often treated as separate entities, they can, in fact, form a partnership and symbiotic relationship, more specifically in Vietnam, to protect illegal business such as piracy.

6.5.1 Vietnam

Vietnam has a dual illegal protection system of illegal business activities based on corruption. Vietnamese illegal protection rackets are dominated by corrupt law enforcers, especially the local police, and by illegal gangs called *Giang Ho* (pronounced as "Yang Ho" which literally means "river," figuratively taken to mean living a "crazy life," a gangster). The Vietnamese government has exerted much effort to fight gangsters that tend to undermine its anti-corruption drive. According to some informants, legal and illegal businesses in Vietnam, particularly in big cities such as Ho Chi Minh, are usually "protected" through bribery of government law enforcers led by the local police and by the local gangs or *Giang Ho*. The corruption of the police is supported by some research findings, but corrupt practices of the *Giang Hos* are less documented owing to a lack of data, but their illegal activities are well known to many Vietnamese, especially to businessmen.[2] Thirty percent of 1000 respondents polled in a Transparency International's 2013 international survey, for instance, said they had paid bribes to one or more of eight public services in Vietnam and considered the police force as the most corrupt of 12 institutions in the country.[3] The alliance of some corrupt police officers and *Giang Ho* becomes apparent when local police would remain silent and refuse to intervene whenever a complaint against the harassment of gangsters is reported by businessmen. A former head of a company in Vietnam recalled that he reported to the district and then to the city police of the harassment and beating of gangsters against his workers and no one intervened. It only stopped when he approached the gangsters' top boss, Nam Cam, and paid a higher protection money to secure his business.[4] In many cases, the police, the underworld led by the *Giang Ho*, and traders can forge a network based on corruption and bribery to persist in illicit business. The involvement of this dual system in business protection racket through corruption has made the illegal piracy trade more difficult to abolish. Both groups provide piracy traders advice and tips on impending government law enforcement actions, raids, and confiscations of discs. The illegal gangsters or *Giang Ho*, whose leaders have connections with the local police and some government bureaucrats, can either directly participate in the illegal trade as producers and distributors or indirectly as protectors of the trade such as providing tips of an impending raid or assisting traders in facilitating illegal payoffs with some traders complying government regulations.

---

[2] For a detailed description of the illegal and criminal activities of Giang Ho in Vietnam, especially in Ho Chi Minh City, read "Gangster's Paradise" at http://www.thanhniennews.com/society/gangsters-paradise-15866.html.

[3] http://www.johnib.wordpress.com/tag/transparency-international/page/2/

[4] vietnamnet.com, 4 April 2013.

The *Giang Hos* have their own informal organization. The members of the organization are usually poor young local thugs, ex-convicts, or unemployed who have experience in the underworld. The *Giang Ho* usually has its own turf and operates territorially like controlling a particular district in Ho Chi Minh City. One *Giang Ho* can either be in competition or allied with other *Giang Ho*. And gangsters have bosses or leaders who are influential people and who have strong connections with the police and government bureaucracy. The famous case of Ho Chi Minh's overall *Giang Ho* boss, Truong Van Cam, also known as Nam Cam, is an illustrative case how widespread *Giang Hos* operate illegal activities in the city in alliance with the police and some top government officials. Nam Cam was said to be the overall leader of the gangsters in Ho Chi Minh City engaging in various illegal activities and protection rackets. More than 150 people went on trial with him for murder, gambling, and bribery.[5] His case shows how *Giang Ho* is well connected with law enforcers in their illegal activities. His coconspirators include 13 police officials, 3 prosecutors, 3 journalists, Vietnam's former deputy security minister, its deputy national prosecutor, and the head of the state-owned broadcasting company. His execution together with his accomplices is an indication of the determination of the Vietnamese government to fight corruption and mobsters in the country. But even before the trial against Nam Cam was opened, news reports said a new generation of Ho Chi Minh City mobsters with such names as Dat Long Hair, Nam Fire, Xuan Leprosy, and Tuan Malaria had begun skirmishing over the spoils of Nam Cam's casino empire, indicating how the underworld of *Giang Hos* has well permeated the illegal culture of Vietnam.[6]

Giang Ho members usually approach both legal and illegal traders and offer protection and security for their businesses in exchange of a regular bribe or protection money. Traders, according to informants, can either accept or reject their offer depending on their social status, political connection, and attitude. If they have strong connections with the government, they can drive away the *Giang Ho* from their establishment and ask the police to step up their protection of their businesses in exchange of a higher bribe. But it is common for many businessmen in Vietnam to just keep the dual protection racket system to secure their trade against those who intend to disrupt business operations. In optical disc trade, the *Giang Ho* can provide advance tips of an impending raid or coordinate with the local police and regulators to make a compromise deal to avoid confiscation of discs. In some cases, the *Giang Ho* themselves engage in counterfeit business. In one Vietnamese news, for instance, a group of gangsters or *Giang Ho* was apprehended by the police for engaging in manufacturing and sale of fake beer in Ho Chi Minh. So if gangsters are not directly involved in the illegal trade, they serve as protectors or intermediaries between government law enforcers and traders. The *Giang Ho* does not, however, operate in industrial parks and industrial zones as they are directly safeguarded by the national government against illegal protection system according to informants.

---

[5] See "Nam Cam: Vietnam's Godfather" at http://www.news.bbc.co.uk/2/hi/asia-pacific/2794607.stm.

[6] See "Court sets out to free a city of corruption" at http://www.theage.com.au/articles/2003/03/09/1047144868386.html.

6.5.2 *Philippines*

Unlike Vietnam, the Philippines does not have a dual illegal protection system based on corruption and bribery. The strict dichotomy between legal and illegal businesses is the general rule in the country. Legal businesses which registered in the government generally do not need to bribe both the police and the local gangsters. They only need to bribe the police and government officials for protection against prosecution if they engage in illegal activities such as a big retail business engaging in smuggling to get cheap supplies abroad or a legitimate optical media producer engaging in illegal replication of discs beyond the license given by the Optical Media Board (OMB). The involvement of gangsters in protection racket of illegal trade is not a dominant system in the Philippines. There are no organized *Giang Hos* in the Philippines which are involved in protection rackets in both legal and illegal trade such as those in Vietnam. Of course, there are some local thugs who demand money and offer protection to some businesses in the Philippines. Some members of the New People's Army (NPA) engage in extortion racket asking some businesses "revolutionary taxes." But these are only few cases and the traders can always call the police or the military to stop their extortion activities. Thus protection racket by gangsters in the Philippines can be considered isolated cases and not part of dominant illegal culture as in the case of Vietnam.

The protection racket in the Philippines is usually controlled by the police and government law enforcers and usually against illegal business and not against legitimate establishments, unless of course, if they engage in something illegal. The underworld or organized crime in the Philippines does not usually engage in protection rackets against legal and illegal businesses like in Vietnam. Instead, it usually engages directly in illegal business activities such as drugs, human trafficking, smuggling, and other illegal activities and rarely in protection rackets in competition with the local police. Thus the protection of the illegal optical disc trade in the Philippines is primarily done by the police and other government law-enforcing agencies without much involvement of local gangsters.

6.6 Appropriating the Protection Money in Piracy

Corruption or the giving of a regular bribe or protection money by illegal traders to government regulators and law enforcers especially to the local police is a major reason why no enforcement action is done against piracy. The amount of bribe given by traders to law enforcers in optical disc piracy trade is usually proportional to the amount of the capital and the degree of risk involved in the illegal transaction: the higher is the amount of capital and risk involved, the higher is the bribe for the law enforcers or public authorities. Thus, if a Filipino trader is a producer-supplier and involved in the importation of replicating equipment or discs from China and/or in mass duplication or burning of pirated discs, the stakes would be high since the investment or capital of the illegal business would usually involve millions of pesos. This can also be true to a Vietnamese trader/owner of illegal optical discs factory. The value of the replicating equipment, raw materials, and other expenses for the business would be costly; hence proper connections and bribe money are needed to avoid the unnecessary loss of capital. In Quiapo Barter Trade Center Complex, the top producers-suppliers of pirated discs are said to be silent millionaires whose networks include a vast network of distributors, suppliers of raw material, retailers, "loaders," workers, technicians, and law enforcers who are dependent on their piracy business. The value of the replicating equipment and computer burners themselves are already expensive, and thus losing them together with the thousands of discs in an uncoordinated raid would be devastating to the trade and implies poor business decision on the part of the producers. Thus, the bribe in this case is usually high and sustained to avoid unnecessary loss of capital and profit due to surprise raids and confiscations of piracy goods and equipment by law enforcers. In an interview, one Quiapo top producer-supplier said that he lost one million pesos worth of discs and equipment due a surprise raid by the police in the barter trade area.

Protection money or bribe can, however, be subject to negotiation between traders and law enforcers, depending on the duration and status of the illegal alliance: the longer is the alliance, the more negotiable is the bribe as friendship and camaraderie influence the relationship between the police and traders. The newer and lesser intimate is the alliance, the more demanding would be the law enforcers led by the police on the amount and frequency of the bribe. This usually happens in sidewalk vending or small retail piracy.

Small retail piracy trade involves lesser capital and risk compared to production piracy; thus the bribe is generally lower and may not be regular, although it also depends on the size and amount of discs involved in transaction. The large- and medium-sized retail outlets invest more money for discs than small and mobile retail outlets. Therefore, the bribe of the large- and medium-sized shops is higher compared to small retail stores or stalls. In the Philippines, there are medium- and small-sized retail outlets. The medium-sized retail piracy shops are usually found in rented store spaces with roll-up doors like those found in the Quiapo Barter Trade Center Complex or in rented space along the sidewalks. They can also be found in rented shops in small- and medium-sized malls in Metro Manila or in big Philippine cities. The big ones are, of course, registered CD–DVD shops or large CD–DVD section found in big malls or shopping centers in urban centers.

6.7 Nonenforcement and Corruption Patterns in the Philippines and Vietnam

This section illustrates some common patterns of corruption and nonenforcement of optical media law in the Philippines and Vietnam. It analyzes six important areas where corruption and bribery are usually observed in these two countries, namely, in (1) production piracy, (2) transactions in the importation and transport of pirated discs and equipment in airports, (3) retail piracy, (4) sale of pirated discs in Philippine malls, (5) government antipiracy agency, and (6) judicial proceedings in courts. Owing to some limitations of data regarding corruption in optical disc piracy in Vietnam, the section focuses more on the Philippine case. Moreover, some of these patterns may have changed through time due to the evolving nature of the piracy trade.

6.7.1 Corruption in Production Piracy

Production piracy is the reason why retail piracy exists. There will be no illegal discs to sell by distributors and retailers if there is no constant replication of counterfeit discs by illegal optical disc plants either from abroad or within the country. Since production piracy entails big capital and investment on the part of illegal producers-suppliers of discs, corruption network and nonenforcement in this area are always fueled by regular and high amount of bribe to protect the trade. The International Intellectual Property Alliance's (IIPA) 2009 Special 301 Report identified around eight optical disc plants in Vietnam with an estimated production capacity of at least 42 million discs per year, exceeding the local market demand (IIPA 2009 Special 301 Report, p. 349). In the absence of strict monitoring and strict regulation with regard to the manufacturing and replication of discs by optical disc plants, even a legitimate disc factory which is supposed to produce blank discs was caught by Vietnamese police manufacturing counterfeit optical media discs of various kinds (IIPA 2012 Special 301 Report, footnote no. 17). Based on interviews of some traders in Ho Chi Minh City, illegal optical disc factories do exist in Vietnam. According to some traders, the pirated discs that they sell come from factories clandestinely located just outside the city. Some buy these discs through distributors located in one popular street in Ho Chi Minh known as the "Quiapo" of Vietnam. Others who know the location of these factories buy directly from the main sources due to their cheap wholesale price. By latest inspection, one can notice that most mobile vendors and CD–DVD shops no longer sell imported discs from China. An important indicator is that the disc cover no longer bears some Chinese characters indicating their origin. This confirms the USTR and IIPA assessments that the focus of Vietnamese authorities in their drive against piracy is the imported discs, particularly from China, rather than the locally manufactured discs—which explains why imported Chinese discs no longer flood the local market. According to informants, the logo on the cover of the disc such as "Simba" suggests that the high-quality digital copies are made inside the country. Many big CD–DVD shops sell this type of beautifully packaged discs with clear digital content bearing this type of manufacturing logo. Mobile vendors, however, sell discs with a different manufacturing logo which are usually of poorer quality, suggesting that the source of counterfeit discs is not only one but several factories. Vietnam used to import illegally counterfeit optical media discs from China through bribery with custom officials in the China–Vietnam borders. But lately, following the global trend of outsourcing, big illegal suppliers and producers linked with big crime syndicates find it cheaper and safer to export their replicating plants instead of pirated discs in countries "friendly" to piracy and vulnerable to corruption where they can both manufacture illegal discs for the local market and at the same time export some to neighboring countries. This confirms the IIPA's assessment that the optical disc plants in Vietnam are manufacturing discs beyond the demand of the local market, implying that these plants are exporting pirated discs to other countries. In its 2013 Special 301 Report, the IIPA observed that Vietnamese-sourced pirate products have already reached in recent years in Asia, North America, and even Eastern Europe (IIPA 2013 Special 301 Report, p. 288).

Vietnam, being proximate to China and its law enforcement susceptible to corruption and bribery, becomes an ideal place for illegal optical disc plants owned by Chinese or foreign producers and their Vietnamese cohorts. According to informants, producers usually follow the legal process of importing replicating equipment and setting up a disc factory in the country. But once established in the country, producers or owners of these factories usually shift to illegal activities by manufacturing pirated discs for the local market and abroad. This could not be done, according to informants, without the cooperation of some corrupt public officials, law enforcers, and illegal groups who conspire—because of bribe money—to circumvent the copyright law and provide protection for this illegal production of counterfeit CDs and DVDs.

The ease that illegal factories can manufacture illegal discs in Vietnam as well as the ease of Vietnamese traders in CD–DVD shops selling pirated copies of movies and music can immediately suggest that some corrupt groups must have protected this type of activity against raids, confiscations of discs, or closure of the shops. It is unusual for an overt illegal business activity like the sale of counterfeit discs in big registered establishments not to get noticed by the economic and local police. Anything illegal that is done publicly is usually protected by some unscrupulous law enforcers, members of the underworld, and other authorities who have established alliances with illegal traders. In Vietnam, the bigger is the business establishment that does illegal business, the higher is the protection money. The strategy of some corrupt government regulators or enforcers in order to extract bribe is usually to create regulatory difficulties for firms, much more if these firms do illicit acts. But the illegal protection system would ease up the legal and bureaucratic pressures for those who engage in illegal activities in Vietnam.

In the Philippines, production piracy is a little bit complicated compared to Vietnam as the Philippines is far from China and archipelagic in territory and, thus, requires the use of airports or harbors in transporting illegal discs and equipment from one province to another. Thus corruption in airports and in the Bureau of Customs is rampant in the country. In the Philippines, there are three types of pirated discs being sold in the local market: those which are imported from abroad, usually from China; those which are manufactured in the country by illegal optical disc plants; and those which are locally burned or duplicated by local producers-suppliers such as those in the Quiapo Barter Trade Center Complex. The optical media law in the Philippines explicitly criminalizes the illegal manufacturing, mastering, and burning of copyrighted media without the proper registration and licensing from the local government and from the Optical Media Board. Despite this prohibition, production piracy continues with the cooperation of corrupt law enforcers in the country. The problem with piracy is that this enterprise is a mixture of legal and illegal dimensions. Some aspects of this trade are legal such as some of its raw materials can be sold legally in legal establishments such as the purchase of empty discs, CD or DVD cases, computer burners, etc., although the law requires a license when bought in large numbers, or availing of the Bureau of Customs brokerage system. Two or three years ago when the Quiapo Barter Trade Center Complex was still an open piracy and imported Chinese discs flooded the Philippine market, Maranao Muslim producers-suppliers in Quiapo imported discs from China using the legal brokerage system in the Bureau of Customs. According to informants, producers-suppliers would call their contacts in China to buy the latest discs in big warehouses in Guangzhou, Guangdong Province, and hire a broker to ship the illegal goods to the Philippines through international airports. Upon reaching the Philippines, another legal broker transports them to the designated warehouses in Quiapo. The broker's inside contacts in the airport and Bureau of Customs will take care of the bribe and protection money to ensure that the discs will reach their destination. The bribe is usually computed per number of disc, such as 1 or 2 pesos per disc. Thus if the total of imported discs, for instance, is 50,000, then the bribe would be 50,000 or 100,000 pesos. The type of discs imported from China was usually those DVDs which contain more movies in discs such as 12 in 1, 24 in 1, etc., which require a more advanced replicating technology not found in the Philippines.

Another type of discs is those which are manufactured by illegal optical disc plants inside the country. Like Vietnam, outsourcing of piracy has become a pattern in the Philippines. This type of source of illegal discs has become more popular as direct importation from China has diminished. Replicating equipment is imported into the Philippines through corruption of some officials of the Bureau of Customs (BOC) in the Port Area of Manila. They are loaded in containers and misdeclared in the BOC. The OMB, in an interview, has admitted that it is difficult to monitor the arrival of various goods and intercept any imported replicating equipment as well as pirated discs. The spot checking is only done in random and not thorough and regular to sort out the illegal goods. In addition, the x-ray machines could not identify if these goods are indeed illegal or not. The bureau is laden with networks of corrupt officials and illegal groups engaging in smuggling which protect the importation of illegal replicating machines for piracy. The smuggling of replicating machines for piracy is only one of the many smuggling activities inside the BOC. Another strategy, according to the OMB, is similar to that of Vietnam. The replicating equipment enters the country as legal shipment allegedly for a legitimate optical disc plant. But once it entered the country, illegal producers would bribe regulators and law enforcers to set up their illegal disc factories. What they only need are the master copies or discs abroad often sent through courier mixed with legal goods or downloaded through the Internet to create pirated copies. The IIPA estimated that there were around 10 optical disc plants in the Philippines and was uncertain whether these plants were properly monitored by the OMB (IIPA 2008 Special 301 Report, p. 300). In 2011, one Quiapo Maranao producer-supplier of pirated discs claimed in an interview that there are illegal plants in the country, highly protected by top law enforcers and politicians, where local suppliers get their pirated discs aside from their privately burned discs in the enclave.

Pirated discs for the local market may not only come from illegal disc factories; there is a probability that they may come also from unauthorized copies of legal producers. According to the OMB chair, the agency has specified the steps and requirements for the legal production of optical discs. Inspections are also done by the OMB to ensure compliance. But there is no assurance that there are no loopholes in the system. The OMB cannot monitor completely the activities of legal producers 24/7. Just like in Vietnam, a government inspector can be bribed by the trader-producer when he/she inspects the disc factory. Although violations are found in the factory, the inspector would report compliance. With corruption network at work in government agencies tasked to fight piracy, the probability that legal producers too may engage in piracy is not farfetched. There is high reward for the legal producers to engage in piracy. They can sell the discs at a very low price but with high profit margin as these copies are untaxed by the government. Pirated discs which are manufactured by illegal optical disc plants are usually delivered to big Maranao producers-suppliers connected with the Quiapo piracy network in Manila who distribute them to various retail outlets in the Philippines.

The third type of pirated discs is those which are replicated locally in the Quiapo Barter Trade Center Complex in Manila. Counterfeit DVDs containing single English film are usually produced in the enclave. After the preproduction stage or after the producer has a complete picture of the total copies to be produced for each title, he/she proceeds to the production stage. In an interview, a former OMB chairman believes that the enclave has no capacity to reproduce the master copy using huge and expensive replicating machines with each line capable of producing as many as 40,000 copies per day. He cites two reasons: (1) these machines are very expensive. One machine, usually imported from Germany, costs around P60–P80 million, and the OMB does not believe the QBTCC producers can afford to buy this; (2) each machine of this type requires at least a space of 600–700 square meters (m^2), and the geographical space in the enclave is limited to house these machines. Thus, the OMB believes that enclave producers only use computer burners to reproduce fake optical media discs which, according to the Chairman, have a poorer quality compared to those made in the huge replicating machines. Most pirated discs are said to have been supplied by syndicates or Chinese triads and enclave sellers are said to receive them through consignment, payable in 15 days. If raided, the syndicates replace the confiscated discs with new ones.

Informants in the Quiapo enclave, however, told a different story. Though QBTCC does not have huge replicating machines used by big companies, it has high-speed replicating equipment or burners which can reproduce thousands of copies per day from the master copy. Because the producers in the enclave always avail of the latest technology in replicating machines, reproduction of the master copy into thousands and thousands of copies a day or within a shorter period of time can be made possible. Each replicating machine without being attached to a personal computer can reproduce at least 25 copies. And since one producer normally has more than one set of this type of machine, orders from local and provincial distributors are often met with dispatch. The total number of copies for each title is already predetermined by the producer after getting the orders of provincial distributors and big retails through mobile phone text or call.

According to informants, there are two kinds of protection money given by traders in the QBTCC before it was ordered closed by authorities in 2011: (1) the protection money given daily by sidewalk traders to local policemen patrolling the area and (2) the protection money given weekly by producers and top traders to the block commander and to some top law enforcers. The latter is a common fund collected from all financiers, producers, distributors, and owners of legitimate stalls or stores in the enclave. The producers have learned to use computer technology when giving bribes to law enforcers. Instead of hiring a liaison, the producers would more directly deposit the weekly protection money to the ATM account of the law enforcers. This procedure also provides protection for the police commander against "buy-bust" operation by other law enforcers not aligned with the trade network. The practice of depositing the bribe in ATM accounts and the use of cellular phones to alert them of the incoming protection money have simplified the transaction and flow of information between the police and the traders. According to a bank teller, it is a normal banking practice for some policemen to maintain ATM bank accounts to receive deposits. It helps that deposit slips do not require the depositors to write their name on it; thus, the anonymity of the source of funds is kept.

The regular protection money is given to law enforcers by big-time retailers, distributors, and producers who occupy legal spaces in the enclave's commercial areas. These law enforcers are the local and top police officers in Metro Manila and the agents of National Bureau of Investigation (NBI) and the Criminal Investigation and Detection Group (CIDG). According to a producer, the buildings or condominiums in the QBTCC, except those occupied by Christians, are organized into associations based on ethnicity and kinship. Each building is an organized group of suppliers, distributors, or sellers with a Maranao leader who is also informally linked with other leaders, especially on matters related to the informal optical media business network. These leaders normally agree among themselves how much protection money each legal owner or lessee of a store or stall should contribute. According to him, the monthly contribution for each trader in the barter center before it was "closed" in July 2011 was usually around 500 pesos (around US$13) per month. Thus, if each building has fifty (50) traders, then the monthly protection money would reach twenty-five thousand pesos (P25,000) for one small building only. If one multiplies this amount to the number of buildings occupied by optical media entrepreneurs, then the protection money would indeed be substantial. According to an informant, this bribe is either be given in cash to law enforcers or deposited in designated automated teller machine (ATM) bank accounts.

6.7.2 *Corruption in Airports*

Imported pirated discs and equipment could not be sent to the Philippines and the locally manufactured fake discs could not reach their provincial destinations without the participation of some corrupt airport and airline personnel. According to a producer-supplier, the pirated discs packed in boxes are delivered from the Quiapo piracy enclave in Manila to the domestic airport by the "loader." This loader has a network of contacts among airport officers, law enforcers, and airline personnel. These discs are usually loaded in the luggage section of the plane. If intercepted, the loader negotiates with the airport officials involved and secretly gives them bribe money for the release of the illegal goods. The amount of the bribe money usually depends on the value of the load. The protection money is usually a percentage of the value of each disc. If the loader, for instance, offers 1 peso per disc as bribe, then a 10,000 disc load could amount to 10,000 pesos as bribe money. Some corrupt airline personnel also receive bribe money from the loader in order that the discs could be loaded safely on the plane. When the loaded discs reach their destination, the provincial distributor who ordered the shipment will assume the role of the loader in bribing some airport and airline officers so the load would reach the local market.

Despite the "closure" of the Quiapo Piracy Center by Mayor Alfredo Lim and OMB Chair Ronnie Ricketts in 2011, the Muslim enclave continues to operate secretly according to key informants and distributes pirated discs in bulk orders to the provinces and regions in the Philippines through airport facilities. Quiapo, being the heart of Manila, is a strategic place for the distribution of pirated discs in the country, being proximate to airports, harbors, and Chinese businesses. The closure only affected the open retail piracy in the area, but production or burning of discs, distribution and sale of pirated discs, according to informants, still continue in the enclave, although done clandestinely with different strategies. According to them, traders now put CCTV cameras and hired security guards to spot law enforcers entering the enclave and disrupt the clandestine sale of discs. Regular buyers and retailers know which "closed" stores with roll-up doors sell wholesale pirated discs.

6.7.3 Corruption in Retail Piracy

The retail piracy in the Philippines is mostly found in makeshift stalls in the sidewalks, while in Vietnam, they are mostly done in CD–DVD shops. The small retail outlets in the Philippines are usually mobile stalls found in the public markets, sidewalks, kiosks, and other public spaces in big cities. They also include the ambulant vendors who sell pirated discs through their vans or cars in private parking, "sari-sari" or variety stores who sell some pirated discs with their main retail items, and the "backpackers" who sell pirated discs door-to-door in residential areas or to pedestrians. In Vietnam, particularly in Ho Chi Minh City, retail piracy is generally found in two areas: either in legitimate CD–DVD shops or in mobile sidewalk vending. The CD–DVD shops in Vietnam are further classified into two: the big or medium-sized shops and big CD–DVD sections in big bookstore–grocery stores which are usually owned by companies or the small-sized shops which are usually household enterprises owned and operated by families and their relatives. One can easily distinguish them by the size of the space of the shop, the number of discs displayed, and the number of hired employees. Large- and medium-sized shops are

Fig. 6.4 An inside look of a medium-sized registered CD–DVD shop in Ho Chi Minh City selling all pirated music and film discs (Image courtesy of the author)

usually managed by employees with uniforms, while small shops have fewer discs and are operated by family members. As a rule, big DVD firms pay a higher bribe compared to small shops since they are more visible to the public and government regulators. The audacity of big registered stores in Ho Chi Minh City to sell pirated discs implies that a higher amount of protection money has already been assured to the local and government law enforcers who may object to the sale of pirated discs without the necessary license (Fig. 6.4).

Retail piracy in the Philippines and Vietnam cannot survive without corruption and bribery since vendors, especially sidewalk hawkers, do not just violate the zoning ordinance but also the copyright law. It is twice illegal than just vending legal goods in illegal spaces. Sidewalk vending is generally considered illegal since it occupies a public space which the law or the local zoning ordinance defines as illegal. Violation of this law carries with it a fine and/or imprisonment. But the case of sidewalk vending of pirated discs is quite different from those who sell legal items such as fruits or food in the sidewalk. It violates not just the zoning law with its occupation of the public space but also the copyright law which prohibits the sale of counterfeit optical media discs. The first type of vending violates only one law, but the second one violates two important laws. With the educational campaign of the government against piracy, the vending of pirated discs tends to attract more attention from law enforcers compared to vending of legal products in the streets. Thus, the latter tends to demand more bribe from traders than the former. Local policemen have their own way of assessing how much protection money is needed to allow vending pirated discs in the sidewalks. Through their regular inspections of the area, they know which stalls or stores in a particular vending area are profitable and thus require a higher bribe or protection money. Moreover, many policemen who are involved in the protection racket of piracy trade know that vending of

Fig. 6.5 Sidewalk vendors selling pirated discs near a police station in the Philippines (Image courtesy of the author)

pirated discs is usually more profitable than vending other products. The profit of retail piracy is usually 100 %. If a DVD movie costs 40 pesos in the sidewalk, the buying price of the retailer would more likely be 20 pesos in a wholesale price in the Quiapo Barter Trade Center Complex (Fig. 6.5).

To avoid arrest and confiscations of their discs, ambulant vendors who occupy the sidewalks usually give daily protection money to the police of the nearby police outpost patrolling the area. While buying some counterfeit discs for the purpose of this study, the author saw a policeman receiving 100 pesos from the seller as daily protection money. The seller revealed to him later that a local policeman personally collects—and sometimes through an errand boy—one hundred pesos (P100) from ambulant vendors of counterfeit discs in the area. Since their goods are illegal and vending on the sidewalk is prohibited by law, vendors cannot object to this corrupt police practice. In fact the Metro Manila Development Authority (MMDA) bans all sidewalk vending and confiscates all goods and structures that impede public space. Protection money given by sidewalk vendors of fake discs to the local police is an assurance of continuity of this illegal trade. This is also confirmed by a policeman who informed the author that his group collects regular protection money from Muslim sidewalk vendors who sell counterfeit discs at night in the province of Rizal.

Once in a while, according to one police informant, the local policemen receive orders from their commanders to confiscate only specific types of counterfeit discs, like pornographic discs. At times, the local police can directly engage in raiding trading posts of counterfeit discs. However, this is often done for accomplishment report purposes because the police are mandated by law to take enforcement action against the illegal optical media trade, especially discs which contain pornographic materials. In this type of confiscation, the targets are normally the small-time retailers or the sidewalk vendors. One policeman narrated how their team raided the stores and stalls for counterfeit pornographic discs, took some pictures for documentation, submitted an accomplishment report to their regional office, and took some confiscated discs for themselves and for their friends.

The Case of Aamira

Aamira, 28 years old, a CD–DVD retailer, sells pirated discs, together with their relatives, in a small makeshift stall beside a public waiting shed. She came from the province of Agusan in Mindanao and married a Muslim whose uncle is a *datu* and the head of the local Muslim association in the area and who has strong ties with the local government officials and police. She said that it was her husband's relative *datu* who has secured permission from the municipal hall and assigned to them the space for her stall. A distributor usually visits their stall and provided them with pirated discs which come from Quiapo. She said that they give a weekly protection money of P100 to the local police to prevent confiscation of their discs. But she said that there are times that their discs are raided despite paying the protection money. She suspected that some law enforcers are engaged in "recycling" where the confiscated discs in raids are sold to other traders in other places (Fig. 6.6).

Fig. 6.6 At the *left* is Aamira's makeshift stall beside a public waiting shed (Image courtesy of the author)

The Case of Jose

Jose, 40 years old, a former tricycle driver, rents a small shop in a municipality near Metro Manila. Since his store is located in an inner street near the highway and adjacent to a tricycle terminal, people can easily notice it and buy some latest music and film discs. Some CD and DVD covers with plastic were displayed at the entrance of his store. He said he rents the shop for P100 per day. He buys his discs once or twice a week or as the need arises from the Quiapo Barter Trade Center Complex in Manila. Despite the closure of the retail shops in the area, Quiapo, he said, continues to operate secretly as the source of pirated discs in Metro Manila and nearby provinces. He supports his family by selling pirated CDs and DVDs. Since his business is illegal, he needs to be "friendly" to law enforcers. In order to survive in the piracy trade, he has to dole out some bribes or protection money to the authorities. He said he has to give a weekly bribe *(tong)* to some members of the local police of the municipality; otherwise, they would come and confiscate his discs. He also gave a certain amount as monthly bribe and a sack of rice to some policemen of the Criminal Investigation and Detection Group (CIDG). Finally, he needs to bribe some agents of the Optical Media Board (OMB) who would come once in a while to visit his shop. He said he really needed higher sales to offset the cost of the rent and of the protection money to enforcers (Fig. 6.7).

The Case of Nguyen

Nguyen, 20 years old, is an ambulant vendor of pirated CDs and DVDs in one of the districts in Ho Chi Minh City. He came from the northern part of Vietnam. He first

Fig. 6.7 The entrance of Jose's counterfeit CD–DVD store showing various pirated discs from Quiapo Barter Trade Center Complex (Image courtesy of the author)

came to Ho Chi Minh alone by train and joined his brothers in the city who work as factory workers. He bought his counterfeit discs at a wholesale price in a factory located in the outer part of Ho Chi Minh. He bought the DVDs for 5000 VND and sells it for 10,000 VND, earning a 100 % profit. He said he purposely use a pushcart for ambulant vending as this provides him mobility to move around the city and to evade the police. In 2008, Vietnam banned sidewalk vending especially to streets near the center of the city. Thus, sidewalk vendors, especially those with mobile stalls, usually sell their goods at the outskirts of the city. Although his little business is very profitable, it is also a difficult one since he needs to avoid the harassment of the local police. His trade has violated the law against sidewalk vending as well as the copyright law by selling pirated discs. So he is always on alert to evade corrupt law enforcers or gangsters who are up to collect some bribes from his daily earnings. But when cornered by these corrupt police personnel or gangster, he said he has no choice but to give a bribe to allow him to avoid arrest and loss of discs (Fig. 6.8).

6.7.4 Corruption in Philippine Malls

Corruption and nonenforcement can also happen in retail piracy in small- or medium-sized malls in Metro Manila and other cities in the Philippines. Because of the memorandum of agreement forged by the OMB with the owners of large and well-known malls in Metro Manila which prohibits the selling and buying of counterfeit optical media, the sale of retailing fake discs has stopped. Virra Mall in Greenhills, for instance, which was once a major retail outlet of counterfeit discs from Quiapo, has now disallowed the sale of fake optical media goods in its retail stores because of this agreement between the OMB and mall operators. However, this agreement between the OMB and big mall operators has not stopped the retail network of the informal optical media trade. Some retailers simply transferred to small and medium malls which have no agreement with the OMB and are tolerant of the informal trade. Thus, the IIPA's 2007 Special 301 Report has noted that many of the vendors of counterfeit discs in the Virra Mall, for instance, merely transferred to Metrowalk, a medium-sized mall, under the same security coordinator as that of Virra Mall (IIPA 2007 Special 301 Report: Philippines, p. 382). Though big malls such as Shoe Mart (SM) and Robinsons prohibit the sale of pirated discs, smaller or family malls proliferating in Metro Manila and in the provinces allow it. Many of these types of malls are part of the distribution networks of Quiapo Barter Trade Center Complex. Therefore, the OMB has concentrated its effort to raid these smaller malls. According to the OMB chair in an interview, he and his agents do weekly raids on smaller- or medium-sized malls.

To prevent outright detection, according to informants, the strategy of the retailers is to mix the sale of counterfeit discs with legal goods in the beginning and would later evolve into the sale of purely optical media depending on the tolerance

Fig. 6.8 Nguyen (hidden) with his pushcart and customers in a highway in Ho Chi Minh City (Image courtesy of the author)

level of the mall administration. Some mall personnel, according to informants, are in cahoots with the traders in the sale of fake discs. With protection money, some security personnel allegedly conspire with the retailers in protecting the illegal business from law enforcement. A television footage shown by *TV Patrol World* last December 2007 has shown security guards restraining the OMB chair and his agents from entering and confiscating the displayed counterfeit discs in the retail stores which makes one wonder why these guards behaved in such a suspicious manner. The OMB, after all, is authorized by law to seize counterfeit optical media and arrest vendors.

6.7.5 Corruption in Government Antipiracy Agency

The Office of the Optical Media Board (OMB) is a mediating network that links opposing and affiliated alliances to informal optical disc trade. This government agency is designated by copyright law to fight and curb optical media counterfeiting. Its chairman has vast discretionary power on when and how to apply the law. However, this power is conditioned by other networks that help him secure his appointive position in the government. The balancing act of the OMB chair to maintain his position as well as to reconcile the opposing and allied networks to the informal optical disc trade network can indicate how the legal and the illegal networks can intertwine to sustain their illegal business operations.

For one, the chairman's position is highly dependent on the network of local movie producers, artists, and powerful personalities. Although it is the president of the Philippines who will make the official appointment, favorable recommendations from this group are necessary to be nominated for the position. In particular, the association of local producers of Philippine movies, music, and other optical media has their own vested interest to protect: they are the big losers to the informal trade network with the high cost and risk in producing legitimate optical media products. Statistics show that the local movie industry and the government are losing millions of money in earnings and revenues because of counterfeit optical media business. For this reason, it is logical that the local producers would recommend somebody as OMB chair who can reverse this trend and protect their legitimate business interest.

This expectation can be realized by the OMB and OMB chair alone. The office itself is small compared to other government agencies. The salary of the OMB chair is not that attractive. The agency has limited resources. It has a few office personnel, officers, and agents. It only receives a low annual budget. It does not also have a well-equipped machinery to fight the powerful informal trade network in Quiapo. To maintain his/her appointive job, the OMB chair has to satisfy the expectations of the local producers of optical media. But this seems to be difficult to achieve given the well-entrenched network of the informal trade in the local and international market. Thus the OMB chair needs the cooperation of the informal optical media producers and traders to help him/her satisfy the public expectations and produce results in the drive against copyright infringement. In this sense, he/she is forced by circumstance to make compromises with rule breakers to accomplish his/her job satisfactorily. It is for this reason, according to local informants, that the OMB chair went to Quiapo and met with the producers and top traders of counterfeit optical media to establish "gentlemen's agreement" with them: the producers or suppliers will not illegally copy and sell the Filipino movies currently shown in local cinemas, especially those films shown in Metro Manila Film Festivals. In exchange, the OMB will not conduct raids against traders in Quiapo. According to one producer-informant, the original deal is that Quiapo producers and traders would only counterfeit original Filipino films in festivals after 1–2 months they are shown in cinemas. This was, however, later modified, and grace period was reduced to at least 2 weeks, after some producers find the original agreement adverse to their business interest. To implement this informal agreement, according to informants, the producers themselves monitor their ranks for possible breach. This agreement has apparently worked to improve the earnings of the movie industry and increase the government revenues. Data show that the box office revenues of local films grew by 40 % to 1.437 billion in 2006 from P1.025 billion in 2005.[7]

Another powerful allied network of the informal trade network which strongly influences the OMB chair and makes his position more desirable and highly reward-

[7] Cf. January–December 2006 Accomplishment Report, Film Development of the Philippines.

ing despite its low salary is the network of powerful non-Muslim producers who own the local plants that pirate foreign and local Filipino movies. This is a powerful network which is said to have strong political connection that goes up to Malacañang according to one producer-supplier. This hidden network of powerful politicians also exerts a strong influence on the OMB chair. One informant has alleged that this hidden network provides the chair thousands of pesos as monthly protection money. If this is true, the OMB chair then faces a conflict of interest. This protection money, according to the informant, would then prevent him from vigorously raiding Quiapo where Maranao producers or suppliers purchase regularly in large scale from these OD plants owned and controlled by powerful politicians. These powerful producers of local plants would lose money if the OMB would conduct relentless raids in Quiapo. And the OMB chair would therefore lose his/her monthly protection money if he/she conducts raids without the consent and knowledge of the OD plant owners.

Aside from the legal network of local Filipino producers and artists and the illegal network of Quiapo traders and producers of local OD plants, another allied network is influencing and pressuring the OMB chair in job—the international networks of American piracy watchdogs—the International Intellectual Property Alliance (IIPA), an American nongovernment coalition of all intellectual property (IP) industries in the United States and the United States Trade Representative (USTR) Office. Being a signatory of the Trade-Related Aspects of Intellectual Property (TRIPS) of General Agreement on Tariffs and Trade (GATT) and being part of the watch list of violators of intellectual property law, the Philippines faces trade sanctions if it fails to curb this informal optical media trade in the country. The OMB, being the Philippine government's lead agency against copyright infringement, is obliged to implement the optical media law and to satisfy the demands of these international monitoring agencies of the United States. This is another powerful legal network that can affect the current configuration of the illegal network of the optical media counterfeiting in the Philippines that the OMB chair has deal with shrewdly without disturbing his alliances with the producers of local OD plants and with the Muslim producers, suppliers, and traders in Quiapo.

6.7.6 Corruption in Courts

According to the IIPA 2007 Special 301 Report, the Philippine court system does not deter the replication and sale of counterfeit optical media in the country. "Court cases drag on for years and rarely result in successful or criminal convictions" (p. 382). In Quiapo, the court has yet to convict with finality a trader involved in the reproduction, distribution, and sale of fake optical media.

One legal procedure in the Philippine judicial system which does not deter the production and sale of counterfeit optical media, according to the IIPA report, is in the area of search warrants. The IIPA noted many irregularities in the issuance and service of search warrants. Unexplained delays in the issuance and service of search warrant are mentioned in the report as a common problem. In a recent case, for instance, it noted that a judge took 6 days to issue a search warrant that compromised a raid (IIPA 2007 Special 301 Report).

The IIPA report, being written from the normative perspective of jurisprudence, fails to account the underlying reason of the irregularity in the issuance of search warrants. Informants say that the delay in the issuance of search warrants is connected to the conspiracy between producers and top traders and some judicial and law enforcement personnel. According to one producer, the informal optical media network has contacts and connections in the local courts. At times, according to him, the application for a warrant to a particular building in Quiapo—one probably hiding sensitive equipment like replicating machines or illegal discs—is intentionally and constantly placed at the bottom of the pile of applications by some corrupt court personnel. That is why, according to him, some people in the enclave would wonder why this particular building is always excluded from the series of raids by law enforcers. Sometimes the powerful "hidden network" of producers of local optical disc plants would intervene to prevent raids against some buildings in the enclave or in the illegal OD plants outside Quiapo. According to a policeman, the law enforcer or warrant officer can intentionally delay the service of the warrant. The officer has the discretionary power when to serve the warrant within the period specified by the judge. Thus, if this police officer is connected with the informal trade network, he/she would intentionally delay the serving of the search warrant as a strategy to give ample time for the traders to hide their equipment and discs before the raiding team can confiscate them.

6.8 Nonenforcement and Raids Against Piracy

Nonenforcement of laws can also happen in the giving of tips by law enforcers to rule breakers (Marx 1981) and, in the case of optical disc piracy, to illegal traders. Raids tainted with corruption are done not in accordance with the letter and spirit of the official law but in accordance to whims and caprices of big traders or producers-suppliers of pirated discs and in coordination with their corrupt protectors in the government. Tips of an impending raid may come from the block commander of the local police, corrupt antipiracy government agents, or gangsters in the case of Vietnam. Some traders in Vietnam confirmed this leak of an impending raid through tips of corrupt law enforcers or gangsters. In the Philippines, the giving of tips or leakage of information on impending raids is acknowledged by the OMB chairman himself. In an interview, a former OMB chairman acknowledged that there might be some "moles" or corrupt agents in the agency who leaked information to traders on when and where the next raid will take place. To avoid this leakage of information, the OMB chair said that the date of raids maybe known by OMB agents, but the site of the raid is kept secret. He revealed that the exact site is known by agents and deputized law enforcers only at the moment when they are about to depart from the OMB office for their raiding mission.

But is it merely the lack of precautionary measures on the part of the OMB that causes leakage of information of an impending raid? Or is it because of the protection money given by traders to unscrupulous law enforcers—including some OMB personnel—that induces this information leak?

The latter seems to be the case in the Philippines, especially during the "golden years" of the Quiapo piracy network. According to some informants, the producers or top traders are always forewarned of the impending raids because of their network ties with the top and local police officers. The local police chief who usually receives regular protection money from the producers often relays to the latter any news of an impending raid in the area. Besides, the OMB needs to coordinate first with the top police commanders in Camp Crame before getting a backup police force to provide security and to help its raiding team in confiscating counterfeit discs, paraphernalia, burners, or replicating machines in the area. Camp Crame, in turn, will inform the block commander of the impending raid. Before the OMB can proceed with the raid, a tip by some unscrupulous law enforcers on the purpose and magnitude of the raid has already alerted the traders. The investment for the informal optical media trade is huge, and the government agents who are aligned with the illegal trade know the effect of unannounced raids on the capital and investment of the producers-suppliers. Thus, the producer's prior knowledge of an impending massive raid is necessary before the commander can proceed with the confiscation of discs in the area. According to some informants, producers and law enforcers sometimes agree to stage "harmless" raids to provide the police and the OMB a good accomplishment report and hide the network alliance between law enforcers and law breakers. These raids are "harmless" in a sense that traders only displayed a few new titles on the day of the raid. Most of those confiscated are the old unsold discs. This is also a pattern in Vietnam according to informants. The traders are sometimes given a tip or forewarned of an impending raid; thus the old and unsold discs are displayed just before the expected hour of the raid. The new ones are already kept in safe places beyond the reach of the raiding enforcers.

Information from a few informants verifies that such raids to seize discs, burners, or replicating machines by the OMB or by the police are at times staged or orchestrated, with the consent and knowledge of the producers. This happens when the heat or pressure from international piracy watchdogs like the IIPA or USTR as well as from the top government leadership becomes unbearable. Since some top traders and law enforcers coordinate with one another in the informal trade, they have regular contact and communication through their mobile phones. According to some informants, the producers determine when and how this type of raid will be conducted in the trade area. To make the raid look real and believable to foreign observers and bystanders, and as stated above, the producers often allow confiscation of their counterfeit discs and even burners and replicating machines—but most of them are either old, obsolete, or defective. In addition, the producers may not inform some of their distributors and retailers in the area to further make the raids look "natural" and not staged. Thus, some raids in the area are shown in television reports and footages as "real" with retailers resisting the confiscations of their retail goods by deputized agents or by the so-called hakot boys (errand boys) of OMB away from the stalls and stores. To help their distributors and retailers cope with the financial loss brought on by the raid, the producers later approach their co-traders to ask them how many discs were lost. On the next day, the producers usually replaced them with new stocks and supplies which are payable in friendly terms. With the new and fast replicating machines or high-speed burners hidden away from the staged raid, thousands of new fake discs per minute can be duplicated in just 1 day to replenish the lost supplies and stocks of their retailers and distributors. This type of raid in Quiapo was finally stopped when Mayor Alfredo Lim of Manila ordered the piracy hub to be closed on July 1, 2011—although it may have continued in some trading areas.

"Business as usual" is often the atmosphere the day after a raid by the OMB and the police. Thus one wonders whether these raids are really genuine law enforcement effort or a bogus one, only done for the sake of complying the police's annual accomplishment report. The traders seem to know what to do before and after a raid to maintain their business.

Looking closely at the system of raids done by law enforcers against optical disc piracy, one can basically classify raids into two general categories depending on the intention of the law enforcers when the raid is conducted. A raid can be either illegitimate or legitimate. A raid can be illegitimate when it is done different from what the official law requires to address an illegal or criminal act. It is done by enforcers in order to extract a bribe or material favors from violators of the law. Three of this type of raids are the "announced" and "unannounced" raid or "hulidup," and "recycling" raid. Finally a "pressured" raid is legitimate but somehow not fully genuine in a sense that it is not done sincerely and voluntarily by law enforcers but done out because of political pressure.

6.8.1 The "Announced" Raid

One illegitimate or bogus type of law enforcement agreed upon by law enforcers and traders is the "announced" raid. A raid can be "announced" if law enforcers and piracy traders agree in advance that a confiscation of discs and/or replicating equipment will be conducted on a specific date or time. This is both done in the Philippines and Vietnam. According to informants, this is the most common type of raids conducted by law enforcers. The law enforcers such as the police or officers of the OMB or MIC and the traders, usually through tips, know of an incoming raid and confiscation of discs which is scheduled at a specified date and time for purposes of accomplishment report. Because this type of raid is known in advance by the traders, there is ample time for the latter to prepare and hide the new stocks and discs and bring out the old ones for confiscation of the raiding team. In Quiapo Barter Trade Center Complex, the producers-suppliers would have enough time to hide their burners and replicating equipment and discs in a safer place, away from the reach of the raiding team. Only old replicating equipment and old titles are placed conspicuously in the shop for law enforcers to confiscate. More often, the tip of an impending raid is sent through a text or call in mobile phones. Usually law enforcers and illegal traders keep each other's mobile phone numbers for purposes of communication and coordination purposes of their illegal partnership. In one town near Metro Manila, the chief of police and the Muslim head, or *datu*, would usually agree electronically through mobile text when the raid would be conducted by the police for accomplishment report which is beneficial for both parties. In this instance, one will notice that traders would usually show less resistance when the raiding team arrives to confiscate their discs. In the author's hometown in Mindanao, he got a reliable information from his friend, who is close to the local enforcers, that indeed the confiscated discs are old titles and copies and are distributed by some raiding agents to their friends after the raid. Intentional or announced raid is beneficial for both law enforcers and traders. This could not be done if there is no prior friendly alliance established between them. Otherwise, the raid can be unannounced which can be disastrous and highly unfavorable to traders as this implies a heavy loss of new discs for retailers or replicating equipment for producers.

6.8.2 The Unannounced Raid: The "Hulidup"

Traders are always on a lookout of "unannounced" raid as this can happen without prior notice. In the Philippines and Vietnam, a common strategy is used by CD–DVD shops to avoid loss of discs, especially the new ones, in case a sudden raid is conducted against their establishments. In all shops in both countries, the author noticed that the discs are hidden either in a stock room or place of their store or in a safer place away from their vending table. What is prominently displayed at the entrance or inside the shops and vending tables are all empty disc covers or cases bearing the title and wrapped with plastic. In the Philippines, when a buyer has chosen a DVD or CD title to be bought, the seller usually goes somewhere to get the disc. In Ho Chi Minh City, some shops even displayed empty original disc covers or cases with government stickers to camouflage the sale of pirated discs and mislead inspectors and raiding teams. In this case, the store can appear to be totally legal and licensed. But informants say that if a buyer chose to purchase these original titles, the trader or employee of the shop would offer him/her the counterfeit copies at the paying counter with clear digital content at a very low price, usually ten times cheaper than the original. Thus the buyer ends up buying the pirated ones instead of the original.

The most typical kind of "unannounced raid" is what is commonly termed in the Philippines as the "hulidup" (a contraction of two words: caught [*huli*] and *hold-up* [robbed]). This raid implies abuse of power and bribery. A violator is caught in the act by the law enforcer or police committing something illegal and criminal. The arresting officer usually magnifies the offense to the violator and threatens him with immediate arrest and imprisonment if he/she does not give a bribe. In this type of corruption, there is no prior alliance between the violator and law enforcers. Thus the encounter can be hostile and threatening, and the corrupt law enforcers are only after the bribe of the violator. In optical disc piracy trade, unintentional raid or "hulidup" is usually done by the police or other government agents against sidewalk vendors, mobile vendors, or small retailers of pirated discs where protection is usually low. The arrested trader or vendor usually pays the demanded bribe by the police in exchange of the release of the pirated discs and immunity from arrest. In Vietnam, some members of the *Giang Ho* can protect by providing mobile vendors with tips against this type of police raids. But in some cases, the *Giang Ho* operating in the area can also act as the agent of the local police, threatening vendors of arrest and seizures of discs by their accomplice policemen if they do not give the demanded bribe. Based on interviews of some traders, the government law enforcers who engage in "hulidup" in the Philippines are some corrupt members of the local Philippine National Police (PNP), Criminal Investigation and Detection Group (CIDG), National Bureau of Investigation (NBI), and Optical Media Board (OMB), all belonging to government agencies which are tasked by law to fight piracy. One time, some disgruntled agents of the OMB created a blog and accused their OMB chair of receiving P250,000 every 2 weeks or half a million pesos per month. The blog alleged that the chair did not close his office door and was seen receiving the bribe money by some of these agents. They were also asking why a truck with boxes of pirated discs which was just impounded in the OMB was suspiciously released. They also alleged that the OMB chair has an agent who goes around to solicit bribes from traders and retailers. Those who fail to pay the demanded bribe would become the target of the OMB's raid or "hulidup." The blog contained scanned documents to support the allegations. Of course the chair denied all these accusations in a press release. Later the blog became unavailable. The allegations in the blog contain a grain of truth. The amount of protection money mentioned in the blog is also the amount of bribe, according to one Maranao producer-supplier in Quiapo Barter Trade Center Complex, given to a former OMB chair as the monthly protection money in order to allow big-time piracy producers and distributors to operate illegally and minimize raids. Some informants also confirmed that the OMB is also involved in protection racket. In Vietnam, it is usually the unscrupulous local and economic police, with the participation of *Giang Ho*, who usually conducted unannounced raid or "hulidup."

An unintentional raid or "hulidup" can also happen, particularly in the Philippines, when there is a change of assignment or leadership among law enforcers. It is public knowledge that during this transition period, the PNP commanders assigned to the different areas around the country are also changed. Normally, the police officers who are close to the new PNP chief or the new top commanders would replace the old set of officers. In Quiapo Barter Trade Center Complex before it was "closed," the block commander is usually replaced when he/she has not reached the "quota" of the protection money or there is reshuffling of command at the top. In this case, the new commander does not know the existing arrangement concerning protection money between producers and the former commander. In this case, according to the informant, it is normal that the new police commander conducts an unannounced raid in the enclave without the prior knowledge of the producers. This raid is intended to indirectly inform the producers and sellers of the enclave who is in control of the area at the moment. This suggests the need to form a new network between the key players of piracy and the new set of officers of the police jurisdiction. People who know the illegal practices of policemen call this strategy as *nagpapakilala*, meaning "introducing oneself" (as the new boss)—an indirect way to let piracy operators know who is in charge. It also signals the need for a new bargaining agreement on the allotment of protection money. This is similar to other illegal activities by law enforcers like "jueteng" (numbers game) or lewd shows in night clubs which enjoy police protection. The new police commander sends his men to stage an unannounced raid to introduce himself to illegal operators as a way of inviting them to form a new illegal network relationship.

According to informants, this change of leadership can sometimes create confusion especially among traders if this is done without prior notice. The traders wonder why a raid was done despite the fact that they have just given their protection money. According to them, the old commander, in order to still continue to enjoy the regular bribe, would deliberately fail to inform the producers and key traders of the new leadership and thus cause an unannounced raid.

As already mentioned, an unannounced raid can be a result of a failed negotiation between traders and law enforcers. When the trader refuses to give the demanded bribe by law enforcers through their agents or bagmen, he/she becomes a potential target of an unannounced raid.

6.8.3 The "Recycling" Raid

The third type of illegitimate raid which is not as common compared to the "announced" or "hulidup" is the "recycling" raid. This type of raid is conducted by corrupt agents of the law enforcement agencies either against traders who failed to provide the demanded protection money or bribe, or they simply want to earn extra money by confiscating discs from one group of traders and sell them to other friendly group of retailers. In this sense, the confiscated discs are "recycled" or resold from one group to another. This implies that the previous alliance of a group of corrupt enforcers with one group of traders has eroded and new partnership with another group has emerged with increased protection money and benefits. One must note that other benefits can include expensive gifts during special occasions such as Christmas in the Philippines and non-monetary benefits such as sacks of rice, expensive wine, or goods. This type of raid is obviously done with the personal discretion of corrupt law enforcers and unauthorized by law. The official law requires that the confiscated discs must be preserved in the government agencies to be used as evidence in prosecution against the arrested traders.

6.8.4 The "Pressured" Raid

An ideal legitimate raid must be one that is done regularly by law enforcers with the intention of truly implementing the official law. A "pressured" raid is not done voluntarily by law enforcers with the intention of enforcing the majesty of law. A pressured raid is a legitimate raid. The only problem is that it is not done by law enforcers freely and voluntarily with a sincere motive of putting an end to piracy because it stifles creativity and destroys the economy, but done because of some pressures from either the top government officials, stakeholders, antipiracy organizations, or the USTR. Since corruption has become part of the law enforcement system in the Philippines and Vietnam, it is often difficult to determine whether a raid is illegitimate or legitimate merely by judging its appearance. What really determines the legitimacy of the raid is the real motive of the law enforcers. If the raid is done with all honesty and full determination of the law enforcers to implement the official law and stop piracy despite the meager government resources, then it can be considered a truly legitimate raid and a genuine enforcement of the optical media law. A legitimate raid is one that really creates an impact and dent on the illegal trade of piracy. One big legitimate but pressured raid is one that happened in Quiapo on July 1, 2012, when Mayor Lim and OMB Chair Ronnie Ricketts were pressured by stakeholders and the US government to close down the notorious open piracy in Quiapo. Although it is really difficult to determine what really transpired during the negotiations between the former Mayor of Manila, Alfredo Lim, the OMB, the Quiapo piracy producers-suppliers and distributors, and stakeholders, the massive raid and closure of the QBTCC in 2011 were by all indication of a legitimate raid and law enforcement. After the mayor had given the traders 1-month grace period, the open piracy in Quiapo and sale of pirated discs in the area came to a halt. Policemen were immediately deployed in the area after the "closure" to ensure that illegal shops would no longer continue their open retail piracy. The "closure" has showed that if there is honesty and really strong determination of authorities to enforce the law without corruption, the illegal piracy trade can be minimized.

The OMB and MIC and other law-enforcing agencies have done legitimate raids against illegal traders in the past. But most of these raids often target pirated discs rather than replicating facilities. Raids which target pirated discs of retailers rather than replicating machines, even though legitimate and done with honesty, are not sufficient means to stop piracy if the big illegal factories remain untouched and protected by corrupt government authorities. That is why regular operation resumes after every raid by the OMB or other government agencies. High-speed replicating machines and burners can immediately replenish the confiscated discs even within hours after the raid. Raiding the illegal factories and replicating equipment with the illicit motive of material gain on the part of the law enforcers is what is needed to cripple the illegal trade of piracy. But before this can happen, the government bureaucracy and enforcement system must be cleansed with corrupt elements and effective surveillance and monitoring system against unscrupulous law enforcers in state agencies must be instituted by the government to put an end to the nonenforcement of the Optical Media Law in the Philippines and Vietnam.

6.9 Summary

The chapter has shown sociologically that the nonenforcement of the optical media law and the persistence of widespread and open production and sale of illegal optical discs in the Philippines and Vietnam is largely facilitated by the illegal networks between some corrupt law government authorities led by the local police and the illegal traders with the participation of gangsters especially in the case of Vietnam. It has illustrated that patterns of corruption, nonenforcement of the copyright law, and bribery can be found in the area of production and distribution of illegal local and imported discs, in shipment of illegal discs in airports and port area, in the sale of pirated discs in small- and medium-sized malls especially in the Philippines and in sidewalks, in courts, as well as in the conduct of raids by law enforcers. The amount of bribe or protection depends on the capital and investment involved in the illegal trade as well as length of the partnership. Usually, the higher is the investment and risk involved in the trade, the higher is the bribe money. In Vietnam where dual informal protection system for businesses exists, illegal disc traders have to deal with both corrupt law enforcers and *Giang Ho* or gangsters who are in most cases in cahoots with one another. In the Philippines, the illegal traders usually deal only with corrupt government authorities led by the police without the intermediary of the gangsters for added security in their business. Finally, corruption and nonenforcement also happen in the conduct of raids by the government agencies and law enforcers. Because of the illegal alliance between traders and government agents, raids are often illegitimate such as the "announced raid," the "unannounced raid" or "hulidup," and the "recycling raid." A legitimate raid is one that is done honestly, voluntarily, and in accordance with the official law. Although a "pressured raid" is legitimate, it is far from the ideal legitimate raid as it is done with a motive of complying with the orders of higher authorities or complying with trade agreements or succumbing to pressures by stakeholders, antipiracy groups, and the USTR. Most raids done by authorities of both countries often target retail piracy and pirated discs rather than production piracy and replication facilities that continuously supply counterfeit optical media discs in the market; thus they hardly provide an impact in government's fight against piracy. This chapter has shown that what the letter of the official law say "it is" is not what some unscrupulous government authorities say "it is" in actual implementation, especially when the government's law enforcement system is colonized and influenced by corruption and bribery.

References

Aguilera, R. V., & Vadera, A. K. (2007). The dark side of authority: Antecedents, mechanisms, and outcomes of organizational corruption. *Journal of Business Ethics, 77*, 431–449.

Alatas, S. H. (1968). *The sociology of corruption: The nature, function, causes, and prevention of corruption*. Singapore: Donald Moore Press.

Alatas, S. H. (1977). *The myth of the lazy native*. London: Frank Cass.

Alatas, S. H. (1990). *Corruption: Its nature, causes and functions*. Avebury: Albershot.

Alatas, S. H. (1999). *Corruption and the destiny of Asia*. Petaling Jaya: Prentice-Hall.

Brown, M. K. (1991). Nonenforcement: Minor violations and disturbances. In C. Klockars & S. D. Mastrofski (Eds.), *Thinking about the police*. New York: McGraw-Hill, Inc.

Deflem, M. (1995). Corruption, law, and justice: A conceptual clarification. *Journal of Criminal Justice, 23*(3), 243–258.

Hodgkinson, P. (1997). The sociology of corruption – Some themes and issues. *Sociology, 31*(1), 17–35.

Hyslop, J. (2005). Political corruption: Before and after apartheid. *Journal of Southern African Studies, 31*(4), 773–789.
IIPA (2007). International intellectual property alliance 2011 special 301 report. www.iipa.com. Accessed 2 Dec 2014.
IIPA (2008). International intellectual property alliance 2011 special 301 report. www.iipa.com. Accessed 5 Dec 2014.
IIPA (2009). International intellectual property alliance 2011 special 301 report. www.iipa.com. Accessed 6 Jan 2015.
IIPA (2012). International intellectual property alliance 2011 special 301 report. www.iipa.com. Accessed 10 Jan 2015.
IIPA (2013). International intellectual property alliance 2011 special 301 report. www.iipa.com. Accessed 6 Feb 2015.
Jain, A. K. (2001). Corruption: A review. *Journal of Economic Surveys, 15*(1), 71–121.
Johnston, M. (1994). *Comparing corruption conflicts, standards and development.* Conference paper, prepared for the XVI World Conference of the International. Political Science Association, Berlin.
Jong-Sung, Y., & Khagram, S. (2005). A comparative study of inequality and corruption. *American Sociological Review, 70*(1), 136–157.
Khondker, H. (2006). Sociology of corruption and 'corruption of sociology': Evaluating the contributions of Syed Hussein Alatas. *Current Sociology, 54*(1), 25–39.
Law No. 36/2009/QH12. (2009, June 19). Amending and supplementing a number of articles of the law on intellectual property (promulgated by the order no. 12/2009/L-CTN of June 29, 2009 of the President of the Socialist Republic of Vietnam). http://www.wipo.int/wipolex/en/details.jsp?id=6566. Accessed 4 Nov 1914.
Marx, G. T. (1981). Ironies of social control: Authorities as contributors to deviance through escalation, nonenforcement, and covert facilitation. In D. H. Kelly (Ed.), Deviant behavior, a text-reader in the sociology of deviance. New York: St. Martin's Press.
Pavarala, V. (1993). Corruption as a site for contested meaning: Elite constructions in India. *Qualitative Sociology, 16*(4), 405–422.
The age.com.au. (2003, March 10). Court sets out to free a city of corruption. http://www.Theage.Com.au/articles/2003/03/09/1047144868386.html
The Hungarian Gallup Institute. (1999). Basic methodological aspects of corruption measurement: Lesson learned from the literature and pilot study. http://www.unodoc.org/pdf/crime/corruption_hungary_rapid_assess.pdf. Accessed 2 Dec 2014.
Vietnamnet.com, Special-Reports. (2013). Warning over the penetration of criminals into state agencies. http://www.english.vietnamnet.vn/fms/special-reports/73176/warning-over-the-penetration-of-criminals-into-state-agencies.html. Accessed 6 Dec 2014.
Widmalm, S. (2008). *Decentralisation, corruption and social capital: From India to the West.* New Delhi: SAGE Publications India Pvt Ltd.

Chapter 7
Tracing Media Piracy: Current and Future Trends

7.1 The Evolving Nature of Media Piracy and Globalization

Emerging theories in sociology of technology seek to find a middle ground that tries to reconcile this dualism between society and technology. These theories acknowledge that technologies and societies are engaged in a mutually constitutive relationship (Bijker 1995; MacKenzie and Wajcman 1999). Technologies are not mere tools of human actors (social determinism, e.g., [Bijker 1987]) nor do they predetermine universally social systems and cultural systems as a whole (technological determinism, e.g., [Winner 1998]). In itself, technology can be politically and morally neutral. But it can be "ambivalent and can drift as a result of decisions made by many different actors, and the need to integrate into pre-existing social and technological contexts" (Holmstrom and Stalder 2001). "The design and use of technologies are simultaneously shaped by and reshape processes of cooperation and conflict among groups within society" (Fleischmann 2006, p. 77).

Counterfeiting and piracy are not fixed forms of rule-breaking phenomenon but evolving crimes that ride on with the technological development of society. Through the years its form constantly adapts to the social environment and existing technology in order to circumvent regulation. Before the advent of digital technology and the Internet, piracy is limited in scope and primarily intended for personal and noncommercial consumption. Artists and copyright holders lost some royalties and sales but not as massive with today's peer-to-peer sharing or mass production of CDs and DVDs of copyrighted songs and films. The latest technologies of the global age have made interaction, transaction, and replication easier, fast, and more convenient. Technologies are not just mere tools in digital media piracy but indispensable material networks that allow humans to accomplish and maintain the crime of piracy.

Aside from technology, piracy also thrives in a favorable social and economic milieu. Today, there is no greater force that fuels media piracy to greater growth than globalization. Globalization is a complex term to define and describe. And not all scholars believe that the process of globalization is taking place today. But for

V.O. Ballano, *Sociological Perspectives on Media Piracy in the Philippines and Vietnam*, DOI 10.1007/978-981-287-922-6_7

some who believe and assume a globalist perspective, they see globalization as a pervasive phenomenon that affects all forms of business or commerce such as the intellectual property trade. The American sociologist George Ritzer (Ritzer 2011) defines globalization as a "transplanetary process(es) involving increasing liquidity and growing multi-directional flows as well as the structures they encounter and create" (p. 2). This definition understands the processes of globalization as affecting not only some groups or organizations, nations, or states but social structures of many nations around the globe. Moreover, it emphasizes reduction of global integration and the growing "liquidity" of the world by globalization's multidirectional flows which make reality more diverse and in a state of flux.

"Liquidity" is a metaphor used by some globalists to explain the growing flexibility and mobility of things, caused by the current processes of globalization, particularly by the advancement of technology. Its opposite is "solidity" in which people, things, and places "harden" over time and are, therefore, "heavy" and difficult to transport. Liquidity simply means that goods, information, and places are increasingly becoming light and, thus, easy to transport from one location to another. In short, things become "liquid and fluid which enable them to flow" to different locations with the capacity to change their forms in order to adapt to the environment. With the process of globalization and technological innovation, things have become lighter, flexible, and faster to move and adapt to the environment. The huge analog computers which are too bulky and heavy to move in the 1970s, for instance, became smaller personal digital computers in the 1980s and became much lighter, faster, and more powerful in the 1990s and 2000s with tablets, smartphones, iPads, and other miniature devices equipped with broadband Internet connections. In media piracy, the heavy and big VHS and cassette tapes containing counterfiet songs and films in the 1980s and 1990s were being replaced by much lighter and smaller USBs, online files, and other cloud-storing computer applications.

Playing an important role in the globalization and liquefaction of the world is technology. The metaphor of "liquefaction" and the idea that technology make things unstable and turn them into "liquids" which pass through barriers and flow to various directions and dimensions of social life can be a more appropriate image to describe the current struggle between copyright infringers and copyright owners and regulators. Technologies are not moving toward consuming less power. Small size increases speed. And increased speed with the use of powerful small transistors called chips increases efficiency (Koepsell 2009, p. 160). Today's technology "liquefies" any thing that is traditionally understood as fixed, stationary, and solid in jurisprudence and law, law enforcement, or property rights. Technological innovation challenges existing laws and provides more loopholes and cracks to their implementation, enabling opportunists and resisters such as infringers to pursue their illegal trade and activity.

Technology is morally neutral. It can be used for regulation, social resistance, or any form of illegality. It can exhibit agency by reshaping the relationships and interaction among people in the social world (Law 2006, p. 78). It can act as an interface among bounded social worlds, allowing productive communication between these distinct social worlds (Star 1989; Strauss 1978, 1984). Peer-to-peer sharing through the Internet and digital technology, for instance, is an illustration of how various unconnected networks of users can unite in one network site and how a legal online service can also be used for illegal purposes. P2P can unite various online networks around the globe in a website with a common software technology such as the BitTorrent and allow users to share files and copyright materials whether legally or illegally. Mobiles or smartphones which are intended for legal transaction and communication can be used by pirate producers, distributors, and retailers for illegal purposes such as producers receiving orders of pirated discs from provincial distributors or contacting a supplier in mainland China to import high-quality DVDs or media boxes. The fast technological innovation and globalization's liquidity have intensified the growth of piracy and flow of counterfeit goods in the world. In its 2014 Special 301 Report, the USTR acknowledged that the "problems of trademark counterfeiting and copyright piracy continue on a global scale and involve mass production and sales of a vast array of fake goods, including counterfeit semiconductors, medicines, health care products, food and beverages, automobile parts, such as air bags, aircraft parts, apparel and footwear, toothpaste, toys, shampoos, razors, electronics, batteries, chemicals, sporting goods, motion pictures, and music" (USTR 2014), p. 18).

7.2 Trends in Media Piracy Follow the Trends in Technology

Actor–network theory (ANT), an established approach in the sociology of science and technology investigates the interaction between human relationships and technological systems in understanding social issues in informational society. Contrary to popular social network approaches to rule breaking that follow the classical epistemological dichotomy between human and nonhuman actors, ANT, as applied in this study, sees material networks as entwining with various human and social networks in the maintenance of the informal optical media piracy trade. Seen from this perspective, the act of "pirating" copyrighted media will not be made possible by human actors alone but by conglomeration of both human and material actants, with technology playing a crucial role in maintaining the entire piracy network. The Internet, replicating machines, televisions, DVD players, and high-tech gadgets like mobile phones, personal computers, and other information and communications technologies and their related networks, in addition to ecological, cultural, and social networks, form one complex infringement system.

Media piracy is a technological and complex form of deviance which cannot be done without the indispensible use of the latest information and computer technologies. The access of the infringers to the latest technology makes unauthorized reproduction and distribution of copyrighted optical media easier and faster. Technology allows divergent networks to communicate and to merge. In media piracy, technology enables infringers to adapt and adjust their strategies to evade detection and law enforcement. It enables "pirates" to adopt their strategies and networks and overtake copyright legislation and the relevance and effectiveness of existing laws and powers of law enforcement agencies. The problem lies not so much on the inadequacies of copyright legislations and enforcement mechanisms but the wide gap between the optical media law and media piracy created by the fast-evolving technology that provides more storage and copying power, thus enabling copyright infringement easier to perform. In the Philippines, for instance, the Videogram Regulatory Board (VRB) was created by law to fight the growing cassette and videotape piracy. With the advent of digital technology and shift to digital piracy, the law and VRB became obsolete as optical disc piracy became popular. The Philippine Congress created a new law, the Optical Media Law of 2003, and established the Optical Media Board (OMB) to curb media piracy in CD, VCD, and DVD formats. Before the OMB can create a dent to massive optical disc piracy in the country, a new technology emerged with the increased Internet penetration and popularity of the mobile phone, cloud, and broadband technologies—peer-to-peer and cyberlocker media piracy—which make the current optical media law obsolete and the OMB lacking in jurisdictions and regulatory powers against online piracy. In Vietnam, the fast introduction of new technologies facilitated by *Doi Moi* and renewed ties and trade with the United States have also overtaken the scope of the local copyright law, power of law enforcement agencies, and the capacity of local courts to deal with infringement cases. The current growth of cyberlockers and peer-to-peer sharing sites facilitated by the growing Internet penetration and widespread adoption of the broadband technology in mobile phones, for instance, has overwhelmed the Vietnamese government efforts to curb online media piracy. The table below can provide an overview of the past, present, and future trends in media piracy with regard to the type of technology, computer, format, mode of distribution, and popular type of infringement (Table 7.1).

7.2.1 *Analog Technology and China in the 1980s*

The videocassette recording (VCR) was introduced in the mid-1970s. It was introduced by Sony with the creation of the Betamax in 1975. The VHS was introduced by the Victor Company of Japan (Japan Victor Company, or JVC) and supported by JVC's parent company, Matsushita Electric, and other major electronics companies.

Table 7.1 Brief overview of the current and future trends in media piracy

	Timeline			
Category	1980–1989	1990–2010	2010 onwards	Future direction
Type of technology	Analog VCR	Digital	Digital, cloud, and nano	Advanced nano and quantum computing
Type of computer	Analog	Digital	Digital and nano	Quantum
Media formats	Cassette/videotapes	CDs and VCDs	DVDs, files, cloud	Cloud and new emerging formats
Mode of distribution	Face to face	Face to face, online file sharing	Cloud file sharing and more	Systems based
Popular type of media piracy	Cassette/VCR	Optical disc peer-to-peer (P2P) sharing	Peer-to-peer (P2P), cyberlocker, and new modes of piracy	Quantum media piracy

> About a year after the introduction of Betamax, the Japan Victor Company (JVC) began selling a home recording machine that used a VHS (video home system) format that was non-compatible with Betamax. JVC believed that a 2-hour machine would be more appealing to consumers than the 1-hour Betamax. Thus, within 2 years of its introduction, the lower-priced, longer recording VHS VCR controlled 57 % of the U.S. VCR market. Betamax's share of the market started to drop in 1986. Sony then announced in 1988 that it would begin manufacturing VHS VCRs. Within 2 years of its introduction, the lower-priced and longer-recording VHS controlled 57 % of the U.S. VCR market. (Levy 1989, p. 24)

> Betamax's market share dropped to 5 % by 1986, forcing Sony and its partners to stop producing Betamax while the VHS continued to dominate the VCR market (Browne and Johnson 2000, p. 6). The competition between Betamax and VHS increased innovation in the fields (Browne and Johnson 2000, p. 6). Indeed, "the VCR became the largest segment of the massive global consumer electronics business in the 1980s" (Cusumano et al. 1992, pp. 1–2).

It continued to dominate the consumer electronics in the United States, Europe, and Asia during this period.

With joint ventures between China and Japanese firms, the VCR also became popular in China. With favorable investment policies offered by the Chinese government to foreign firms in the early 1990s, Japanese and other VCR and electronics multinationals built their factories in China. But the presence of these foreign firms in China did not, however, result in control of the Chinese market as technology transfer (TT) policies of the Chinese government made it easy for Chinese electronics firms to acquire and innovate the analog technology of these foreign firms. As a result, top Chinese electronics firms were then able to overtake the Japanese and foreign firms in terms of sales of electronics, especially with regard to television sets, VCR recorders and players, and other consumer electronic products (Marukawa 2004). In one instance, China experienced overproduction of these products particularly television sets which resulted in their massive exports to its neighboring Southeast Asian countries that included the Philippines and Vietnam, prompting the United States to accuse China for violating antidumping laws. But this overproduction, however, popularized home viewing in Southeast Asia (SEA) which eventually became the main consumers of pirated music and video cassettes in the late 1980s and early 1990s.

7.2.2 *The VCR and the Rise of Analog Media Piracy*

The introduction of the analog VCR technology changed the viewing habits of consumers particularly those in SEA countries. Sony invented the first VCR for home use. With the introduction of home music and videos and the popularity of the televisions, cassettes, players, and recorders, the viewing habits of Asian consumers changed from viewing videos or movies in cinemas or movie houses to home viewing of their favorite films using the Betamax or VHS. This triggered a high demand for video and music cassettes for home viewing and listening. With the weak copyright protection regime operating in China and SEA in the 1980s, analog media piracy in cassette format flourished during this period, prompting the USTR to include China and some Southeast Asian countries at the top of its Special 301 Special watch lists. The production of VCR recorders has made media piracy in cassette formats possible.

China's adoption of the analog and VCR technology did not only increase its exports in electronic products but also in pirated tapes and cassettes to satisfy the high demand for copyright content for consumers' VCR equipment. Together with the exports of counterfeit products, pirated films and music in cassette formats were exported to neighboring countries of Southeast Asia and other parts of the world. In the 1980s, Hong Kong was the largest pirate market of Chinese counterfeit products in East Asia and also became the center of video piracy during this period. Then this market was transferred to Singapore which became the piracy capital of the world in the early 1980s (Peters 1986). However, with the intense pressure from regulators and lobby groups, piracy eventually declined in Singapore and the analog piracy capital was transferred to Indonesia and finally to Thailand in the late 1980s and early 1990s (Paradise 1999). The Philippines became part of this piracy loop of imported pirated video and music cassette tapes in the 1990s.

Media piracy during this period had limited scope and distribution. Copyright infringement was primarily focused on music and home videos or movies. And the distribution system is primarily dependent on face-to-face transaction and communication and not in digital space as the Internet and digital technology were only introduced in the 1990s. Thus, media piracy during this period consisted mainly of unauthorized copying of new films, videos, and recorded local and foreign music for noncommercial purposes, although commercial sales of pirated cassette tapes were sold in some authorized sidewalk stalls and stores usually mixed with other legal goods. The main carriers or distributors of "master copies" are vacationing immigrants or overseas workers as in the case of the Philippines and Vietnam. Upon reaching their home countries, these copies were being duplicated by the locals with the use of recorders (VCR). They were also shared and sold informally to friends and relatives. There was no systematic and widespread production, distribution, and retail of pirated films during this period. The primary players of media piracy during this era are overseas workers and immigrants who brought with them copies of new films unreleased in their home countries. In the Philippines, the returning overseas Filipino workers from the Middle East would usually bring home new movies in Betamax and VHS formats and duplicate them upon reaching their country. The production was small scale and the distribution was limited to personal acquaintances. But it had an impact to the legitimate store selling original copies of films in Betamax and VHS formats. Unreleased foreign films were viewed then in advance by people who bought the illegal copies. Thus, authorities became alarmed of this type of copyright infringement. In the Philippines, for instance, the former President Ferdinand Marcos issued Presidential Decree No. 1987 which created the Videogram Regulatory Board (VRB) in order to combat the growing video piracy in the Philippines from the 1980s to early 1990s.

7.2.3 *Shift to Digital Technology in the 1990s*

The digital technology is the evolution of analog architectures. The important reason of the technological shift to digital technology is the limitation imposed by analog technology and its incompatibility with the growing use of digital computing. One limitation of the analog technology is that the Betamax and VHS device and format can deteriorate through constant use. Moreover, analog devices such as VCRs, tape players, and record players record data linearly from one point to another which makes replaying, copying, and duplication tedious and time consuming. And lastly, the analog technology of the Betamax and VHS was incompatible with the growing popularity of digital computing and computer devices in the 1990s. Analog computing does not use binary system which is the heart of digital and computer technology. Moreover, huge analog computers were constructed using electronic components, the mechanical integrators being replaced with capacitor charging circuits after 1945. "In an analog computer, quantities are represented using a continuous physical medium such as shaft rotation or electrical voltage. Digital computers, on the other hand, use a discrete representation of state" (Care 2008).

The analog technology became incompatible with digital technology in the 1990s resulting in its demise. A digital system is different from the analog. It uses numbers to represent a concrete object or an abstract idea: "Digitization is the process of transforming the object or idea into a numerical code. The baseline of digital technology is a coding system with only two numbers — 1 and 0 — hence the term binary. Each numerical place in the system is a bit."[1]

The Internet which uses the digital technology was created primarily for research in US universities and not for commerce. Thus, its protocols were open, unsecured, and not designed to hide (Lessig 1999, p. 39). But in 1991 with the creation of the World Wide Web led by Tim Berners-Lee and supported by numerous people across the globe, the Internet became commercially available. Throughout the early 1990s, the World Wide Web grew to become the foundation of Internet navigation today. It has become the largest file sharing network ever created (Smith and Gross 2011). The Internet and digital technology have made access, reproduction, distribution, or sharing of copyrighted media wider in scope, cheaper, and easier to perform. Computers and rewritable media virtually eliminated the costs of reproducing works because bits do not require any significant tangible resources. Web 1.0—based on client–server functionality—put Internet service providers in the role of content distributors, while Web 2.0—encompassing peer-to-peer, YouTube, social networking, and related technologies—put that power into the hands of netizens (Menell 2012, p. 1553).

As already mentioned, media piracy before the introduction of the Internet was limited. Those who intend to reach a large copyright content and audience had to go through content industry producers and intermediaries. And film, television, radio,

[1] www.nedcc.org

recording, publishing, and broadcast industries controlled distribution and acted as gatekeepers of their own copyrighted works and screen out unauthorized copying and sharing. Due to the relatively limited distribution channels (e.g., theaters, licensed broadcasters, bookstores, record stores), copyright owners could easily detect unauthorized content (Menell 2012, p. 1552). Because copyright infringement was tedious, costly, and easy to detect, media piracy in the analog age of the late 1970s and 1980s was limited and confined mostly to noncommercial infringement—such as home viewing, copying, or recording using VCR equipment.

But digital technology and the Internet changed all these in the 1990s. With a more advanced technology with faster speed, greater storage, wider scope, more efficient computing, and cheaper to perform, media piracy has reached a massive and commercial scale that posed a serious challenge to stakeholders, regulators, and law enforcers. Physical presence is no longer necessary to acquire illegally large amount of copyrighted materials. The advanced capabilities of digital technology provide infringers more options to pirate copyrighted materials with more hiding abilities to evade law enforcement. The peer-to-peer (P2P) file sharing networks on the Internet, for example, can enable users to "publish" or "share" files of various kinds copyrighted digital media and protect them with a ready-made sharing infrastructure that is difficult to block and even harder to track (Johnson et al. 2008).

7.2.4 Digital Technology and Digital Online Piracy

The introduction of the Internet and digital technologies replacing the analogy technology of the VCR had resulted basically in two types of digital media piracy. The first is the digital optical disc piracy for countries with less Internet penetration and digital online piracy for economies with wide Internet penetration, particularly to those with high mobile phone and broadband Internet subscription and with weak copyright protection regime.

A new development in piracy that is slowly replacing the optical disc piracy is the digital online piracy. With the global spread of the Internet, media piracy gradually shifted in computing techniques, format, and strategy. The unauthorized media viewing and sharing in digital discs such as CDs and DVDs have gradually migrated to online file sharing in countries with high Internet or broadband penetration: the physical piracy of the digital disc is now being transformed gradually into a digital online piracy in the cyberspace. The geographical network and locus of the main distribution of digital media have now slowly being transferred from the temporal space of the sidewalk and illegal CD–DVD shops to the virtual space of the Internet. The number of Internet users in the world has been doubling a hundred times since the introduction of the World Wide Web in 1991. As of June 2011, the world had 2.4 billion Internet users with an estimated 35 % having fixed broadband and 15 % with mobile broadband connection (IIPA 2013 Special 301, p. vi).

Since the Internet is a worldwide center for the exchange of information, the quality of the content in a website will determine the number of its visitors. Thus, sharing copyrighted materials publicly such as videos, songs, movies, books, games, etc., has become a popular strategy for websites or P2P sites to attract more visitors and to gain more subscriptions and advertising revenues (Rengifo Garcia 2014). A study by Envisional in 2011 revealed that 23.76 % of all worldwide Internet traffic is copyright infringing with 11.4 % illegal BitTorrent downloading; 5.1 % illegal downloading from infringing distribution hubs; 1.4 % illegal video streaming; and 5.8 % other peer-to-peer (P2P) file sharing (eDonkey, gnutella) or Internet protocols, such as Usenet, that are used for file sharing (cited in IIPA 2013 Special 301 Report, p. vi).

The USTR's Special 301 Annual Report for 2014 identified some of the recent types of the digital media piracy on the Internet: unauthorized retransmission of live sports telecast over the Internet; piracy using mobile phones, tablets, flash drives, and other mobile technologies; emergence of pirate servers, or "gray shards"; playing copyrighted video games that are made available through hacked software or circumvention of technology protection measures in an unauthorized cloud-based servers; and the sale and development of devices that allow for the circumvention of technological protection measures (TPM) (USTR 2014 Special 301 Annual Report).

The current trends in media piracy are highly powered by nanotechnology. Hard drives used as memory in computers consume more power and have more chance of failure than solid-state memory that doesn't have any moving parts. With nanotechnology, these problems are overcome. Nanotechnology has made mobile phones, tablets, and notebooks faster, better, and more robust.[2] It has greatly improved the density of solid-state memory of computers and allows small devices or computers such as tablets, iPads, or iPad mini to take up less space and battery power and to less likely be damaged if device is dropped (UnderstandingNano.com). Nanotechnology has improved the speed and storage of digital technology and computing. The current media piracy utilizes the nano's power, speed, and miniaturization of computing for infringement. The current cloud technology, P2P file sharing protocols, and cyberlockers which are also used by pirates are now using nanotechnology's power and speed, making it more difficult for law enforcers and regulators to curb media piracy. Noncommercial file sharing of MP3s has made a tremendous dent in record sales. BitTorrent and cyberlockers make even large digital files—such as high-definition feature films—relatively easy to find and transmitted across the Internet (Menell 2012).

7.2.5 *Peer-to-Peer Sharing Media Piracy*

The technology that is most synonymous with Internet digital piracy is peer-to-peer (P2P) file sharing. Some of these P2P sites are multi-platform sites, but they are said to encourage illegal sharing of copyrighted materials such as music, films, video games, spreadsheets, etc. P2P file sharing is a specific Internet-based technology

[2] "Faster, more efficient, more robust: Nanotechnology in computers, mobile phones, and more" at http://www.nanostart.de/en/nanotechnology/nanotechnology-information/692-faster-more-efficient-more-robust-nanotechnology-in-computers-mobile-phones-and-more.

that allows computer users with P2P software to connect with each other to seek and share digital content. It consisted of a remote central server that facilitated the searching of users' files (music in the form of Mp3s) and the establishment of a connection between those who seek the file and those who have it available for download. The P2P software called BitTorrent allows users to create "torrent files" to help direct other users to establish a connection to specific file on the computer (Fung and Lakhani 2013, p. 383). Internet connection speed is said to be an important predictor of P2P file sharing. Because of fast connection, broadband users are more than 50 % more likely to share than those on a dial-up connection (30–19 %). Therefore, as "Internet connection speeds continue to increase, it seems likely that more and more users will flock to P2P networks and file sharing applications" (Johnson et al. 2008, p. 5). This is one important reason why illegal file sharing of copyrighted media through P2P sharing has become more popular in digital nano devices such as tablets or mobile phones with fast broadband Internet connections.

P2P file sharing has been cited often by the USTR and the IIPA lately in their yearly Special 301 reports as one of the most dangerous types of copyright infringement on the Internet. IIPA Special 301 Report for 2013, for instance, identified some of these infringing multiplatform sites encouraging illegal sharing such as ThePirateBay.se (Sweden), kat.ph (formerly Kickasstorrents.com), 23 IsoHunt.com (Canada), Baixe de Tudo (Brazil), Xiami (China), Usenext.com (Germany), Blubster (Spain), Extabit.com (Netherlands), etc.

The concept of P2P file sharing has a long history. It actually extends back almost four decades to the US Department of Defense development of ARPANET. But P2P file sharing came popular only during the dot.com boom and the rise of Napster. Between its debut in 1999 and its eventual failure in 2001, Napster enabled tens of millions of users to share MP3-formatted song files (Johnson et al. 2008, p. 5). In the decade since peer-to-peer (p2p) file sharing site Napster emerged in 1999, the Recording Industry Association of America (RAAA) estimated that the music sales in the United States have dropped 47 %, from $14.6 billion to $7.7 billion. It also estimated that between 2004 and 2009 alone, an approximately 30 billon songs were illegally downloaded on P2P sharing networks.[3] After Napster was shut down by a US court for infringement, new brands of P2P networks which are more sophisticated and evasive from law enforcement emerged with the advancement of nanotechnology and cloud computing.

7.2.5.1 BitTorrent (BT) File Sharing

A particular type of P2P file sharing which is resistant to regulation is BitTorrent. BitTorrent (BT) has become one of the most popular peer-to-peer (P2P) protocols on the Internet which allows the unauthorized sharing of copyrighted materials by its users. BT's popularity is primarily due to "its fundamental advantages over traditional client–server architecture in terms of self-scalability, reliability, fairness,

[3] http://www.riaa.com/faq.php

and cost–efficiency" (Sarjaz and Abbaspour 2013, p. 86). As described by its website, BitTorrent offers an ultrafast delivery, breaking big files down into small pieces or tiny bits and downloading them piece by piece from one or many different sources, allowing users to use less bandwidth and making downloads a lot faster. BitTorrent software also synchronizes files directly between devices and requires no accounts and no file size limits, and its transfer speeds never throttled, making its peer-to-peer sharing shift and easy.[4]

BitTorrent's (BT) capacity to share big files is said to have caused greater financial losses to the movie industry. The financial losses to the movie industry due to P2P are said to be severe and long-lasting because "(1) distributing the digital form of pirated movies is much easier; (2) copyright holders or movie publishers can do very little to prevent distribution over P2P networks, and they usually respond passively; and (3) pirated movies exist even before their official release since the Telesync (TS) version of movies shot in the cinema can be easily produced" (Kwok 2004). Despite BT's assurance that its P2P file sharing is not intended for infringing, it is widely believed that most of the digital media shared in BT such as films, songs, e-books, and video games are unauthorized. A study by the University of Ballarat in Australia in 2012 revealed that only 0.3 % or 3 cases of the total 1000 torrent files examined as sample were determined to be not infringing, while the 11 % was likely infringing and the remaining 890 files were definitely infringing.[5]

The response of authorities and antipiracy groups to the threat of BitTorrent is torrent poisoning or the act of intentionally sharing corrupt data or using different kinds of attack to slow down BitTorrent downloads: "Clients such as ZipTorrent are an indication to this attempt; the goal of ZipTorrent is to slow down popular downloads as much as possible" (Sarjaz and Abbaspour 2013, p. 86). A number of Internet service providers (ISPs), for instance, block or throttle traffic associated with P2P systems using a simple, fast approach known as port filtering. But BT and other P2P networks using the latest technological sophistication are, however, quick to respond to this regulation to continue to pursue their copyright infringement and hide their traffic and illegal activities. In response to port filtering, P2P clients were quick to use ports associated with other services (web traffic, email traffic, etc.) to exchange data, blending P2P traffic with other legal traffic, making it more difficult for authorities to regulate them (Johnson et al. 2008, p. 2).

7.2.5.2 P2P and Online Piracy in the Philippines and Vietnam

Owing to slow Internet connection and low Internet penetration, P2P file sharing of digital media in the Philippines is not as intense compared to other piracy hotspots in the ASEAN such as Vietnam. But the use of the BT for downloading digital media, especially music, is one of the highest in the world. In a study by

[4] See www.bittorrent.com.

[5] See Cheng (2012): "Only 0.3 % of files on BitTorrent confirmed to be legal" at http://arstechnica.com/tech-policy/2010/07/only-03-of-files-on-bit-torrent-confirmed-to-be-legal/.

Musicmetric in 2012, its Digital Music Index showed that the Philippines ranked 10th among the top 10 countries with most BT music downloads. As many as 8.3 million BT downloads originated from the Philippines for the first half of 2012 out of the total 403 million BT downloads during this period.[6] Although Internet access outside Metro Manila is not yet established, Internet penetration in the cities continues to grow and Internet piracy is growing along with it through P2P file sharing services according to the IIPA. BitTorrent is among the most popular P2P file sharing protocols for Internet users in the country (IIPA 2013 Special 301 Letter to USTR February 8, 2013, p. 201). Because the Internet infrastructure in the Philippines is not yet well established, the P2P domains used in the Philippines for infringing are basically located outside the country. The infringing website kat.ph was the lone P2P site identified by the IIPA and USTR as being located in the Philippines. But it was, however, ordered closed by the Intellectual Property Office (IPO) of the Philippines in 2013 and was forced to migrate to kickass.to in mid-2013 to continue its infringing activities (2014 IIPA Special 301 Report: Philippines, p. 201).

Compared to the Philippines, Vietnam has a more serious problem with P2P piracy. With an Internet penetration and connection faster than the Philippines, the USTR and IIPA identified numerous infringing websites using the P2P technology in Vietnam whose domains are located inside and outside the country. This is understandable as the "vast majority of remaining websites dealing in copyright content are unlicensed, including streaming and download sites, blogs/forums, video streaming sites, search engines, deep-linking sites, cyberlockers, and social networks are said to deliver unlicensed copyright content" (2014 IIPA Special 301 Report).

An increasing Internet and mobile penetration plus the popularity of the broadband technology has increased tremendously illegal trade and sharing of copyright files online. In 2012, for instance, the International Telecommunication Union (ITU) estimated that 39.5 % of Vietnamese use the Internet—35 million users (including more than 4.5 million fixed broadband subscriptions). Mobile subscriptions have exploded, with Vietnam well surpassing the 100 % penetration mark and boasting 134 million mobile subscriptions as of the end of 2012. 3G mobile Internet users reached more than 16 million in late 2012 (18 % of the country's population) (IIPA 2014 Special 301 Report: Vietnam, p. 78).

Indeed, the Philippines and Vietnam's P2P and online digital piracy are fast increasing in network. With the growing popularity of mobile devices with broadband connection in these countries, it will only take a short time for Internet media piracy to dominate in Vietnam and the Philippines if authorities would not move fast to curb online infringement and to manage creatively the power of the latest digital and nanotechnology to mediate and facilitate copyright infringement.

[6] Cited in Villavicencio (2012): "Philippines has 10th highest BitTorrent downloads in the world — report" at http://www.interaksyon.com/infotech/philippines-has-10th-highest-bittorrent-downloads-in-the-world-report

7.2.5.3 Deep Linking or Hyperlink Piracy

Internet search engines can also be a means of disseminating pirated digital media on the web. These search engines show hyperlinks where surfers from one website pass the home page of another and go directly to the relevant content. They provide users with deep links to infringe music files and torrent links from unauthorized sources. Some Chinese search engines have been accused of deep linking by the IIPA and the USTR. The search engine Gougou was reported to "actively" provide users with deep links to infringe digital media to surfers in China. Baidu, China's biggest search engines, was also labeled by the US government as a "deep linking" hub spewing out location details about where pirated content is stored online. Baidu has become increasingly popular with the Chinese population for its MP3 indexing abilities with its "MP3 Search" which provides algorithm-generated links to millions of undoubtedly illicit copyright tracks hosted by others or by the so-called deep linking. In 2008, Baidu was sued for around $9 million by Sony BMG, Universal Music, and Warner Music for providing so-called deep links to copyright music tracks, but a court has ruled that providing search results does not breach copyright law, clearing China's biggest search engine of wrongdoing.[7] Another popular global website which engages in deep linking and is listed in the "notorious markets" for piracy by the USTR is the BitTorrent tracker site The Pirate Bay which is known for providing hyperlinks to pirated music, films, video games, and other unauthorized copyright materials to its users and subscribers.

The Philippines has no local popular search engines with deep linking, but Vietnam with its strong online connection and high Internet penetration has websites engaging in providing deep links to pirated materials. The most famous of them is Vietnam-based social media site Zing.vn which is blacklisted by US authorities for infringing and deep-linking music portals, although the report noted that the parent company, VNG, is in talks with rights holders to turn the site into an authorized digital music platform.

7.2.5.4 Media Box and Circumvention Technologies

Nanotechnology's capacity to increase storage capacity of digital devices has made possible the creation of media boxes which can store copyrighted media for unauthorized use or sharing. Media box piracy, as documented in IIPA reports, remains a serious issue, and China is the main source and manufacturer of this type of technology and is exporting this across Asia and other parts of the globe.

Media box piracy is a new business model which originated from China. It facilitates remote and unauthorized access to copyrighted music videos, karaoke, audiovisual, and other creative materials. These boxes are capable of playing high-definition content. They are loaded with large quantities of pirated works and

---

[7] "IFPI Loses "Deep-Linking" Case Against Baidu" at https://torrentfreak.com/ifpi-loses-deep-linking-case-against-baidu-100126/

are configured to facilitate the user's access to websites featuring unlicensed content (2014 USTR Special 301 Report, p. 19). These boxes are being manufactured in China and exported to overseas markets such as Hong Kong, Indonesia, Malaysia, Taiwan, Thailand, Vietnam, and throughout Asia. One of the well-known products called AsiaBox, for instance, is a media box that enables streaming and downloading of online audio and visual content. And a total of 70 applications are made available at the "Apps Market" of AsiaBox for installation. Moreover, AsiaBox provides online streaming of content from sites like PPSLive and PPStv which are popular P2P online services in China. The IIPA identified three different companies distributing AsiaBox in Malaysia, Singapore, and Taiwan. But AsiaBox can also be used in countries such as Japan, Australia, Hong Kong, China, and elsewhere. Rights holder groups know that the country of origin of the product is China, though the details of manufacture are unavailable (IIPA 2013, Special 301 Report: China, p. 38).

Aside from media boxes, technologies for circumvention which come from China are also popular. These are invented to circumvent access controls employed by copyright owners to manage access to their works and services and avoid unauthorized use and sharing (2014 IIPA Special 301 Report). The digital rights management (DRM), for instance, is a generic term for access control technologies which are used by hardware manufacturers, publishers, copyright holders, and individuals to try to impose limitations on the usage of digital content and devices,[8] although circumvention is allowable for some purposes such as attaining program-to-program cooperation or engaging in encryption research and computer security testing as long as the end goal is legal. An early example of a DRM system was the content scrambling system (CSS) employed by the DVD forum on film DVDs. CSS used a simple encryption algorithm and required device manufacturers to sign license agreements that restricted the inclusion of features, such as digital outputs that could be used to extract high-quality digital copies of the film, in their players. The future of DRM is said to be the UltraViolet. This DRM platform has a database that stores all of your digital purchases. When you insert a disc or open a downloaded file, your credentials are checked before the file plays. This DRM is expected to alter how music, movies, TV shows, or books are consumed because of the IPR safeguard against media piracy.[9]

The protection technology such as the DRM by copyright owners is not, however, a guarantee that media piracy can be prevented. Since piracy rides on the current technology, infringers use the same technology to create anti-circumvention technologies. Thus, converters, DRM removal, and other anti-circumvention software and devices mostly from China can remove DRM and other protection technologies to allow unauthorized use and sharing. Authorities and copyright and IP

[8] See "DRM Protection, Need Removal or not" at http://www.m4vconverterplus.com/drm-removal/drm-protection-removal.html.

http://www.m4vconverterplus.com/drm-removal/drm-protection-removal.html

[9] See "Outlawing Distribution of DRM Circumvention Technology" at https://wikispaces.psu.edu/display/IST43213/Outlawing+Distribution+of+DRM+Circumvention+Technology.

owners are now pushing for legislations against anti-circumvention technologies. The USTR is now pressuring China to stop manufacturing and exporting anti-circumvention technologies and devices (2014 USTR Special 301 Report: China).

7.3 Future Trends

The current trends such as P2P file sharing, deep linking, cyberlocker, and emergence of pirate servers or "gray shards"[10] will continue albeit in different forms and techniques due to advancement in technology. But new forms of copying and sharing of copyrighted materials will continue to arise depending on technological advancement and how antipiracy regulators and groups would react to curb the current infringement strategies. The optical disc piracy will still continue in developing countries especially those with low Internet penetration. But online digital media piracy will definitely continue to intensify with the increasing Internet connection world wide. This time the online Internet media piracy will now be migrating in mobile devices such as smartphones or tablets with the growing popularity of the broadband technology.

The future of media piracy lies in the development and adoption of new technology such as nanotechnology and quantum technology. The problem with piracy such as infringement is that it takes advantage of the current computing system, enjoying similar benefits enjoyed by legal users. Regulators and stakeholders would be facing more difficult obstacles in fighting piracy due to the new computing powers provided by the emerging nanotechnology and eventually quantum computing which make piracy easier to perform and hide from law enforcement. Nanotechnology, for instance, has miniaturized computers, hard drives, computer applications, and devices. The once bulky, room-filling monstrous computer equipment and devices are now being reduced to handheld or mobile computers with broadband connections such as tablets and iPads. With the continuing nano research and nanoengineering, computer storage, application, and networking would continue to grow fast and efficient and computer equipment and devices to further shrink until they reached their fundamental physical limits.

Conversely, nanotechnology is the application of scientific and engineering principles to make and utilize very small things. Researchers who try to understand the fundamentals of these size-dependent properties call their work nanoscience, while those focusing on how to effectively use the properties call their work nanoengineering. Nanotechnology is the understanding and control of matter at the realm of

[10] "Players of cloud-based entertainment software access these unauthorized servers to play copyrighted games that are made available through hacked software or circumvention of technological protection measures, which are used by rights holders to control unauthorized access to, and prevent unauthorized copying of, protected content" (2014 USTR Special 301 Report, p. 21).

1–100 nm.[11] "A nanometer is one billionth of a meter."[12] The prefix "nano" means "one billionth," or 10–9, in the international system for units of weights and measure. A sheet of paper is about 100,000 nm thick.[13]

Nanotechnology is the future of cloud computing. Researchers and writers are now talking of nano servers as the future of cloud computing. With the growing Internet penetration and digitalization of the world, the need for many data centers, space, and energy will surely double up in the coming years. Thus, some researchers believe that they can shrink down servers to atomic level using nanotechnology and reduce energy levels in the processing information. Thus, they think of miniaturizing all server components onto a chip for greater storage power and flexibility[14] (Storage Servers, 31 October, 2013). With nanotechnology's miniaturizing power which enables servers and various forms of data storage system to contain huge data, infringers can now upload, download, store, or share in blinding speed large amounts of files containing various types of copyrighted music, films, video games, and other forms of optical media never seen before in the history of media piracy. Unlike the VCR and optical disc piracy, sharing and trading of optical media in the cyberspace would not just be in individual or few titles but in combos or in large collections of optical media.

Aside from storage power, nanotechnology can also provide infringers with extra option and power to maintain anonymity and avoid detection from authorities. With its miniaturizing power which can reduce objects or things in nanometers, nanotechnology can provide infringers that necessary cloak to hide their illegal activities from authorities. It can also enable them to create new software and other nanodigital programs to circumvent the various protection systems set up by stakeholders and copyright industries.

7.4 Digital Spying and Hacking

With greater digitalization of data and reliance of business and industries on the Internet, the greatest threat faced by IP industries including copyright industries is not just counterfeiting or illegal downloading, sharing, and reproduction of some copyright products and services but a wholesale theft of the entire intellectual property of companies through digital spying and systematic hacking. The hacking of Sony Entertainment which resulted in the theft and unauthorized uploading on the Internet of the company's digital and intellectual property and secrets, including

---

[11] See Jones: "Nanotechnology" at http://physics.about.com/od/nanotechnology/p/nanotechnology.htm.

[12] A meter is about 10 % longer than a yard.

[13] See Bellis: "Introduction to Nanotechnology" at http://inventors.about.com/od/nstartinventions/a/Nanotechnology.htm.

[14] "Nano Servers are the future of Cloud Computing says research!" at https://storageservers.wordpress.com/2013/10/31/nano-servers-are-the-future-of-cloud-computing-says-research/

theft of some new and unreleased films, only illustrates that piracy in the future could include not just target-specific type of infringement such as unreleased films but the entire creative wealth of business companies as well. Piracy in the future would not just be on “retail” but wholesale!

Computer espionage has a history almost as long as that of the modern Internet. In the late 1980s, the German hacker Markus Hess and several associates were recruited by the KGB to penetrate computers at American universities and military labs. They made off with sensitive semiconductor, satellite, space, and aircraft technologies. Today, China, Israel, and Russia are reportedly the most aggressive about stealing secrets. But China is playing a game of a different magnitude and is now considered the worst offender. In its Special 301 Annual Report of 2014, the USTR accused China of spying and stealing trade secrets inside and outside China in order to provide competitive advantage to Chinese state-owned and private companies against their competitors (2014 USTR Special 301 Report, p. 31). Because of its aggressive innovation and technology development program, China becomes the most likely suspect of any “wholesale” and sophisticated hacking. In the Sony hacking, some experts believe that China with its friendly relation with North Korea could probably be behind the attack against the company. North Korea and its hackers could not have been that sophisticated in cyber attack—assuming that the FBI findings on this incident are true—without the support and training of Chinese hackers and digital experts.

The leaking of new and copyrighted materials especially films can take different ways. It is usually done either through illegal procurement of unreleased copy of new films from unscrupulous film jurors, illegal camcording of new movies in movie houses, or illegal procurement of edited materials of unreleased films in post-production houses. With the Sony hacking, a new source of camcords can be secured through hacking. The hacking has resulted in massive illegal downloading of “The Interview” and other new and unreleased films of Sony. Thus, the procurement of master copies or camcords of new films to be uploaded on the Internet for media piracy, i.e., illegal reproduction and duplication and sharing, is now being expanded from the temporal space to cyberspace.

In today’s digital age, the greatest threat of legitimate business including optical media is computer hacking and digital spying. As Internet penetration spreads throughout the world, piracy and counterfeiting would shift more gradually from spatiotemporal space to the cyberspace.

The jungle warfare in the cyberspace is totally different from the temporal space. Counterfeiters and pirates employ evasive hacking techniques to steal copyright products. The attack of Sony by North Korea may be politically motivated to protect the honor of their leader Kim Jung Un, but the hacking incident revealed that the counterfeiting of films and other media products can be done online by a group of anonymous hackers. Offense is said to be easier than defense in the cyberspace. Hackers can devise new evasive strategies without prior clues to legitimate anti-hacking groups to break into computer systems and steal information and data they want from media companies. In sociology, real power is not possessed but exercised through strategies, tactics, and other manipulative schemes. Cyber security experts may be well prepared and always on a lookout against cyber attack and hacking, but it is always difficult to track and predict when and how hacking can take place.

Master copies of film piracy are used to be taken from jurors in Oscars or other film awarding bodies who leaked advanced copies of new films or through illegal camcording in movie houses, but now advanced and unreleased copies of digital media can be stolen through computer spying and hacking.

The change of infringing techniques is not only occurring in stealing master copies but also in the replication and distribution of pirated optical media. Instead of physical distribution with the use of optical discs, the exchange of optical media is now taking place more in the cyberspace and peer-to-peer sharing.

7.5 Quantum Computing and Machine-Mediated Piracy?

If nanotechnology would make media piracy greater storage, flexibility, anonymity, power, and quantity of pirated goods and services, quantum technology and computing would even push the frontiers of copyright infringement to an unimaginable scale guided by artificial intelligence. With another 10–15 years of developing quantum computing, it is expected that artificial intelligence could now make decision as to what and how to infringe copyright materials in a massive scale and shortest speed: "Conventional computers cannot make decisions, as humans do, but quantum computers can eventually use programs based on quantum mechanics to see multiple possible outcomes to any given problem and combine information from each to formulate solutions."[15] If quantum computing becomes fully operational, expect that artificial intelligence can take the lead on how to pirate optical media and other copyright goods and services. And since infringement is committed by machines with quantum computing that shields the human network that operates them from criminal and administrative liability, prosecution and regulation by authorities would be very much difficult in a cyberspace with a computing world dominated by machines and artificial intelligence. The theory of technological determinism which sees technology as fully determining and controlling society which has long been rejected by many sociologists of technology would be proven correct after all with the advent of quantum computing and quantum media piracy. Instead of people, machines and artificial intelligence would then take the lead in collecting, analyzing, and computing data and programs to achieve a wholesale infringement of a wide array of not just optical media but all types of materials and processes covered by copyright and IPR laws. Regulators and human "pirates" would not then be the frontline networks in this new global copyright war but artificial intelligence and material networks of regulators and infringers.

[15] "Forecasts From the Futurist Magazines" at http://www.wfs.org/Forecasts_From_The_Futurist_Magazine

7.6 Regulating the Internet and ICT

The complexity of online business and transactions on the Internet poses a serious challenge to law enforcement. As the operations and networks of the Internet, the interconnection of legality and illegality would also become more complex. Empirical knowledge through research and prudence must guide authorities and stakeholders in regulating the Internet. The fate of the US bills Stop Online Piracy Act (SOPA) and PROTECT IP Act (PIPA) is a lesson for regulators not to be too enthusiastic to regulate the Internet without understanding its business, political, and social landscape.[16] The interconnection network between legal and illegal on the Internet is so intimate and intricate that regulating the illegal aspects of it may greatly affect the legal ones. The US economy is currently built on the idea of innovation which is greatly facilitated by the Internet. Thus, too much regulation of the Internet to fight piracy with the intention of enhancing the growth of the US economy may just result to an unintended and opposite effect of stifling legal networks and businesses as well as creativity and the overall goal of encouraging innovation in the creative economy. Some groups who oppose exaggeration of revenue losses of US IP industries based on inadequate methodology of their studies and magnified by inaccurate reporting in the media have valid concerns: if the US legislators are fed with bogus and inaccurate data on the effect of piracy to the US economy, new legislations would inaccurately address the problem. Instead of objectively identifying and solving the negative impact of piracy in the US economy, it might only exacerbate the current problem with sound empirical basis.

Counterfeiting and media piracy can also be considered as an unintended consequence of the ongoing competition between service providers of the Internet and its allied technologies against content providers of these technologies. Many of these are mostly US multinational information technology (IT) and telecommunication corporations with manufacturing plants and subsidiaries abroad vying for greater sales of their technologies in the market of IP-consuming countries like the Philippines and Vietnam. Some of these such as computer hardware and software are the very same technologies used by users and pirate producers for illegal downloading, sharing, and reproduction of optical media for piracy trade. The United States and its top allied countries cannot just impose regulation on the exportation of the high-tech products of these multinationals as they are also one of the major drivers of American economy that provide employment and revenues in the homeland. The US government cannot just regulate Internet use and connection and the sale of computers, mobile phones, replicating machines, DVD, and Blu-ray duplicators, burners, or software used in downloading, copying, or converting files—material things which are usually used in optical disc piracy—which are legitimately sold by big American IT or information and communications technology (ICT) companies. In the first place, ICT-exporting countries like the United

[16] See Condon, S. "SOPA, PIPA protests spur Congress to rethink bills" at http://www.cbsnews.com/news/sopa-pipa-protests-spur-congress-to-rethink-bills/.

States would be the first to ensure that trade barriers in the exportation and sale of these high-tech technologies abroad are minimized or removed. In Vietnam, for instance, the United States introduced provisions in the BTA to open the Vietnamese economy to the entry and sale of American ICT technologies as well as copyright products such as optical media. Vietnam's accession to the WTO sponsored by the United States has further paved the way to friendly trade policies that facilitate the importation of ICT to country at the expense of copyright products which become vulnerable to counterfeiting given the weak IPR protection system in the country.

One can, therefore, see two patterns of trade policies and laws with regard to ICT and IP being structured by US and IP-exporting countries in developing countries. One pattern is establishing a set of trade policies that allows the exportation of ICT technologies, and the other is one that protects the IP technologies which are being carried by these ICT technologies in a newly established high-tech market of developing countries. Applying the basic tenet of the normative pluralism theory, one can then see various normative standards or ways of doing business within one technology industry. The trade policy conflict between IT, ICT, and copyright industries provides counterfeiting and piracy loopholes to persist in their illegal operations. Since each of this type of industry such as the ICT technology business has various intermediating legal networks such as software and application for downloading, virus security, social networking, etc., which are dependent on the Web, the Internet cannot just be regulated, curtailed, or censored by the authorities without affecting big online business interests. And yet the Internet is the major source of pirated materials carried or processed by big IT and ICT multinational companies.

Aside from the Internet, other ICT devices and equipment which are sold legally are also used for optical media piracy trade. Suspending the sale of these popular items would not be possible and would be met with great resistance from other multinational manufacturers. As already mentioned, the piracy trade is a network of legal and illegal components; it uses a mix of legal and illegal goods for its preproduction, production, and postproduction stages. In the preproduction stage, i.e., communication equipment such the cell phone is usually used to contact the illegal source of the master copy or get bulk orders from distributors in various regions in the country. The Internet is indispensible at this stage for the producers to know the latest upcoming movies from Hollywood or local cinema or popular music and other media content to be burned or replicated. In the production stage, personal computers, burners, stampers, CD or DVD printers, and duplicators and other equipment for the production of pirated discs are also indispensible. In the postproduction stage or the marketing, sale, and distribution stage, ICT equipment such as the cell phone is also necessary for communication purposes as well as portable DVD players for retailers to test the pirated discs in retail stores or stalls. All these ICT equipment are all legally available in the market. In fact, most of these technologies are provided by American multinational corporations. American companies such as Apple supply the popular iPhones or smartphones with both communication and Internet capabilities Fig. 7.1.

Big multinational corporations selling these ICT hardware, providing their home country employment and revenues, would be the first to be affected and to oppose

Fig. 7.1 An electronics store in Ho Chi Minh City selling latest models of US mobile phones and accessories (Image courtesy of the author)

such move. Regulating the sale of replicating technologies can only apply if the existing markets of these ICT multinational corporations are not greatly affected. This is particularly true with regard to the sale of recording or copying equipment in the United States. Although the market for recorders or duplicators in the United States is gradually disappearing due to the government's drive against piracy and new style of copying television programs, the sale of this type of technology continues in the developing countries such as in SEA where piracy activities thrive. Thus, burners, CD printers, CD and DVD duplicators, and players which can be used for illegal copying are legally sold by legitimate high-tech companies.

7.7 The Role of China in Piracy

Tracing the evolution of media piracy vis-à-vis the growth of technology would not be complete without mentioning the role and participation of China in manufacturing and distribution of IT and consumer electronic products necessary for viewing, copying, and distributing or sharing copyrighted media products and services. Since China became the beneficiary of Foreign Direct Investment (FDI) of high-tech multinationals in the late 1970s up to the present, the growth in technological innovation of the country has reached an unprecedented height. Top high-tech multinational companies particularly from Japan and the United States investing are setting up their manufacturing hubs for their latest technological and creative products and services in China with the purpose of penetrating the huge Chinese market. With the outpouring of foreign high technology since the transformation of its economy from centrally planned to market economy, China is in the best position to engage in counterfeiting and media piracy, starting with joint ventures with top Japanese electronics firms such as Masushita which manufactures the VCRs in the 1980s, with American giants such as IBM to promote digital technology in the 1990s, and with Internet American companies in the 2000s onward. With these joint ventures and partnerships, the Chinese government is clever enough not to be outsmarted by strategies of foreign multinationals to gain control of the local market. After these top high-tech firms established their manufacturing hubs and subsidiaries in China, the Chinese government made a series of moves to protect the local market such as tolerating counterfeiting and using joint ventures to encourage technology transfer, putting up market barriers to foreign products and services, creating difficulties for foreign multinationals after being established in the country, as well as empowering Chinese firms to outcompete foreign firms to control the local market.

China is not a newcomer with regard to media piracy, particularly video piracy. With the introduction of the VCR which allowed the copying and distribution of films, Hong Kong became the destination of Chinese pirated analog films and videos in the 1970s. China also became the dominant market of Hollywood films replicated and distributed illegally in video formats and shown in numerous video halls (popular between the mid-1980s to mid-1990s) around the country (Castells and Cardoso 2013). With underdeveloped local film industry, the lowering of prices of televisions sets and video players and recorders in the late 1980s and the government's regulation against ideologically inappropriate, morally decadent, and sexually explicit content in videos, the venue of film viewing in China shifted from the popular public viewing in video halls to private viewing in residential homes. People then preferred to rent or buy cassette tapes to view films in their residence (Johnson et al. 2014). Thus, the demand for more new videos and films for home viewing instead of mass viewing in video halls emerged, resulting in an underground economy of videocassette piracy in Betamax and later in VHS format. This underground video piracy trade went overseas as China exported thousands of cheap television sets, VCR players, and recorders in Southeast Asia and other parts of the world.

The birth of the Internet and digital technologies has even facilitated the greater participation of China in media piracy trade. Since the popularity of the CD, VCD, and DVD formats in the late 1990s, China is the main exporter of high-quality optical discs in SEA including the Philippines and Vietnam. China's joint ventures with the United States and foreign IT and ICT multinationals have made the country the major manufacturing hub and exporter of CD and DVD players and recorders, computer burners, duplicators, and other consumer electronic and computer devices which could be used for optical disc piracy. Through imitation and technology transfer, China became the main exporter of replicating machines for optical disc piracy in SEA and other parts of the world.

The theory that China, not the United States, is actually the original leader of technological innovation in the world and is now only reclaiming this title by engaging in technological innovation through imitation and intellectual property counterfeiting is gaining ground if one examines China' policy on technology transfer (TT) and IPR protection. China has always been behind the media piracy trade from the analog technology era up to the current nanotechnology age.

China, the leading country in counterfeiting goods and services and media piracy in VCR and digital technologies, is also the front-runner in copyright infringement using the nanotechnology with its huge investment on nano research and development together with Taiwan, South Korea, and the United States. It would be no surprise then if China can maintain its belligerent status as the number one counterfeiting nation and would eventually overtake the United States as the leader in copyright traffic on the Internet as well as in technological innovation. Nanotechnology's power to miniaturize and empower data storage can provide Chinese infringers more power to upload, store, and share massive copyrighted materials. More storage means that more unauthorized media materials can be stored for illegal uploading, downloading, and sharing.

The latest IIPA and USTR Special 301 reports indicated that China continues to lead in media piracy by continuously adapting to new technologies such nanotechnology to avoid law enforcement. Its current innovation to pursue media piracy which is powered by nanotechnology is the "media box." "Media box" which is the recent new mode of media piracy can contain massive copyright materials such as films and music in just a small storage device. The manufacturing, distributing, and using of "media boxes" is a recent phenomenon in media piracy initiated by China. Media boxes are generally manufactured in China and exported to overseas markets particularly throughout Asia. These boxes "can be pre-loaded with hundreds of high-definition (HD) motion pictures prior to shipment; loaded with content upon delivery; or plugged directly into Internet-enabled TVs, facilitating easy access to remote online sources of unauthorized entertainment content including music, music videos, karaoke, movies, and TV dramas."[17]

7.8 China's Future Involvement in Piracy

China's involvement and leadership in piracy and counterfeiting including media piracy will continue and intensify until it establishes its own IP industry which is ready to compete or overtake the US IP industries. If we analyze China's economic development plan, we can infer that counterfeiting plays an important role in protecting its local business from foreign intrusion and at the same time achieving its goal of regaining its old glory as the world's leader in innovation,

[17] IIPA's Letter to Susan Wilson February 7, 2014, pp. ix–x

intellectual property, and technology. China has always been in a regular feature in the watch lists of the USTR since the creation of the Special 301 Annual Report in 1989. Since its ascension to WTO in 2001, China has agreed to comply with the USTR's demand to reform its IPR regime and with the international standards set by TRIPS and other international IPR treatises. More than 20 years had passed but China is still leading in USTR's piracy Priority Watch List. More often China says "yes" in public forums to USTR's recommendations but does otherwise in actual life such as agreeing to implement the protection of patents and copyright laws but engages in spying and stealing of trade secrets of multinationals in its homeland as well as tolerating massive online and physical media piracy. The United States, on its part, cannot afford to bully and antagonize China on this regard as it aims to find ways to penetrate and dominate the biggest potential market for American IP products in the world. With a huge growing middle class and massive Internet users, China is expected to be the world's biggest market for American IP exports, particularly for entertainment and digital media goods and services. The transfer of technology through imitation, counterfeiting, or stealing of trade and IP secrets as well as enhancing the cloned technology through indigenous innovation seems to be China's overall path to economic modernization. This is also the underlying reason why it opposes any form of strict IPR regime—such as the one demanded by the US—that stifles technology transfer (TT) and Chinese innovation.

China's resistance to fully comply with the TRIPS and USTR's IPR recommendations must, therefore, be seen within a larger context. Piracy improves the short-term competitiveness of Chinese firms and facilitates technology transfer. Piracy and counterfeiting can, then, be seen as part of the grand plan of China to overtake the United States not just as the largest economy of the world but as the global leader in innovation, science and technology, and eventually in IP. Counterfeiting and piracy seem to serve only as a strategic means for China to protect the Chinese economy from foreign intrusion and to facilitate technology transfer that will ultimately dislodge the United States as the leader in innovation and in the global intellectual property trade. Thus, the slow implementation and nonenforcement of TRIPS and the recommendations of USTR on piracy can be a delaying tactic to allow technology transfer to happen in the meantime and to prepare Chinese IT and IP firms to build their own brands which can outcompete foreign brands. For this reason, China's counterfeiting such as media piracy would continue—albeit expressed in various forms and adapted to the latest available technology—despite the USTR's repeated warnings until such time that China would be able to compete legally with the United States in the IP sector.

China is used to be the "sleeping giant" and a "sleeping innovation leader." But since it started to reform its economy in 1978 from a centrally planned economy to market economy and to focus on improving science and technology, China is now moving toward its old leadership post in the world economy and innovation business. In fact, some top Chinese multinationals such as Huawei Technologies and Lenovo computers are now leading global suppliers of high-tech products and services.[18] By engineering a unique brand of technology transfer which combines both illegal (e.g., counterfeiting or stealing trade or technology secrets) and legal means (e.g., joint ventures) to imitate or induce technology transfer from top Japanese, American, and foreign high-tech multinationals, China is on its way to reoccupy its post as the world's leader in innovation and technology, challenging the United States' current global position. The market-enhancing reforms since the late 1980s have increased the entry of foreign and private firms to China and stimulated competition in most manufacturing subsectors.[19] Many high-tech multinational corporations have invested in research and development (R&D) facilities in China which enhanced Chinese innovation capability. Moreover, China has adopted a range of policies designed to create "indigenous innovation" and reduce dependence on the United States and the West for advanced technologies. This includes government procurement, competing technology standards, and requiring technology transfer from multinational corporations in return for market access (Segal 2013). Chinese scientists who are included in the prestigious Science Citation Index rose to 9.5 % in 2010. China can now boast the world's fastest supercomputer, according to the semiannual TOP500 official listing of the world's fastest supercomputers. The Tianhe-2 or Milky Way-2 clocked in at number one with a performance of 33.86 petaflops per second or more than 20,000 trillion calculations per second.[20]

China's determination to collect technology by all means in order to emerge as the world leader in innovation is noteworthy. Although the United States remains the world leader in science and technology at the moment, China is projected to overtake the United States and advanced countries in terms of innovation and technology by 2030.[21] China's progress in spending on research and development (R&D) can overtake the United States in 10 years (Segal 2013).

With China's determination to surpass the United States as the leader in science and technology, one will witness more piracy and theft of intellectual property of the United States both offline and online and eventually dislodge the American hegemonic leadership in IP trade. Thus, the world will continue to witness piracy and counterfeiting especially in the area of scientific research and technological development through digital spying and hacking of trade secrets, inventions, and patents. The target of Chinese counterfeiting would, then, expand beyond entertain-

---

[18] China's best known multinationals may not be comparable to giant US MNCs such as Coca-Cola, McDonalds, Apple, or Pfizer, but the growth of Chinese MNCs in terms of total revenues is consistently climbing. Twelve Chinese companies were included in Fortune's Global 500 list in 2001. And only a decade later, in 2011, that number rose to 61 (including four with headquarters in Hong Kong). China now ranks third on the global list, only slightly behind Japan but well behind American firms. Please see Shambaugh: "Are China Multinationals Really Multinational?" at http://www.brookings.edu/research/articles/2012/07/10-china-multinationals-shambaugh.

[19] See "Supporting Document 2: China's Growth through Technological Convergence and Innovation" p. 163 at http://www.worldbank.org/content/dam/Worldbank/document/SR2–161–228.pdf.

[20] "China Boasts World's Fastest Computer"

http://www.voanews.com/content/china-boasts-worlds-fastest-computer/1683465.html

[21] Word Bank Supporting Report 2, p at http://www.worldbank.org/content/dam/Worldbank/document/SR2–161–228.pdf

ment media in the future and would include research findings and materials in universities, think tanks, and research centers in the United States. In just one of the most recent cases of industrial spying, US prosecutors charged three Chinese scientists at New York University School of Medicine with illegally sharing research findings with a Shenzhen institute and a Shanghai medical technology company (Segal 2013). In copyright realm, media piracy would not just be in retail process but wholesale and massive. The insinuation that China may have something to do with the hacking of North Korea on Sony—if proven to be factually true—can have a solid basis as China is the only country next to the United States which is technologically capable of doing so against advanced corporate computer systems of Sony. If China's aggressiveness in innovation through counterfeiting and piracy is not properly addressed by the United States, China will surely be on its way to dominate the IP global trade and install itself as the new IP hegemon or leader in the world.

7.9 Summary

This chapter has shown that media piracy will not decline but will intensify with the technological development and innovation. Piracy rides on the latest technology to increase power and capabilities. With limited capabilities of the VCR technology introduced by Sony and later replaced by VHS by Sony's competitors, media piracy is limited mainly to home viewing and recording in the late 1970s and 1980s. Copyright distribution during this period has limited channels and copyright holders can monitor infringement. But when digital technology and the Internet were introduced in the 1990s, media piracy in digital formats became widespread and commercially available in CD, VCD, and DVD disc formats for countries with low Internet connection.

The introduction of nanotechnology in digital computing and Internet services which miniaturize and empower data storage and increases speed has even make media piracy more convenient, easier, and cheaper. The current media piracy forms are now supported by the combined power of digital and nanotechnology. These include the P2P file sharing, especially BitTorrent, deep linking, cyberlockers, media boxes, and other online services that store copyrighted materials for unauthorized use. The battlefield between infringers and authorities has now gradually shifted from the temporal space of makeshift sidewalk stalls for pirated DVDs or illegal CD–DVD shops to the cyberspace of the Internet, particularly in mobile devices with the increasing power of the broadband Internet. To curb piracy requires regulating the Internet, the main source of infringing materials. But legality and illegality are so intimately intertwined in the cyberspace that regulating some aspects of the Internet can affect legal services and, thus, the conflict between Internet service providers and content providers as well as regulators and Internet users. The fate of SOPA has illustrated how Internet regulation can be a thorny issue in the current battle against piracy.

Through this evolution of technology and piracy, China played an important role. Since the VCR era, China has always facilitated the growth of counterfeiting and piracy.

The ultimate goal of China is to regain its old post as the global leader in innovation and technology. Combining both legal and illegal means such as joint ventures and piracy, China was able to appropriate foreign technology and build its own technological innovation. If China's aggressiveness in innovation and technology transfer through piracy, digital hacking, and spying would remain unchallenged by the United States, China would surely be on its way as the new hegemon or leader in the global IP trade.

References

Bijker, W. (1987). The social construction of bakelite: Toward a theory of invention. In B. Wiebe, T. Hughes, & T. Pinch (Eds.), *The social construction of technological systems: New directions in the sociology and history of technology*. Cambridge, MA: MIT Press.

Bijker, W. (1995). *Of bicycles, bakelites, and bulbs: Toward a theory of sociotechnical change.* Cambridge, MA: MIT Press.

Browne, C., & Johnson, D. (2000). VCR development, diffusion and impact. http://www.smecc.org/video/vcr_development_diffusion_impact.pdf. Accessed 21 Dec 2014.

Care, C. (2008). From analogy-making to modeling: The history of analog computing as a modeling technology. Ph.D. thesis. Department of Computer Science, University of Warwick. http://go.warwick.ac.uk/wrap/2381. Accessed 4 June 2015.

Castells, M., & Cardoso, G. (Eds.). (2013). *Piracy cultures: How a growing portion of the global population is building media relationships through alternate channels of obtaining content.* University of Southern California: USC Annenberg Press.

Cusumano, M., et al. (1992). Strategic maneuvering and mass-market dynamics: The triumph of VHS over beta. *Business History Review*, *66*, 51–94.

Fleischmann, K. R. (2006). Boundary objects with agency: A method for studying the design-use interface. *The Information Society*, *22*(2), 77–87. Doi: 10.1080/01972240600 567188.

Fung, W. M. J., & Lakhani, A. (2013). Combatting peer-to-peer file sharing of copyrighted material via anti-piracy laws: Issues, trends, and solutions. *Computer Law and Security Review*, *29*(4), 382–402.

Holmstrom, J., & Stalder, F. (2001). Drifting technologies and multi-purpose networks: The case of the Swedish cashcard. *Information and Organization*, *11*(2001), 187–206. Doi: 10.1016/S1471-7727(01)00004-5

IIPA (2013). International intellectual property alliance 2013 special 301 report. www.iipa.org. Accessed 2 June 2014.

IIPA (2014). International intellectual property alliance 2014 special 301 report. www.iipa.org. Accessed 4 May 2015.

Johnson, E. M., McGuire, D., & Wiley, N. D. (2008). The evolution of the peer-to-peer file sharing industry and the security risks for users. http://cds.dartmouth.edu/digital/assets/images/30750383.pdf. Accessed 2 Dec 1914.

Johnson, M. V., et al. (Eds.). (2014). *Piracy cultures: Cinema and moving image culture for the twenty-first century*. New York: Bloomsbury Academic.

Khondker, H. H. (2006). Sociology of corruption and 'corruption of sociology': Evaluating the contributions of Syed Hussein Alatas. *Current Sociology*, *54*(1), 25–39. Doi: 10.1177/0011392106058832.

Koepsell, D. (2009). Let's get small: An introduction to transitional issues in nanotech and intellectual property. *Nanoethics*, *3*(2), 157–166.

Kwok, S. H. (2004). File sharing activities over BT networks. *ProQuest*. http://www.informatik.uni-trier.de/~ley/pers/ht/k/Kwok:Sai_Ho.html

Law, J. (2006). *Notes on the theory of the actor network: Ordering, strategy and heterogeneity.* Lancaster University: Centre for Science Studies and the Department of Sociology. http://72.14.235.104/search?q=cache:2PB8bauNIMYJ:www.lancs.ac.uk/fss/sociology/pa Accessed 20 Sept 2007.

Lessig, L. (1999). *Code: And other laws of cyberspace*. New York: Basic Books.
Letter of IIPA to Susan Wilson (2014). http://www.iipa.com/pdf/2014SPEC301COVERLETTER.pdf. Accessed 1 Jan 2015.
Levy, M. (Ed.). (1989). *The VCR age: Home video recorders and mass communication*. Newbury Park: Sage Publications.
MacKenzie, D., & Wajcman, J. (1999). Introductory essay: The shaping of technology. In D. MacKenzie & J. Wajcman (Eds.), *The social shaping of technology* (2nd ed.). Buckingham: Open University Press.
Marukawa, T. (2004). Towards a strategic realignment of production networks: Japanese electronics companies in China. In *Regional strategies in a global economy: Multinational corporations in East Asia* (pp. 99–117). München: Iudicium-Verl. ISBN: 389129848X.
Menell, P. S. (2012). *Judicial regulation of digital copyright windfalls: Making interpretive and policy sense of Viacom v.* YouTube and UMG Recordings v. Shelter Capital Partners. UC Berkeley Public Law Research Paper No. 2049445. Available at SSRN: http://ssrn.com/abstract=2049445 or http://dx.doi.org/10.2139/ssrn.2049445
Paradise, P. R. (1999). *Trademark counterfeiting, product piracy, and the billion dollar threat to the U.S. economy.* Westport: Quorum Books.
Peters, W. (1986). Toward negotiating a remedy to copyright piracy in Singapore. *7Nw.J. Int'l. L & Bus, 561*, 1985–1986. http://scholarlycommons.law.northwestern.edu/5EA1BC14-1762-41C0-A156-478520C1DCC3/FinalDownload/DownloadId-A635F15668990900187F5BE342023D7C/5EA1BC14-1762-41C0-A156-478520C1DCC3/cgi/viewcontent.cgi?article=1207&context=njilb. Accessed 15 March 2015.
Rengifo García, E. (2014). Toward the extension of obligations to other intermediaries in the internet (Hacia La Extensión De Las Obligaciones De Otros Intermediarios En Internet) (December 9, 2014). Revista La Propiedad Inmaterial Número *18*, 2014. Available at SSRN: http://ssrn.com/abstract=2535829
Ritzer, G. (2011). *Globalization: The essentials*. Malden: Wiley-Blackwell.
Sarjaz, B. S., & Abbaspour, M. (2013). Securing BitTorrent using a new reputation-based trust management system. *Peer-to-Peer Network Application, 6*, 86–100. Doi: 10.1007/s12083-012-0141-y.
Segal, A. (2013). The challenge of China as a science and technology superpower. http://www.theguardian.com/science/political-science/2013/oct/11/china-science-superpower. Accessed 23 Jan 2015.
Smith, M. S., & Gross, T. (Eds.). (2011). The history of file sharing: Where did it begin? http://www.brighthub.com/computing/smb-security/articles/67395.aspx
Star, S. L. (1989). The structure of ill-structure solutions: Boundary objects and heterogeneous distributed problem solving. In M. Huhns & I. Gasser (Eds.), *Distributed artificial intelligence* (Vol. 2, pp. 37–54). London: Pitman.
Strauss, A. (1978). A social world perspective. *Studies in Symbolic Interaction, 1*, 119–128.
Strauss, A. (1984). Social worlds and their segmentation processes. *Studies in Symbolic Interaction*, *5*, 123–139.
USTR (2014). United States trade representative 2014 special 301 report. www.ustr.gov. Accessed 7 May 2015.
Winner, L. (1998). Prophets of inevitability. *MIT's Technology Review*, *101*(2), 62.

Erratum to: Sociological Perspectives on Media Piracy in the Philippines and Vietnam

Vivencio O. Ballano

Erratum to:
V.O. Ballano, *Sociological Perspectives on Media Piracy in the Philippines and Vietnam*, https://doi.org/10.1007/978-981-287-922-6

The original version of this book was missing the second affiliation of the book author. The second affiliation is updated in the current version as below:

Vivencio O. Ballano
St. Paul University
Quezon City, Philippines

Polytechnic University of the Philippines (PUP)
Santa Mesa, Kalakhang Maynila, Philippines

The updated online version of this book can be found at
https://doi.org/10.1007/978-981-287-922-6

V.O. Ballano, *Sociological Perspectives on Media Piracy in the Philippines and Vietnam*, https://doi.org/10.1007/978-981-287-922-6_8

Index

V.O. Ballano, *Sociological Perspectives on Media Piracy in the Philippines and Vietnam*, DOI 10.1007/978-981-287-922-6

The manufacturer's authorised representative in the EU is Springer Nature Customer Service Centre GmbH, Europaplatz 3, 69115 Heidelberg, Germany. If you have any concerns regarding our products, please contact ProductSafety@springernature.com

Printed and bound by CPI Group (UK) Ltd, Croydon, CR0 4YY
25/09/2026
02222896-0007